THE SHAPE OF BIBLICAL LANGUAGE:

Chiasmus in the Scriptures and Beyond

THE SHAPE OF BIBLICAL LANGUAGE

Chiasmus in the Scriptures and Beyond

John Breck

With an Afterword by Charles Lock

ST. VLADIMIR'S SEMINARY PRESS
Crestwood, New York 10707-1699
1994

Library of Congress Cataloging-in-Publication Data

Breck, John, 1939–
    The shape of biblical language : chiasmus in the Scriptures and
beyond / John Breck.
        p.   cm.
    Includes bibliographical references and index.
    ISBN 0–88141–139–6
    1. Bible—Criticism, form. 2. Bible—Language, Style.
3. Chiasmus. I. Title.
BS511.2.B74   1994
220.6'6—dc20   94–30129
                                                                        CIP

ISBN 0-88141-139-6

The analysis of 3 Maccabees has been adapted from the author's
Introduction to 3 Maccabees in *The New Oxford Annotated Bible:
New Revised Standard Version*, copyright © 1991 by Oxford
University Press, Inc., and is used by permission.

PRINTED IN THE UNITED STATES OF AMERICA

For Lyn

"Beauty is truth,
truth beauty,"

that is all ye know on earth,
and all ye need to know.

— *Keats*

CONTENTS

ABBREVIATIONS

AJSL – *American Journal of Semitic Languages and Literatures*
Arndt and Gingrich – Arndt & Gingrich, *A Greek-English Lexicon
of the NT and Other Early Christian Literature* (Chicago,
Cambridge, 1957).
ATR – *Anglican Theological Review*
BASOR – *Bulletin of the American Schools of Oriental Research*
Bib – *Biblica*
BS – *Bibliotheca sacra*
BTB – *Biblical Theology Bulletin*
CBQ – *Catholic Biblical Quarterly*
DBSup – *Dictionnaire de la Bible, Supplément* (1926-)
EJ – *Encyclopaedia Judaica* (1971)
esp. – especially
Gk – Greek
Heb – Hebrew
IDB – *Interpreter's Dictionary of the Bible*
IDB-S – *Interpreter's Dictionary of the Bible, Supplement* (1976)
Int – *Interpretation*
JBC – *The Jerome Biblical Commentary* (1968)
JBL – *Journal of Biblical Literature*
JQR – *The Jewish Quarterly Review*
JR – *Journal of Religion*
JTS – *Journal of Theological Studies*
KJB – *King James Bible*
Ling Bib – *Linguistica Biblica*
Migne, P.G. – J.P. Migne, *Patrologiae cursus completus, series graeca*
NEB – *New English Bible*
NJBC – *The New Jerome Biblical Commentary* (1990)
NKJV – *New King James Version*
NovT – *Novum Testamentum*
NT – *New Testament*

NTS – *New Testament Studies*
OT (AT) – Old Testament
PG – Migne, *Patrologia Graeca*
RSV/NRSV – *Revised Standard Version/New Revised Standard Version*
STZ – *Schweitzerische Theologische Zeitschrift*
SVTQ – *St. Vladimir's Theological Quarterly*
TJE – *The Jewish Encyclopedia* (1909)
TWNT – *Theologisches Wörterbuch zum Neuen Testament*
UF – *Ugarit-Forschungen*
VT – *Vetus Testamentum*
ZKT – *Zeitschrift für katholische Theologie*
ZNW – *Zeitschrift für neutestamentliche Wissenschaft*
ZThK – *Zeitschrift für Theologie und Kirche*
// – parallel(s)

Abbreviations for books of the Bible, according to the *NRSV*

PREFACE

A quiet revolution is presently under way in the field of biblical studies. For the past several decades, small numbers of scholars have been exploring the *shape* or literary structure of scriptural passages in order to determine more precisely and more fully the author's intended *meaning*. Their investigations have led to an exciting and promising discovery about the way in which major sections of the Bible were composed.

It has long been recognized that biblical writers made use of a rhetorical pattern known as "chiasmus," a literary form consisting of two or more parallel lines structured about a central theme. Only recently has it become apparent that chiasmus is one of the most frequently occurring patterns in both the Old and New Testaments, and that its detection and proper analysis open new and significant avenues toward understanding the author's message. The aim of this book is to introduce the reader to this pattern and to demonstrate its importance for the task of biblical interpretation. By learning the laws that govern chiasmus, virtually anyone with a minimal sense for the flow of language can read the Scriptures with new depths of pleasure and comprehension. For those who come to the text with faith, they can discover that in the rhetorical shape of biblical language, beauty and truth are mutually expressive.

Biblical authors of both Testaments used a variety of literary forms to compose their works. Common narrative served as a vehicle for story-telling and for reporting sequences of events. To express feelings of suffering, lament or jubilation, on the other hand, or to transmit divine promises and warnings, psalmists, prophets and apostolic writers alike drew on an assortment of poetic forms that had been shaped chiefly by Semitic peoples over a period of several centuries.

Most of these forms involved some type of symmetry, producing balance or "parallelism" among the several elements of a literary unit. The ancient Hebrews perfected this pattern, later known as *"parallelismus membrorum,"* that carries over to the New Testament, especially to the Johannine Gospel and Epistles. No one can read the psalms or prophetic oracles without sensing the harmonious repetition that occurs between successive lines. The author's concern to create this effect, however, is not simply a matter of aesthetics. Whether the second line of a Hebrew couplet expresses an idea synonymous with the first line or antithetical to it, semantic and syntactic balance between the two serves in a unique and powerful way to convey the author's meaning. This suggests that form in Hebrew literature is essentially functional: the "shape" of a biblical passage plays a substantial role in conveying its message.

Literary critics have given a great deal of attention to the characteristics of Hebrew composition and have provided biblical scholars with precious insights into the connection between an author's style and his message, between the shape of a biblical passage and the sense it conveys. The impetus provided by this research is what has led a small number of specialists to focus particularly on "chiastic" structures. Commonly defined as inverted parallelism ("Beauty is truth, / truth, beauty"), chiasmus has usually been treated as a literary curiosity, interesting as a technique of composition but of little significance for the work of exegesis. As studies of the pattern accumulate, however, it becomes increasingly evident that chiasmus is one of the most common and significant rhetorical forms of both Testaments. And because of its unique shape or literary configuration — based on inverted parallelism but involving a concentric, spiraling flow as well — it provides a hermeneutic key that is indispensable for a proper interpretation of the biblical writings.

As true as this is, we should stress from the outset that rhetorical analysis does not stand alone. Full and proper interpretation of the Scriptures requires a variety of complementary approaches, including the sciences known as form, redaction and genre criticism, together with insights provided by reader-response dynamics and structuralism. Some of these methods are discussed briefly in the first section, insofar as they bear on our topic. The main focus of this present study, nevertheless, is the phenomenon of chiasmus itself, and the usefulness of chiastic analysis for simplifying and adding precision to the arduous task of biblical exegesis.

The purpose of the following chapters, then, is twofold: to demonstrate the pervasiveness of chiasmus, not only in the Hebrew and Christian canons, but in later religious and secular literature as well; and to spell out the distinctive characteristics of the pattern that point toward the author's intended meaning. To an extent that has never been fully appreciated, biblical authors wrote according to the laws of this ancient and universal literary form. To read the Word of God with understanding, we need to read it according to the principles by which it was composed. The purpose of this study is to elucidate those principles, and thereby to serve as both an introduction and a guide to a "chiastic reading" of the Scriptures.

The cumulative evidence for chiasmus as a major rhetorical form throughout the canon (and beyond) is overwhelming, although legitimate questions may well be raised about the exact "shape" of any particular literary unit. I would like to stress that the analyses offered here represent only a modest beginning to what requires a great deal of further study. Some interpreters would prefer to see different structures within a given pericope, while others might deny that the passage contains any chiastic pattern whatsoever. On the other hand, those who reject chiastic analysis as fanciful, arbitrary, or simply "unconvincing" (Bultmann, *Johannes-Evangelium*, followed by numerous reviewers of chiastic studies published by Lund, Welch, Ellis, and others), need to make their case. They need to demonstrate convincingly that the patterns of concentric parallelism which we term "chiasmus" are in fact coincidental, unintentional, or non-existent.

We begin in Part I with a detailed discussion of the basic features of Hebrew poetry before turning to the "concentric parallelism" that characterizes chiasmus as such. A question we want to keep in mind is this: How does *form* express *content*? How does the rhetorical shape of a biblical passage serve to convey its meaning?

In Part II we focus on a broad selection of passages from the Gospels and Epistles, to illustrate the authors' use of chiastic structuring and its importance for interpreting the sense of the text. It will become apparent that entire works (e.g., the Gospels of Mark and John, 1 Corinthians), as well as individual "micro-units," were composed according to this same rhetorical model.

Part III then traces the "persistence" of chiasmus from intertestamental Judaism to the hymnography of the early Church, through medieval religious poetry, and down to contemporary works as diverse as an English oratorio and an American newspaper column.

Here as well the concentric parallelism of chiastic structures serves to focus the reader's attention on the author's major theme.

The Conclusion takes up the question of the conscious and unconscious use of chiasmus, and further discusses its significance for the task of biblical exegesis. My purpose throughout is to define this literary phenomenon as precisely as possible and to illustrate its importance for discerning the literal meaning of the text. But at the same time I hope to convey to the reader something of the delight that I have experienced in detecting and analyzing these intriguing and intricately woven rhetorical patterns. Read "chiastically," the Scriptures reveal a beauty and vitality that is otherwise lost. As I have noted elsewhere, "The frequency with which chiasmus occurs in the biblical writings, together with the relative ease with which it can be detected, make of it a key that virtually anyone can use to gain access to the all too often hidden treasures of the Scriptures. There may be no more effective way to promote an ongoing renewal in biblical studies today than to teach and encourage the lay people of our various confessions to read Scripture according to the same principles by which it was composed."[1]

Often chiastic structuring appears more clearly in the Greek than in translation, and I have relied for the original on the 26th edition of the Nestle-Aland *Novum Testamentum Graeca*. Where indicated, English translations are taken from the *RSV* or *NRSV*, otherwise they are my own. (For technical reasons, Greek accents, breathing marks and the "iota subscript" have been omitted throughout.)

Acknowledgements

A mong the many people who have aided me in this project, including colleagues, students and friends, I wish to acknowledge with genuine gratitude at least the following: Stewart Armour, Prof. Peter Cowe, Rev. Dr. Frederick Harm, Cynthia Hartman, Prof. Susan Ashbrook Harvey, Prof. Veselin Kesich, V. Rev. Paul Lazor, Prof. Charles Lock, Prof. William MacBain, Prof. Paul Meyendorff, Prof. Thomas Oden, Prof. Raymond Oliver, V. Rev. Anthony Scott, and Kenneth Sivulich. To these must be added my former and present students who have contributed significantly to my appreciation of literary form in biblical composition: Vladimir Aleandro, Michelle Amack, John Barnet, William Congdon, Mary Sweazey

Cowles, John Dibs, Ludwig Djaparidze, Rev. Nabil Hanna, Nancy Holloway, André Issa, Esther Juce, Walter Ray, Nicholae Roddy, and Rev. Peter San Filippo.

Miss Eleana Silk, Librarian of St. Vladimir's Orthodox Seminary, spent untold hours formatting the examples of chiasmus in these pages and otherwise purging bugs and clearing debris, and to her I am most grateful. The laborious work of preparing the text for publication was done by Amy Odum and Martin A. Christiansen, and to them, too, go my heartfelt thanks. Charlotte Rodziewicz made a skillful and major contribution to the burdensome task of proof-reading the entire text. And Judy Ellis very kindly provided me with her structural analysis of St. John's Gospel that is included here as Appendix II.

A particular word of appreciation goes to Professor Peter F. Ellis, whose advice and encouragement have been matched only by his consideration in entrusting to me a wealth of materials relevant to this study. To the Rev. Dr. John Gerhard, S.J., I owe an equal debt for his kindness in sharing with me so generously the fruits of his ground-breaking studies in parallelism and "alternating" symmetries.

Special thanks goes in addition to my son Michael, whose interest in literary analysis has made him a valued teacher as well as a willing pupil.

As important as the help and encouragement of each of these collaborators has been, my deepest appreciation is for the patience, insight and enthusiastic support of my wife, Lyn, and to her I dedicate this book with abundant love and affection.

Crestwood, New York
Advent, 1993

ENDNOTE

[1] "Biblical Chiasmus: Exploring Structure for Meaning," *BTB* xvii/2 (1987), p. 74.

Part One:

CHIASMUS, A KEY TO THE SCRIPTURES

1. NEW DIRECTIONS IN BIBLICAL CRITICISM

How are we to *read* the Bible?

The question invites a reply that expresses an attitude: we should read it with respect, with devotion, with curiosity, perhaps even with awe. Certainly these are appropriate responses. Our concern in this present study, however, is not with attitudes, but with the approach we use. Should we read Scripture the same way we read a newspaper? Or a novel? Or a poem? Or is there some other approach by which we can sound the depths of the biblical message, to perceive what the Church's spiritual elders called its "theandric" quality, its inner nature as a work of both human intention and divine inspiration?

To answer this question, we will concentrate on another which is still more basic: what is the "shape" of biblical language? Given the fact that the meaning of a literary text is expressed by semantic and syntactic relationships — that is, by the "form" of the passage — we want to ask about specific principles of composition that biblical writers drew upon in order to convey their message. That inquiry defines the purpose of this book. For once we understand those principles, then we will be able to *read* the Scriptures appropriately. We will read them as they were intended to be read (and heard) by the biblical authors themselves, rather than through the lens of our own arbitrary presuppositions.

The author of a novel usually adopts the traditional narrative or story form of expression: providing a setting, introducing characters, developing the plot, working toward a climax, and ending with a conclusion that draws the elements of the story together into a coherent whole. The movement of narrative or story telling is basically horizontal or chronological, proceeding in a line from past to future. "Flashbacks" may add interest and detail to the story, but they still conform to the pattern of thematic development from beginning to end, from first word to last. We are so accustomed to this pattern, that any deviation from it tends to confuse us. Poetry, both metric and free, is the despair of many people today, primarily because they have never acquired a sense for reading a poem as something other than narrative. Yet a good poem expresses meaning not so much through linear development of theme as through what we might call "holistic impression." It speaks in thought-images that focus from a variety of perspectives upon the specific aspect of reality and experience the poet seeks to evoke. Every phrase, every line, every strophe is structured so as to impress a particular, comprehensive truth upon the mind and the heart of the reader. In addition, poetry possesses a "self-referential" quality which enables each word or phrase to illumine every other. However much it may "tell a story," its basic movement is concentric rather than linear, flowing from and about, as well as toward, its central theme. Like the petals of a flower, the language of a poem unfolds from, yet leads the eye back to, its vital core.

Prose and poetry can express their message in a variety of ways. While any meaningful passage conforms to some degree to the laws of narrative, the ultimate sense of an author's work is not necessarily expressed by its conclusion. A "whodunit," of course, must adhere to the linear principle of narrative flow, in order to preserve suspense until the end. Other more noble forms of literature, on the other hand, often convey their meaning as a poem does, by repeatedly reflecting the author's primary theme with a variety of images and nuances. This is as true of a Dostoievsky novel as it is of a Shakespeare sonnet. As we shall discover, it is also true of much of the Hebrew and Christian Scriptures, whether they were composed as poetic pieces (psalms, hymns, prophetic oracles) or as narratives (most of the Pentateuch, Gospels, and Epistles).

Before we turn to the structure or "shape" of biblical language, it would be helpful to recall briefly certain methods of Old and New Testament interpretation that have been in vogue since the mid-nineteenth century. Developed especially by European Protestant exegetes, these methods have contributed in a very significant and positive way to our understanding of the "literal" sense of Scripture.

In general usage, the expression "literal sense" refers to "the intention of the author": what he or she intended to convey by the writing in question.[1] The science of exegesis, applying certain "hermeneutic" or interpretive principles to passages of Scripture in order to set forth their meaning, was practiced by the rabbis and Qumran sectarians long before the time of Christ. As a Christian discipline, it dates from the earliest years of the Church's existence. If Irenaeus and Origen were concerned to decipher portions of the Christian Gospels and Epistles whose sense was no longer evident in their day, the apostles before them felt obliged to apply interpretive methods to the Old Testament, which was of course their Bible, in order to discern in the history of Israel various events and encounters that prepared God's people for the coming of the Messiah. In every age, then, whether ancient or modern, those who attempt to interpret biblical passages are dealing with documents from earlier generations. As a result, many details of the accounts are less than self-evident and need to be clarified.

To meet this need, scholars since the sixteenth century Protestant Reformation have investigated with increasingly sophisticated tools the historical, archaeological and philological background of biblical texts. The advent of the "historical-critical method," however, came only with the Enlightenment and its emphasis on the primacy of reason over revelation. As this methodology has developed since the nineteenth century, a distinction has usually been made between "lower" and "higher" criticism. The former refers to the process of determining the original wording of biblical documents. Since there are no known autographs of apostolic writings in existence, reconstituting the most authentic Greek text must be done by comparing a number of different manuscripts and, by applying specific criteria, selecting the reading that seems most original, thereby "establishing" the text.[2] Higher criticism, on the other hand, refers to determination of the literary form or genre of the passage, the historical circumstances that led to its composition, and the meaning the author sought to convey to his readers.

Under the influence of Hegel and Darwin, Protestant biblical scholars of the late nineteenth century developed an approach to the study of scripture that was at once dialectic and evolutionary. The composition of individual writings was explained as the result of historical conflict and resolution. Far from being the work of single authors, the Gospels and even the Epistles were held to be highly composite. Exegetes borrowed from literary criticism the method of source analysis, by which it was possible to distinguish behind the received text different layers of tradition, both written and oral. Out of this procedure there developed the "Two-Source Hypothesis," which holds basically that similarities between the first three Gospels are to be explained by the fact that Matthew and Luke each used Mark and a second source (known as "Q" from the German word *Quelle* or "source"), a document — presuming it was written — which is now lost, but which originally contained parables and other sayings of Jesus.[3]

With the advent of source criticism, biblical studies became essentially *disintegrative*. Their primary focus shifted from the message of the passage to discovery and analysis of its individual components. This is not a negative judgment but merely an assertion that the chief aim of historical criticism was to discern behind the existing text the various sources or elements of tradition that underlie it. This method was perfected by students of the Old Testament such as Wellhausen and Gunkel, and of the New, such as Dibelius and Bultmann. The method of "form criticism" or "form analysis" (*Formgeschichte*) extended source analysis by discerning within those sources individual units of oral tradition. Martin Dibelius identified these as "paradigms" (edifying stories that focus on a specific action or teaching of Jesus; Bultmann's "apothegms"), "parenesis" (ethical exhortations), "novelle" (generally, miracle stories), and "legends." To these can be added other units of tradition underlying pre-existing sources, such as kerygmatic, liturgical and catechetical elements.

The apparent success of form criticism led naturally to the question of composition: how did a given biblical author utilize the various sources and units of tradition at his disposal? Was he a mere compiler, doing nothing more than receiving, arranging and editing his materials? Or did he play a significant role in the actual composition of the writing that bears his name? Or was the real "author" of the work in question in fact a group or "school" of persons, each of whom had a hand in shaping the document as it appears in our canon? The science of "redaction criticism," (*Redaktionsgeschichte*) given special prominence by Willi Marxsen in his work on the Gospel of Mark, attempts to answer questions such as these. Redaction analysis, also known as "composition criticism,"[4] aims to determine the process by which a Gospel writer, for example, drew upon and reshaped his various sources in order to realize his literary achievement. While form criticism concentrates on the origin and shape of individual, underlying units of tradition, redaction criticism takes a more global view by asking how each writing expresses the unique theological stance of its author. While it is still "disintegrative" in its basic approach, it marks an important shift in modern biblical studies. Like the Fathers of the Church before them, redaction critics focus less on the medium and more on the message. Thanks to their work, the way has been opened to new approaches that go still further toward recovering a typically patristic reading of the biblical text, one which is holistic rather than fragmenting.

With introduction of the "new literary criticism," biblical scholarship has come full circle, at least in terms of nomenclature. But rather than revert to a quest for individual sources lying behind a given biblical work, exegetes who use this method today are investigating the *meaning* of the text, in relation not so much to the author and his intention as to the *reader and his or her response.*

Like other methods of modern biblical analysis, "reader-response criticism" is a stepchild, the offspring of secular literary criticism. Its main features can be summarized as follows.[5] Basic to reader-response criticism is the idea that a literary work is a "bipolar virtual entity." This means that any given writing is incomplete — it is in a virtual or potential, rather than an actual state — until it is read and assimilated. In the jargon of the discipline, each literary composition is constituted of an "artistic pole" and an "aesthetic pole." The first refers to the creative labors of the author in composing the work. For that work to be complete, however, it must be "received": it must be appropriated by the reader, who brings both imagination and understanding to the text. So-called "narrative criticism" dovetails with the reader-response approach. It treats the narratives of the Gospels and Acts as stories that conform to the laws of narrative prose. But it also shares the conviction that the real story can be interpreted in an infinite number of different ways, depending on how it is received by the reader.[6] What the reader in fact reads is merely the narrative account. The actual *story* unfolds as the reader applies understanding and insight to the narrative, thereby producing a work of art of his or her own creation.

There is no question that narrative and reader-response criticism have greatly enhanced our understanding of the way "stories" function. They very rightly stress the potential nature of any literary work, insofar as its full realization depends upon reception and assimilation by a responding reader, whose own creative energies play a vital role in giving meaning to the story. But therein, as well, lie the limits and an inherent weakness of the method. Literary critics speak of the "indeterminacy of text and reader." In other words, any text is capable of bearing an infinite number of interpretations, depending on who the reader is, or even on the reader's change of mental state from first to second reading. Indeed, pressed to its logical conclusion, the principle of text-reader indeterminacy implies that a story is forever changing, even as it is being read. The question naturally arises as to the ultimate source of the story's *meaning*. If we abandon altogether the traditional view that the text contains and communicates its own specific sense or message, and affirm that meaning is dependent on the reader's interpretation rather than upon the author's "intention," then we risk falling into an unrelieved relativism. What the reader brings to (or imposes upon) the story becomes more important than the author's intention in composing it and the community's purpose in preserving and transmitting it.

A serious reader-response approach, therefore, will acknowledge that meaning is controlled by the text itself. Accordingly, it will attempt to preserve a balance between the sense intended by the composer and the sense perceived by the interpreter. It is a difficult balance to maintain, however, and all too often the "literal" sense of a passage is sacrificed in the interests of "reader-response" dynamics.

2. REDISCOVERING CHIASTIC PATTERNS

Although many literary critics today would argue otherwise, *biblical interpretation must have as its primary goal elucidation of the literal meaning of the text.*[7] This is the necessary first step toward any attempt to unfold what has traditionally been called the "spiritual sense" of Scripture, which we can define as the Word addressed by God *through the text* to the church and world of today. To discern the literal meaning, biblical interpretation must insist upon a holistic reading, much as literary criticism proposes. This does not imply, however, that we should reject the findings of form and redaction criticism. Insofar as they enable us to isolate and analyze stages in the growth of a specific biblical tradition, these disciplines are indispensable for recovering the literal meaning of a given passage. Nevertheless, like literary criticism they can also divert our attention from the literal sense and prevent us from discerning the actual principles by which the author composed his work. When this happens, they betray their intended purpose and need to be complemented by some other approach. The question is, what other approach can prove really fruitful? Given the limitations inherent in historical-critical analysis and literary criticism, how in fact are we to discover the literal sense of a biblical passage?

One of the most fruitful means is to examine the literary structure or *shape* of both individual passages and entire compositions that make up the biblical corpus. This approach, known as rhetorical criticism (or analysis), has been curiously neglected even by literary critics.[8] In the remainder of this book, we want to focus on a particular rhetorical pattern, common to both Testaments, that in many cases reveals clearly and precisely the central theme the biblical author sought to develop and communicate to his readers. That pattern is known as *chiasmus,* a form of inverted parallelism that focuses about a central theme. Before illustrating its usage throughout the Scriptures, we should begin with a preliminary description of chiastic structuring and compare it with other forms of parallelism found in both poetry and prose.[9]

It is axiomatic that the form or structure of a given literary work serves as an important vehicle for its content. Consequently, the author of that work, whether it be an epigram or an epic novel, chooses the particular linguistic structure that best expresses the meaning he or she wants to communicate.[10] To proclaim a message that comes to light with the unfolding of events in chronological sequence, an evangelist chooses the gospel form, while Paul and others find the apostolic letter more appropriate for developing theological themes and drawing out their ethical consequences.

Form and redaction criticism, however, have made clear the great extent to which gospel narrative is used to express theological ideas, and how thoroughly the apostolic letters presuppose and reflect the teachings of Jesus. Every biblical writing, in fact, combines proclamation with recitation, in order to fulfill its task of witnessing to the person of Christ and to the significance of his life and work. The major literary forms, in other words, are not "pure" but are invariably mixed. In both gospels and epistles narrative is combined with hymnic confessions, catechetical instructions, liturgical fragments, etc., and the combination reveals new depths of meaning. Beginning with oral or written tradition, a biblical author selects those elements that best suit his purpose of proclamation and exhortation, then he shapes them through a process of editing and interpretation. The result is a unique work and a unique witness, one that complements other writings in the apostolic corpus because it offers fresh insight into the *meaning* of those teachings and events that he recounts. To understand an author's message, then, it is of the greatest importance that we come to understand his method: precisely how and by inference why he edits, interprets, and thereby reshapes the material he has received.

One indispensable way to attain this elusive end is to study the structure of individual literary units in light of the overall composition. Structural analysis of New Testament texts has proven beyond any doubt that most if not all of their authors, like many of their Hebrew and Jewish predecessors, relied heavily on chiasmus (also called "chiasm") to produce their literary work. Nils Lund initiated the most recent wave of interest in this area back in 1942, with the publication of *Chiasmus in the New Testament*.[11] In the early 1960s, Albert Vanhoye analyzed in exhaustive detail the "concentric symmetry" of the Epistle to the Hebrews.[12] More recent works by Peter Ellis have investigated the parallel and chiastic structuring of Matthew's gospel, the Pauline epistles, and, most significantly, the Gospel of John.[13] In this last work, Ellis drew upon the unpublished doctoral dissertation of John Gerhard, S.J., to show that the entire Fourth Gospel is structured according to the laws of chiasmus.[14] In so doing, he offered an important corrective to the commonly held opinion expressed by John Welch: "Although the individual sections of the Gospel of John are chiastic, the book as a whole is not."[15] While a good many Johannine scholars had recognized that certain short passages of the Gospel were structured chiastically, they did not recognize that the evangelist consciously wove his traditional material into a pattern that makes of his total work an extraordinarily beautiful, seamless robe.

Rediscovery of chiasmus, one of the most important rhetorical forms in biblical literature, is already having a major impact on the way we read Scripture. Lund, Ellis, Welch and a host of other scholars have detected chiastic patterns in small, isolated units as well as in whole compositions. They have rightly sensed the intimate connection that exists between rhetorical form and thematic content, between the structure of a literary passage and its theological meaning.

What, then, is this rhetorical form that we term "chiasmus"? Unfortunately, the answer depends to a large extent on whom we ask. Even among specialists in the field, there is little agreement as to the exact definition of chiasmus and the characteristics of chiastic patterns. Before we turn to a more detailed analysis of those patterns, then, it would be helpful to note the following definitions.

"Parallelism," as we shall see in detail in the next section, refers to a correspondence established between two (or occasionally three[16]) lines of prose or poetry. Such correspondence can involve semantic and syntactic elements (i.e., similar verbal or grammatical usages), or it can be established through repetition of certain sounds (assonance or rhyme). The term "chiasmus" is used today to refer to a variety of different patterns whose common denominator is symmetrical structure involving some form of inversion: the reversing of word order in parallel phrases. An example would be the pattern A:B:B':A'.[17] Here the propositions A and B are reflected as in a reversed, mirror image by the propositions A' and B'. One of the clearest examples is 1 John 4:7-8,

A : for *love* is of *God*,

   B : and everyone who loves is born of God and knows God.

   B': The one who does not love does not know God,

A': for *God* is *love*.

Here A (love/God) is reflected as in a mirror by A' (God/love). The parallelism is constituted by identical terms, placed in inverted order. The same is true of B-B', yet here the element of *antithesis* is introduced: loves — knows // does not love — does not know. To distinguish this antithetical form from direct parallelism, we can use a double prime ("): A:B:B":A'.

Scholars refer to such a pattern as "chiastic" (from χιαζειν, to mark with crossed lines) because it can be represented by the Greek letter "chi" (χ):

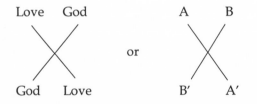

Strictly speaking, however, this pattern represents inverted parallelism rather than chiasmus. For *authentic chiasmus produces balanced statements, in direct, inverted or antithetical parallelism, constructed symmetrically about a central idea.*

The uniqueness of chiasmus, as distinct from other forms of parallelism, lies in its focus upon a *pivotal theme*, about which the other propositions of the literary unit are developed. It therefore presupposes a *center*, a "crossing point," illustrated by the letter chi (χ), which gives us the figure

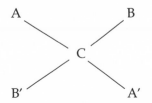

The image of concentric circles, rather than that of parallel lines, illustrates this characteristic most clearly. For in most cases of biblical chiasmus, as we shall see further on, the parallel themes focus upon and derive their meaning from the center. Any number of parallel statements may be arranged about that focal point, giving, for example, the pattern A:B:C:**D**:C':B':A'; and the center itself can consist of two or more lines in parallel, e.g., A:B:**C:C'**:B':A'. The essential characteristic of genuine chiasmus remains the pivot (in this case, D or C-C') about which the whole is centered. Chiasmus, then, may best be described by the expression *concentric parallelism*.[18]

Such parallelism can be constituted by the repetition of similar terms and phrases, as in the above example from 1 John. Or, especially in longer sections, it can depend upon the repetition of basic themes or ideas. The Gospel of John, for example, has been shown to be divided into a Prologue, followed by twenty-one "sequences" or sections, of which the last mirrors the first, the twentieth mirrors the second, the nineteenth mirrors the third, and so forth.[19] While these long sections contain few verbal parallels (exact repetitions of terms or phrases), they do nevertheless reflect parallel themes and ideas. Thus sequence 1 (Jn 1:19-51) speaks of Jesus' first coming and includes the witness offered by John the Baptist, together with introduction of Simon Peter, two unnamed disciples and Nathanael. Sequence 21 (Jn 20:19-21:25) speaks of Jesus' second coming, and includes the witness of Thomas; and again Simon Peter, two unnamed disciples and Nathanael are present. (Nathanael, significantly, appears nowhere else in the New Testament.) This clear thematic parallelism leads to important conclusions concerning the relation of John 21 to the rest of the Gospel, a question we consider later on. The point to be stressed here is that parallel structuring can be achieved by the repetition of *themes* or *ideas* as well as by the repetition of verbal expressions.

Because of its central focus, chiasmus accentuates the main idea or theme the writer is concerned to convey to his readers. It serves, therefore, as an indispensable key for determining the literal sense of a scriptural passage. We can easily illustrate this point by referring to the Prologue of the Fourth Gospel. If readers accept the paragraph divisions suggested, for example, by the *New Revised Standard Version* (*NRSV*), then it would be reasonable, perhaps inevitable, that they understand the central theme of the Prologue to be the incarnation of the Logos or Word of God as affirmed in v. 14: "And the Word became flesh and lived among us...". Because most interpreters throughout the history of the Church have taken this affirmation to be the core of the author's message in this passage, they have waged an interminable debate over the meaning of v. 9: "The true light, which enlightens everyone, was coming into the world." If v. 14 refers to the incarnation, then v. 9 — clearly announcing the arrival within history of the eternal Word — must refer to a "pre-incarnational" coming. Thus we find in the Church Fathers, and in modern interpreters as well, the notion that v. 9 speaks of the presence of the Word in the Old Testament, much as Paul in 1 Corinthians 10 declares that the rock that gave forth water to the children of Israel "was Christ."

If we read the Johannine prologue according to its inherent chiastic structure, however, the tension between vv. 9 and 14 is resolved, and we discover that the author's focus is not what it may at first have seemed. The chiastic center of John 1:1-18 is not v. 14, but vv. 12-13: "But to all who received him, who believed in his name, he gave power to become children of God...."[20] The focus of the "literal sense" of this passage, then, is not incarnational but *soteriological*. Like the concluding verse of ch. 20, it expresses the fundamental purpose for which the Gospel was written: to proclaim salvation through Jesus Christ to those who believe in him as Messiah and Son of God. Accordingly, vv. 9 and 14 must be read as *parallel affirmations of the one incarnation in the flesh* of the eternal divine Word. This is borne out by the fact that this central passage, vv. 9-14, is surrounded by two parallel references to the witness of John the Baptist. And, as we shall see later on, the first verses of the prologue stand in direct parallelism with the last verses.

The whole is thus structured according to the laws of chiasmus. If we fail to detect that structure, we inevitably miss the central theme of the passage and run the risk of distorting its message altogether. To interpret Scripture fully and accurately, therefore, it is of the utmost importance that we detect the presence and function of chiastic patterns wherever they occur.

3. THE SHAPE OF BIBLICAL LANGUAGE

Although chiasmus was used abundantly in the prose of the ancient Semites, it appears to have originated in their poetic literature. Recent studies of Sumero-Akkadian and Ugaritic literary texts has unearthed its roots in the third millennium before Christ.[21] In order to appreciate its role in Hebrew and early Christian writings, it would be useful to recall some of the basic characteristics of Hebrew poetry and the place of chiasmus within it.[22]

Unlike classical Western poetry, Hebrew verse makes little use of meter or rhyme. Beauty and meaning come to expression rather through flexible rhythm and balanced phrases. The Anglican Bishop Robert Lowth of Oxford was one of the first modern scholars to study Hebrew poetry in any depth.[23] Detecting in its structure a balance of ideas and themes, he noted that the basic poetic unit consists of paired half-lines which express a single theme in complementary ways. Words or phrases in the first line are balanced directly or antithetically with expressions in the second line. This paralleling effect led Lowth to coin the technical expression *parallelismus membrorum* or parallelism of members, the basic formal characteristic of Hebrew poetry.[24]

Scholars who have built upon Lowth's work use a variety of technical terms to designate the different components of prose as well as poetic texts. For our purposes we need to keep in mind the following definitions and usages, grouped under the main headings of (1) "parallelism" and (2) "chiasmus."

(1) *Parallelism:* a balance of both thought and form between successive members of a literary unit that provides a feeling of

completeness or "closure."[25] The simplest model consists of two half-lines that constitute a "line" or "verse" (e.g., "O God, thou knowest my folly, / the wrongs I have done are not hidden from thee." // — Ps 69:5).[26] The half-line is also called a "stich" or "hemistich" (from the Greek *stichos* or "line"), or a "colon" (Greek *kolon*, "member" or "part"). Two parallel half-lines thus form a verse, referred to as a "distich," a "bicolon," or a "couplet." Units of verse formed of three stichs or cola are termed "tristich" or "tricola," and so forth. Sets of lines form thought-units, and are referred to as "strophes." A combination of two or more strophes makes up a "stanza."

Basic to Hebrew poetry is the juxtaposition of two (and occasionally three) short clauses, or half-lines, with the first ending in a pause and the second in a full stop:[27]

> Blessed is the man who fears the Lord, /
> who greatly delights in his commandments. //
> (Ps 112:1)
>
> The eyes of the Lord are in every place, /
> keeping watch over the evil and the good. //
> (Prov 15:3)

Some scholars[28] refer to the hemistich or half-line as a "verset." We shall adopt this practice in order to avoid confusion with lines of liturgical verse of variable length ("stichs"), or with the less poetic images evoked by the terms "colon" and "cola." For the sake of convenience, however, we shall retain "bicolon," "tricolon," etc.

The basic unit of verse in Hebrew poetry is the bicolon or couplet. Lowth attempted to classify relationships between the two lines of a couplet by describing the way balance — semantic and syntactic symmetry — is created among their various elements. His categories, accepted by most students of the genre until the early 1980s, included "synonymous," "antithetical," and "synthetic" parallelism. By synonymous parallelism, he meant repetition of a thought or sentiment by the use of synonymous terms or equivalent syntactic structures. Antithetical parallelism, on the other hand, expresses contrast or opposition (e.g., "Some take pride in chariots, and some in horses, / but we take pride in the name of the Lord our God" // — Ps 20:7). In synthetic parallelism the theme is developed from the first line to the second, expressing different but complementary ideas (e.g., "The fear of the Lord is the beginning of knowledge; / fools despise wisdom and instruction." // — Prov. 1:7), or building one thought upon another similar to it (e.g., "Know that the Lord is God! / It is he that made us, and we are his; / we are his people, and the sheep of his pasture." // — Ps 100:3). Let us look for a moment at the manner in which these categories are usually described and illustrated; then we shall see how the recent investigations of scholars such as James Kugel and Robert Alter have improved our understanding of the way Hebrew verse functions.

Countless examples of the poetic couplet can be found in the Psalms and prophetic works of the Old Testament.[29]

> I will bless the Lord at all times; /
> his praise shall continually be in my mouth. //
> (Ps 34:1)

> The heavens are telling the glory of God; /
> and the firmament proclaims his handiwork. //
> (Ps 19:1)

> A voice cries:
> "In the wilderness prepare the way of the Lord, /
> In the desert make straight a highway for our God." //
> (Isa 40:3)

This last example illustrates several important points about Hebrew parallelism. (1) Often the poetic unit is introduced by an element that stands outside the parallel structure. This non-metrical word or phrase is called "anacrusis" (from the Greek *anakrouein*, to "thrust off"). Anacrusis can comprise a full sentence or phrase as in the above example; or it can include only a word, as in the address "Children" or "Beloved" (1 Jn 2:18; 4:7), or in Paul's repetition of "brethren" (1 Thess 2:17, etc.). (2) Syntactic elements in a couplet tend to stand in parallel, strengthening the impression of balance:

wilderness	prepare	way	the Lord
desert	make straight	highway	our God.

(3) Most important is the fact that the parallelism usually expresses some form of *thought progression*. Rather than simply repeating the sense of the first line by the use of synonymous terms, it expresses gradation: *the second line intensifies, specifies or completes in some essential respect the thought or feeling expressed in the first line.* Long recognized but little appreciated, this characteristic is a basic feature

of Hebrew poetry. Referring again to the above example from Isaiah 40, we see that the general term "wilderness" becomes in the second line the "desert," the verb "prepare" is specified by its counterpart "make straight," and "the way of the Lord" becomes "a highway for our God."[30] In the Psalter, this pattern of thought progression creates a magnificent crescendo effect. This is particularly notable in the doxological hymns 146-150,

> Praise the Lord! /
> Praise the Lord, O my soul! //
> I will praise the Lord as long as I live; /
> I will sing praises to my God while I have being! //
> (Ps 146:1-2)

Examples of this progressive or *climactic parallelism*,[31] in which the second line amplifies, intensifies or explains the first, can be found in prose as well as in poetry (correspondences are indicated in italics):

> I will *bring* you into the *wilderness* of the peoples, /
> and *there* I will *enter into judgment* with you
> face to face. //
> (Ezek 20:35)

> Ascribe to the Lord, O heavenly beings, /
> Ascribe to the Lord glory and strength. //
> (Ps 29:1)

> ...concerning the *word of life*, and the *life* was *made manifest* / and we have seen and bear witness and proclaim to you / the *eternal life* which was with the Father and was *made manifest* to us. //
> (1 Jn 1:1)

Although we indent the example from Psalm 29 to indicate that it is written as verse, the convention is somewhat artificial. The balance and forward movement of the passages from Ezekiel and First John make it clear that our rigid distinction between prose and poetry is overdrawn. Studies have recently shown that Hebrew prose, including the seemingly pedestrian formulations of Levitical law, often relies on elaborate parallelism to convey its deeper meaning.[32]

The opening couplets of Psalms 19 and 34, given above, are examples of so-called *direct* or *synonymous parallelism*. The thought of the first line is simply repeated in the second by means of synonyms: e.g., "bless/praise; Lord/his; at all times/continually" (34:1). Compare the following psalm verses:

> O Lord, rebuke me not in thy anger, /
> nor chasten me in thy wrath! //
>
> (Ps 38:1)

> Make me to know thy ways, O Lord; /
> teach me thy paths. //
>
> (Ps 25:4[5])

Numerous examples of this kind can be found in the Pentateuch and prophetic books, as well as in the Psalter; although as we shall see, no two lines of Hebrew verse are, strictly speaking, synonymous.

The penitential Psalm 51:10-12 offers another interesting example:

> 10: Create in me a clean heart, O God, /
>   and put a new and right spirit within me. //
> 11: Cast me not away from thy presence, /
>   and take not thy Holy Spirit from me. //
> 12: Restore to me the joy of thy salvation, /
>   and uphold me with a willing spirit. //

Here the link-word "spirit" provides the common theme. This unit, however, stands at the center of the psalm and constitutes its pivotal focus. The entire composition (taking vv. 18f as a later liturgical addition) in fact represents a chiastically structured tri-colon: A:B:A'. Beginning with an attitude of contrition ("Have mercy!") and a confession of guilt, built about the threefold reference to "sin" and "iniquity" (vv. 2, 5 and 9), the psalmist moves to the focal idea in vv. 10-12: three couplets, of which the first and the third speak of the human spirit, whereas the second or conceptual center expresses the fervent desire not to be cast away from the divine presence, but to partake of the Holy Spirit of Yahweh. As Weiser states it, this key verse (v. 11) expresses the longing for "an organic relationship which will permanently link" the worshiper's life to God.[33] This is then followed by the "vow" (vv. 13-17) consisting of a "sacrifice" of praise and a final word of contrition (see Psalms 7:17 and 66:13-15). The overall pattern is thus: A (sin/contrition),

B (spirit/Spirit), A' (praise/contrition). The chiastic structuring reveals the thematic center to be the psalmist's appeal for a renewed spirit through the indwelling of God's own Spirit, a theme that foreshadows the prophetic promise of transformation of the human heart and spirit under the new covenant to be established in the post-exilic age (Jer 31:31ff; Ezek 36:26f; cf. 1 John 3:24; 4:13).

Antithetical parallelism, as we noted earlier, expresses contrast or opposition. This pattern occurs very often in Proverbs.

> A wise son makes a glad father, /
> but a foolish son is a sorrow to his mother. //
> (Prov 10:1)

Here the contrast is marked by the adjectives "wise/foolish," and by the change from "glad father" to "sorrow to his mother." Similarly:

> Soundness of heart is the life of the flesh, /
> envy is the rot of the bones. //
> (Prov 14:30)[34]

A particularly beautiful example appears in Isaiah 54:7-8 (The indentation of successive versets is to facilitate reading from one half-line to its prime complement: from A to A', B to B', etc.).

> A : "For a brief moment I forsook you,
>   B : but with great compassion I will gather you.
> A': In overflowing wrath for a moment I hid my face from you,
>   B': but with everlasting love I will have compassion on you,"
> C : says the Lord, your Redeemer.

Significant here is the intensification or "heightening" from A to A' and from B to B'. A brief moment in which God forsakes Israel as an expression of divine judgment is dramatically augmented by the image of his "overflowing wrath"; and the "brief moment" becomes a "moment" of prolonged anguish during the period of exile, when Yahweh hides his "face" (his presence) from his people. Yet his "compassion" which brings about their release from captivity is similarly augmented to a declaration of "everlasting love." The alternation of antithetical lines in this passage expresses the tension between divine justice and loving tenderness in a way impossible to render otherwise.

Antithetical statements appear with special frequency in polemical writings, such as the First Epistle of John. In many cases they can be divided into couplets, suggesting the influence Hebrew poetry exercised on the Johannine author:

> A : Whoever knows God listens to us. /
> A": Whoever is not of God does not hear us. //
>   (1 Jn 4:6bc)

More often antithetical statements are arranged in the form of a quatrain:

> A : He who says he is in the light yet *hates his brother* /
>   B : is *in the darkness* until the present time. //
>
> A": He who *loves his brother* abides in the light /
>   B": and in him/it there is *no cause* for *stumbling*. //
>   (1 Jn 2:9f)[35]
>
> A : He who *works righteousness is righteous* /
>   B : just as he *is righteous*. //
>
> A": He who *works sin* is of the devil, /
>   B": for the devil *has sinned* from the beginning. //
>   (1 Jn 3:7f)

Antithesis also lies behind the rhetorical questions of Romans 8:31-35,

> A : If God is for us,
> A": Who is against us?
>
> A : It is God who justifies;
> A": Who is to condemn?

Finally we may note *inverted parallelism*, where members of the second line of a couplet correspond to those of the first line, but in reversed order, providing a mirror image. The most straightforward and familiar example from the Gospels is probably:

> the last shall be first /
> and the first, last. //
>
> οι εσχατοι πρωτοι /
> και οι πρωτοι εσχατοι. //
>   (Mt 19:30; 20:16; etc.)

This example from the prophecy of Zechariah typically combines inversion with anacrusis:

> As *I* called and *they* would not hear, /
> so *they* called, and *I* would not hear, //
> says the Lord of Hosts.
>
> (Zech 7:13f)

The following examples are structured according to the pattern a:b / b':a'[36]

> They stirred him to jealousy with strange gods, /
> with abominable practices they provoked him to anger. //
> (Deut 32:16)

> For he peers from the heights of heaven, /
> the Lord from sky to earth looks down. //
> (Ps 102:19[20])[37]

In each case, the verb is placed at the extremities of the couplet: stirred / provoked; peers / looks down. The inversion tends to stress the central elements: strange gods / abominable practices; heights of heaven / the Lord. And again there is what Kugel terms "differentiation," with B "going beyond" A.

Other examples of inverted parallelism appear in the form a: b: c / b': c': a', or, as in Psalm 19:1, in the form a: b: c / c': b': a' (translated literally):

> The heavens are telling the glory of God /
> and his handiwork proclaims the firmament. //

Here "handiwork" is the direct object of the verb "proclaims," representing a complete inversion.[38]

Inverted parallelism is often described as chiastic, but this is a misnomer insofar as it is missing a central "pivot" or focal point. A good example from the Gospels, in which the middle couplet does serve as the thematic center, is the famous "Johannine thunderbolt" that appears in Matthew 11:27-28.

> A : *All things* have been *delivered* to me by my Father;
> B : and no one knows the *Son* except the *Father*,
> B': and no one knows the *Father* except the *Son*
> A': and *all those* to whom the Son chooses to *reveal* him.[39]

A : παντα μοι παρεδοθη υπο του πατρος μου,

B : και ουδεις επιγινωσκει τον υιον ει μη ο πατηρ,

B': ουδε τον πατερα τις επιγινωσκει ει μη ο υιος,

A': και ω εαν βουληται ο υιος αποκαλυψαι.

Whereas in the central couplet the nouns are inverted (Son/Father, Father/Son), in A:A' parallelism is achieved through the inversion of the verbs (delivered/revealed). This could be considered chiastic insofar as B:B' expresses the central message of the passage, which is the reciprocal knowledge of Father and Son. Note once again that inversion tends to stress the central versets, B:B'. The line between this and A:B:A' chiasmus is very fine indeed.

A variant of this pattern similarly relies on the two middle versets to form the conceptual center. In this case, if the concentric pattern is not detected, the passage simply defies intelligent exposition. The following is translated literally.

> A: Give not what is holy to dogs
>
>   B : nor throw your pearls before swine,
>
>   B': lest they trample them under their feet
>
> A': and turning, tear you to pieces ("rend you").
>
>   (Mt 7:6)

Translators of the *RSV/NRSV* clearly missed the inversion, which follows a pattern common in ancient Greek and Roman rhetoric, referred to as *hysteron-proteron* or "last-first."[40] They render the last line "and turn to attack you" (*NRSV:* "and turn and maul you"). This implies that the action is accomplished by the swine. The Greek, however, uses a verb (ρηγνυμι) that can only refer to an attack by the dogs, mentioned in line A. The real meaning of the passage cannot be discerned unless we read it "spirally," from the extremities toward the center (A → A' → B → B'): "If you give what is holy to dogs, they will turn on you; if you throw pearls before swine, they will trample them under foot."

To the minds of the ancients, accustomed as they were to the *hysteron-proteron* model, this inversion would have posed no problem. For they were trained throughout their school years to *read from the center outward and from the extremities towards the center.* As Augustine Stock has stressed,[41] under the ancient Greek educational system, carried over intact into Latin culture, children learned the alphabet forwards, then backwards, then from the extremities towards the middle: alpha-omega, beta-psi...mu-nu. They proceeded to analyze texts in the same manner, in order to detect and understand their inverted parallelism and chiastic structure. Similarly, reflecting the hysteron-proteron model, when two questions were asked in succession, an answer was given to the second question first; and only then was the first question answered.[42] Reading "chiastically," then, was as natural for them as reading according to narrative development is for us.

The origin of the hysteron-proteron pattern may lie with Homer, who possibly adapted it from a more ancient concentric parallelism inherited from early Semites. In any case, it was a common feature familiar to all students of Greek rhetoric, and it explains how simple direct parallelism could develop into the highly sophisticated chiastic structures we shall be looking at shortly. Another example of it in the New Testament is Philemon 5:

A: I hear of your love,
   B :   and of the faith,
   B':   which you have towards the Lord Jesus
A':   and all the saints.

If the inversion and hysteron-proteron principle are not recognized here, Philemon's faith appears to be placed both in the Lord Jesus and in all the saints. Read according to the meaning Paul intended, the passage declares: "I hear of your love for all the saints, and of the faith which you have towards [in] the Lord Jesus."[43]

Of course the aim of the interpreter should not be to transform Hebrew poetic forms (many of which carry over into the New Testament) into narrative. Ideally, the modern student of Scripture will come to master the principles behind those forms as one masters the syntax of a foreign language. At times, however, while attempting to perceive the "shape" of a biblical passage, it is necessary to transform it into a more familiar structure.[44]

In addition to these examples of "internal" parallelism, in which the correspondence between form and content occurs within the poetic unit,[45] we can speak as well of "external" parallelism. Here the correspondence is created between such units, as it can be between couplets or entire strophes. Isaiah 6:10, for example, combines two internal direct parallelisms with an external inverted parallelism, and concludes with anacrusis:[46]

> Make the *heart* of this people fat, /
> and their *ears* heavy, /
> and shut their *eyes*; / /
> lest they see with their *eyes*, /
> and hear with their *ears*, /
> and understand with their *hearts*, / /
> and turn and be healed.

One of the most interesting findings in recent study of Hebrew poetry is the pattern called variously "the two-way middle" or "double-duty modifier."[47] Structured usually as a triptych, the central line of this pattern can — and should — be read both with what precedes and with what follows it. A good example is Dahood's translation of Psalm 86:12,

> I will thank you, my Lord, my God,
> with all my heart
> I will indeed glorify your name, O Eternal!

Here the psalmist declares, "with all my heart I will give thanks and glorify the Lord," but with a refinement that could not otherwise be expressed.

A still more sophisticated example of this form appears in Isaiah 11:9b (again, Dahood's translation):

> For the earth shall be filled with
> the knowledge of Yahweh
> shall be like the waters covering the sea.

The central verset, "the knowledge of Yahweh," serves as the object of the first verset and as the subject of the last. In addition, the author has employed a technique known as "enjambement" or "run-on." This indicates that an idea continues from one line of a couplet to the next. As simple as the above tricolon may seem, it is a masterpiece of poetic elegance. In fact, it combines inversion (earth/sea / / be filled/be like) with enjambement and the double-duty modifier, to produce a particularly beautiful example of chiasmus.

Before we consider the phenomenology of chiasmus, however, it is necessary to stress the importance of *inclusion* in parallel structures. We noted above that in addition to balance, parallelism provides a feeling of "completeness" or "closure." This is a standard feature of the A:B couplet (A..... / B..... //), but it is an equally significant factor in longer passages of both poetry and prose.

Inclusion, also known as the "envelope effect," is created by paralleling the first and last elements of a given literary unit. In the brief quatrain 1 John 4:7-8, it is formed by the inversion of two key nouns: "love is of God // God is love." In longer passages it serves either to complete the thought by recapitulating the initial theme (as in Jn 1:1, "the Word was with God" // 1:18, "the only Son was in the bosom of the Father"), or to set the passage off from its context and indicate that it constitutes a distinct unit of thought. An example of this latter usage would be Judges 4:2 and 4:23-24. Here inclusion is provided by repetition of the name of Israel's enemy, "Jabin the king of Canaan" — once at the beginning of the passage and three times at the end — although the account itself focuses rather on Sisera, the general of Jabin's army, and Sisera's female adversaries, Deborah and Jael.

In the New Testament inclusion can involve the repetition or reversal of an action (Mk 8:10b and 13b: Jesus got into the boat and departed; cf. 7:24a and 31; 9:2-3 and 9-10, Jesus ascends/descends the mountain) or a phenomenon (Mk 4:37, the wind and sea threaten the disciples, // v. 41, the wind and sea obey Jesus). Or it can mark off a unit of discourse by repeating, inverting or otherwise modifying key themes (Jn 13:33-34, go-command-love, // 14:31, command-love-go; Rev 9:1f, the "star" [angel] of the Abyss // 9:11, the angel of the Abyss [cf. the repetition of "Amen" in Rev 7:12]; Mk 12:28a, Jesus' adversaries argue with him, // v. 34c, Jesus' adversaries dare not ask him any questions; 1 Cor 10:1-13, spiritual food and drink of Israel, // 11:27-34, spiritual food and drink of the Church).[48]

Inclusion is often created by a paralleling of the first and last elements of a passage which is entirely structured according to the laws of parallelism, as in the pattern A:B:C:C':B':A'. On the other hand, A:A' can just as easily stand alone, representing the only parallelism within an entire section. An example would be Matthew 22:15-46, that begins with the Pharisees taking counsel together as to how they might entangle Jesus in his talk, and closes with the statement that "no one was able to answer him a word" nor dared ask him further questions. In like fashion, Jesus' parables are often set off by inclusion. Matthew 13:44, for example, begins an independent series of brief "parables of the Kingdom," which opens with the "treasure" hidden in the field and, in 13:52, closes with the "treasure" of the householder.

In each of these cases, "inclusion" is a literary device that serves to mark the beginning and end of a unit of thought. (In the Gospels particularly, it can also indicate that a given pericope originally stood as an independent element of early oral tradition; cf., for example, Mk 7:1-23, 24-31, and 32-37.) The device served an essential purpose at both the oral and the written stages of early church tradition. On the one hand, stories conveyed orally are more easily retained when they begin and end with the same or a similar theme. A conclusion that repeats the opening words or ideas of a given teaching aids both understanding and memorization. Then again, ancient Semitic and Greek manuscripts used none of the conventional symbols and spacing we are so accustomed to finding in modern written works. In order to indicate clearly where a passage begins and ends, biblical authors had to resort to some convention other than paragraphing and punctuation marks. The accepted convention was precisely "inclusion," the effect of enveloping a discrete unit of thought by reverting at the end to the ideas or images evoked at the outset.

Further on we shall see that, as with all forms of parallelism, the tendency is not merely to repeat or reflect in A' what was already stated in A. Rather, inclusion incorporates an element of *intensification* from A to A', such that the conclusion is "more than" the beginning: it rounds out or fulfills the major theme(s) of the passage as a whole. For this reason, it continued to find a place in both poetry and prose, even after the invention of punctuation and paragraphing.[49] Inclusion, then, is not merely a practical device used to facilitate the telling or reading of an element of tradition. It serves to *complete* that tradition as well as to frame it. Accordingly, analysis of the movement from the first to the second element of an inclusion (from A to A') is essential for discerning the meaning of the entire passage.

(2) *Chiasmus:* a rhetorical form in which key words and concepts are constructed in synonymous, antithetical or inverted parallelism about a central theme. The term "chiasmus" should be restricted to strophes of at least three lines, arranged about a pivot or conceptual center, such as A:B:A', A:B:C:B':A', A:B:C:C':B':A', etc.

The essential characteristic of chiasmus, once again, is the *pivotal center*. Normally this will be the "conceptual center," the focus of meaning for the entire strophe. It can also function, however, as a mere turning point or hinge, linking two parallel lines or parallel passages. A good illustration of this latter case is John 10:6, "This figure Jesus used with them, but they did not understand what he was saying to them." This verse functions as "C" in the A:B:C:B':A' arrangement of John 9:39-10:21.[50] It has no particular theological content and serves merely to mark the transition between the first part of the parable (Jesus as the Shepherd) and the last part (Jesus as the Door).[51]

Attempts to classify poetic chiasmus, as distinguished from chiasmus in longer prose passages, have met with a fairly high degree of success. The examples that are most frequently recognized and discussed, however, hardly cover all examples of the genre. Writers in antiquity drew upon it almost instinctively. The form served to express their theme, and consequently it remained flexible, assuming an almost limitless number of variations. The following list, therefore, includes only the most frequently encountered chiastic patterns.[52]

The foundation of chiastic structure is the inverted (or "introverted") bicolon.[53] Thus 1 John 4:7f again:

> (a) love   (b) is   (c) of God
> (c) for God   (b) is   (a) love.

A particularly interesting example appears in John 14:1, where the inversion is evident only in the Greek:

> πιστευετε εις τον Θεον /
> και εις εμε πιστευετε. //
>
> You believe in God /
> believe also in me // *or*
> and in me you also believe //[54]

The simplest form of chiasmus, properly so-called, is the chiastic monocolon, a single line in which three elements balance according to the pattern a:b:a'.

> Have mercy upon us, O Lord, have mercy upon us.
>   (Ps 123:3)
>
> A garden locked
> is my sister, my bride,
> A garden locked...
>   (Song 4:12).

In the first example the petition centers about the divine name. In the second, the third element ends with the complementary descriptive phrase, "a fountain sealed," illustrating climactic parallelism. This a:b:a′ form is also termed "pure" or "mirror" chiasmus, in that it involves word-for-word repetition, usually in reverse order.[55]

So-called "complete" chiasmus — where each term of the first verset is matched by a corresponding synonymous or identical term in the second — follows the same pattern of reversal. It, too, is based on the inverted bicolon. An example that many would term chiastic is found in Genesis 9:6,

> Whoever *sheds* the *blood* of *man*
> by *man* shall his *blood* be *shed*.

And again, in Revelation 3:7,

> ...who *opens* and *no one* will *shut*,
> and *shuts*, and *no one opens*.

Genuine chiasmus, however, centers about a third element:

> *I will cover*, when you are blotted out, the *heavens*
> And I will darken their stars
> The *sun* with a cloud *I will cover*...
> (Ezek 32:7)[56]

1 John 5:7-8, read literally, forms a complete chiasmus:

> *Three are* the *witnesses:*
> the Spirit and the water and the blood,
> And the *three* in the *one are* (i.e., are at one, they agree).

> τρεις εισιν οι μαρτυρουντες,
> το πνευμα και το υδωρ και το αιμα,
> και οι τρεις εις το εν εισιν.

The chiastic tricolon is a favorite device of the apostle Paul. The A:B:A′ pattern is well illustrated by the long passage, 1 Corinthians 12-14. Here A and A′ pivot about the central theme B, each elaborating the same idea in a different way:

A = 12:1-30 (varieties of spiritual gifts);

B = 12:31-14:1b (love as the highest spiritual gift; note the *inclusion*: "earnestly desire the higher gifts" // "earnestly desire the spiritual [gifts]"); and

A′ = 14:1c-40 (spiritual gifts: tongues and prophecy).

The A:B:B':A' tetracolon can be considered chiastic, as we saw earlier, when the propositions B:B' serve as the conceptual center of the passage. When translated literally, 1 John 3:6 offers a clear example,

A :   Everyone who abides in him

   B :   does not sin;

   B':   Everyone who does sin

A':   has neither seen him nor known him.

Here the focus is upon the reality and consequences of sin. The parallel between A and A' is achieved by the fact that to "abide" in God is equivalent to "seeing" and "knowing" him.

A far more common form is the A:B:C:B':A' chiastic pentacolon. This pattern is normative for the entire Fourth Gospel and occurs as well in the First Epistle.

A :   No one who is *born of God*

   B :   *commits sin,*

      C: for his [God's] seed abides in him,

   B':   and he is not able to *commit sin,*

A':   because he is *born of God.*

(1 Jn 3:9)

The central affirmation of this strophe is "C," affirming that the "seed of God" (the Spirit) dwells in those who are "born of him," referring most likely to members of the Johannine community who have been "reborn" through baptism.

Another example (1 Jn 1:6-7) includes antithetical parallelism:

A :   If we say *we have fellowship with* him

   B :   and (yet) *walk in the darkness,*

      C :   we lie and do not do the truth.

   B":   If we *walk in the light* as he is in the light,

A":   *we have fellowship with* one another...

The chiastic pattern concludes with anacrusis in the form of a central doctrinal affirmation: "and the blood of Jesus his Son cleanses us from all sin." The effect of the chiastic arrangement is to focus attention on C, the hypocrisy of the author's opponents, who claim to be in perfect fellowship with God while nevertheless committing sin (which in the context of this writing means denial of Jesus Christ as Messiah, Son of God and Savior : 1 Jn 4:2,14; 5:1; etc).

This five-fold pattern, common throughout the New Testament, occurs with equal frequency in the Hebrew Bible. It is there that we should seek its origins. An excellent example is Jeremiah 2:27c-28 (*RSV*):

A : In the time of *their trouble* they say,

    B : *"Arise* and *save us!"*

        C: But where are your gods that you made for yourself?

    B': Let them *arise,* if they can *save you,*

A': In the time of *your trouble.*[57]

Other types of chiasmus that can be illustrated from both the Old Testament and the New include the hexacola, the heptacola, the octacola, and the decacola.[58] Note, for example, the salvation oracle, Isaiah 60:1-3, presented in the form of a perfectly balanced chiastic decacolon.

A : Arise, shine;

    B : for your light has come,

        C : and the glory of the Lord

            D : has risen upon you.

                E : For behold, darkness shall cover the earth,

                E': and thick darkness the peoples;

            D': but the Lord will arise upon you,

        C': and his glory will be seen upon you.

    B': All nations shall come to your light,

A': and kings to the brightness of your rising.

The center of the oracle serves as an antithetical pivot between strophe I: fallen Zion exhorted to arise and receive "light / the glory of the Lord," and strophe II: the universal vocation of Israel, called to radiate the light of Yahweh among the nations and disperse the darkness in which they dwell. Here once again narrative flow is combined with an intensifying, concentric movement that focuses the attention of the reader (or hearer) upon the central theme: through a risen and renewed Israel, the peoples who dwell in darkness (cf. Isa 9:1ff) will behold the glory of the coming Lord. However deep the darkness that envelopes them, through Israel's witness "kings and nations" (the Gentiles) will share in the life-giving light.

4. FROM SYNONYMOUS PARALLELISM TO THE RHETORICAL HELIX: The "What's More" Factor

In his book, *The Idea of Biblical Poetry*, James Kugel defends a thesis that has won wide acceptance among literary critics. He begins his study by describing the basic feature of biblical verse as two short clauses that constitute a "parallelistic line," giving the pattern ...../ .....//, which he terms A and B. Rejecting altogether Lowth's category of "synonymous parallelism," Kugel insists that all parallel structures are essentially "synthetic" or "climactic," progressing in thought from A to B. The thrust of his argument is summed up in the formula, "A is so, and what's more, B." The second verset of a couplet, in other words, never merely repeats the meaning of the first verset; it almost always *represents an advancement in the form of heightening, intensifying, specifying, elevating, or "seconding."*

> The notion of parallelism with which we began conceived of it basically as an emphatic, elevating feature, 'seconding.' Sometimes what B added to A was significantly different, a definite going-beyond in force or specificity; sometimes A and B were related in a manner best expressed by some subordination in English ('when,' 'if,' 'just as'); sometimes B's 'what's more' was a reassertion of A via the most conventional pairs.[59]

Kugel insists upon B's "subjoined, emphatic character," which, "more than any aesthetic symmetry or paralleling..., is at the heart of biblical parallelism."[60] Through careful analysis of numerous passages, he arrives at the conclusion that the "A, and what's more

B" pattern is so basic a feature of virtually all Hebrew literature that the distinction between prose and poetry should be regarded as simply a matter of degree: "...there are not two modes of utterance [poetry and prose], but many different elements which elevate style and provide for formality and strictness of organization."[61]

Robert Alter's work, *The Art of Hebrew Poetry*, which appeared four years after Kugel's study, takes issue with this thesis by its very title. Alter perhaps exaggerates Kugel's rejection of the idea of a specifically poetic form in Hebrew literature, but his corrective is welcome and justified. The characteristics that determine a poem, he holds, include "a verbal sequence [with] sustained rhythm, that...is formally structured according to a continuously operating principle of organization."[62] As his work makes incontestably clear, such poetic form is prevalent throughout the Hebrew Bible.

The studies by Kugel and Alter confirm the theory that biblical parallelism is never truly "synonymous." The "What's more" factor — describing a movement of intensification, specification or completion from A to B — describes the very essence of Hebrew poetry and prose. What is true of the Hebrew Bible in this respect is true as well of much of the writings of the early Church. Gospels, Epistles and other New Testament and post-apostolic works likewise structure both poetic and prose passages according to the "What's more" principle. This will become especially apparent further on when we examine the christological hymn of Philippians 2:5-11 and the overall structures of the Gospels of John and Mark. For the present, we want to underscore the significance of this principle for an appreciation of chiasmus as it appears generally throughout the New Testament.

Thus far we have seen how chiasmus in passages of both Testaments depends upon the movement from A to B through a process of inversion: "love is of God / for God is love" //. The movement from A to B in this strophe (1 Jn 4:7f) achieves intensification (from God as the source of love, to love as God's very essence), and specification (from God as the source of love, to God as the embodiment of the love he communicates). It also expresses completion: the affirmation "God is love" answers the question why one must love in order to be "born of God."

Alter refers to such intensification and completion by the appropriate term "focusing."[63] The technique was used, for example, by the author of the Balaam oracle (Num 24:3f), who produced a "step" effect by employing "palilogical" parallelism: repeating in the second line one or more words of the first line to create an echo. Different means to produce the focusing effect were employed by the psalmists and prophets, as well as by wisdom writers.[64] A superb example of *incremental repetition*[65] with focusing, which incorporates narrative movement into a basically poetic structure, appears in the Song of Deborah (Judg 5:24-31). Here the Israelite heroine Jael brings down the Canaanite general Sisera, who ventured into her tent to seek refuge:

> Her hand reached for the tent peg, /
> her right hand for the workman's hammer. / /
> She hammered Sisera, cracked his head, /
> smashed and pierced his temple. / /
>
> Between her legs he kneeled, fell, lay, /
> between her legs he kneeled and fell, /
> where he kneeled, he fell, destroyed! / /[66]

Intensification or focusing, however, can be equally well expressed through the use of chiasmus. The following is the *RSV* translation of Psalm 8, arranged to represent the versification of the Hebrew. For the usual convention of indicating parallel lines by the letters A:B:C, etc., we substitute numbers to show more clearly how the entire passage focuses upon the central couplets 0:0'.[67]

> 4 : O Lord, our Lord, /
>   how majestic is thy name in all the earth! / /
>   3: Thou whose glory above the heavens is chanted /
>   by the mouth of babes and infants, / /
>   2 : thou hast founded a bulwark because of thy foes, /
>   to still the enemy and the avenger. / /
>   1 : When I look at thy heavens, the work of thy fingers, /
>   the moon and the stars which thou hast established; / /
>   0 : what is man that thou art mindful of him, /
>   and the son of man that thou dost care for him? / /
>   0': Yet thou hast made him little less than God, /
>   and dost crown him with glory and honor. / /
>   1': Thou hast given him dominion over the works
>   of thy hands /
>   thou hast put all things under his feet, / /
>   2': all sheep and oxen, /
>   and also the beasts of the field, / /

3′:   the birds of the air [heavens], and the fish of the sea, /
      whatever passes along the paths of the sea. //

4′:   O Lord, our Lord, /
      how majestic is thy name in all the earth! //

The inclusion in 4:4′ appears to involve a simple repetition of the doxology. As so often, however, appearances are deceptive. The song begins with praise of Yahweh, Lord and Master of creation. The couplets of 3, 2 and 1 exalt God's glory and might, then focus upon his creative work within the cosmos. The conceptual or thematic center of the psalm is the rhetorical question of 0, together with its "answer" in 0′. For a reason known ultimately to God alone, he has created human beings ("son of man" refers to individual persons) in his own image (reflecting the ancient theme formulated in Gen 1:26) and bestowed upon them the dominion that properly belongs to himself as Lord and Creator. From this point, the movement of the psalm passes to a specification of that dominion in 2′ and 3′, then concludes with a verbal repetition of the opening doxology.

This conclusion, nevertheless, involves far more than mere repetition. If the song begins with praise of the Lord for his work of creation, it concludes with a similar cry of praise for his loving condescension that grants to human persons dominion over the created world. *The entire semantic context*, in other words, *provides the closing doxology with new meaning*. Although the words are identical, their sense has been substantially altered from the opening couplet to its closing counterpart. And that altering, like the progression from verset to verset in a single couplet, involves intensification, specification, and conclusion.

By virtue of its chiastic structure, the psalm describes a movement of intensification in several directions. Within the couplet there is "focusing" through specification from A to B (foes → enemy-avenger; work of your fingers → moon and stars; man [generic] → son of man [the particular individual], etc.). A similar focusing or intensification occurs from the first strophe (4-0) to the second (0′-4′). The opening glorification is followed by a *descending* movement from creation as a whole to the specific human creature. From 0′, the movement is *ascending*, from the affirmation of the dominion accorded to human beings, to specification of that dominion as lordship over every other creature in the heavens and beneath the sea. Then there is as well a "narrative movement" from line to line that describes a thematic flow from beginning to end.

This forward movement from verset to verset, from strophe to strophe, and from beginning to end, is complemented by another that is more difficult to conceptualize. It is, however, the most characteristic movement of the chiastic pattern. We have already encountered numerous examples of chiasmus in which the parallel couplets derive their meaning from the center. Taking the penta-colon as an example (A:B:C:B':A' or 2:1:0:1':2'), we have noted that 0 represents the conceptual or thematic center, about which the couplets 2:2' and 1:1' are constructed according to various laws of parallelism. This structure we have termed "concentric parallelism," keeping in mind that the "parallel" phrases almost always conform to the "what's more" principle.

To describe the concentric aspect of chiastic parallelism, it seems appropriate to speak of a *spiraling*, or more precisely, a *helical* effect that on the one hand produces the forward or focusing movement from line to line and strophe to strophe, and on the other provides *meaning* to the passage by focusing upon 0, its thematic center. This helical movement — from the extremities toward the center, with intensification or heightening — can be illustrated by the following diagram:

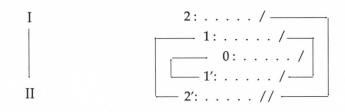

[Read: 2 → 2' → 1 → 1' → 0]

Applying this schema to Psalm 8, we note first of all the inclusion between 4 and 4' which represents an intensification or focusing from strophe I (= 4-0) to strophe II (= 0'-4'). Similar focusing is achieved between the other parallel couplets: 3:3' (glory above the heavens → literally, birds of the heavens; infants [the lower echelon of human life] → all sea-life [the lower echelon of animal life]); 2:2' (foes and enemies → domestic and wild animals); and 1:1' (work of thy fingers → works of thy hands; moon and stars → all things). Yet the whole achieves meaning by reference to the center, 0:0' (What is the human creature? → little less than God, crowned with glory and honor). Although the *RSV* separates 0 and 0', placing them in different strophes, they clearly belong together as the thematic focus of the entire psalm.

There is, then, a further *concentric, spiraling movement* characteristic of chiastic parallelism that leads, according to the above diagram, from 2 to 2', then from 1 to 1', to focus upon 0. This can be illustrated by referring once again to 1 John 3:9.

> 2 : No one who is born of God
> > 1 : commits sin,
> > > 0 : for his seed abides in him,
> > 1': and he is not able to commit sin,
> 2': because he is born of God.

Here the first verset (2-1) is augmented and specified by the last (1'-2'). Consequently the passage can be read as a spiral that moves toward the center (2 → 2' → 1 → 1' → 0): "No one who is born of God — (precisely) because he is born of God — commits sin; and he is not able to commit sin, for God's seed abides in him." This example of concentric parallelism thus describes a *helical* movement, both forward and concentric: from 2 to 2', from 2' to 1, and from 1 to 1', to arrive at the center, 0.

This is admittedly an unusual case. Ordinarily the spiraling or helical effect would be created simply by reading from strophe I to II (that is, from 2-1 to 1'-2'), concluding with 0:

> 2 : No one who is born of God /
> 1 : commits sin, //
> 1': and he is not able to commit sin, /
> 2': because he is born of God; //
> 0 : for (God's) seed abides in him.

Given 0 as the focus of meaning in the passage, it is also possible to read it *from the center outward*, from 0 to I to II:

> 0 : (Because) God's seed abides in him,
> 2 : no one who is born of God
> 1 : commits sin,
> 1': and he is not able to commit sin
> 2': because he is born of God.

It happens exceptionally that this passage can be worked out in terms of its concentric structure to make perfectly good sense in English translation. Normally this is not possible. The spiraling or helical effect is provided not by literal "narrative" reading from 2 to 2' to 1, etc., but rather by a *conjunction of two distinct movements* within the passage: the "what's more" intensification from verset to verset and from strophe to strophe, and the *implied* movement about the thematic center. Reconsider Jeremiah 2:27c-28,

    2 : In the time of their trouble they say, /
        1 : "Arise and save us!" / /
            0 : But where are your gods that you made for yourself? / /
        1': Let them arise, if they can save you, /
    2': in the time of your trouble. / /

The cry for help in strophe I (i.e., 2-1) is answered by God's challenge in strophe II (1'-2'), on the basis of the ironic question (0) that gives meaning to the entire passage: their gods which they made for themselves do not exist! The passage thus constitutes a ringing condemnation of idolatry. Its movement once again is both forward and circular, moving from strophe I to II, while being grounded in 0.[68]

In 1 John 1:6-7, which we examined earlier, there is a similar focusing: a progression of intensification or specification from the versets in the first half of the passage to their antithetical parallels in the second half.

    2 → 2': If we say we have fellowship with him →
        we have fellowship with one another...

    1 → 1': and yet walk in the darkness →
        If we walk in the light as he is in the light,
                                        (1 Jn 1:6f)

In both 2-2' and 1-1' the thought progresses from "deception" (πλανη) to "truth" (αληθεια), a basic theme of the entire epistle.[69] That this progression constitutes as well the central theme of the author's argument is confirmed by the focal affirmation 0: "we lie and do not do the truth." Once again the helical movement is evident. Whether we begin from the extremities and move toward the center, or move from the center outward, the primary focus is upon 0: hypocrisy is incompatible with the truth. This theme occurs repeatedly throughout the epistle and reflects the author's concern to bring

moral conduct in line with doctrinal profession. Although the antithetical structure of the unit precludes the kind of "inward-outward"
reading that was possible with 3:9, it nonetheless exhibits similar
characteristics insofar as the spiraling movement from 2 to 2' to 1,
etc., *reveals the author's intended meaning.*

Many longer passages of both prose and poetry are also structured in such a way as to focus upon the central element. Yet they,
too, combine a forward, narrative development with this concentric
flow, to produce a double movement from beginning to end and from
the extremities toward the center. The resultant helical "shape,"
which can be found in a great many New Testament passages, occurs
as well in a variety of Hebrew literary genres. The following examples
include a psalm, passages of "historicized prose fiction,"[70] a well-
known prophetic oracle, and a striking passage from the Fourth Gospel.

Psalm 72 is a coronation hymn that implores God's blessings of
justice, righteousness and material well-being upon the king and,
through him, upon the people. It concludes with v. 17 (the last three
verses, 18-20, constitute a doxological conclusion to Book Two of the
Psalter) and is set out here, in the *Revised Standard Version*, so as to
illustrate its chiastic structure.

5 : Give the king thy justice, O God /
    and thy righteousness to the royal son! //
    May he judge thy people with righteousness /
    and thy poor with justice! //

    4 : Let the mountains bear prosperity for the people, /
        and the hills, in righteousness! //

        3 : May he defend the cause of the poor
            of the people, /
            give deliverance to the needy, /
            and crush the oppressor! //

            2 : May they fear thee while the sun endures, /
                and as long as the moon,
                throughout all generations! //

                1 : May he be like rain
                    that falls on the mown grass, /
                    like showers that water the earth! //

> 0 : In his days may righteousness flourish, /
> and peace abound, till the moon
> be no more! / /
>
>   1': May he have dominion from sea to sea, /
>   and from the River to the ends
>   of the earth! / /
>
>   2': May his foes bow down before him, /
>   and his enemies lick the dust! / /
>   May the kings of Tarshish and of the isles
>   render him tribute, /
>   may the kings of Sheba and Seba bring gifts!/ /
>   May all kings fall down before him, /
>   all nations serve him! / /
>
>   3': For he delivers the needy when he calls, /
>   the poor and him who has no helper. / /
>   He has pity on the weak and the needy, /
>   and saves the lives of the needy. / /
>   From oppression and violence he redeems their life; /
>   and precious is their blood in his sight. / /
>
> 4': Long may he live, may gold of Sheba
> be given to him! /
> May prayer be made for him continually, /
> and blessings invoked for him all the day! / /
> May there be abundance of grain in the land; /
> on the tops of the mountains may it wave; / /
> may its fruit be like Lebanon; /
> and may men blossom forth from the cities
> like the grass of the field! / /
>
> 5': May his name endure for ever, /
> his fame continue as long as the sun! / /
> May men bless themselves by him, /
> all nations call him blessed! / /[71]

The thematic center, 0 (v. 7), expresses the hope that the king's reign will produce the cardinal blessings of righteousness and peace. This theme is developed in a variety of ways from 5 to 5', but the relation of the second parallel statement to the first is in each case one of intensification or specification. Thus:

5 → 5′: God grants the king to rule the people with justice; →
God grants the king himself eternal fame and blessings.

4 → 4′: The mountains bear prosperity and the hills righteousness; →
The mountains bear grain and the land fruit.

3 → 3′: The king defends and delivers the poor and needy,
he crushes the oppressor; →
The king delivers, pities and saves the needy, he redeems them
from oppression and violence.

2 → 2′: The oppressors fear the king forever; →
Foes, enemies, and the kings of the earth and all nations submit
to Israel's king.[72]

1 → 1′: The king is likened to water: rain and showers on the earth
(suggesting fertility and prosperity); →
The king rules over the waters: seas and the (Euphrates) River,
to the ends of the earth.

0 : Through the blessing and prosperity of the king, the righteous
can live in peace and prosperity.

Intensification or heightening occurs as well within individual strophes of the psalm, particularly in the tricola of 3 and 4′ (defend → deliver → crush; life → prayer → blessings).

Finally, a "spiral" reading, from 5 to 5′ to 4 to 4′ ... to 0, gives a similar sense of intensification and specification, leading toward a conclusion expressed as the hope for peace and prosperity: from justice and blessings bestowed upon the king, to the cosmic blessings that accrue from his reign, to the defense and redemption of the poor and needy, to the king's victory over all oppressors and foreign adversaries, to his dominion over all the earth, to the benefits that will pour forth upon the righteous who are subject to him. Thus from verset to verset, from strophe to strophe, and from the extremities toward the center, the psalmist's artistry, as well as his message, is displayed in magnificent fashion through elaborate use of the "what's more" principle.[73]

That same principle is at work throughout the Hebrew Scriptures. *Genesis 32:24-32*, for example, exhibits the same characteristics in reporting the struggle between Jacob and the divine messenger. The passage could be read as a simple etiological explanation for the Israelite practice described in v. 32. The real significance of the account, however, is revealed by its chiastic structure: bestowal upon Jacob of the name "Israel."

> 2 : And Jacob was left alone; and a man wrestled with him until the *breaking of the day*. When the man saw that he did not prevail against Jacob, *he touched the hollow of his thigh;* and Jacob's thigh was put out of joint as he wrestled with him.
>
>> 1 : Then he said, "Let me go, for the day is breaking." But Jacob said, "I will not let you go, unless you *bless me*." And he said to him, *"What is your name?"* And he said, "Jacob."
>>
>>> 0 : Then he said, "Your name shall no more be called Jacob, but Israel, for you have striven with God and with men, and have prevailed."
>>
>> 1': Then Jacob asked him, *"Tell me, I pray, your name."* But he said, "Why is it that you ask my name?" And there he *blessed him*. So Jacob called the name of the place Peniel, saying, "For I have seen God face to face, and yet my life is preserved."
>
> 2': The *sun rose* upon him as he passed Penuel [*sic*], limping because of his thigh. Therefore to this day the Israelites do not eat the sinew of the hip which is upon the hollow of the thigh, because *he touched the hollow of Jacob's thigh* on the sinew of the hip.

Using the principles thus far established, the reader can easily detect the forward and spiral movements that characterize this passage. Note as well the inversion that exists within the parallel sections: e.g., the last line of 1 ("What is your name?" / "Jacob") is virtually repeated, but with a reversal of roles, in 1' (Jacob asked, "Tell me...your name").

> 2 → 2': Jacob's thigh is put out of joint; →
> The Israelites refuse to eat the sinew of the hip because the man (God) touched the hollow of Jacob's thigh.
>
> 1 → 1': Jacob demands a blessing, the man of God asks his name; →
> Jacob asks the man's name and receives a blessing, having "seen God face to face" and lived.
>
> 0 : Jacob receives a new name, signifying "God rules," as the divine act that foreshadows establishment of the Israelite Confederation.

The helical effect (the combined forward and spiral flow) produces movement from the struggle and its practical consequences in

Israel's eating habits, through request for and bestowal of a blessing, to the further bestowal of a "new name" as a consequence of Jacob's successful struggle with God. Intensification, specification and conclusion are here again clearly apparent.

Of the many other narrative passages in Genesis that could be cited to illustrate typical chiastic structure and its helical movement, one of the most interesting is *Gen 39:1-23*, the story of Joseph and Potiphar's wife. Because of the close verbal parallels between corresponding sections, it is worth quoting the passage in full (*RSV* translation):

> [The passage typically begins with an introductory statement, a form of anacrusis: "Now Joseph was taken down to Egypt, and Potiphar, an officer of Pharaoh, the captain of the guard, an Egyptian, bought him from the Ishmaelites who had brought him down there."]

3:   (vv. 2-3): *The Lord was with Joseph,* and he became a *successful* man; and he was in the house of his master the Egyptian, and his master saw that *the Lord was with him,* and that *the Lord caused all that he did to prosper* in his hands.

    2:   (vv. 4-6): So *Joseph found favor in his sight* and attended him, and he *made him overseer* of his house and put him *in charge of all* that he had. From the time that he made him overseer in his house and over all that he had the Lord blessed the Egyptian's house for Joseph's sake; the blessing of the Lord was upon all that he had, in house and field. So he left *all* that he had in Joseph's charge; and having him *he had no concern for anything* but the food which he ate. Now Joseph was handsome and good-looking.

        1:   (vv. 7-10): And after a time *his master'*s wife cast her eyes upon Joseph and said, "Lie with me." But he refused and said to his master's wife, "Lo, having me my master has no concern about anything *in the house* (*beth*), and he has put everything that he has in my hand; he is not greater *in this house* than I am; nor has he kept back anything from me except yourself, because you are his wife; *how then can I do this great wickedness,* and sin against God?" And although she spoke to Joseph day after day, he would not listen to her, to lie with her or to be with her.

O: (vv. 11-12): But one day, when he went into the house *to do his work* and none of *the men of the house* was there in the house, she caught him by his garment saying, *"Lie with me." But he left his garment in her hand, and fled and got out of the house.*

O': (vv. 13-15): And when she saw that he had *left his garment in her hand, and* had *fled out of the house,* she called to *the men of her household* and said to them, "See, he has brought among us a Hebrew to insult us;[74] he came in to me to *lie with me;* and I cried out with a loud voice; and when he heard that I lifted up my voice and cried, *he left his garment* with me, *and fled and got out of the house."*

1': (vv. 16-20): Then she laid up his garment by her until *his master* came home, and she told him the same story, saying, "The Hebrew servant, whom you have brought among us, came in to me to insult me; but as soon as I lifted up my voice and cried, he left his garment with me, and fled out of the house." When his master heard the words which his wife spoke to him, *"This is the way your servant treated me,"* his anger was kindled. And Joseph's master took him and put him into the *prison (beth-sohar),* the place where the king's prisoners were confined, and he was there in *prison.*

2': (vv. 21-23a): But the Lord was with Joseph and showed him steadfast love, and *gave him favor in the sight of the keeper of the prison.* And the keeper of the prison *committed to Joseph's care all* the prisoners who were in the prison; and *whatever* was done there, he was the doer of it; the keeper of the prison *paid no heed to anything* that was in Joseph's care,

3': (v. 23bc): because *the Lord was with him;* and *whatever he did, the Lord made it prosper.*

The passage is framed by affirmation of the Lord's presence and his active bestowal of success upon his servant Joseph. The blessings that pour forth from God accrue both to Potiphar and to the prison keeper, leading them to place *all things* in Joseph's hands (2 → 2', note the emphatic repetition of "all" and "anything"). In the following sequence, the storyteller has sketched a masterful portrait of Potiphar's wife, contrasting her lustful abandon with Joseph's scrupulous concern to honor the trust his master has placed in him. (The ethical problem is posed not so much by the enticement to an illicit sexual act as by the fact that the woman is Potiphar's possession: "nor has he kept back anything from me except yourself...".) Joseph's question, both plaintive and indignant, "How then can I do this great wickedness?," is balanced by the woman's deceitful assertion, "This is the way your servant treated me!" Her none too subtle implication is that the husband, as much as Joseph himself, is to blame for her injury, since he brought the slave to the household in the first place (v. 14), and as his master Potiphar is responsible for Joseph's actions (vv. 17-19). This heaping of guilt upon her spouse, as well as upon the supposed seducer, works admirably. Potiphar, who had given Joseph authority over all his household, now throws him into prison (note the parallel between "house" [*beth*] in 1 and "prison" [*beth-so-har*] in 1'). In language that is nearly identical to that of vv. 4-6, the narrative continues (vv. 21-23a) by affirming the Lord's presence with Joseph in prison, together with the favor the Lord bestows upon him and his works. Like Potiphar, the prison keeper responds by placing in Joseph's care all responsibility for the daily routine, to the point that he too "paid no heed to anything" that was in Joseph's care.

There is definitely an intensifying, forward movement to the sequence — a spiraling effect from the extremities toward the center — although it is somewhat less apparent than in the narrative of Jacob's struggle with the angel.

> 3 → 3': The Lord causes Joseph to prosper in his master's house. →
> *Because* the Lord was with him, Joseph prospers even in prison.

> 2 → 2': Joseph is given all responsibility because he has found favor in Potiphar's sight. →
> Joseph is given all responsibility because the Lord was with him and showed him his steadfast love.

> 1 → 1': Joseph's righteous refusal. →
> The woman's self-serving lie leads to Joseph's imprisonment.

> 0 → 0': The innocent Joseph flees the seductress. →
> The woman impugns his innocence with her lie.

Here, however, the vital message of the passage is located at the extremities rather than in the center. While the reader's interest may well focus on the exchange between Joseph and the woman, and the latter's artful weaving of an elaborate lie, the author intends the story to communicate a single truth: that despite adversity in the form of temptation and betrayal, Joseph is protected by the presence of the gracious Lord. In fact his trials become the occasion for ever greater blessings. The moral of the story, then, has little to do with sexual propriety and avoiding temptation. It is rather an affirmation that however adverse the circumstances surrounding his people, God remains unfailingly faithful. Righteousness will eventually, but inevitably, receive its reward.

Turning now to the book of Samuel and the David cycle, we may consider still another literary unit structured according to the laws of chiasmus or concentric parallelism. *1 Samuel 18:14-30* focuses upon the lie conjured up by Saul in v. 22, by which he attempts to destroy David:

> And Saul commanded his servants, "Speak to David in private and say, 'Behold, the king has delight in you, and all his servants love you; now then become the king's son-in-law'."

The passage is too long to present in full, but the following schema should enable the reader to detect here as well the forward and spiral movements of intensification, specification and conclusion.

5 → 5′: vv. 14-15 // vv. 29-30.

4 → 4′: vv. 16-17 // vv. 27-28.

3 → 3′: v. 18 // v. 26.

2 → 2′: vv. 19-20 // v. 25.

1 → 1′: v. 21 // vv. 23-24.

0 : v. 22.

Note the inversion with heightening that occurs from 3:3′ (David's protest / Saul's invitation that he become his son-in-law) to 1:1′ (Saul's invitation, revealed as a snare / David's stronger protest). Here again, the movement from the extremities toward the center is one of intensification.

A further example is the salvation oracle found in the prophet *Ezekiel, 36:24-28*. Jeremiah had already prophesied the establishment of a new covenant with the remnant of God's people, one in which Torah should be "written upon their hearts" (Jer 31:31-34). Building on this same promise, Ezekiel's oracle proclaims that the covenant sealed by the indwelling power of the Spirit of Yahweh will effect a thoroughgoing moral transformation in the lives of the people. Through the use of chiasmus, Ezekiel balances in parallel affirmations two major priestly motifs: purification by lustral water, and the effusion of God's Spirit.

3 : *I will take* you from the nations
      and *gather you* from all the countries
      and *bring you into your own land.*

  2 : *I will sprinkle clean water upon you*
        and you shall be *clean* from all your uncleanness
        and from all your idols I will *cleanse* you.

    1 : *A new heart* I will give you,

      0 : and a new Spirit I will put within you;

    1': and I will take out of your flesh the heart
          of stone and give you *a heart of flesh.*

  2': *And I will put my Spirit within you*
        and cause you to *walk* in my statutes
        and be careful to *observe* my ordinances.

3': *You shall dwell in the land* which I gave to your fathers
      and you shall be *my people*
      and *I* shall be *your God.*

Although at first reading the oracle appears to be written as straightforward narrative prose, its tight chiastic structure provides the balance, the sustained rhythm, and the "continuously operating principle of organization" that determine Hebrew poetry.[76] Once again the movement from strophe to strophe, as from the first half to the second half of the passage, effects that heightening or "going beyond" so characteristic of the genre. Three ascending promises in 3 (take → gather → bring) and 2 (I will sprinkle → you shall be clean → I will cleanse) express God's work to be accomplished by the parallel promises of 2' and 3'. And the spiral movement leads from exterior to interior, from the outer world to the inner life, from re-establishment of the remnant in the land of their fathers to re-creation of a covenant written on the heart through the indwelling of the Lord's Spirit.

3 → 3': The people will be taken, gathered from the nations and
led back to their own land. →
The people will dwell in the land of their fathers, "You shall be
my people, I shall be your God."

2 → 2': They will receive cleansing from idolatry through purify-
ing lustrations. →
They will receive the gift of God's own Spirit for moral
transformation.

1 → 1': God will give them a new heart. →
God will remove their heart of stone and replace it with a heart
of flesh.

0 : The basis of their new life, national and personal, is the *new
Spirit* God will put within them.

With the balance expressed between water and Spirit in 2:2',
together with the concentric focus upon the "new Spirit" as the
transcendent power by which the transformation from a "heart of
stone" to a "heart of flesh" is accomplished, it is little wonder that
the early Church interpreted this passage typologically, as a prophetic image of the regeneration bestowed through Christian Initia-
tion. Although Ezekiel probably understood the object of God's
action to be a collective "you," referring to the remnant as a whole,
his oracle could very well be read as a description of the intensely
personal Christian experience which is given through baptismal
incorporation into the Body of Christ.

A final example can be taken from the Fourth Gospel account of
the empty tomb. As in the Synoptic tradition, John's narrative of
Jesus' crucifixion, burial and resurrection seems to be woven together from units that were originally independent. One such unit
apparently consists of *John 20:3-10*, a passage that has no direct
parallel in the first three Gospels.

All four evangelists identify Mary Magdalen as a (John: *the*) first
witness to the empty tomb. According to the Fourth Gospel, she
comes early on the first day of the week, she sees the stone rolled
away from the tomb, and — although it is only implied in v. 2 — she
notices that "they" have stolen away Jesus' body. She then runs and
announces her finding to Peter "and the other disciple, the one
whom Jesus loved." The following account — unique to this Gospel

— describes the reaction of Peter and the Beloved Disciple: they run to the tomb to see for themselves.

> 4: Peter then came out with the other disciple, and they went toward the tomb.
>
>> 3: They both ran, but the other disciple outran Peter and reached the tomb first;
>>
>>> 2: and stooping to look in, he saw the linen cloths lying there,
>>>
>>>> 1: but he did not go in.
>>>>
>>>>> 0: Then Simon Peter came, following him,
>>>>
>>>> 1': and went into the tomb;
>>>
>>> 2': he saw the linen cloths lying, and the napkin, which had been on his head, not lying with the linen cloths but rolled up in a place by itself.
>>
>> 3': Then the other disciple, who reached the tomb first, also went in, and he saw and believed; for as yet they did not know the scripture, that he must rise from the dead.
>
> 4': Then the disciples went back to their homes.

By its concentric structure, the passage conveys a dual message. On the one hand, it provides two valid (i.e., male — Deut 19:15) witnesses to the fact that the tomb was empty and the gravecloths were lying in a particular way. On the other, it establishes the Beloved Disciple as the first to reach the tomb and witness the linen cloths, and as the first to "believe": "he saw and he believed" is the foundational experience of those who encounter the Johannine Jesus and receive him as Lord and Son of God (1:34,39,46; 20:25-28). Yet at the same time, the evangelist affirms Peter's "primacy" among the disciples by having him enter the tomb first. The parallel with ch. 21 is clear, where the Beloved Disciple is the first to recognize the risen Lord, yet it is Peter who leaps into the water and swims to meet him.[76] The evangelist's concern, however, is to stress the *priority of the Beloved Disciple's witness, relative to that of Peter*. Accordingly, he structures the passage to emphasize the point that Simon Peter "followed" the primary eye-witness who lies behind Johannine tradition.

4 → 4': An implied heightening from "Peter and the other disciple,"
to "the disciples": the Beloved Disciple
is on a par with Peter because of his witness
and belief.

3 → 3': The other disciple *outran* Peter →
The other disciple *saw and believed*.

2 → 2': The linen cloths →
The linen cloths and the napkin.

1 → 1': The Beloved Disciple did not enter the tomb →
The Beloved Disciple entered the tomb.

0: Simon Peter *followed* the Beloved Disciple.

Chiastic parallelism in this passage enables the biblical author to express a complex set of affirmations concerning the tomb, the gravecloths, the witness of the disciples, and the relationship between Peter, chief of the disciples, and the Beloved Disciple, the implied leader and primary authority within the Johannine communities. The helical movement, with heightening or intensification from the first statement to its "prime" complement, conveys to the Gospel's readers the point that Petrine "primacy," while acknowledged, is of less importance than the witness of the disciple who "sees and believes."

With this sort of analysis there is a constant danger of introducing into the discussion cumbersome neologisms in an effort to express concisely and clearly new and difficult concepts. The specific movement of concentric parallelism, however, calls for a label, even at the risk of straining the already overburdened vocabulary of taxonomy.

We have noted that the forward, narrative movement of a chiastic pattern is complemented by the concentric flow toward and away from its center of meaning, 0. This twofold movement describes an upward spiraling motion characteristic of a *helix*, a three-dimensional spiral that progresses in parallel sweeps about a central axis. The most appropriate image for this phenomenon is that of a "conical helix," in which movement begins from a broad base, then spirals upward toward the point that represents the conceptual center. Presupposing an A:B:C:D:C':B':A' pattern, for example, A:A' are both farther apart from each other and farther from the central axis than B:B'. This means that B:B' are *heightened* relative to A:A', as C:C' are, relative to B:B'. The "point" or D is both the concluding point of the upward movement and the central axis of the cone. Thus it serves as the "conceptual center" that both ends and gives structure to the movement as a whole. This can be illustrated by the following figure:

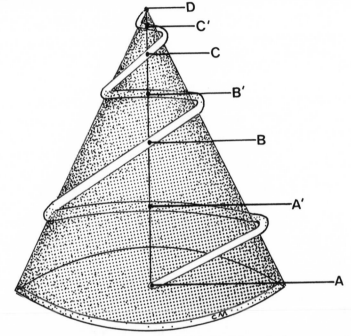

With this image of a "rhetorical helix" in mind, we can summarize the various movements of chiastic structures under the following six points. Although the "what's more" and helical characteristics are not equally evident everywhere, they are sufficiently typical of both prose and poetic units that they can be considered normative for biblical chiasmus.

1. The second verset of a line intensifies, specifies or completes the first: A → B (A ...../ → B...../ /).

2. The second parallel line or couplet intensifies, specifies or completes the first: 2 → 2'; 1 → 1'; or A → A'; B → B'.

3. The second strophe of the chiastic pattern intensifies, specifies or completes the first: I → II.

4. The first strophe "descends" toward 0, the conceptual center, whereas the second strophe "ascends" from it.

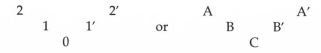

5. Movement from line to line produces a chronological or thematic narrative flow, "from beginning to end," "from A to Z": $2 \to 1 \to 0 \to 1' \to 2'$.

6. Finally, progression from line to line also describes a spiral or, more accurately, a helical movement from the extremities (inclusion) toward the thematic center: $2 \to 2' \to 1 \to 1' \to 0$.

Chiasmus has been commonly described as a reversing of terms or themes in synonymous, antithetical or synthetic parallel phrases. We have seen that such a description is at best inadequate. In the first place, the concept of parallelism itself needs to be reinterpreted so as to reflect the actual characteristics of Hebrew poetry. It should not be confused with its counterpart in Greek verse, which depends heavily on meter and rhyme. This is true for the New Testament as well as the Old, since the rhetorical patterns of Israel were taken over and adapted by Christian writers, including those whose mother tongue was Greek.

In the second place, we have found that the basic flow of the chiastic pattern is twofold: forward through some form of focusing; and concentric, deriving its meaning from the middle term 0. This double movement describes what may be called a *rhetorical helix: a three-dimensional spiral that progresses with increasing intensity about a central axis or focus of meaning.* The examples of chiastic structuring in the New Testament which we consider in Part II demonstrate that there as well this helical movement marks a progression of thought toward intensification, specification or completion, and thereby it serves to draw the reader's attention to the literal sense of the text.

5. THE VALUE OF CHIASMUS

In the following chapters we examine a selection of passages from the New Testament and early Christian hymnography, in order to illustrate how various writers employed the chiastic structure to convey the essence of their message. Before we turn to those specific examples, however, we need to address briefly a frequently raised question.

If the Hebrew, and later the Christian author relied so heavily on chiasmus, what was the benefit they and their readers derived from it? Is the device purely aesthetic, an artistic sophistication that serves no particular function other than to display the ingenuity of the writer? Or does it in fact, as we have maintained, play a vital role in conveying the meaning of God's Word? Related to this is a second question: What precisely is the importance of recognizing chiasmus where it occurs? Why should the reader bother with the intricacies of Hebrew poetry and make the effort to detect its influence on passages of Scripture, whether in the Old Testament or the New?

The benefits of chiastic and related rhetorical forms were in fact many, both to the biblical author and to his reader. Ancient writing made no use of paragraphs, punctuation, capitalization or spacing. These are late conventions, like the chapter divisions and versification of the New Testament which were made only in the thirteenth and sixteenth centuries respectively. Ancient authors were obliged to organize the internal format of their works by other means. One of these was the envelope technique or *inclusion:* the framing of a literary unit by placing the same key terms or themes at the beginning and at the end. Concentric parallelism was especially useful for providing *stress*, by repeating key expressions or by balancing related syntactic elements. Chiasmus, finally, served to focus the reader's attention on the core of the author's message. By reading the passage concentrically, the reader was drawn into its circular flow, as an object is drawn toward the center of a vortex.

Equally important was the *mnemonic* benefit of parallelism and chiasmus. The ancients learned by rote. They listened to a master, then repeated his instruction in unison (a practice one still finds today in the Koran schools of Moslem countries). There were no notebooks, no pen and paper or other devices to relieve the student of the burden of memorizing what was taught. Parallelism and especially chiasmus facilitated this process by repetition and by focusing on a central theme. Once the student had in mind the first half of a simple bicolon or a complicated chiastic structure, it was a relatively easy matter to recall the rest. In addition, the paralleling of themes facilitated *antiphonal recitation*, an important element in Hebrew and early Christian liturgical worship.

Finally, we should not underestimate the *aesthetic* value of these forms. As John Welch so aptly expressed it, "More then than now, beauty was synonymous with form." [77]

To detect parallel and chiastic structures is no less important for today's exegete or, indeed, for any reader of Scripture. Failure to do so has led interpreters to weave some rather fantastic theories to explain apparent irregularities in the composition and style of individual biblical writings. As a result, more energy than we like to admit has had to go into correcting the mistaken conjectures of those who have gone before us.[78] One of the most egregious — because so widely accepted — examples in modern New Testament study is the so-called "displacement theory" concerning the arrangement of material in the Fourth Gospel. A brief example, which we develop further on, illustrates this point very clearly.

In his commentary on the Gospel of John, Rudolph Bultmann advanced a displacement theory which was taken up and variously modified by many of his students.[79] They noted that the healing at the pool in ch. 5 is alluded to again in 7:21-23. This and other factors seemed to point to a "displacement" in Johannine materials. In addition, it was difficult to explain why the author should interrupt the flow of ch. 6 — the multiplication of bread and its explanation in the Bread of Life discourse — with the apparently unrelated narrative of Christ walking on the water.

Once the chiastic structure of the Gospel is recognized, however, the problem is solved. The core of the entire writing is in fact the walking on the water (6:16-21), representing the New Exodus.[80] This paschal theme is then complemented by the surrounding miracle and discourse, each of which is explicitly eucharistic. These passages flank the central theme like the side panels of a triptych. Then the concentric movement continues backwards and forwards, paralleling the healing of ch. 5 with the allusion to it in ch. 7. The displacement theory, therefore, is not only unnecessary. It is a definite obstacle to a proper understanding and interpretation of the Gospel.

Other examples appear below. This one noted here should suffice to show how very important detection of parallel and chiastic structuring is to the task of exegesis and, for that matter, to any reading of the Scriptures.

Although studies of these rhetorical forms have been fairly widely published in recent years, they seem to have had little impact on the work of Bible translators. Dahood and others have rendered portions of the Psalms in such a way as to represent the concentric parallelism, but the real work of translation in this regard has barely begun. Although at first literal translations of these forms might appear strange to modern readers, the advantages in conveying precise meaning and poetic beauty certainly outweigh any temporary inconvenience.

Above all, however, respecting the literary form of biblical passages goes far towards throwing light on the literal sense of the text. Understanding and elucidating that sense remains the exegete's primary task.[81] The beauty of chiasmus lies in the fact that its form expresses its meaning with such directness and clarity. The surest way to discover and proclaim that meaning, then, is to proceed by a thoroughgoing analysis of the form by which that meaning is conveyed.

ENDNOTES

[1]Today biblical scholars sometimes use "literal sense" to designate the meaning that the text itself conveys, even if that is other than the original intention of the author. The text is thus seen as in some respects autonomous, expressing its meaning through the reader's "response" to it. We discuss this theory further on.

[2]Thanks to the prodigious efforts of text critics such as Eberhard and Erwin Nestle, Kurt Aland, Matthew Black and Bruce Metzger, together with researchers at the Institute for New Testament Textual Research in Münster, W. Germany, the latest critical edition of the *Greek New Testament* (Nestle, 26th ed.) is far more accurate than, for example, the text(s) used by representatives of the exegetical schools of

Alexandria and Antioch during the third and fourth centuries. This holds true even if the so-called "Majority Text" ultimately proves to be closer to the original apostolic writings than the predominantly Egyptian text type that forms the basis of the Nestle edition. See Z.C. Hodges and A.L. Farstad, *The Greek New Testament According to the Majority Text* (2nd ed.) (Nashville: Nelson, 1985) p. ix-xliv; and on the whole question, B.M. Metzger, *The Text of the New Testament* (New York: Oxford, 1964; third enlarged ed., 1992).

[3]For an introduction to and reconstruction of the "Q" document, see I. Havener, *Q. The Sayings of Jesus* (Wilmington, DE: Michael Glazier, 1987).

[4]A distinction is often made between "redaction" and "composition" analysis or criticism, the former referring to the editorial activity of the author, the latter to his actual compositional efforts in producing what is essentially his own work. As Marxsen has pointed out, however, "redaction criticism" properly considers both of these aspects.

[5]A fine, readable account of this and other forms of literary criticism, structuralism, etc., can be found in T. J. Keegan, *Interpreting the Bible* (New York: Paulist Press, 1985). I am indebted to Keegan's study for portions of the following summary. For more detail on the method itself, see J.P. Tompkins, ed., *Reader-Response Criticism* (Baltimore: Johns Hopkins, 1980); and for specific application, G.A. Phillips, "This is a Hard Saying. Who Can Be Listener to It?: Creating a Reader in John 6," *Semeia* 26 (1983) p. 23-56. Indispensable for a true appreciation of the contributions literary criticism has offered to modern biblical studies are the recent works by R. Alter, *The Art of Biblical Narrative* (New York: Harper Basic Books, 1981) and *The Art of Biblical Poetry* (New York: Harper Basic Books, 1985); see as well Alter and F. Kermode (eds.), *The Literary Guide to the Bible* (London, 1987). For other introductions to the various interpretive methods we have mentioned, see the following: O. Kaiser & W. Kummel, *Exegetical Method* (New York: Seabury, 1981); N. Perrin, *What is Redaction Criticism?* (New York: Fortress, 1970/79); and the Fortress Press "Guides to Biblical Scholarship" on historical-critical method, literary criticism and structural exegesis.

[6]J. Navone defines "narrative theology" as "the sustained reflection of the theologian on the way we react to and appropriate the story of Jesus into our own stories." "The life of Jesus and his community of faith," he continues, "is a story, the universal story of all human persons, whether they know it or not." *Gospel Love. A Narrative Theology* (Wilmington: Michael Glazier, 1984) p. 15. See as well T.W. Tilley, *Story Theology* (Wilmington: Michael Glazier, 1985). Both works ground "narrative theology" in a narrative-critical approach to the Gospels.

[7]Some of the most creative interpretive work on biblical texts today is in fact being done by literary critics who would hardly consider themselves to be professional biblical scholars. Robert Alter is an outstanding case in point. Less satisfying is the recent work of G. Josipovici, *The Book of God. A Response to the Bible* (New Haven: Yale U. Press, 1988). Although filled with insights from a literary-critical perspective, the book is oddly out of step with modern biblical research, relying as it does on the original *King James Version* and holding to such untenable theories as the Johannine authorship of Jn 7:53-8:11, the pericope of the woman caught in adultery. (His argument is based on the envelope effect created by the parallel stonings of the adulterous woman and of Jesus in 8:59. While this may explain why a later editor inserted the passage in its present context, it hardly counters the overwhelming evidence for its non-Johannine authorship. See the arguments presented by B. M. Metzger, *A Textual Commentary on the Greek New Testament*, [New

York: United Bible Societies, 1975], p. 219-222; and R.E. Brown, *The Gospel According to John*, vol. I, [New York: Doubleday, 1966], p. 335f.). Josipovici's study decisively, if unwittingly, confirms the need for a theological and historical-critical, as well as literary, approach to the Bible.

[8]Again, Robert Alter is a noteworthy exception. For other highly useful contributions in the area of rhetorical criticism by specialists of Hebrew prose and poetry, see the works of M. Dahood and J.L. Kugel, listed in the bibliography.

[9]Some of the material in this and following sections is drawn from my article, "Biblical Chiasmus: Exploring Structure for Meaning," *BTB*, 17:2 (1987), p. 70-74, and is used with the kind permission of the editor.

[10]The Catholic theologian David Tracy has stated this as follows: "There are no pure ideas free of the web of language. There are no pure messages. Whatever message comes, whatever subject matter is understood, comes by means of its form, whether the text is as short as a proverb or as long as an epic." *Plurality and Ambiguity. Hermeneutics, Religion and Hope*. (San Francisco: Harper & Row, 1987, p. 43); quoted in W.H. Kelber, "Gospel Narrative and Critical Theory," *BTB*, 18:4 (1988), 131. Kelber's essay deals with "the stumbling block to our comprehension of the gospel narratives," which he sees as "their narrative emplotment." Despite its heavy use of jargon, the article offers a useful examination of the positive and negative aspects of narrative criticism, including structuralist and deconstructionist approaches.

[11]University of North Carolina Press. Lund had been working on chiastic structuring well before 1930. See his articles, "The Presence of Chiasmus in the Old Testament," *AJSL* 46 (1930), p. 104-126; "The Presence of Chiasmus in the New Testament," *JR* 10 (1930), p. 74-93; and "Chiasmus in the Psalms," *AJSL* 49 (1933), p. 281-312.

[12]*La structure littéraire de l'Epître aux Hébreux* (2nd ed.), (Paris: Desclée de Brouwer, 1976).

[13]*Matthew: His Mind and His Message* (Collegeville: The Liturgical Press, 1986); *Seven Pauline Letters* (Collegeville: The Liturgical Press, 1982); and *The Genius of John: A Composition-Critical Commentary on the Fourth Gospel* (Collegeville: The Liturgical Press, 1984).

[14]This arrangement is summarized below, II.3.A and Appendix II.

[15]"Chiasmus in the New Testament," in J.W. Welch, ed., *Chiasmus in Antiquity: Structures, Analysis, Exegesis* (Hildesheim: Gerstenberg Verlag, 1981), p. 242.

[16]See J.T. Willis, "The Juxtaposition of Synonymous and Chiastic Parallelism in Tricola in Old Testament Hebrew Psalm Poetry," *VT* 29:4 (1979), p. 465-480, who offers cogent reasons why the psalmist occasionally resorted to the three-line form or "tricolon," including "a natural attraction for triads" characteristic of the Israelite mind, and the use of this form in the cult.

[17]Read "A, B, B-prime, A-prime." This pattern is accepted as chiastic by most commentators. In addition to Lund, see M. Dahood, art. "Chiasmus," *IDB-S* (Nashville: Abingdon, 1976) p. 145; and J. Staley, "The Structure of John's Prologue: Its Implications for the Gospel's Narrative Structure," *CBQ* 48:2 (1986), p. 241-264. A.R. Ceresko, "The A:B::B:A Word Pattern in Hebrew and Northwest Semitic, with Special Reference to the Book of Job," *UF* 7 (1975), p. 73-88; "The Chiastic Word Pattern in

Hebrew," *CBQ* 38:3 (1976), p. 303-311; and "The Function of Chiasmus in Hebrew Poetry," *CBQ* 40:1 (1978), p. 1-10, also considers the A:B:B':A' pattern to be chiastic and offers examples from Ugaritic sources as well as from the Hebrew Scriptures.

[18]Vanhoye, A. Di Marco ("Der Chiasmus in der Bibel, 1. Teil," *LingBib* 36 [1975], p. 21-97) and others speak of "concentric symmetry." While accurate, the expression is less precise, since the existence of parallel phrases (verbal or thematic) is basic to chiasmus.

[19]See P. Ellis, *The Genius of John*, p. 14f for an outline of the sequences of the Fourth Gospel, and Appendix II of this present study.

[20]M.E. Boismard, *Le prologue de S. Jean* (Paris: Cerf, 1953) established this point, which has been accepted by many interpreters, but hardly by all. On the structure of the prologue, see A. Feuillet, *Le prologue du quatrième évangile* (Paris: Desclée De Brouwer, 1968), esp. ch. 2; A. Di Marco, "Der Chiasmus in der Bibel, 3 Teil," *LingBib* 39 (1978) p. 37-85, esp. p. 75; and the important study by R.A. Culpepper, "The Pivot of John's Prologue," *NTS* 27 (1980) p. 1-31; together with our discussion in II.3.B.

[21]See R.F. Smith, "Chiasm in Sumero-Akkadian," in Welch, *Chiasmus in Antiquity*, p. 17-35; J.W. Welch, "Chiasmus in Ugaritic," *ibid.*, p. 36-49; and J.C. de Moor, art. "Ugarit," *IDB-S*, p. 928-931, for an overview of recent studies of Ugaritic texts and their relationship to the OT.

[22]For general introductions to this field, see the articles "Poetry, Hebrew," by N.K. Gottwald in *IDB* vol. 3, 829-838; and M. Dahood, *IDB-S*, 669-672, with their bibliographies on specific rhetorical forms; also A. Fitzgerald, art. "Hebrew Poetry" in *JBC* (1968), p. 238-244, and *NJBC* (1990), p. 201-208. A good introduction, with definitions of technical terms, is provided by W.G.E. Watson, "Chiastic Patterns in Biblical Hebrew Poetry," in J.W. Welch, *Chiasmus in Antiquity*, p. 118-168. A brief outline can also be found in *The New Oxford Annotated Bible*, ed. H.G. May and B.M. Metzger (New York: Oxford, 1973), p. 1523-1529; and in the *NRSV* version (New York: Oxford, 1991), p. (NT) 392-397. For more technical studies, see W.L. Holladay, "The Recovery of Poetic Passages of Jeremiah," *JBL*, 58 (1966), p. 401-435; and A.R. Ceresko, "The Function of Chiasmus in Hebrew Poetry," p. 1-10. Particularly useful is M. Dahood's three volume commentary on the Psalms (Garden City: Doubleday, 1966, 1968, 1970). More recently, significant advances in our understanding of the way Hebrew poetry functions have been made by M. O'Connor, *Hebrew Verse Structure* (Winona Lake, IN: Eisenbrauns, 1980); J.L. Kugel, *The Idea of Biblical Poetry. Parallelism and its History* (New Haven: Yale U. Press, 1981); and R. Alter, *The Art of Biblical Poetry* (New York: Harper Basic Books, 1985). Alter rejects Kugel's conclusion that the distinction between Hebrew prose and poetry is one of mere degree (implying, in fact, that "poetry" is a misnomer); but the two works complement each other and should be studied together. Particularly on the question of "divergences" in parallel structures in Hebrew poetry, see A. Berlin, *The Dynamics of Biblical Parallelism* (Bloomington, Ind.: Indiana U. Press, 1985).

[23]Lowth's *Lectures on the Sacred Poetry of the Hebrews*, published in Latin in 1753, appeared in English translation in 1787. A new edition, with notes by Calvin E. Stowe, was published in 1829 by Crocker and Brewster (Boston), and J. Leavitt (New York). Lowth's most important work is the commentary *Isaiah: A New Translation with Preliminary Dissertation* (1778; London: Dodsley and Cadell), in which he offers a fuller explanation of Hebrew poetic forms. For an historical overview and evaluation, see A. Baker, "Parallelism: England's Contribution to Biblical Studies," *CBQ* 35:4 (1973), p. 429-440.

[24]In his commentary on Isaiah, Lowth states: "The correspondence of one verse or line with another, I call parallelism. When a proposition is delivered, and a second subjoined under it, equivalent or contrasted with it in sense, or similar to it in the form of grammatical construction, these I call parallel lines; and the words or phrases, answering one to another in the corresponding lines, parallel terms" (p. x-xi, quoted by J. Muilenberg, art. "Biblical Poetry," *EJ*, vol. 13, cols. 671-681, quote col. 672). Lowth's classifications of "synonymous," "antithetical" and "synthetic" parallelism have been rightly criticized by scholars such as Kugel and Alter. No one, however, denies that Lowth's investigations led to a major breakthrough in our understanding of Hebrew poetic forms. See his introductory "Dissertation" in the 1829 edition, p. i-lxxiv.

[25]Holladay, "The Recovery of Poetic Passages of Jeremiah," p. 406ff, distinguishes two basic structures in Hebrew poetry: "balance" and "sequentiality." He prefers the term balance "to indicate a correspondence or identification, of whatever sort, between any given components of poetry, whether they be units, cola, lines, or stanzas." Sequentiality, on the other hand, refers to components arranged in sequential order. While the distinction is useful, it is somewhat misleading. Passages, whether poetry or prose, can be structured according to both balance and sequence; and "parallelism" more adequately expresses the kind of symmetry that is basic to chiasmus.

[26]Notice the inverted parallelism in this example: verb (knowest) — object (folly) // object (wrongs) — verb (not hidden). The numbering of the Psalms follows the Hebrew psalter unless otherwise noted.

[27]See J.L. Kugel, p. 1f.

[28]B. Hrushovski, art. "Prosody," *EJ* vol. 13 (New York: MacMillan, 1971), cols. 1195-1203 ("introduction" and "principles of biblical verse"), followed by R. Alter.

[29]Numerous definitions and examples are given by Mary Sweazey (Cowles) in the introduction to her Master of Divinity thesis, "A Chiastic Study of the First Epistle of John," St. Vladimir's Orthodox Theological Seminary, Crestwood, N.Y., 1986. This study, presently being revised for publication, offers a thorough and convincing analysis of chiasmus in 1 John, both in individual units and in the Epistle as a whole.

[30]This illustration is based on the English translation of the Masoretic text (the LXX and NT renderings omit the second reference to "desert"). A similar example is Isa 53:1, "Who has believed what we have heard? / And to whom has the arm of the Lord been revealed?" // The second line represents a gradation upon the first in that "heard" is augmented by "revealed," and "what we have heard" is specified by "the arm of the Lord." Compare the parallelism with intensification characteristic of the following doxological couplets: "Blessed be the Lord, the God of Israel / who alone does wondrous things. // Blessed be his glorious name forever; / may his glory fill the whole earth! Amen and Amen!" // — Ps. 72:18f. Countless other examples could be given from the prophets, the psalms and other Hebrew writings, and several of the most characteristic are noted below.

[31]Specialists also distinguish "formal" (often referred to as "synthetic") parallelism and link it closely to the climactic pattern. In formal parallelism, the second line merely advances the thought of the first but with no repetition of content. An example commonly cited is Ps 14:1, "The fool says in his heart, / there is no God." The only justification for calling this "parallelism" is the fact that it forms a couplet

followed by a clear caesura (a pause or stop). Authentic parallelism, however, must balance terms or ideas, whether or not it expresses gradation in thought.

[32]Y.T. Radday, "Chiasmus in Hebrew Biblical Narrative," in J.W. Welch, *Chiasmus in Antiquity*, p. 50-115, analyzes key prose passages from the Hebrew Bible, beginning with the most recent and proceeding to the more ancient. He contends that the older prose texts exhibit more conscious chiastic structuring than do the more recent, and therefore he suggests that the presence of chiasmus can help with dating a given passage. The evidence does not clearly support this view, but his study, especially on the chiastic rendering of Leviticus and Numbers, is highly useful.

[33]A. Weiser, *The Psalms: A Commentary* (Philadelphia: Westminster Press, 1962), p. 407.

[34]Translation of I.M. Cassanowicz, art. "Parallelism in Biblical Poetry," *TJE* vol. 10, p. 520-522.

[35]The contrast between B and B' is between "being in the darkness" and "having no cause for stumbling," implying that one is "in the light."

[36]Lower case letters indicate the distinct semantic or syntactic elements in a particular verset; A and B represent the first and second verset respectively.

[37]Kugel's translation, *ibid.*, p. 20. See his discussion of inverted forms, which he identifies as chiastic, p. 19f.

[38]See J. Muilenberg, art. "Biblical Poetry," *EJ* col. 671.

[39]This passage also illustrates a characteristic of Semitic poetry known as *epiphora:* repetition of the same words or sounds at the end of successive lines (A-B, "my Father," "the Father"). *Anaphora*, or repetition of the same words or sounds at the beginning of successive lines, is broken in this case, because in the Greek original the "no one knows" of B-B' is arranged in inverted order: B = "and no one knows the Son except the Father"; B' = "nor the Father (does) anyone know except the Son." Alter, *Poetry*, p. 64, gives a more comprehensive definition of anaphora: "the rhetorically emphatic reiteration of a single word or brief phrase, in itself not a syntactically complete unit." As an example, he offers "Soldier, bid her farewell, bid her farewell," where the repetition creates reinforcement, from simple leave-taking to what will become a permanent separation if the soldier dies in battle.

[40]See J.W. Welch, "Chiasmus in Ancient Greek and Latin Literature," in his *Chiasmus in Antiquity*, p. 250-268, who discusses this pattern in detail.

[41]See A. Stock, "Chiastic Awareness and Education in Antiquity," *BTB* 14:1 (1984), 23-27; and H.I. Marrou, *A History of Education in Antiquity* (New York: Sheed & Ward, 1956).

[42]A simple example of this form would be, Question: "Do you like it here? Would you prefer to be home?"; Answer: "I would prefer to be home, but I do like it here." An interesting NT example of the model is found in Mk 3:22-30, where Jesus answers *in reverse order* two charges made by the Jerusalem scribes. V. 22a = the charge that Jesus is possessed by Beelzebul; v. 22b = the charge that he casts out demons by the prince of demons. The latter charge is answered first in vv. 23-27 (a house divided against itself cannot stand); then the former charge is answered in vv. 28-30 (the scribes' initial accusation represents blasphemy against the Holy Spirit).

[43]See R.E. Man, "The Value of Chiasm for New Testament Interpretation," *BS* (1984), p. 146-157, esp. p. 152. M.H. Lichtenstein, "Chiasm and Symmetry in Proverbs 31," *CBQ* 44 (1982), p. 202-211, shows that Prov 31:6-7 "may be viewed either as a framed chiasm..., or as a case of *hysteron proteron*" (210).

[44]J. Kugel, *Poetry*, p. 40f, rightly warns against the practice of "redistribution" (from diaeresis or "dividing in two," a term attributed to Theodore of Mopsuestia): recombining the elements of juxtaposed versets to make a single statement. This practice, Kugel states, is based on the false notion that the biblical writer began with a single sentence, "then, via distribution, made it into two parallel halves. Redistributing them into a single assertion intends to find out what was 'really' meant." What was "really" meant, however, can only be determined by respecting the movement of thought from the first verset to the second.

[45]For an exhaustive listing of these forms within single verse lines of classical Hebrew, see W.G.E. Watson, "Internal or Half-Line Parallelism in Classical Hebrew Again," *VT* 29:1 (1989), p. 44-66, and the references to his previous studies, n. 1.

[46]Example given by N.K. Gottwald, *IDB* III, p. 833.

[47]Discussed by M. Dahood, *IDB-S*, p. 670f. See also his article, "A New Metrical Pattern in Biblical Poetry," *CBQ* 29:4 (1967), p. 574-579.

[48]See below for discussions of these passages and the chiastic arrangements within them.

[49]The phenomenon of inclusion is still apparent today, even in such popular compositions as news magazine articles. It is often a key feature of the brief, tightly structured pieces composed by syndicated columnists. For a striking example, see below, "Chiasmus Today," III.9.

[50]This passage is a subsection of Ellis' sequence 14, Jn 9:1-10:21. See his *Genius*, p. 165f.

[51]Yet even here it should be noted that "C" is not without significance for the entire section, insofar as it stresses the failure on the part of Jesus' adversaries to grasp the meaning of his parabolic images. Since the theme of the "Jews" misunderstanding is central to this portion of the Gospel (chs. 8-10), this brief hinge-verse, 10:6, still serves to some degree as the thematic center of 9:39-10:21.

[52]This list is drawn in part from Watson's "Chiastic Patterns in Biblical Hebrew Poetry," p. 123ff. The interested reader will find there an excellent presentation of the various patterns that appear in chiastic form.

[53]The first to label this construction was John Jebb: "There are stanzas so constructed, that, whatever be the number of lines, the first shall be parallel with the last; the second with the penultimate; and so throughout, in order that it looks inward, or, to borrow a military phrase, from flanks to centre. This may be called introverted parallelism." Jebb, *Sacred Literature*, London 1820; quoted in Lund, *Chiasmus in the New Testament*, p. 37.

[54]The form *pisteuete* is both indicative and imperative. The verse can be translated as though the first phrase were a statement ("You believe in God") and the second a command ("[therefore] believe also in me"). The inversion, however, suggests another possibility, according to which both verbs would be read as indicatives: "[Since] you believe in God, [therefore] you also believe in me;" or as imperatives: "Believe in God, [therefore] believe also in me." In either case it would

represent still another Johannine declaration of Jesus' divinity: to believe in God is, *ipso facto*, to believe in Jesus as God. It would therefore be affirming what is stated a few verses farther on: "Whoever has seen me has seen the Father" (14:9).

[55]For examples of "split-member" and "partial" chiasmus in monocola and bicola, see Watson, p. 124f.

[56]Translation by Watson, p. 128.

[57]D.C. Fredericks, "Chiasm and Parallel Structure in *Qoheleth* 5:9-6:9," *JBL* 108:1 (1989), p. 17-35, has recently pointed to a similar pattern in Ecclesiastes, where the center is a double proposition, C:C'. Here a dramatic contrast is created between the extremities (frustrations of wealth, personal tragedy // frustrated desire, vanity) and the conceptual center with its theme of joy and blessedness.

[58]D. Grossberg, *Centripetal and Centrifugal Structures in Biblical Poetry* (Atlanta: Scholars Press, 1989), p. 39, detects an eightfold structure in Ps 124: A-A' (YHWH), B-B' (man), C-C' (animal), D-D' (water). This pattern is common in the NT: see, e.g., Mk 5:24b-34, analyzed below.

[59]Kugel, *Poetry*, p. 171.

[60]P. 51.

[61]P. 85. S.A. Geller, "Theory and Method in the Study of Biblical Poetry," *JQR* 73:1 (1982), p. 65-77, objects sharply to what he perceives to be Kugel's polemical "unconcern for taxonomic exactness that is in keeping with his disdain for description and classification," extending "even to the basic differentiation between 'prose' and 'poetry' assumed by Lowth" (p. 75).

[62]This is in fact the definition given by B.H. Smith, *Poetic Closure* (Chicago, 1968), whom Alter quotes on p. 6. The key elements here are sustained rhythm and a continuously operating principle of organization, which imply the presence of a form of meter "separating it from a 'ground' of less highly structured speech and sound," Smith, p. 23f.

[63]*Poetry*, p. 20 and *passim*.

[64]Cf. Jer 7:34; Isa 45:12; and Job 30:10, which Alter translates, "They despised me, drew away from me, / and from my face they did not hold back their spittle" //, p. 21.

[65]Defined by Alter as verbatim repetition with an added element, *Poetry*, p. 23f.

[66]Alter's translation, *Poetry*, p.43f. His exposition of this passage is a masterpiece of literary analysis. Cf. Gen 6:5-17, with incremental repetition from vv. 5-7 to v. 13 to v. 17, expressing respectively God's regret at having created humankind, his determination to destroy all flesh, and his vow that "everything that is on the earth shall die!"

[67]I am grateful to my former student, Rev. Nabil Hanna, for suggesting this use of numbers. In Parts II and III we revert to the more familiar use of letters; but this is occasionally complemented by summaries using numbers, in order to stress the focusing movement from the extremities toward the center. The letter arrangement has the effect of highlighting the envelope or inclusion (A:A'), whereas the numbers more clearly indicate the spiral movement towards the central focal point. A system is needed that will emphasize both of these elements with a single set of indicators.

[68]Cf. Deut 32:37f, "Then he will say, 'Where are their gods, / the rock in which they took refuge, // who ate the fat of their sacrifices, / and drank the wine of their drink offering? // Let them rise up and help you, / let them be your protection!' " // This is an example of direct parallelism, constructed as three lines of two versets each, but it is not chiastic. The Jeremiah oracle, while conveying the same message, resounds with far greater power, precisely because of the concentricity of its parallelism and the heightening effect from strophe I to strophe II.

[69]Cf. 4:6, and the opposition between the "spirit of truth" and the "spirit of deception."

[70]The expression is used by R. Alter, *The Art of Biblical Narrative*, p. 24, and refers to the fact that the biblical authors sought not only to express theological meaning, but to exploit as well their own consummate literary skill, in composing their accounts of Israel's sacred history. Alter states: "Perhaps this is the ultimate difference between any hermeneutic approach to the Bible and the literary approach that I am proposing: in the literary perspective there is latitude for the exercise of pleasurable invention for its own sake, ranging from 'microscopic' details like sound-play to 'macroscopic' features like the psychology of individual characters," (p. 46.)

[71]J.S. Kselman, "Psalm 72: Some Observations on Structure," *BASOR* 220 (1975), p. 77-81, divides the psalm into five strophes (1 = vv. 1-4; 2 = vv. 5-8; 3 = vv. 9-11; 4 = vv. 12-15; and 5 = vv. 16-17) and analyzes the parallelism in strophes I and III, together with the inclusion represented by vv. 1-2 and 15-17. He concludes: "the Hebrew poet was capable not only of working with line-by-line parallelism of the bicolon and tricolon, but of creating a wider, more complex symmetry through chiasmus, inclusion and other techniques" (p. 79).

[72]The chiastic structure of this psalm confirms the Masoretic reading in v. 5: "May they fear thee," rather than "May he live," despite the shift from third to second person.

[73]The studies dealing with chiasmus in the Psalms seem to multiply daily. In addition to Dahood's commentary, see M. Girard, *Les Psaumes. Analyse structurelle et interprétation*, Vol. I, 1-50 (Montreal: Belarmin / Paris: Cerf, 1984); and P. Auffret, "'Allez, fils, entendez-moi!' Etude structurelle du psaume 34 et son rapport au psaume 33," in *Eglise et Théologie* (A Review of the Faculty of Theology, St. Paul University, Ottawa, Canada) 19/1 (1988), p. 5-31, who stresses the "concentric symmetry" characteristic of the genre. For a study of the intricate "scribal exercises" represented by the so-called "alphabetic" psalms, and their concentric patterns, see B. Lindars, "The Structure of Psalm CXLV," *VT* 27/1 (1977), p. 23-30.

[74]Alter translates more appropriately, "to dally with us" (*Narrative*, p. 107-111). This better preserves the contrast between "to do his work" of v. 11 and the woman's accusations in vv. 14 and 17.

[75]For further basic examples of poetic elements in Priestly tradition, see J.S. Kselman, "The Recovery of Poetic Fragments from the Pentateuchal Priestly Source," *JBL* 97:2 (1978), p. 161-173. Other prophetic passages also display chiasmus within a narrative framework and thus qualify as "poetry": see, e.g., R. Pesch, "Zur konzentrischen Struktur von Jona 1," *Bib* 47 (1966), p. 577-581; and J. de Waard, "The Chiastic Structure of Amos V.1-17," *VT* 27 (1977), p. 170-177. De Waard shows how chiastic sub-units can be contained within a larger chiastic arrangement, a phenomenon frequently encountered in the NT. He also raises the important question, which

we consider further on, of the *conscious* or *unconscious* use of the "spatial arrangements" of words and phrases typical of concentric parallelism.

[76]See R.E. Brown's discussion of "the role of the Beloved Disciple in xx 3-10 in relation to Peter," *The Gospel According to John*, vol. 2 (New York: Doubleday, 1970), p. 1004-1007.

[77]*Chiasmus in Antiquity*, p. 14.

[78]Note the perceptive remark of Yehuda Radday, in J.W. Welch, *Chiasmus in Antiquity*, p. 91: "When confronted with a painting by Picasso of a woman half of whose head is *en face* and whose other half shows her in profile, would anybody dare propose that the painter was forgetful, that he painted the two halves in different periods of his lifetime or that one half was painted by the artist himself and the other by a disciple? Only in biblical criticism does one encounter such theories and one wonders to whom they make sense."

[79]*Das Evangelium des Johannes*, Göttingen, 1964, p. 154f. Bultmann was not the first to argue for such a rearrangement of gospel materials, nor was he the last; but he is certainly the most influential. In his discussion of the Prologue, he dismisses Lund's work with the comment, "(L's attempt) to explain the plan of the Prologue from the principle of chiasmus is not convincing," p. 2, n. 3.

[80]The evidence for this analysis is given in Part II.3.C, below.

[81]Once again, this is not to say that the final aim of biblical interpretation is to uncover the author's own intended meaning. Such is and should remain the initial task of the exegete. But exegesis must ultimately lead beyond the literal sense to discern the "spiritual sense" of the text: the message God addresses to the church and world in each new generation through the Word of Scripture. For the relation between the literal and spiritual senses in the history of exegesis, see J. Breck, *The Power of the Word*, chs. 1-3.

PART TWO:

CHIASMUS IN THE
NEW TESTAMENT

1. SYNOPTIC NARRATIVES

A. Peter's Confession of Faith

At this point we turn to specific examples of chiastic structuring in the New Testament gospels and epistles. The first passage to consider is the familiar "confession of Peter" which appears in each of the three Synoptic Gospels.[1] We plan to examine it in some detail, since it offers an excellent illustration of the way in which Matthew has taken up Mark's witness and modified it for theological reasons by structuring it chiastically. As we shall discover through other examples, Matthew has a penchant for altering his Markan source in this way, thereby shaping the tradition to express his own theological point of view.

Our purpose, then, is to show how Matthew utilized and altered the more primitive Markan tradition, and to draw some conclusions as to how the restructuring of this passage in the First Gospel changed its conceptual center and thereby changed its meaning. No attempt is made to resolve all of the difficult exegetical problems raised by Matthew 16:13-20. Our concern is more with the redactional history of this passage than with its theological implications.[2]

The historical authenticity of Peter's denial of Christ is attested by the fact that all four evangelists assure their readers of Peter's rehabilitation. In every gospel but Matthew's, this rehabilitation is accomplished after the resurrection, either by an angel-messenger or by the risen Lord himself.

In Mark 16:5-7 "a young man" at the tomb tells the women that "the crucified one" (τον εσταυρωμενον) is risen, and he instructs them to "go, tell his disciples and Peter" to meet Jesus in Galilee, where their mission began. Whether this refers to a resurrection appearance or, as some have suggested, to the parousia,[3] its effect is to distinguish Peter from the other disciples by emphasizing his unique position: και τω Πετρω. This is supported by Luke 24:34 ("the Lord has risen indeed, and has appeared to Simon"), and still more directly by 1 Corinthians 15:5 ("...He appeared to Cephas, then to the Twelve"). In the former instance, the Emmaus disciples hear the testimony of "the Eleven and those gathered with them." Although Luke presents the Emmaus encounter as the first resurrectional appearance to disciples other than the women, he lets the reader understand that a prior appearance had occurred to Simon, thereby distinguishing him both from the "Eleven" (of whom he was, of course, a member) and from the others. Paul's tradition likewise sets Cephas off from the rest of the Twelve. Luke and Paul share with Mark, then, a common concern to show that Peter, who denied Christ at the time of the trial, has been made a privileged witness to the resurrection.[4]

The Johannine equivalent of this rehabilitation process occurs in ch. 21 of the gospel. By soliciting a threefold affirmation of love, the risen Lord demonstrates his forgiveness of Peter's threefold denial, and in the process he reinstates him as the chief pastor over the flock of believers. Although the Good Shepherd (10:14) is taken away from his sheep, he does not leave them leaderless. On the one hand he promises to be present with them in the person of the Spirit-Paraclete (14:16f,18,26; 16:7,13-15); on the other, he communicates particular — and apparently unique — pastoral authority to Simon Peter by the commission, "Feed my sheep" (21:15ff).

Matthew appears to know nothing of these various traditions. Whereas Luke 22:31-34 stresses Peter's coming temptation, Matthew 26:30-35 follows Mark in declaring that "you will all fall away." Matthew's account of the empty tomb omits all reference to Peter (compare Mt 28:7 with Mk 16:7), as do his stories of the resurrection appearances. How are we to assess these factors? Is Matthew simply uninterested in those elements of the early tradition which affirm that the risen Christ appeared first to Peter? Can he be unaware of the tradition which augmented that earliest proclamation (1 Cor 15:3-5) by affirming that Peter received from the risen Jesus both forgiveness for his denial and restitution as leader of the Twelve?

A close examination of Matthew's form of the Petrine confession (16:13ff) shows quite the contrary. It is there that Peter receives both divine approval and divine authority to assume the pastoral charge which, according to the implicit or explicit witness of the other gospels, he received only after Jesus' resurrection.

The Markan account of Peter's confession includes five separate elements: 8:27-28 = the popular conception of Jesus; 8:29 = Peter's confession of Jesus as Messiah; 8:30 = Jesus' charge to secrecy; 8:31 = the first passion prediction; and 8:32-33 = Peter's refusal to accept the suffering and death of Jesus as Son of Man, followed by Jesus' rebuke (the "Satan-word").[5] As a result of Markan redaction, the first three elements form a unit, as do the last two. The former begins with an introductory statement (anacrusis) that locates the confession geographically: "And Jesus went on with his disciples to the villages of Caesarea-Philippi." Verse 27b begins the unit containing the confession and the charge to secrecy. The whole passage is structured in simple direct parallelism, while the "what's more" principle of focusing through specification is evident from A to A' and from B to B'.

A : And on the way he asked his disciples,
   "Who do people say that I am?" (v. 27b)

B : And they told him,
   "John the Baptist, and others (say) Elijah,
   and others one of the prophets." (v. 28)

A': And he asked them,
   "But who do you say that I am?"

B': Peter answered and said to him,
   "You are the Messiah." (v. 29)

C: And he charged them
   to tell no one about him. (v. 30)

The typically Markan (Semitic) repetition of "and" (και) links v. 31 to the foregoing unit: "And he began to teach them...". Luke avoids any such break between the two units, joining them by the participle "saying" (ειπων, 9:22). This produces a smooth transition which forges Lk 9:18-22 into a single unit ending with the passion prediction. Luke also omits the mutual rebuke between Peter and Jesus in order to pass directly to the saying about the Cross and its consequences for discipleship (9:23-27).[6]

The only other significant point at which Luke differs from Mark is in the setting of the confession. No mention is made of Caesarea-Philippi; he states rather that "Jesus was praying alone [and] the disciples were with him" (9:18a). This is a frequent theme of the Third Gospel that marks crucial moments in Jesus' ministry.[7] As a

Lukan redactional device, therefore, it in no way calls into question the hypothesis that Luke relied on Mark as his source for the confession scene. Luke changes Jesus' question to "Who do the multitudes (οχλοι) say that I am?" But as with the "people" (οι ανθρωποι) of Mark 8:27, this refers generally to those outside the immediate circle of the Twelve. In the disciples' reply to Jesus' initial question, Luke reflects the popular belief that one of the former prophets would rise from the dead to herald the new, messianic age. He augments the force of Jesus' command to silence (v. 21) and (with Matthew) "corrects" Mark's "after three days" to "on the third day" (v. 22).

As for the confession itself, Luke has Peter declare, "You are the Christ of God" (τον χριστον του θεου). This confessional formula occurs indirectly in 4:41 ("Son of God" / "Christ") and again in 23:35, where the taunting rulers unwittingly profess Jesus to be "the Christ of God, his Chosen One!" (ο χριστος του θεου ο εκλεκτος). Once again, however, nothing of this warrants the conclusion that Luke relied upon any source other than the Gospel of Mark to compose his account of Peter's confession.

Turning to Matthew's account, we find the matter to be far more complicated. A glance at a synopsis shows that Matthew has inserted into the Markan outline three verses of material that constitute Jesus' reply to Peter's confession (16:17-19). He marks a clear break after the charge to silence (16:20) by beginning the passion prediction with "From that time on" (Απο τοτε).[8] In addition, he has made several small but important changes in the Markan source that tighten Mark's A:B:A':B' parallelism and transform C, the charge to silence, into the second term of an inclusion: A ("asks his disciples") // C ("admonishes the disciples"). The overall structure may be clearly seen from the following arrangement of the Greek text of Matthew 16:13-16, and 20, the verses that represent a modified version of Mark's tradition.

A : Ελθων δε ο Ιησους εις τα μερη Καισαρειας της Φιλιππου
ηρωτα τους μαθητας αυτου λεγων·
τινα λεγουσιν οι ανθρωποι
ειναι τον υιον του ανθρωπου;

B : οι δε ειπαν·
οι μεν Ιωαννην τον Βαπτιστην, αλλοι δε Ηλιαν,
ετεροι δε Ιερεμιαν η ενα των προφητων.

A': λεγει αυτοις·
υμεις δε τινα με λεγετε ειναι;

Β': αποκριθεις δε Σιμων Πετρος ειπεν·
    συ ει ο χριστος
    ο υιος του θεου του ζωντος.

C : τοτε διεστειλατο τοις μαθηταις
    ινα μηδενι ειπωσιν
    οτι αυτος εστιν ο χριστος.

A : Jesus asks his *disciples*, "Who do *people* say
the Son of Man is?" (v. 13).

   B : They reply, "John the Baptist, Elijah, Jeremiah
   or one of the prophets" (v. 14).

A': Jesus asks, "Who do you say that I am?" (v. 15)

   B': Simon Peter answers, "You are the Messiah,
   the Son of the living God" (v. 16).

C (A"): Jesus admonishes the *disciples* to tell no one
(*no person*) that he is the Messiah.

In Matthew, Peter's confession is preceded by Jesus' warning concerning the leaven of the Pharisees and Sadducees (16:6). The fact that Mark preserves the more primitive account is shown by the personal reference to Herod,[9] rather than to the Sadducees, together with the intervening healing story, 8:22-26. This latter account Matthew omits, perhaps because of its somewhat unrefined imagery ("spittle," "walking trees"), but more likely because he wishes to move directly from the discourse on leaven — with its condemnation of the false teaching of those who reject Jesus — into Peter's extraordinary confession of Jesus as Messiah and Son of God.[10] Attempting to improve on the rather clumsy Markan account ("they had forgotten to bring bread...they had only one loaf with them," 8:14), Matthew changes his source to imply they had no bread at all (Mt 16:5), thereby making a smoother introduction into the double allusion to the leaven and to the multiplication of bread. With these images of "true and false bread," implying true and false teaching, Matthew moves directly on to the ultimate confession of truth about Jesus, made by the first-called of the disciples.[11]

The changes Matthew introduces into the tradition he received from Mark's Gospel can be summarized as follows.

16:13 — Matthew modifies Mark's account of the setting of Peter's confession by changing "(surrounding) villages" to "the region" of Caesarea-Philippi. The city itself thus becomes the locus at which Jesus of Nazareth is proclaimed to be Messiah and Son of God. Caesarea-Philippi was a major Hellenistic city, the most important Gentile center in northern Palestine. Having just recounted Jesus' condemnation of Jewish leaders who refused to recognize his Lordship, Matthew proceeds to situate Peter's confession in a major Gentile metropolis. He also incorporates the place-name into the first strophe of his account to emphasize the geographic setting (cf. Mk 8:27, "on the way"). By opening the scene with the participle "coming" (ελθων; Mk reads εξηλθεν), he focuses attention immediately on Jesus' question, composed of two lines of nine syllables each that balance "men" with "Son of man" (Mark and Luke read, "Who do men say that I am?").

16:14 — In Mark, Peter's confession is prepared in 6:14-16, where Herod hears of Jesus' renown as a preacher and healer. Popular opinion identified Jesus with John the baptizer, with Elijah, or with the awaited eschatological prophet.[12] Peter's confession in Mark 8:29 affirms that Jesus is to be identified with none of these figures, since each of them was understood to be a mere precursor.[13] Rather, he is ο χριστος — not "Christ" or "the Christ," but "Messiah," the "anointed one" announced by the prophets, who fulfills God's promise to redeem his people.

Matthew, however, omits the Markan reference to Elijah and the prophets in his parallel passage, 14:1-2. Here Herod himself declares that Jesus is "John the Baptist raised from the dead." This "confession" is the central focus for Matthew, since John's presumed resurrection serves as a prophetic image of Jesus' own resurrection, which will be announced for the first time in 16:21, following the true confession by Peter.

In 16:14, Matthew adds to the list of popular assumptions concerning Jesus' identity the name of the prophet Jeremiah. Jeremiah was not expected to return as was Elijah, nor was he viewed as a type of the eschatological prophet.[14] Nevertheless, his appearance in the Matthean account is consistent with his place in the evangelist's overall proclamation. Matthew is the only New Testament author to cite the name of Jeremiah,[15] and he quotes or alludes to his prophecy some fourteen times, of which the majority are unique to his gospel.[16] Occasionally he appeals to Jeremiah to build his polemic against Jewish religious leaders who have proven to be "false shepherds" to their people.[17] The change from one servant to several in the parable of the wicked tenants (Mt 21:33ff; Mk 12:1ff) may also reflect Matthew's special interest in Jeremiah, if Mt 21:35 can be read as an allusion to Jer 20:2. In this case, the one servant of the parable who was beaten would refer to Jeremiah himself. Be that as it may, Matthew seems to find in Jeremiah's message and his suffering the characteristics of the true prophet, who would naturally serve as a type or prophetic figure of Jesus, the suffering Messiah.[18]

16:15-16 — Jesus' question, "Who do you say that I am?" (υμεις δε τινα με λεγετε ειναι;) is the only fixed element in the Synoptic accounts of this scene. The reply is given by "Simon Peter" (Mark and Luke read simply "Peter"). Although Jesus first attributes the unusual name "Cephas" (*Kepha*, Greek: *Petros*) to Simon only two verses later in 16:18, Matthew has previously referred to him as Peter six times.[19] On two of those occasions he uses the expression "Simon, called Peter" (4:18; 10:2). This apparent anachronism is only one indication that vv. 17-19 constitute an independent unit, either composed by Matthew, or representing primitive Aramaic tradition that Matthew has inserted into his Markan source.

Simon Peter's confession comprises two messianic titles, "Christ" and "Son of God." As throughout the Synoptic tradition, the most frequent christological title in Matthew is "the Son of Man," used by Jesus as a self-designation. Matthew reports the use of other titles, both single and composite: "Son of David"[20] and "Lord / Son of David."[21] In 22:42, Jesus indirectly identifies himself as both "Messiah" and "Son of David." As for the title "Son," it occurs alone in 11:27 and 24:36, passages that represent a bridge between Jesus' use of the familiar epithet "Abba," and the "Father-Son" theology that comes to fullest expression in the Fourth Gospel.

By appealing to Old Testament prophecy, Matthew attempts from the outset of his gospel to show that Jesus of Nazareth is the Messiah awaited by Israel. It seems quite probable that the Markan tradition concerning Peter's confession is ultimately based upon an actual dialogue between Jesus and his disciple,[22] although its original form may be impossible to recover. At a turning point in the Galilean ministry, Simon declared Jesus to be Messiah. This declaration was answered by the charge to silence, which stands in Mark as an example of the "Messianic secret."[23]

Matthew expands that original confession in order to draw together in Peter's declaration the full significance of Jesus' messianic work and his filial relationship to his "Father in heaven" (a typically Matthean expression[24]). From the beginning Jesus is named "Emmanuel," "God with us," in fulfillment of prophecy.[25] In the infancy narrative he is designated God's Son, the personification of Israel (2:15). At his baptism (3:17), and again at the transfiguration (17:5), the heavenly voice (bat-qôl) proclaims him publicly to be "my beloved Son,"[26] a composite announcement based on Gen 22:2; Ps 2:7; and Isa 42:1. Since the discovery of the Dead Sea Scroll known as 4 Q Florilegium, it has become clear that at Qumran — and presumably in other pre-Christian Jewish milieux — the title "Son" or "Son of God" was used of the Davidic or Royal Messiah.[27] Commenting on the verse, "I will be a father to him and he shall be my son," the author of the florilegium identifies the "son" as "the Branch of David." This designation is from Jeremiah 23:5; 33:15, and perhaps accounts for the frequent occurrence in Matthew of the title "Son/Son of God" to signify Jesus' authority to proclaim the word of the Kingdom and to cast out demons (8:29, the demons confess him to be "Son of God").

That Matthew intends the title "Son/Son of God" to designate Jesus' divine origin as well as his divine authority is clear from his references to those who "worship" him. In the temptation scene, Jesus quotes Deuteronomy 6:13 (LXX), declaring "You shall worship (προσκυνησεις) the Lord your God and him only shall you serve" (4:10 // Luke 4:8, from Q?).[28] Yet Matthew repeatedly emphasizes the worship accorded to Jesus: by the Magi (2:2,8); by the leper (8:2, where Matthew alone specifies προσεκυνει αυτω); by the ruler (9:18, unique to the First Gospel); and by the Canaanite woman (15:25, omitted by the parallel in Mk 7:25). Although the RSV reads simply "kneel" in passages such as 8:2 and 20:20, the expression προσκυνησαν αυτω and its equivalents clearly have the force of "worship" throughout the First Gospel. In Matthew's unique appearance of the risen Jesus to the women (28:9f // Jn 20:14ff?), they seize his feet and "worship" him. In 28:17, also unique to Matthew, the Eleven meet Jesus in Galilee, and they too "worship" him.[29]

The key verse in this regard, however, is 14:33, where Jesus rescues the drowning Peter. As Peter begins to sink into the raging water (the symbol of chaos and death), he cries out in the archetypal Christian prayer, "Lord, save me!" In response, Jesus lifts him up and rebukes him for his doubt (cf. 28:17b). As they get into the boat, the wind ceases. The other disciples worship Jesus and declare, "Truly you are (the) Son of God" (αληθως Θεου υιος ει).[30] At the crucifixion, the title "Son of God" is spoken by the taunting crowd (27:40,43); and finally, in the same form as the disciples' confession of 14:33, it is uttered by the centurion and other observers: "Truly this man was (the) Son of God" (27:54).

The true parallel to Peter's confession in Mt 16:16, however, is the inadvertent "confession" of Caiaphas, the Jewish high priest, at Jesus' trial: "I adjure you by the living God (του θεου του ζωντος), tell us if you are the Christ, the Son of God"; to which Jesus replies, "You have said so" (συ ειπας, 26:63f). Compare these two formulas:

16:16 συ ει ο χριστος ο υιος του θεου του ζωντος.
You are the Christ, the Son of the living God.

26:63 συ ει ο χριστος ο υιος του θεου.[31]
You are the Christ, the Son of God.

The fact that Matthew strengthens the high priest's question ("I adjure you") so that he utters the oath "by the living God," makes it evident that the parallel is intentional. Peter, the leader of the *ekklesia*, the church or assembly of believers, confesses openly and confidently what the high priest, leader of the Jewish people, refuses to acknowledge.[32] From the baptismal declaration (3:17) to Caiaphas' question (26:63), we come full circle; and the mid-point at which Matthew's christology comes to its most complete and sublime expression is seen to be the confession, unique among the gospel authors, pronounced by Peter in the name of the Twelve (16:16).

For our purposes it is important to note that Matthew inserts into the Markan outline of Peter's confession what amounts to *a parallel confession on the part of Jesus*. In reply to Simon's declaration, Jesus pronounces a blessing upon him; he bestows upon him the name Peter, signifying his role as the "rock" upon which the Church is to be founded; and he offers him "the keys to the Kingdom of heaven," to indicate the nature of his pastoral ministry.

We noted earlier that the secondary character of these verses is clear from the fact that while Simon receives the name Peter only in 16:18, he has already been called Peter elsewhere in the gospel, and already in 16:16 he is designated Simon Peter. More telling, however, is the parallel structure of vv. 17-19. Following the introductory phrase (anacrusis), each verse represents a strophe of three lines, beginning with a thematic statement (A), followed by antithetical qualifying phrases (B-B").

(v. 17) αποκριθεις δε ο Ιησους ειπεν αυτω·
    A : μακαριος ει, Σιμων Βαριωνα,
    B : οτι σαρξ και αιμα ουκ απεκαλυψεν σοι
    B": αλλ' ο πατηρ μου ο εν τοις ουρανοις.

(v. 18) A : καγω δε σοι λεγω οτι συ ει Πετρος,
    B : και επι ταυτη τη Πετρα
      οικοδομησω μου την εκκλησιαν
    B": και πυλαι αδου ου κατισχυσουσιν αυτης.

(v. 19) A : δωσω σοι τας κλειδας
      της βασιλειας των ουρανων,
    B : και ο εαν δησης επι της γης
      εσται δεδεμενον εν τοις ουρανοις,
    B": και ο εαν λυσης επι της γης
      εσται λελυμενον εν τοις ουρανοις.

(v. 17) And answering, Jesus said to him,
    A : "Blessed are you, Simon Bar-Jonah,
    B : for flesh and blood did not reveal (this) to you,
    B": but my Father (who is) in the heavens.

(v. 18) A : And I tell you that you are Peter,
    B : and upon this rock I shall build my Church,
    B": and the gates of Hades shall not
      withstand it.

(v. 19) A : I shall give you the keys to the Kingdom of heaven,
    B : and whatever you bind on earth shall be bound in heaven,
    B": and whatever you loose on earth shall be
      loosed in heaven.

While we cannot discuss in detail the meaning of each element in Jesus' reply, the following observations should clarify the structural relationship between 16:13-16, 20 and 16:17-19.

Several factors point to the Matthean authorship of vv. 17-19:[33] (1) the typical and frequent usage in Matthew of the expressions "blessed" and "my Father who is in the heavens"; (2) the term *ekklesia*, that only Matthew among the evangelists uses (18:17, twice); and (3) his allusion to "the keys to the Kingdom of heaven" to be held by Peter after the resurrection (future tense: δωσω σοι), together with the power of "binding and loosing." Each of these expressions, however, could have originated with Jesus himself. Although Mt 6:9 // Lk 11:2 have suggested to some interpreters that the original form of the Lord's Prayer began simply with "Father," the longer phrase has Semitic coloring and could well be authentic. The term *ekklesia* appears in the Septuagint to designate the assembly of believers or "congregation" (*qahal*), and finds a parallel in the *edah* of Qumran (for example, 1QSa 3, "Men of his [God's] Counsel who keep his Covenant"). As for the "Keys to the Kingdom," the expression was current in intertestamental Judaism and would have been immediately comprehensible to Jesus' hearers (Isa 22:22 offers the closest parallel, including the authority to "open and shut" or "admit or refuse").[34]

To whatever degree we can hear the *ipsissima verba Jesu* in these verses, they have doubtlessly been shaped by Matthew to accord with his overall proclamation. However we are to interpret the enigmatic reference to "binding and loosing,"[35] for example, it seems that Matthew creates a deliberate contrast between the "scribes and Pharisees, hypocrites!" who "shut (κλειετε) the Kingdom of heaven against men" (23:13),[36] and Peter, who alone (16:19) or "collegially" (18:18) uses the keys (κλειδας) to admit the faithful into the presence of God.

For our immediate purposes, the significant point is that Matthew's redactional effort yields an overall structure in 16:13-20 that thoroughly transforms the Markan original, and *shifts the conceptual or thematic center from Peter's confession to Jesus' reply in v. 17*. The resultant A:B:C:B':A' pattern is as follows:

A : Ελθων δε ο Ιησους εις τα μερη Καισαρειας της Φιλιππου
(13) ηρωτα τους μαθητας αυτου λεγων
τινα λεγουσιν οι ανθρωποι
ειναι τον υιον του ανθρωπου;

(14) οι δε ειπαν·
οι μεν Ιωαννην τον Βαπτιστην, αλλοι δε Ηλιαν,
ετεροι δε Ιερεμιαν η ενα των προφητων.

B : λεγει αυτοις·
(15) υμεις δε τινα με λεγετε ειναι;

(16) αποκριθεις δε Σιμων Πετρος ειπεν·
συ ει ο χριστος
ο υιος του θεου του ζωντος.

C : αποκριθεις δε ο Ιησους ειπεν αυτω·
(17) μακαριος ει, Σιμων Βαριωνα,
οτι σαρξ και αιμα ουκ απεκαλυψεν σοι

αλλ' ο πατηρ μου ο εν τοις ουρανοις.

B': καγω δε σοι λεγω οτι συ ει Πετρος,
(18) και επι ταυτη τη πετρα οικοδομησω μου την εκκλησιαν
και πυλαι αδου ου κατισχυσουσιν αυτης.

(19) δωσω σοι τας κλειδας της βασιλειας των ουρανων,
και ο εαν δησης επι της γης
εσται δεδεμενον εν τοις ουρανοις,
και ο εαν λυσης επι της γης
εσται λελυμενον εν τοις ουρανοις.

A': τοτε διεστειλατο τοις μαθηταις
ινα μηδενι ειπωσιν οτι αυτος εστιν ο χριστος.

A : (13) Now when Jesus came into the region of Caesarea-
Philippi he asked his *disciples*, "Who do *men*
say that the Son of Man is?"
(14) And they said, "Some (say) John the Baptist, *others*
Elijah and *others* Jeremiah or one of the prophets."

B : (15) He said to them, "And who do you say that I am?"
(16) And answering, Simon Peter said, *"You are the
Christ, the Son of the Living God."*

C : (17) And answering, Jesus said to him,
"Blessed are you, Simon Bar-Jonah,
for flesh and blood did not reveal (this) to you,
but my Father (who is) in the heavens.

B': (18) And I tell you that *you are Peter*,
and upon this rock (*petra*) I shall build my Church,
and the gates of Hades shall not withstand it.
(19) I shall give you the keys to the Kingdom of heaven,
and whatever you bind (forbid/retain?) on earth
shall be bound in heaven,
and whatever you loose (permit/remit?) on earth
shall be loosed in heaven."

A': (20) Then he strictly ordered the *disciples*
to tell *no one* that he is the Christ.

The parallels appear still more clearly in the following outline:

A : Jesus' question addressed to his disciples. →

A': Jesus' prohibition addressed to his disciples.

B : Peter's confession of Jesus as Messiah
   and Son of God. →
B': Jesus' authority bestowed upon the Church *surpasses* all
   Messianic expectation.

C : Jesus affirms that Peter's confession is grounded in
   divine revelation.

[Matthew alone repeats the messianic confession in the command
to silence.]

The effect of Matthew's arrangement, once again, is *to shift the
central theme from Simon's confession to Jesus' reply.* The conceptual center
now becomes Jesus' assertion that the confession is possible only by
virtue of *divine revelation.* In 11:25-27 Matthew records (with Luke)
Jesus' word, "No one knows the Son except the Father, and no one knows
the Father except the Son and any one to whom the Son chooses to reveal
him." In the case of Simon Peter, it is the Father who reveals the true
identity of the Son, not only as Messiah, but as "Son of the living God."

On the basis of this double confession, Jesus bestows the name
Petros: it is upon Peter himself, and not merely upon his confession
of faith, that Jesus will found his Church. This Church, built upon a
rock (*petra;* cf. 7:24), will prevail even against the gates of Hades,
which signifies both the realm and the power of corruption and
death.[37] While it would be anachronistic to read "the institutional
Church" back into Matthew 16:18, there, as in 18:17, *ekklesia* implies
an enduring, structured community in which Christ is present "until
the end of the age" (28:20).[38]

To what extent is the *principle of intensification* operative in the
Petrine confession? Does Matthew, like the author of 1 John, reflect
the influence of Old Testament concentric parallelism, with its typical helical movement? Clearly he does. Focusing between parallel
lines appears as follows:

2 → 2': Jesus' question addressed to his disciples →
   a command issued to the disciples to keep
   silent regarding his true identity.

1 → 1': Peter's amplified version of the traditional
   messianic confession (Christ *and Son*) →
   Jesus' unique "confession" of Peter, with the

promise to establish the Church and to bestow
the "keys."

0: The central focus, which serves as the ground for both
Peter's confession and Jesus' unique response, is Jesus'
affirmation that revelation of his true identity (as
Christ *and Son*) is granted directly by the Father.

The helical movement ($2 \rightarrow 2' \rightarrow 1 \rightarrow 1' \rightarrow 0$) progresses from Jesus'
question and the disciples' popular but erroneous reply, to Jesus'
command to silence regarding his true identity; then from Peter's
true confession of Jesus, to Jesus' answering "confession" of Peter;
and from these complementary confessions to their source and ground
in divine revelation. Intensification and heightening occur from I to II
and from the extremities toward the center: $2{:}2' \rightarrow 1{:}1' \rightarrow 0$ (question /
prohibition $\rightarrow$ Peter's confession / Jesus' confession $\rightarrow$ revelation).

Detection of the chiastic structure Matthew developed in reworking his Markan source makes it possible for us to appreciate
both the process of his redactional work and the shift in focus that
such effort has produced. While Mark and Luke call their readers'
attention to the confession itself, "You are the Messiah (of God),"
*Matthew is concerned rather with Jesus' reply to Peter and the authority
Jesus grants to him.* If Peter represents the entire Christian community
in Mark and Luke, in Matthew (as in John 21), he is singled out and
invested with particular authority and pastoral responsibility. In the
words of the Protestant scholar J.-J. von Allmen, "The New Testament
unquestionably affirms that Peter is the first in the college of the Twelve.
He is first before Christ's passion; he is first after his resurrection."[39]

Peter's "primacy," in Matthew's eyes, is an incontestable fact,
one rooted in and revealed by Jesus' reply to his disciple's inspired
confession. Unconcerned with the question of the "transmission of
authority," Matthew nevertheless presents Peter as the pastoral
leader of the Church, the Apostle who holds the keys to the Kingdom
in the period following the resurrection. While scribes, Pharisees,
and the high priest prevent the people of God from entering into that
Kingdom, Peter — and through him, the Church as a whole — is
granted the power "to bind and to loose," to accord or to deny access
to the Kingdom on grounds of faith and moral conduct (16:16;
18:15-18). This unique Matthean accent declares unequivocally that the
ultimate source of faith in Christ and of authority within the Christian
community is not "flesh and blood," but God himself (16:17).

B. The Temptation of Christ

We have discussed Peter's Confession in considerable detail to illustrate the importance for all exegetical work of detecting and analyzing chiastic structures wherever they appear. In the remaining chapters of Part Two we limit ourselves to a more cursory presentation of examples typical of a variety of New Testament writings, including narrative and discourse material, liturgical units, and parables, of differing lengths and degrees of structural complexity.

Matthew's depiction of the reciprocal confessions made by Jesus and Peter illustrates a tendency of this evangelist to take up Markan material and either tighten its already existing chiastic structure or reframe it from a more simple parallelism into a chiastic pattern. Among the many other passages we could cite, the clearest are perhaps the Temptation (Mt 4:1-11 // Mk 1:12f; Lk 4:1-13), the Transfiguration (Mt 17:1-9 // Mk 9:2-9[10]; Lk 9:28-36), and the Walking on the Water (Mt 14:22-33 // Mk 6:45-52; [Lk omits; cf. Jn 6:16-21]). One further example, the healing of the blind man Bartimaeus, will illustrate an important exception to this rule. There Matthew discards Mark's chiastic structure because of a shift in his own theological program.

Mark's account of the Temptation of Christ is confined to a bare two verses, 1:12-13.

A : And immediately the Spirit cast [Jesus] out into the desert.

   B : And he was in the desert forty days

      C : being tempted by Satan;

   B': and he was with the wild beasts,

A': and the angels were ministering to him.

The Semitic repetition of "and" (Gk. καὶ, Heb. *waw*), together with the introductory formula "immediately" (εὐθύς), are stereotypical features of Markan style (cf. 1:10,18, etc.). Examination of the Greek text confirms that the passage is structured as a chiastic pentacolon:

A : Καὶ ευθυς το πνευμα αυτον εκβαλλει εις την ερημον.

   B : και ην εν τη ερημω τεσσερακοντα ημερας

      C : πειραζομενος υπο του σατανα,

Β': και ην μετα των θηριων,

Α': και οι αγγελοι διηκονουν αυτω.

The principle of focusing through intensification is evident here as well:

2 → 2': The *Spirit drives* Jesus into the desert →
the *angels minister* to him.

1 → 1': He was (και ην) in the *desert* forty days →
He was (και ην) with the *wild beasts*;

0 : He was being tempted by Satan (whose domain is the
desert and whose legions are symbolized by the beasts).

The primary focus is upon the temptation itself. From the extremities towards the center, the parallel phrases define the transcendent agents (Spirit/angels) and provide the setting (the desert as a spiritual wilderness, the archetypal locus of temptation). Heightening is achieved by passing from the action of the Spirit (signaled by the forceful εκβαλλειν), to the service of the angels; and from Jesus' presence in the desert, to his accompaniment by the wild beasts; all of which culminates in the continuous activity of the Tempter (πειρα–ζομενος). Once again, the movement of the passage describes a rhetorical helix: an incremental spiral that draws the reader's attention to the central theme, 0.[40]

Turning to Matthew's account of the Temptation, we note first of all that virtually all of Mark's information is given in Mt 4:1-2, with the exception of the ministering angels, which Matthew places at the end, 4:11.[41] The only Markan detail Matthew omits concerns the "wild beasts," avoided perhaps to tone down the dramatic imagery of his source. Into this framework, Matthew inserts (with Luke — taken probably from "Q") a series of three specific temptations, together with Jesus' response to each. In every instance that response is drawn from Deuteronomy, and has the effect of presenting Jesus as the new, faithful Israel, who withstands the triple temptation to rely upon Satan rather than God for physical nourishment, physical safety, and personal glory.

Luke presents the same three temptations, but he reverses the order of the last two. This serves to place Jesus' word, "You shall not tempt the Lord your God," just before his conclusion, "And when the devil had ended every *temptation*...." Matthew's order, however, produces an incremental effect: from living by the word of God, to refusing to tempt God, to worshiping God alone.

The commentaries discuss the mythological and theological aspects of this passage.[42] For our present purposes, it is enough to indicate the way in which Matthew has introduced a unique if rather loose chiastic structure into the A, B, and A' elements of his Markan source.

A : Then Jesus was *led up* into the desert *by the Spirit* to be *tempted by the devil.*

    B : And he fasted forty days and nights [like Moses, Ex 34:28]; afterwards he was hungry. And the Tempter approaching said to him: *"If you are the Son of God,* order these stones to become bread." But answering, he said: "It is written, 'Man shall not live by bread alone, but by every word that proceeds from the mouth of God.' "

        C : Then the devil took him to the holy city and set him upon the pinnacle of the temple and said to him: *"If you are the Son of God,*[43] cast yourself down; for it is written, 'He will give his angels charge over you, and upon their hands they will lift you up, lest you strike your foot against a stone.' " Jesus said to him: "Again it is written, 'You shall not tempt the Lord your God.'"

    B': Again the devil led him to a very high mountain [cf. Moses, Ex. 19; Deut. 34:1-4] and showed him all the kingdoms of the world and their glory; and he said to him: "All these things I shall give to you if you will fall down and worship me." Then Jesus said to him: "Be gone, Satan! For it is written, 'You shall worship the Lord your God and him only shall you serve.' "

A': Then *the devil left* him, and behold, *angels approached* and were ministering to him.

A → A': The Spirit leads, the devil tempts → The devil leaves, angels minister.

B → B': Material temptation (food) → Material temptation (power).

C: The supreme temptation

Commentators usually interpret the Temptation in one of two ways: as specifically messianic, or as a spiritual testing common to any faithful Israelite. In Beare's words, "Is the basic idea that Jesus is tempted to attain his Messianic ends by false means, or is it that Jesus is tempted to fail in the radical obedience to God that is the duty of every human soul?"[44]

While it is more the former than the latter, the real significance of the passage can only be grasped in relation to its context. The preceding passage recounts Jesus' baptism in the Jordan at the hands of John. Here for the first time the voice of the Father confirms that "This is my beloved Son," an affirmation reiterated at the Transfiguration with the added command, "Listen to him" (17:5). The Matthean form of Peter's confession includes, as we have seen, a double title: Messiah *and Son of God*. The temptations held out by the devil similarly involve Jesus' role as Son of God (4:3, 6). Jesus' final rebuke — "Begone, Satan!" — is a foreshadowing of his rebuke to Peter, who was unable to comprehend the suffering destiny of the one who is both Christ (Messiah) and Son of God. Luke ends his account of the Temptation with the words, "[the devil] departed from him until an opportune time." That time was the crucial moment of Peter's confession, when at the turning point of his public career, surrounded by adoring crowds, Jesus faced the temptation to acquiesce to the wishes of his followers and assume the messianic role they expected of him. Accordingly, both Matthew and Luke have expanded the Temptation account given in skeletal form by Mark, in order to dramatize the struggle that faced Jesus throughout his earthly ministry: the struggle against the temptation to usurp worldly power and authority rather than submit to the Father's will.

The very fact that Jesus is not only "Messiah" but also "Son of God," the beloved Son in whom the Father is well pleased, means that the temptation involves more that the lure of wealth and power. It engages him in a profound spiritual struggle between strength and weakness, exaltation and humility. It necessitates, in fact, an ongoing choice between Jesus as Messiah and Jesus as Servant. This perhaps explains the order of the temptations in Matthew. Luke places the temple scene last, showing that this was the supreme test. Matthew, on the other hand, places it between the other two temptations that offer material benefits: stones transformed into bread to feed Jesus' hunger, and divine worship deformed into devil worship to acquire worldly power and glory. (Note the parallels between Jesus and Moses in B:B'. Like the people of Israel, Jesus is tempted in the wilderness. But whereas fasting and the mountain imagery prepare Moses to receive the revelation of God, Jesus experienced them as demonic temptations.)

The focal point of Matthew's Temptation account, then, is the challenge that Jesus prove his claim to divine Sonship by casting himself down from the pinnacle of the temple, the House of God, the sacred center of the "holy city." This is the only temptation that would lead Jesus to risk his very life, to prove his ultimate trust in God. It is the supreme temptation, repeated only at Jesus' arrest in the Garden of Gethsemane. "Do you think that I cannot appeal to my Father," Jesus admonishes his disciples as they attempt to defend him by force, "and he will immediately send me more than twelve legions of angels?" (Mt 26:53). At this point, the die is cast; in Johannine language, Jesus' "hour" has come. Early on in the Temptation scene, however, this later challenge to his faithful obedience is only foreshadowed. He refuses to put God to the test and declares his total devotion to the one who sent him. And in response, angels draw near and minister to him.

C. The Transfiguration

The account of Jesus' Transfiguration offers a further example of a Matthean refinement of Markan chiasmus.

From the literally historical to the purely symbolic, interpretations of Christ's "metamorphosis" have been as diverse as any in the history of exegesis. To Eastern patristic tradition, the divine, uncreated Light experienced as the culmination of mystical experience is identified with the light that manifested itself from within the person of Christ on Mount Tabor, the traditional site of the transfiguration.[45] According to the witness of Gregory Palamas and the "hesychast" school of contemplative prayer,[46] the light of Jesus' transfiguration is the radiant "energy" of the Divine Trinity that manifests the power of the Kingdom of God within the earthly life of the Son, a vision accessible to the disciples by grace.[47] Popular interpretations of the transfiguration scene in Eastern Orthodox tradition have accordingly stressed the conviction that it was not Christ who was transformed; rather, the eyes of the disciples were "opened" to behold him as he truly is: as the eternal Son of God, the effulgence of the Godhead present in the flesh, the very "Light of the world" (cf. Jn 8:12; Heb 1:3, "He is the radiance of the glory of God").

At the opposite end of the spectrum are those interpretations that understand the transfiguration scene as a misplaced (or proleptic) resurrection appearance, or as a mystical experience granted to Jesus alone and to be understood in purely symbolic terms. According to this latter approach, the "mountain" can no more be geographically located than the mountain of the temptation (the "very high mountain" of Mt 4:8) or the mountain of the Sermon, Matthew 5-7. The presence of the blinding light, therefore, like that of Moses and Elijah, is to be understood metaphorically as a visionary prefiguration in Jesus' own experience of his coming glorification through resurrection from the dead.

If we ask the evangelists what their understanding of the transfiguration was, we arrive at something of a synthesis of these two very disparate approaches. To their mind, the "event" was precisely that: a historically determinable moment in the course of Jesus' earthly ministry that marks a turning point in the Gospel narrative.[48] The sequence in each account is Peter's confession; Jesus' first prediction of his passion, followed by a warning of coming judgment when he will return as the glorified Son of Man; and the transfiguration scene itself. In each instance, the particular cast of the transfiguration account offers important insight into the author's christology.

Over against the opinion of the vast majority of commentators, there can be little doubt that Jesus' statement which concludes his apocalyptic warning is also intended by the evangelists to serve as an introduction to the transfiguration scene: "Truly I tell you, there are some standing here who will not taste death until...". To Mark, whose principal christological title is "Son of God,"[49] and who relegates the visitation of the Son of Man to the future (cf. 14:62), "those standing there" will simply "see the Kingdom of God come with power" (9:1). Luke states even more briefly that they "will see the Kingdom of God" (9:27). Matthew, on the other hand, incorporates the title "Son of Man" into this saying, thereby attaching it, more explicitly than either Mark or Luke, to the apocalyptic imagery that precedes it and to the scene that follows. That Matthew conceives the statement to be a bridge between the coming of the Kingdom and the vision of Jesus transfigured is shown by the fact that he alone makes the unusual change from "Kingdom of God" to "his Kingdom," that is, the Kingdom of Jesus, the "beloved Son."

Other differences in the three accounts further illumine each author's theological stance. Mark's narrative includes typical homely details the other evangelists prefer to omit. In v. 3 he indicates that the metamorphosis affected Jesus' clothing rather than his person; and he adds the comparison "as no fuller on earth could bleach them." While Mark declares that Peter and the others were "terrified" at the vision, Luke tones this down to the simple assertion that Peter did not know what he was saying. Matthew omits the detail altogether; or rather he transposes it to the disciples' response to the divine voice in v. 6.

In Matthew's account, the booths Peter proposes to set up (an allusion to the Jewish feast of Tabernacles) are to be permanent memorials, erected with Jesus' permission to preserve the extraordinary "mountain top" experience. In Mark (followed by Luke), they are proposed out of Peter's confusion and fear provoked by the vision itself.

Then again, Mark concludes his account with the admonition to silence, which serves in the context of his Gospel as an element in the general theme of the "messianic secret." Whereas Luke attributes the disciples' silence to their own initiative, Matthew has Jesus command them to maintain silence "until the Son of Man is raised from the dead." He thereby creates an envelope effect, linking the apocalyptic announcement of the coming of the Son of Man in 16:28 with the resurrectional prophecy regarding the Son of Man in 17:9. This further demonstrates that for Matthew — and by inference, for Mark and Luke as well — the promise that some of those present with Jesus would not die before they beheld the Son of Man coming in his Kingdom, serves as an introduction to the transfiguration scene, where that promise is proleptically realized.

In the person of the radiant Christ, the disciples behold the presence of the Kingdom within human history. This apocalyptic emphasis — foreshadowing the parousia as much as it does the resurrection — carries over in Matthew to the transfiguration scene itself. There Jesus' *face* [i.e., his personal presence] "shone like the sun," an allusion to the *shekinah* or manifestation of divine glory. Thereby Matthew succeeds in linking two originally independent motifs: the apocalyptic imagery of the soon-to-return Son of Man, and the prediction of Jesus' resurrection, which would enable him to be present with his disciples "until the end of the age" (Mt 28:20).

Luke's most important addition to his Markan source concerns Jesus' mission, which is to be fulfilled in the holy city. He alone among the evangelists divulges the content of the discussion between Jesus, Moses and Elijah: they "spoke of [Jesus'] departure (εξοδον, his 'exodus' or death and resurrection) which he was about to accomplish (ην ημελλεν πληρουν) in Jerusalem" (9:31). This points directly forward to the pivot of Luke's Gospel narrative in 9:51, "When the days were fulfilled for him to be lifted up (αναλημψεως),[50] he set his face to go to Jerusalem." The focus here is upon Jesus' coming passion, which the author consistently balances with the promise of his coming glory. Accordingly, he has the disciples awaken from their slumber to behold not only Moses and Elijah, but also Jesus' glory as the Chosen Son of God (9:32,35).[51] Thereby Luke, like the other evangelists, modifies his source to express his chief theological concern in a subtle but significant way. Once again, exquisite literary technique becomes the vehicle for expressing unique meaning.

Turning to the question of structure, we notice first of all that Mark's account of the transfiguration (9:2-10) is presented in chiastic form.

A : (vv. 2-3) Jesus ascends the mountain with his disciples
and is transfigured before them.

   B : (vv. 4-6) Elijah and Moses appear talking with Jesus;
Peter, out of fear, suggests building three booths.

      C : (v. 7) A cloud overshadows them; a voice from
the cloud declares, "This is my beloved Son;
listen to him."

   B': (v. 8) Elijah and Moses disappear; the disciples are
alone with Jesus.

A': (vv. 9-10) Jesus descends the mountain with his
disciples; the charge to silence and promise of
resurrection; the disciples' puzzlement.

Thus Mark achieves a rough parallelism that centers about the heavenly voice and its admonition to pay heed to Jesus' words. The chiastic pattern demonstrates as well that vv. 9 and (probably) 10 are part of the literary unit and should not be relegated to a separate paragraph, as they are in the *RSV/NRSV*.

Matthew (17:1-9) has tightened this structure and created a more extensive parallelism by adding vv. 6-7 to the original narrative.

A : (vv. 1-2) And after six days Jesus took with him Peter
and James and John his brother, and *led them up* into a
high *mountain* by themselves.
And he was *transfigured* before them,
and his face shone like the sun,
and his garments became *white as the light* [shining
forth from Jesus?]

   B : (v. 3) And behold, there *appeared* to him Moses and
Elijah, talking with him.

      C : (v. 4) And Peter responding said to Jesus: "Lord,
it is *good for us to be here*. If you wish,
I will make here three booths, one for you, one
for Moses and one for Elijah."

         D : (v. 5) While he was still speaking, behold, a
bright cloud overshadowed them; and behold, a
voice (came) from the cloud, saying: "This is
my beloved Son in whom I am well pleased;
listen to him."

C': (vv. 6-7) And hearing (it), the disciples fell on
their faces and were *exceedingly afraid*. But
Jesus drew near and touching them said: *"Arise
and have no fear."*

B': (v. 8) And when they lifted up their eyes, they
saw no one but Jesus himself alone.

A': (v. 9) And as they were *coming down* out of the *mountain*,
Jesus commanded them: "Tell no one the *vision* until the
Son of Man has been *raised* from the dead."

Once again, inclusion — the envelope effect — is produced by
the parallelism between 16:28, the Son of Man coming in his Kingdom, and 17:9, the Son of Man raised from the dead. Here the former
verse couples with 17:1 (the Kingdom manifested through Jesus'
transfiguration) to balance the conclusion of the passage (the resurrection of the Son of Man). Intensification is provided as well from the
initial transfiguration on the mountain to the ultimate "transfiguration"
to be accomplished by Jesus' resurrection from death to glory.

The triple imperative "Behold" (ιδου, vv. 3 & 5), unique to the
First Gospel, signals a theophany. In the first instance, Moses and
Elijah (reversing the Markan order to represent more clearly the
sequence Law and Prophets) appear to confirm Jesus as the fulfillment of the Old Covenant; in the latter two, the Sinai theophany of
a cloud and a heavenly voice are transformed into a *christophany*, a
declaration by God himself that Jesus is his beloved Son, who
possesses all authority to speak the divine word (cf. Jn 3:34f).

Into the Markan structure, however, Matthew has inserted vv.
6-7 to create a balance between Peter's response to Jesus, and Jesus'
response to the fearful disciples. The overall pattern is thereby
expanded to A:B:C:D:C':B':A'. Intensification and the helical movement appear as follows:

3 → 3': Ascending the mountain / transfiguration →
Descending the mountain / resurrection.

2 → 2': Appearance of Moses and Elijah with Jesus →
Jesus left alone as fulfillment of the Law
and the Prophets.

1 → 1': Peter offers to honor Jesus with booths →
Jesus consoles the disciples by a touch and by the
word, "Have no fear," (a revelatory formula in
biblical tradition). The command "Rise!"
(εγερθητε) presages Jesus' resurrection,
alluded to in v. 9, (εγερθη).

0 : The conceptual center of the passage is the theophany of
v. 5: Jesus as the New Moses receives heavenly
approbation on the "new Sinai." Like Isaac, he is the
"beloved Son" (ο υιος μου ο αγαπητος; cf. Gen 22:2,
LXX), who will offer his life in sacrifice and be
vindicated through his resurrection.

While Matthew preserves Mark's basic outline and chiastic
structure, he draws on his remarkable literary skill to modify and
add elements that shift the overall focus of the passage. For Mark,
the transfiguration scene serves his fundamental aim to present Jesus
as the Son of God, whose identity and destiny remain concealed from
the disciples even during this sublime theophany. The dominant
theme in the Second Gospel remains the "messianic secret": Jesus
will be finally revealed as Son of God only after his death and the
discovery of the empty tomb.[52] The initial Gospel proclamation,
closing with Mark 16:8, will only become fully intelligible through the
experience of the believing community: those who come to know the
Crucified and Risen One by exercising faithful discipleship in his name.

Matthew takes up the command to silence, but he frees it from
the constraints of the Markan "secret." To his mind, the transfiguration is perceived by Peter and the others as a genuine christophany,
a revelation of Jesus' person and mission as fulfilling the law and
prophets of the Old Covenant. By adding vv. 6-7 to the narrative,
Matthew does more than supplement the original chiastic pattern.
He shows Jesus responding to the disciples with compassion and
consolation (this is the only time Jesus "approaches" others; usually
others "draw near" to him). Yet Jesus does so in such a way as to
confirm his divine authority by the formula "Be not afraid" (μη
φοβεισθε), and to announce his own victory over death by the
command, "Arise!" Such key expressions could be neither misun-
derstood nor overlooked by his readers.

In Matthew's redaction, then, the Transfiguration stands mid-
way between Jesus' Baptism and the Great Commission that concludes the evangelist's proclamation. Beginning with a manifestation

of the Spirit of God, the Son of God and the voice of the Father, the Gospel ends with the command to baptize all nations in the name of the Father, the Son and the Holy Spirit.[53] The transfiguration scene serves to bridge these opening and closing moments in Jesus' earthly ministry. For here too the voice of the Father bears witness to the Son, and — according to patristic interpretation — the radiant light emanating from the person of Christ manifests the presence within him of the Holy Spirit.[54] Whether Matthew himself so understood the transfiguring radiance is another question. Nevertheless, the tripartite confessional thread running through the Gospel from the Baptism, to the Transfiguration and on to the final Commission, enabled patristic theologians to ground their doctrine of the Trinity in the witness of the First Evangelist as much as in that of the Fourth.

D. Walking on the Lake of Galilee

The brief episode of Jesus walking on the water was attached to the feeding of the five thousand in pre-gospel oral tradition. In Mark, Matthew, and the Fourth Gospel the sequence is the same (Luke alone omits the encounter on the lake), and each evangelist situates the tandem miracles in a Passover context.

The feeding in the wilderness points in two directions at once: back to the experience of Israel in Egypt and in the Sinai desert, and forward to the Lord's Supper. Eucharistic imagery is provided by the use of key verbs: Jesus *takes* the bread and *blesses* God; then he *breaks* it in pieces and *gives* it to his disciples to *distribute* to the multitude (Mk 6:41; Mt 14:19; Jn 6:11).[55] Just as Yahweh nourished Israel in the wilderness by raining down upon them "bread from heaven," so Jesus nourishes his followers in a "lonely place" (Mk 6:31f and Mt 14:13, 15; Jn 6:3 situates the feeding on a "mountain," recalling the theophany at Sinai).

These gospel accounts of the feeding of the five thousand inevitably evoked in the collective memory of Jewish Christians the image of Passover and, consequently, of the entire Exodus event, of which the Passover meal served as the historical and theological foundation (Exodus 12-14).[56] The episode of Jesus walking on the water, tied directly to the foregoing feeding, thus represents a "new Exodus" parallel to the crossing of the Red (Reed) Sea. This is all the more evident in John's Gospel, where the following eucharistic discourse on Jesus as the Bread of Life mentions explicitly Moses and the heavenly manna (6:31, quoting the "historical" Psalm 78 with its reference to the Exodus event).

The scene in which Jesus encounters the disciples on the lake, then, is not simply a "nature" miracle or incidental detail to demonstrate his supernatural powers. If both the Synoptic and Johannine traditions preserve it as they do, it is to focus the reader's attention on the role of Christ who, like God of old, leads his people through the maelstrom of suffering and persecution and into the safe harbor of the Kingdom.[57]

In Matthew's account of Peter's Confession, the evangelist creates concentric parallelism by adding the complementary response Jesus addresses to Peter (16:17-19). Similarly, Matthew adds to his Markan source of the Transfiguration the disciples' reaction of fear at the heavenly voice, together with Jesus' reply; and the addition has the effect of tightening the chiastic structure and focusing attention all the more directly on the central theme.

A similar expansion reshapes Matthew's version of the walking on the water. Matthew's tendency is to *shorten* Markan narratives, omitting picturesque but unnecessary details and episodes (such as the "fuller" of Mk 9:3, and the graphic healing of the deaf and dumb man of 7:32-36). When he expands a given account, it is always with the purpose of conveying some further theological insight that speaks directly to the circumstances and needs of his own church community.[58] Thus he adds Jesus' response to Peter's confession, indicating that the keys presented to the disciple are possessed by the whole body of the faithful;[59] and Jesus' compassionate touch and consoling word on the Mount of Transfiguration confirm, both to the disciples and to all those who follow him, that he is the divine Son in whom God is present "until the end of the age."

Matthew similarly expands his Markan source for the walking on the water by adding the unique encounter between Jesus and Peter (14:28-31). Once again Peter is the focus of the passage, yet Matthew presents him in such a way as to symbolize the struggle between faith and doubt, loyalty and betrayal, that engages every Christian believer.

Mark's account appears to be straightforward narrative: Jesus sends off the disciples, dismisses the crowd and retires to pray; before dawn[60] he draws near to the disciples, intending to pass them by;[61] the disciples cry out in fear believing him to be a ghost; he comforts them with the revelatory formula "Take heart, it is I, have no fear" (θαρσειτε, εγω ειμι, μη φοβεισθε); he gets into the boat and the wind ceases; the disciples are amazed "because they did not understand about the loaves...". As so often in Mark, the disciples fail to grasp the real meaning of Jesus' words or actions. This closing to the story highlights once again the motif of secrecy. The narrative flow throughout the passage is evident. Nevertheless, as we shall point out in detail further on, Mark has fashioned this account according to the familiar pattern of concentric parallelism.

Matthew's modifications of Mark's outline include an addition that, as elsewhere, transforms it into a still more tightly woven chiastic pattern (14:22-33; vv. 22-23a serve as an introduction, a sort of extended anacrusis):

[And immediately he made the disciples board the boat and go on ahead of him to the other shore, while he dismissed the crowds. And after he had dismissed the crowds, he went up into the mountain alone to pray.]

A : (vv. 23b-25) When evening came, he was there alone. Now the *boat* was already a good way from land, being battered by the waves because the *wind was against them*. And in the fourth watch of the night, [Jesus] came to them, *walking upon the lake.*

  B : (vv. 26f) Now when the disciples saw him walking on the lake, *they were terrified*, saying "It is a ghost!" and they *cried out* in *fear*. But *at once Jesus* spoke to them, saying: *"Take heart. It is I, do not be afraid."*

   C : (v. 28) And *Peter* replying to him said, "Lord, if it is you, tell me to *come* to you *upon the water.*"

    D : (v. 29a) And he said, "Come!"

   C': (v. 29b) And stepping out of the boat, *Peter* walked *upon the water* and *came* to Jesus.

  B': (vv. 30-31) But when he saw the [strong][62] wind *he was afraid;* and beginning to sink, he *cried out:* "Lord, save me!" And *at once Jesus* reached out his hand and took hold of him. And he said to him, "O man of little faith! *Why did you doubt?"*

A': (vv. 32f) And when they got into the *boat* the *wind ceased*. And those in the boat worshiped him, saying: *"Truly you are the Son of God!"*

As before, verbal and conceptual parallels are indicated by italic characters. Focusing is achieved through a combination of intensification, specification, and conclusion. A → A' represents a movement toward conclusion: from the initial scene with its setting and depiction of the miracle, to the dénouement that consists of two elements, namely the calming of the wind and thus the climax of the miracle; and the disciples' confession, which marks the climax of the entire encounter. B → B' involves specification: from the fear experienced by the whole group of disciples to Peter's fear that betrays his personal anguish and doubt. C → C' represents intensification: from Peter's request to his actual feat of walking upon the water.

The helical movement can be sketched graphically by reverting to numbers to designate the parallel elements:

3 → 3': The wind is against them; Jesus' miracle → The wind is calmed; the disciples' confession.

2 → 2': The disciples' fear; Jesus' self-revelation → Peter's fear and his cry for salvation; Jesus' rebuke.

1 → 1': Peter's request in the form of a challenge → Peter's response as an act of faith.

0 : The whole passage focuses upon the invitation, addressed to Peter, and through him to every Christian soul, to "Come!" to Jesus as the unique source of salvation.

With the encounter between Jesus and his disciples on the Lake of Galilee, Matthew has offered us one of the most finely crafted passages in all of biblical literature. Two external signs or miracles — the walking on the water and the calming of the wind — provide the setting for an inner miracle, the resolution of doubt expressed by the collective confession, "Truly you are the Son of God!" This in turn prepares Peter's own messianic confession in 16:16, "You are the Christ, the Son of the living God!"

Detection of the chiastic, helical movement of the passage enables the reader to perceive within the narrative several different yet complementary levels of meaning. It seems reasonable to suggest, for example, that Matthew intends the disciples in the boat to offer an image of the Church in every age, as it faces external persecution and deals with internal stress and doubt. The Psalmist cried out to God to rescue his life from the watery abyss (18:16; 144:7, "Stretch out thy hand from on high, rescue me and deliver me from the many waters"; cf. Job 9:8; 38:16; Sirach 24:5-6). Both the evangelist and his readers would have had such passages in mind as they meditated on the tradition of Jesus walking upon the waters of the lake. And they would readily link his consoling affirmation, "Take heart, it is I, have no fear," with a similar declaration from the mouth of Yahweh, as he revealed himself to Moses on Mount Sinai.

It may be an exaggeration to claim, as some commentators do, that eucharistic overtones appear in this passage.[63] Nevertheless, the statement "It is I, have no fear," is, as we have pointed out, a formula of self-revelation, one given special prominence in the Fourth Gospel but which goes back to the earliest tradition lying behind the written witness. Can we affirm the "historicity" of the event, then, and hold that the miracle(s) as well as Jesus' self-designation and the disciples' confessional response occurred as they are presented here? This is a tempting question, one that has long been wielded as a two-edged sword in the hands of fundamentalists and skeptics alike. To affirm that Matthew, and the authors of the tradition(s) upon which he relied, expressed truth through literary creativity, that they were artists before they were historians, is a fact that many Christians refuse to acknowledge, fearing that to do so would undermine the foundation of their faith. To insist, on the other hand, that the evangelist's creativity lies in his ability to draw upon and to shape the essential elements of historical fact, of actual occurrences, merely invites the scorn of those who cannot accept the notion that a human being actually walked on water, or that the neat progression of events, from storm and doubt to the calm profession of faith, really "happened that way." The average reader can accept the historical kernel behind a disciple's confession of Jesus as Messiah; he can even give qualified credence to the reality of a "transfigured" Jesus, supposing that the vision of light amounted to an inner, "mystical" perception of the true significance of his person and mission. But to affirm that both Jesus and Peter actually walked upon the water is more than the "modern mind" is inclined to accept.

But aren't we posing a false problem for ourselves when we state the alternatives in this way? We rightly insist that Christian faith is grounded in historical reality. If Christ did not die on the Cross at a moment in *our* time, if his rising from the dead is not similarly a reality within *our* history, and consequently accessible to us within the framework of history, then indeed "we are of all people the most to be pitied." Nevertheless, the most superficial comparison of the parallel narratives in the Gospels makes it evident that each evangelist has shaped tradition in a unique way that expresses his literary genius as much as it does his dependability as a chronicler.

If the Fourth Evangelist could alter the "Jesus tradition" as he did, stamping it so profoundly with his unique style and theological vision, it is because of his conviction that his own words were in fact "spoken" by the Spirit of Truth. This conviction, that the Spirit speaks through human witnesses, in their language and thought-forms but with utter faithfulness to truth or ultimate reality, was shared by Matthew and by the other apostolic writers as well (cf. Jn 16:13f; Mk 13:11; 2 Tim 3:16; 2 Pet 1:20f).

What then of the "historicity" of the narrative of Jesus — and Peter — walking on the water? On the one hand, it is a question that cannot be resolved. The reality, and consequently its truth, transcend the limits of history *per se* and therefore they ultimately defy methods of historical analysis. What we seek, however, is not historical veracity as such, but rather *that truth which reveals itself within history.* Insofar as the account of the walking on the water, from the miracles themselves to the disciples' response of faith, illumines our own experience of the power and authority of Jesus, and shapes our own profession of belief in him and commitment to him, the story possesses absolute and unimpeachable truth. It may well be that the events occurred precisely as they are depicted. The point is, however, that were we somehow to confirm that as fact, it would have no ultimate bearing upon our own life and faith. Only when we incorporate the *meaning* of the narrative into our own experience, our own life and witness, does it acquire *truth* in the fullest sense. The crucifixion and resurrection of Christ have salvific power and significance for us only insofar as they are "appropriated," and made the most basic formative elements in our own spiritual growth, through baptism and sacramental communion with the living Lord. Similarly, events from his life and aspects of his teaching become "ours" only insofar as we appropriate them and build our very existence upon them.

It is this *interiorization of meaning*, accomplished through the activity of the indwelling Spirit, that allows a text composed two millennia ago to speak in our own day a "relevant" word, a word of life. Through the Spirit, the risen Lord continues to issue his invitation, "Come!"; and we continue in the struggle that leads from doubt to faith and from fear to trust. In this sense, then, whether or not every detail of the narrative is historically verifiable, the account of Jesus meeting with his disciples on the waters is true, speaking truth *about* us as well as to us.

This line of reasoning will not satisfy those who confuse truth with historical event. And yet they, too, must acknowledge that the most crucial, precious and formative experiences of our life lie beyond the realm of "history" — experiences such as faith, love and death. Perhaps we can leave the debate at this point with the observation that here as well the "what's more" principle appears to be operative. The Scriptures recount, among other things, historical fact; and *what's more*, they convey that depth and intensity of meaning which we experience as ultimate, transcendent truth.

E. The Healing of Bartimaeus

A key element in Matthew's presentation of the Transfiguration, as we have seen, is Jesus' word addressed to the terror-stricken disciples, "Arise" (εγερθητε). This command is followed by the revelatory formula "be not afraid," and clearly parallels Jesus' reference to the "raising up" of the Son of Man (εγερθη) that concludes the pericope (17:9). In the account of Jesus walking on the waters of the Lake, Matthew has chosen to structure his entire narrative about Jesus' word, also addressed to the disciples, "Come!"

The earliest record we have of Jesus healing the blind man on the road from Jericho, Mark 10:46-52, is crafted in such a way as to place similar commands at the very center. Jesus orders bystanders to summon Bartimaeus: "Call him"; and they comply by using what are virtually technical formulas of consolation and promise: "Take heart, arise, he is calling you." Bartimaeus — an unknown, unnamed "everyman" ("Bartimaeus, son of Timaeus" is a redundancy) — thus becomes the type of all those, Jews and Gentiles, who are led by Christ from darkness to light, from unbelief to faith, and in response "follow Jesus in the Way."

The structure of the passage is as follows:

(V. 46a is introductory: "And they came to Jericho.")

A : (v. 46b-c) As (Jesus) was leaving Jericho with his
disciples and a large crowd, a *blind* beggar named
Bartimaeus, the son of Timaeus, was *sitting* by the roadside.

B : (v. 47) And when he heard that it was Jesus of
Nazareth, he began to cry out and say, "*Jesus,*
Son of David, *have mercy upon me!*"

C : (v. 48) And many *people rebuked him*, telling
him to be *quiet.* But he cried out all the more,
"Son of David, have mercy upon me!"

D : (v. 49a) And *stopping, Jesus* said, "*Call him.*"

E : (v. 49b) And they called the blind man,
saying, "Take heart, arise, he is calling you."

D': (v. 50) And throwing off his cloak and *leaping
up, he came* to *Jesus.*

C′ : (v. 51) And Jesus asked him, *"What do you want* me
to do for you?" The blind man said to him,
"Master, let me receive my sight."

B′ (v. 52a) And *Jesus* said to him, *"Go; your faith has
healed you."*

A′ (v. 52b) And at once he *received his sight*, and he
followed him in the way.

Matthew (20:29-34) makes a number of significant changes in his
version of the incident. As in the case of the Gadarene demoniac, he
doubles the number of the afflicted. In fact, the story appears to be
a doublet of the healing recounted in Mt 9:27-31. Since Matthew
omits Mark's account of the blind man at Bethsaida (Mk 8:22-30),
some interpreters have suggested that his introduction of two blind
men into the framework of Mark's Bartimaeus story represents a
simple conflation of the two traditions. It seems far more likely,
however, that Matthew omits the Bethsaida story because of the
exuberant use Mark makes of dramatic detail: Jesus spits on the
man's eyes, lays hands on him, interrogates him, repeats the gestures, etc. Matthew is averse to such dramatizing, as we have seen
in the Transfiguration narrative. A more plausible explanation for
Matthew's presentation of two blind men and two demoniacs is that
the number satisfies the requirements for a valid witness according
to Jewish law (Deut 19:15; cf. Jn 8:17f).[64]

Matthew also modifies the conclusion to the passage by having
Jesus touch the eyes of the blind men. The healing is effected precisely by his touch, rather than by their profession of faith. Mark's
point, however, is to show that Bartimaeus receives his sight as a
direct consequence of his profession of belief in Jesus as "Son of
David," that is, the Davidic Messiah. By following Jesus "in the
way," Bartimaeus becomes the model disciple and the prototype of
all those who will take up their cross and follow their Lord to the
end. An implicit connection is made between this image of "the way"
and the designation of the Christian pilgrimage as "the Way" in the
Acts of the Apostles (9:2, etc.).

To demonstrate just how and why Mark shaped this tradition as
he did, it would be helpful to indicate the chiastic relationships
within the passage by the following outline:

4 : Bartimaeus is sitting in darkness.

   3 : He seeks "mercy" (healing) from Jesus.

      2 : The people rebuke and silence him.

         1 : Jesus stops and calls Bartimaeus.

            0 : The people declare: "Take heart, arise,
               he is calling you."

         1': Bartimaeus leaps up and comes to Jesus.

      2': Jesus accepts Bartimaeus and encourages him
        to speak.

   3': Jesus has mercy upon (heals) him.

4': Bartimaeus receives his sight and follows Jesus.

We should recall that physical blindness was regarded as a curse from God, either for the sins of the afflicted person or for those of the person's ancestors (cf. Jn 9:2). The crowd consequently feels no moral obligation whatever to respond to Bartimaeus' plea. To the contrary, they attempt to silence him for his audacious efforts to attract the Master's attention. Nevertheless, Bartimaeus displays qualities that conform significantly to the image of the man of prayer depicted by Jesus in his parables. He is perseverant (cf. Mt 7:7f; Lk 11:5-13; 18:1-8); and above all, his appeal is phrased as the most fundamental cry of faith and repentance, "Lord, have mercy upon me!" (cf. Lk 18:13; Mt 14:30). Jesus responds to his petition in a way diametrically opposed to the initial reaction of the crowd: they pass by / Jesus stops; they rebuke and try to silence the blind offender / Jesus invites him to receive healing.

The most striking detail, however, is the transformation in the attitude of the crowd represented by the chiastic center of the narrative. Whereas initially they reacted with scorn and hostility toward Bartimaeus, in response to Jesus' command, "Call him," they become the mouthpiece for words of blessing and consolation similar to those pronounced by Jesus at the Walking on the Water and the Transfiguration: "Take heart, arise!" (cf. Mk 6:50; Mt 17:7).

This focus is lost in both Matthew and Luke. In all three Gospels, this is the last miracle Jesus performs before his entry into the Holy City. In Matthew's version, Jesus is the chief actor throughout the scene: he calls the two blind men, he touches their eyes in a healing gesture, he responds to their plight out of pity. All that is said of the two men themselves is that they received their sight and followed him. They thereby become witnesses to Jesus' messianic power at the threshold of his passion.

Luke retains the Markan emphasis placed upon the blind man's faith: "Receive your sight, your faith has made you well" (18:42); and he concludes his account with a stereotyped formula on the lips of both the healed man and the crowd, affirming that they glorified and gave praise to God. For Matthew, then, the focus is upon the miraculous healing power Jesus possesses, and on the response of the two men who bear witness to it. For Luke, the conclusion is the key element: the healing has as its effect to elicit a particular response on the part of all present. They glorify God, who manifests his power through this Son of David, God's "Chosen One" (cf. Lk 9:35). Thereupon Jesus embarks on the final stage of his journey toward Jerusalem and his "exodus" from this world (9:51).

By creating a chiastic format for his account, Mark produces a remarkably detailed and poignant narrative. As a literary achievement, it rivals Matthew's depiction of the encounter between Peter and Jesus on the Lake. Both stories preserve details that lead the reader to identify with the one who cries out for help. Mercy and salvation come from the Lord and are bestowed freely and compassionately upon those who ask. But again, the vital center of Mark's story is the transformation of attitude that comes over the crowd: "Take heart, arise!" All other elements are structured about this command, and once more there is an evident focusing through intensification:

4 → 4': from darkness, to Light;

3 → 3': from an appeal for mercy, to the merciful healing;

2 → 2': from the crowd's rebuke, to Jesus' invitation;

1 → 1': Jesus stops and invites, Bartimaeus leaps up and comes;

0 : The crowd is moved from scorn to compassion, and to acceptance of a recognized outcast.

Mark's literary genius appears in his ability to present Bartimaeus as a living, longing, tortured, yet hopeful being, whose life is radically transformed by this "chance" encounter with Jesus. Readers of the story feel they *know* this man, and they sympathize with him accordingly. Yet despite the warmth and humor of the detail ("But he cried out all the more...!"), Bartimaeus never overshadows Jesus. Nor is the point lost concerning the change in attitude of those in the crowd. This exquisite balance of gestures and words is primarily due to the *literary structure* of the passage. Once again, a deft use of chiasmus enables the evangelist to couch a profound and complex theological message in a beautifully woven narrative tale.[65]

Endnotes

[1]This term refers to the Gospels of Matthew, Mark and Luke. When "seen together" in the parallel columns of a gospel "synopsis," they reveal remarkable similarities to one another; yet differences are significant enough to eliminate the possibility of simple copying. The solution to the "synoptic problem" is usually given with reference to the "two-source hypothesis" mentioned earlier. It is presumed that Matthew and Luke used Mark and Q (the discourse source), together with special materials (labeled respectively "M" and "L") from their own body of oral tradition. This hypothesis has been modified in a variety of ways, but in its basic outline it remains the most plausible explanation for relations between the synoptic gospels.

[2]Peter Ellis, *Matthew: His Mind and His Message* (Collegeville, MN: The Liturgical Press, 1974/1985) p. 173, very rightly points out that "...the proper key to the theological purposes of any evangelist lies primarily in an analysis of his work as a whole and only secondarily in a comparison between his use of sources and that of another evangelist. The first approach is called the vertical, the second, the horizontal approach." If our focus for the moment is on the horizontal approach, it is merely to indicate how Matthew made use of Markan tradition in presenting his unique interpretation of the meaning of Peter's confession.

[3]*Peter in the New Testament*, ed. R.E. Brown, K.P. Donfried and J. Reumann (New York: Paulist Press, 1973) p. 72, n. 167, gives bibliographical references for this hypothesis.

[4]In Luke, Peter's rehabilitation is prepared in 22:31-33, just prior to the foretelling of his denial. There is a clear parallel here to the account in John 21:15-19, including three common elements: Peter's affirmation of love or faithfulness, allusion to his death, and the pastoral charge. Similarities between Lk 24:34 and 1 Cor 15:5 suggest that the former was originally an independent kerygmatic formula that Luke has inserted into the Emmaus narrative in order to make the point that Simon — and not Cleopas and his companion — was the first witness to the resurrection. If the verse is removed, there results no break in continuity between v. 33 and v. 35. V. 34, λεγοντας...Σιμωνι, fits awkwardly into its present context, especially if 24:12, containing the name Peter, is original. By placing a period after αυτοις in v. 33 and deleting v. 34, we obtain a consistent narrative in which the Emmaus disciples return to Jerusalem and — as two legally "valid" witnesses — testify to the gathered disciples that they have seen and "broken bread" with the risen Lord.

[5]See *Peter in the New Testament*, p. 64-68. E. Dinkler, "Peter's Confession and the 'Satan' Saying: the Problem of Jesus' Messiahship," in *The Future of our Religious Past*, ed. J.M. Robinson, New York 1971, links the Satan-word directly to Peter's confession and holds that the pre-Markan tradition reflects Jesus' refusal of the title "Messiah."

[6]Luke frequently omits elements unfavorable to Peter: in the garden of Gethsemane there is no rebuke of Peter for his failure to keep watch (22:46; cf. Mk 14:37); and at the moment of the denial Luke omits Peter's curse (22:60; cf. Mk 14:71). On the other hand, Luke can add favorable details, such as Peter's confession of sin at

the miraculous catch of fish (5:8). This verse also represents an initial confession by Peter: "Lord" (κυριε).

[7]Thus, 3:21, at Jesus' baptism; 6:12, prior to choosing the Twelve; 9:28, the transfiguration; 22:40-45, Jesus' prayer in Gethsemane; cf. 5:16; 10:21; 11:1; 23:34,46.

[8]The only other usage of this expression occurs in 4:17, marking the beginning of Jesus' proclamation of the Kingdom.

[9]Or "the Herodians," as P[45] W, etc., Mk 8:15.

[10]Luke places the leaven-word, directed against the Pharisees only, in 12:1 as part of a scene of conflict between Jesus and the scribes and Pharisees. Thereby he has Peter's confession follow directly upon the feeding of the five thousand (9:10-17).

[11]Mt 4:18; but cf. Jn 1:40f which grounds the early Church's conviction that Andrew was the first-called of the disciples.

[12]Deut 18:15,18; Ac 3:22; Jn 6:14; cf. Lk 9:8.

[13]Cf. Jn 1:20-25, where John's denial constitutes a veritable confession of Jesus: "I am not the Christ/Elijah/the Prophet." In the Fourth Gospel, John is presented less as the baptizer than as the *witness* to Jesus, the self-sacrificing Lamb of God.

[14]In Mt 21:11 the crowd identifies Jesus as ο προφητης , but no connection is made here with the figure of Jeremiah.

[15]He does so at the beginning of his gospel (2:17, the "slaughter of the innocents"), in the middle (16:14, Peter's confession), and at the end (27:9, the purchase of the Field of Blood with the thirty pieces of silver). Although Isaiah's name occurs seven times, Matthew's references to Jeremiah at these key points may have particular significance.

[16]Mt 2:13 (Jer 26:21-23); 2:18 (31:15); 4:19 (16:16); 7:7 (29:13f); 7:22 (14:14f); 10:5-6 (50:6); 21:13 (7:11); 21:34-36 (7:25f); 23:8 (31:34); 23:38 (12:7; cf. 22:5); 24:2 (7:14); 26:28 (31:31,34); 27:10 (18:2f; 32:6-15); 27:25 (51:35; cf. 2 Sam 1:13-16; 3:29).

[17]Mt 10:5-6; 21:34-36; cf. 23:29f,38. Mt 21:34-36 has changed "a servant / another servant," read by Mark and Luke, into the plural, recalling Jer 7:25, "all my servants the prophets" (cf. 25:4). The false prophets whom Matthew targets are apparently false teachers within the Christian community.

[18]Matthew's inclusion of Jeremiah in the list of popular identifications might also be linked to the tradition of the appearance of Jeremiah to Judas Maccabeus (II Macc 15:13-16). It is worth noting that the addition of the name Jeremiah creates two lines of fifteen syllables each: οι μεν...Ηλιαν / ετεροι ... προφητων. Thus Matthew brings into balance both Jesus' initial question and the disciples' response. While this may have been intentional, however, little can be made of it since the confession itself is structured differently — although it too is clearly rhythmic.

[19]Mt 4:18; 8:14; 10:2; 14:28f; 15:15.

[20]Mt 9:27; 12:23; 20:30; 21:9,15.

[21]Cf. 20:31.

[22]The question of the historicity of Mark's account is well-nigh impossible to resolve. Rather than attributing it to Mark's literary inventiveness, or to a displaced passion (O. Cullmann) or post-resurrection (E. Stauffer) saying, we would do well

to take the fact of such a dialogue at the mid-point in Jesus' ministry more or less at face value. Mark makes it the pivotal moment of his entire narrative; and the Johannine parallel supports its authenticity. See the discussion in *Peter in the New Testament*, p. 64f; and the comments of D. Hill, *The Gospel of Matthew* (Grand Rapids: Eerdman's, 1972) p. 258f.

[23] The parallelism of Mk 8:27-29, together with the fact that Jesus' rebuke to Peter is better suited to a situation in which the disciple denied that the Son of Man must suffer to fulfill his mission, speak against the thesis of E. Dinkler (note 5, above). For the important relation between this scene and the passion narrative, see D. Senior, *The Passion of Jesus in the Gospel of Matthew* (Wilmington, DE: Michael Glazier, 1985) p. 73f.

[24] "My (Jesus') Father in heaven": 5:16; 7:21; 10:32f; 12:50; 16:17; 18:10,19. "Your (the disciples') Father in heaven": 5:45; 6:1,9; 7:11; 18:14(?).

[25] Mt 1:23; Isa 7:14, LXX.

[26] Mark and Luke read "This is my Son" at the transfiguration scene only. At the baptism the voice addresses Jesus directly: "You are..." Matthew has modified the baptismal announcement to manifest Jesus as the (divine) Son to those present.

[27] 4Q Flor 10-13, commentary on 2 Sam 7:11-14. For the translation, see A. Dupont-Sommer, *The Essene Writings from Qumran* (New York: Meridian/World, 1961) p. 313.

[28] The expression προσκυνεω means literally to prostrate oneself before another, but with an attitude of obeisance or worship (see Arndt & Gingrich, p. 723f).

[29] Mt 28:17 omits the object αυτω (thus B D). *The New King James Version* splits the difference, reading "worshipped" in 8:2 and "kneeling down" in 20:20.

[30] Further on we shall discuss the chiastic structuring of this passage as well, and the unique interpretation of the scene that Matthew achieves by virtue of chiasmus.

[31] C* N W, etc. add του ζωντος to complete the parallel.

[32] Mark records a more Semitic form of the high priest's question: "Are you the Christ, the Son of the Blessed?" Luke has the Sanhedrin as a whole pose the question, "Are you the Christ/Son of God?" (22:67,70). Does an historical reminiscence of the coupling of "Christ" and "Son of God" or "Son of the Blessed" account for Matthew's linking of the two in 16:16, with the express purpose of creating the parallel: Peter // the high priest?

[33] See the discussion and bibliographical references in *Peter in the New Testament*, p. 88f.

[34] Cf. III Baruch 11:2, where the archangel Michael "holds the keys of the Kingdom of Heaven." R.H. Charles, *Pseudepigrapha of the Old Testament*, Oxford 1913/1963, p. 359.

[35] Cf. 18:18; Jn 20:21-23. For some recent discussions of this question, see J.D.M. Derrett, "Binding and Loosing (Matt 16:19; 18:18; John 20:23)," *JBL* 102 (1983), 112-117; H.W. Basser, "Derrett's 'Binding' Reopened," *JBL* 104 (1985), 297-300; and, in the same issue, R.H. Hiers, " 'Binding' and 'Loosing': the Matthean Authorizations," 233-250, who concludes that the terms refer to the exorcizing of demons and, by extension, to the authority granted to Peter and others to deal with problems

confronting the church community. While this may explain the "binding," it fails to make sense of the "loosing." A recent, interesting analysis in this discussion has been offered by J. Marcus, "The Gates of Hades and the Keys of the Kingdom (Matt 16:18-19)," *CBQ* 50/3 (1988), p. 443-455, who interprets "binding and loosing" in Mt 16:19 "as declaring forbidden or permitted, i.e., promulgation of authoritative halakah," (452). Peter is granted authority on earth to "distinguish valid from invalid prohibitions," that is, to interpret the law as it changes in the eschatological time of the Church following Jesus' death and resurrection.

[36]Cf. 2 Baruch 10:18, "Moreover, ye priests, take ye the keys of the sanctuary, and cast them into the height of heaven, and give them to the Lord and say: 'Guard Thy house Thyself, for lo! we are found false stewards'." Charles, *Pseudepigrapha*, p. 486.

[37]The more natural reading would be to take κατισχυσουσιν in the sense of "resist" or "withstand." The meaning could be, "the gates of Hades will not withstand the onslaught of the Church," accomplished by Christ's victory over death. On the other hand, J. Marcus, "The Gates of Hades," p. 443f, argues for an active meaning of "prevail": the expression "gates of hades" includes both the city of the dead and its inhabitants, who, in the apocalyptic age following Jesus' death and resurrection, will surge forth through the gates to attack the Church. Peter, however, who will possess the keys to the Kingdom of heaven, will unlock the gates of heaven and release "the kingly power of God." That power will emerge victorious, thereby fulfilling the (uniquely Matthean) petition of the Lord's Prayer, "Thy Kingdom come, thy will be done on earth as in heaven."

[38]See H. Frankemölle, *Jahwebund und Kirche Christi*, Münster 1974, on the significance of the permanent covenant-bond between Jesus and his community as the foundation of Matthean ecclesiology.

[39]J.-J. von Allmen, *La primauté de l'Eglise de Pierre et de Paul*, Fribourg (Switzerland) 1977, p. 96. To argue strictly on the basis of such an affirmation that Peter's authority and pastoral responsibility are transmissible to successive bishops of Rome or to the episcopacy as a whole is more than most contemporary New Testament scholars of any confession are willing to do. The issue of primacy through "apostolic succession" cannot be resolved by exegesis; it is a matter of broader church tradition.

[40]Further on we shall find that this passage is one element in a larger chiastic pattern that includes the first fifteen verses of ch. 1.

[41]See P. Bonnard, *L'Evangile Selon Saint Matthieu*, 2nd ed. (Neuchâtel: Delachaux & Niestlé, 1970), p. 41-44, who discusses Matthew's redactional technique in this passage.

[42]An interesting discussion appears in F. W. Beare's *The Gospel According to Matthew* (Peabody, Mass.: Hendrickson, 1981), p. 104-113; see also his dated but still useful work, *The Earliest Records of Jesus* (Oxford: Blackwell, 1962), p. 42f.

[43]Luke places this identification of Jesus as "Son of God" in the first and third temptations. Thereby he creates a chiastic parallelism that focuses on the image of Jesus set upon the pinnacle of the temple in the midst of Jerusalem. Is it far-fetched to see here an affirmation of Jesus as the locus of true worship (cf. Jn 2:19-21; 4:23f)?

[44]*The Gospel According to Matthew*, p. 105.

[45]On the place of the uncreated light in Orthodox spirituality, see J. Meyendorff,

St. Gregory Palamas and Orthodox Spirituality (Crestwood, NY: St Vladimir's Seminary Press, 1974); V. Lossky, *The Mystical Theology of the Eastern Church* (Crestwood: SVS Press, 1976), esp. chs. 4 ("Uncreated Energies") and 11 ("The Divine Light"); and G.I. Mantzaridis, *The Deification of Man* (Crestwood: SVS Press, 1984), esp. chs. 4-5 on the "mystical experience" and "consummation of deification."

[46]From the Greek term for "silence" or "inner stillness," *hesychia* refers to a tradition of mystical prayer associated particularly with Athonite monks of the 14th century. Originating with Origen, the Cappadocians and Evagrius Ponticus, it focused upon ceaseless repetition of the "Prayer of Jesus" or "Prayer of the Heart," usually formulated as "Lord Jesus Christ, Son of God, have mercy on me, a sinner." Texts on the hesychast tradition were collected by Nicodemus of the Holy Mountain (d. 1809) in the *Philocalia* and remain today an important element of the spiritual tradition of Orthodox Christianity.

[47]Gregory Palamas, "Homily on the Transfiguration" (Migne, *PG* CLI, 448).

[48]Cf. the later witness of 2 Pet 1:16-18.

[49]1:1, taking υιου θεου as original; 1:11; 9:7; 15:39; etc. Throughout Mark's Gospel Jesus is presented as the Davidic Royal Messiah and Son of God. Cf. J.D. Kingsbury, *The Christology of Mark's Gospel* (Philadelphia: Fortress, 1983), p. 47-71.

[50]This is a clear allusion to the ascension (cf. 24:51 and Acts 1:9-11) and, as in Matthew, links the glorification of Jesus through death and resurrection with his parousia as Son of Man.

[51]The *RSV Gospel Parallels* (New York: Nelson, 1957), p. 91, notes the connection between this Lukan image and John 1:14b, "We have beheld his glory, glory as of the only Son from the Father."

[52]Revealed, that is, to his own people, including the disciples. From the beginning of his ministry Jesus is recognized and acknowledged by the demons, as he is by the Gentile centurion who witnesses his crucifixion (Mk 1:24; 5:7; 15:39). Our allusions to the "messianic secret," by the way, are intended to point out a characteristic element of Markan composition. They do not imply acceptance of the thesis of Wrede, Bultmann and other form-critics, that all such injunctions to silence are creations of the post-Easter community, to explain why Jesus was not recognized and acclaimed as Messiah during the course of his public ministry. As indicated in the preceding chapter, there is good reason for taking Peter's confession of Jesus' messiahship at face value.

[53]On the origin and significance of this ancient formula, see J. Breck, *The Power of the Word*, p. 159-171.

[54]Patristic exegesis also sees the presence of the Spirit in the overshadowing cloud.

[55]In John's account, Jesus gives thanks (ευχαριστησας), then distributes the bread himself. As the "Bread of Life," it is appropriate that he, rather than the disciples (who perhaps represent deacons in the Markan and Matthean communities), give the bread to the crowds.

[56]The feeding of the four thousand (Mk 8:1-10; Mt 15:32-39), on the other hand, involves Gentiles (shown by the geographical location and the people's response, "They glorified the God of Israel," Mt 15:31) and reflects the Gentile mission of the early Church.

[57]This is especially clear in the Fourth Gospel, where the account ends with the disciples and Jesus coming "immediately" to their destination (6:21).

[58]A classic example of this is Matthew's modification of Mark's "words of institution" at the Last Supper. Aside from providing balance, reflecting more developed liturgical usage, Matthew adds a theological explanation to the cup-word: "for the forgiveness of sins." Cf. Mt 26:26-29 with Mk 14:22-25.

[59]The whole body, perhaps (although this is not stated) as represented by their ministerial orders (*episkopoi, presbyteroi,* which were synonymous until close to the end of the first century). This seems to be the meaning of the Johannine account, where the power of the "keys" as the authority to forgive and retain sins is bestowed upon the body of disciples, who represent the Church as a whole: Jn 20:23.

[60]The "fourth watch" according to Roman reckoning is between 3 and 6 a.m. The time element is interesting here: from the early evening until morning the disciples are on the sea, struggling against wind and waves. While there is no thought of a tempest (as there is in Mk 4:35ff), one wonders if the hostile waters are meant to represent chaos and death, the watery abyss (*tehom*) of Gen 1:1f, personified as the goddess Tiamat in the *Enuma Elish*. The theme of the ark, common to Genesis and the Babylonian creation myth, suggests such a rapport.

[61]Matthew omits this detail, possibly because it perplexed him as much as it does most modern commentators. Perhaps the best explanation is given by A. Stock, *The Method and Message of Mark* (Wilmington, DE: Glazier, 1989), p. 197f: " 'He meant to pass them by' gives the reason why Jesus comes to the disciples — he wanted to save them. The verb *parerchomai* is strongly linked to the theophany tradition. Jesus' rescue of the disciples reveals something of who he is; he wants to 'pass by' as Yahweh 'passed by' Moses and Elijah....'"

[62]The qualifiers "strong," "very strong," etc. read by some manuscripts are almost certainly secondary additions; but they of course render the sense of the text.

[63]See Wilfrid Harrington's commentary on *Mark* (Wilmington, DE: Glazier, 1979) p. 94. Harrington bases his observation on the connection between this pericope and the multiplication of bread (Mk 6:41).

[64]This is a far more likely explanation for the frequent doublings in Gospel tradition than the widely accepted suggestion made by Rudolf Bultmann that we have to do here with a popular folk motif that insists upon symmetrical groupings: *The History of the Synoptic Tradition* (Oxford: Blackwell, 1963), p. 314-317.

[65]Let me insist once again that the label "narrative tale" implies no judgment whatsoever about the historicity of the events recounted. It merely affirms that the evangelist presents those events with extraordinary literary skill, selecting some elements, rejecting others, and — through his own interpretive genius — weaving the whole into a spare yet powerful story. That such tales are not merely "narrative fiction," however, is due less to the accuracy and completeness with which they report historical events than to the way they reveal to the reader truth about God and about oneself.

2. SYNOPTIC DISCOURSES

A. The Lukan Infancy Hymns

The Lukan infancy narratives contain four recognized hymns unique to the Third Gospel: the "Magnificat" of Mary, mother of Jesus (1:46-55); the "Benedictus" of Zechariah, father of John the Baptist (1:68-79); the "Gloria in Excelsis" of the angels, sung at Jesus' birth (2:14); and the "Nunc Dimittis" of Symeon, pronounced at Jesus' presentation in the temple (2:29-32). To these may be added other hymnic passages such as Gabriel's canticle in honor of John (1:14-17), his hymn of praise to the Davidic Messiah (1:32-35), and the angelic annunciation of Jesus' birth to the shepherds (2:10-11). While these are not "discourses" in the proper sense, they may be most conveniently considered under this heading.[1]

Commentators have long recognized the parallelism that Luke creates between the angelic announcements and the births of John and Jesus. In alternating sequences we read of the annunciation of John to Zechariah and of Jesus to Mary; of the parent's doubtful questioning; of the birth of the children, followed by their circumcision and presentation or manifestation.[2] What has been much less noticed — and in fact ignored in most critical studies of the Gospel — is the use of chiasmus in several of the key passages of the narrative.

Following his opening verses, Luke introduces his readers to the righteous couple, Zechariah and Elizabeth. This initial passage (1:5-6) sets the scene for the encounter between the priest Zechariah and the angel Gabriel, who announces the coming birth of the Forerunner. The following verses reproduce a chiastic pattern whose center or focus is the descriptive canticle of vv. 14-17.

A (7):Elizabeth is barren; conception is humanly impossible.

  B (8-10):Zechariah enters the temple; the people are praying outside.

    C (11-12): the angel appears; Zechariah is afraid.

      D (13): the angel reveals the miracle.

        E (14-15): qualities of the Forerunner.

        E' (16-17): the work of the Forerunner.

      D' (18): Zechariah doubts the miracle.

    C' (19-20): the angel identifies himself; Zechariah is struck dumb.

  B' (21-23): the people are waiting outside; Zechariah comes out of the temple.

A' (24-25): Elizabeth conceives; her conception is a miracle from the Lord.

A form-critical analysis of this passage pressed to its limits would likely excise verses 14-17 as an originally free-floating hymn that was inserted into the narrative at a secondary stage of composition. It is possible to pass from v. 13 to v. 18 with no break in continuity or meaning: " '...your wife Elizabeth will bear you a son, and you shall call his name John.' And Zechariah said to the angel, 'How shall I know this?...'." The canticle itself (vv. 14-17) consists of a carefully crafted set of Old Testament prophecies reworked to describe John as the messianic precursor. It begins by describing the qualities that equip him to fulfill his call: he will bring joy to "many" in Israel; he will be consecrated as a Nazirite prophet; he will be filled with the Holy Spirit "even from his mother's womb." His task consists in preparing the way of the Lord in "the spirit and power of Elijah," by summoning the children of Israel to repentance in the end time (cf. Mal 4:5-6). The content and rhythmic structure of these lines led the editors of the RSV to set them as verse, furthering the reader's impression that they were originally independent.[3]

It may well be, as many hold, that the several Lukan passages concerning John were taken by the evangelist from a "Baptist" source and reworked in such a way as to create a parallel with the annunciation, conception and birth stories of Jesus. The fact that the passage 1:7-25 is structured chiastically, however, with the canticle to John as its thematic center, makes it evident that the canticle is no secondary interpolation. It is the focal point of all that surrounds it, beginning with the promise that the barren Elizabeth would miraculously conceive and ending with the conception itself. Moreover, the entire passage is characterized by the heightening effect we have found so often before.

A → A': The promise →
Its fulfillment.

B → B': The people wait, praying, as Zechariah enters the temple →
The people "wonder" (εθαυμαζον) as he reappears,
unable to speak.

C → C': The angel appears →
The angel reveals himself to be Gabriel, sent to reveal the "good news."
Zechariah is afraid →
Zechariah is struck dumb.

D → D': The angel reveals (μη φοβου) →
Zechariah doubts.

E → E': The qualities of John that equip him for his mission →
The mission itself.

The overall unity of the Lukan composition is further indicated by the fact that the following passage, depicting the annunciation to Mary, is composed in a similar A:B:C:D:E:E':D':C':B':A' chiastic pattern. Here the central theme or focus begins with Mary's bewildered yet rhetorical response to the angel, "How can this be...?" Whereas such a question on the lips of Zechariah led to a rebuke and the punishment of temporary dumbness, in the case of Mary it provides the opening for Gabriel to declare that the child to be born of her will be conceived by the power of the Holy Spirit and thus will be (literally) "the Son of God" (v. 35).

[Vv. 26-27 introduce the passage, a typical usage of anacrusis.]

A (28): The angel comes to Mary and greets her.

B (29): Mary is troubled and questions the angel.

C (30f): The angel prophesies Jesus' birth.

D (32f): He will be great, Son of the Most High and messianic King.

E (34): Mary's question, "How can this be, since I have no husband?"

E' (35ab): Gabriel's answer, "The Holy Spirit will
come upon you, and the power of the Most
High will overshadow you."

D' (35cd): He will be called holy, the Son of God.

C' (36f): The angel prophesies John's birth.

B' (38a): Mary accepts the angel's word (her "fiat").

A' (38b): The angel departs from Mary.

In addition to the inclusion created by the arrival and departure of the angel, intensification is evident in the movement from B to B' (Mary's perplexity → Mary's total acceptance), from C to C' (Jesus' conception, birth and naming → John's humanly impossible conception),[4] and from D to D' (Jesus' designation as "Son of the Most High," a traditional title of the Davidic King, → Jesus' designation as "holy" and "Son of God," in Luke the supreme title of divine Sonship [cf. 22:70]). The thematic center of the passage is the exchange between Mary and the angel. In response to her bewilderment, Gabriel replies that the son to be born of her will be conceived by the power of the Holy Spirit; the son of Mary is thus revealed to be ("ontologically," we might say) the very Son of God.

A similar heightening should be noted between the passages concerning John and Jesus respectively. As Joseph Fitzmyer points out in his exhaustive commentary on the Third Gospel, "Luke has not used parallelism just for the sake of parallelism...there is a step-parallelism at work."[5] Whereas John's parents are described as "righteous" before God (1:6), Mary is "favored" (1:28); Elizabeth's conception is natural, despite her age (1:24), whereas Mary's is miraculous (1:35); John will be "great before the Lord" (1:15), whereas Jesus will be "great" and "Son of the Most High" (1:32); John will be filled with the Holy Spirit from his conception (1:15), whereas Jesus' conception itself will be miraculously accomplished by the Holy Spirit (1:35); etc. This further demonstrates that in its final form the entire infancy narrative is the carefully conceived product of a single mind, an evangelist with exceptional literary skill, who wove together several elements of primitive tradition to create a thoroughly unified if variegated tapestry.

Recognition of chiastic patterning is especially useful as a counterweight to an overly enthusiastic analysis of the hypothetical sources that underlie a given passage. The canticle of Zechariah known as the "Benedictus" (Lk 1:68-79) appears to be composite. Virtually all commentators divide the passage into a first and second stanza, vv. 68-75, and vv. 76-79.[6] Whereas the hymn as a whole seems clearly to be about John, vv. 76-79 pose a special problem since the terminology appears to apply to Jesus as the fulfillment of God's saving work, rather than to John as the forerunner. Some exegetes hold that vv. 76-77 are a Lukan insertion into an originally Jewish Christian hymn; others see the first half of the canticle as a hymn to Jesus, while the second half alone refers to the Baptist.[7]

Whatever the case regarding the sources that underlie the passage, its present structure clearly indicates that Luke intended it to be a unified hymn of praise that speaks of John — and not Jesus — as the fulfillment of the covenant promises enunciated in vv. 72-73. The chiastic arrangement of the text is as follows.[8] Note that Luke has once again opted for the A:B:C:D:E:E':D':C':B':A' pattern.

A (68): Blessed be the Lord, the God of Israel, for he has *visited* (επεσκεψατο) and redeemed his people,

   B (69): and has raised up a horn of *salvation* for us in the house of his servant David,

      C (70): as he spoke by the mouth of his holy *prophets* from ancient times,

         D (71): [promising] salvation from *our enemies* and from the hand of all who hate us,

            E (72): to perform mercy for our fathers and to remember his holy *covenant*,

            E' (73): to realize for us the *oath* which he swore to Abraham, our father,

         D' (74f): that we, being rescued from the hand of *our enemies*, might serve him fearlessly in holiness and righteousness before him all our days.

      C' (76): And you, child, will be called a *prophet* of the Most High; for you will go before the Lord to prepare his ways,

   B' (77): to give knowledge of *salvation* to his people in the forgiveness of their sins,

A' (78f): through the compassionate mercy of our God, when the day shall *dawn* (επισκεψεται) upon us from on high[9] to illumine those sitting in darkness and the shadow of death, to guide our feet into the way of peace.

The structure may be summarized as:

A : Visitation
  B : Salvation
    C : Prophets
      D : Enemies
        E : Covenant
        E′: Covenant
      D′: Enemies
    C′: Prophet
  B′: Salvation
A′: Visitation.

As for the focusing or heightening effect,

A → A′: The past "visitation" of God's intervention in
  Israel's sacred history [referring ostensibly to
  the birth of John, but in Luke's scheme a
  reference is intended to Jesus as well] →
  The eschatological "visitation" of the Dawn
  from on High.[10]

B → B′: Salvation →
  Salvation through forgiveness of sins.

C → C′: The prophets of old →
  The Prophet of the Most High.

D → D′: Salvation from enemies →
  Salvation from enemies in order to serve God.

E → E′: God's holy covenant →
  Fulfillment of the specific oath God swore
  to Abraham.

With the former and future Visitations forming an inclusion, the
canticle progresses through an assurance of salvation, articulated by
the former prophets and actively prepared by the new Prophet John,
to deliverance from enemies that makes it possible for a renewed
Israel to serve the Lord forever "in holiness and righteousness." The
central theme is that of the Covenant, which God sealed with Abraham, and which he faithfully accomplishes "for our sake" (του
δουναι ημιν).

This concentric parallelism not only speaks in favor of the original unity of the hymn and confirms that the entire composition refers to John the Baptist. It also reinforces the argument that Luke himself was the original author of the piece, since it conforms to the same tenfold chiastic pattern that appears in 1:7-25 and 1:28-38.

As a final example of Luke's use of chiasmus in his infancy narrative[11] we may recall the story, unique to this gospel, of Jesus in the temple at the age of twelve (2:41-51a). As worked out by H. J. de Jonge,[12] the pattern is as follows:

A : Mary, Joseph, and Jesus go to Jerusalem (41-42)

    B : Jesus stays in Jerusalem, which is not noticed (43)

        C : His parents seek and find him (44-46a)

            D: *Jesus among the teachers* (46b-47)

        C': His parents, annoyed, reproach him (48)

    B': Jesus' reaction, which is not understood (49-50)

A': Mary, Joseph, and Jesus return to Nazareth (51a)

Although I would analyze the pericope somewhat differently, as set out below, de Jonge has clearly made his point with regard to its chiastic format.

[V. 41: introduction (anacrusis)]

    A (42-43a): Jesus and parents go up to Jerusalem;
    Jesus is disobedient.

        B (43b): Parents do not know what Jesus did.

            C (44): Parents journey on, unconcerned.

                D (45): Parents return to Jerusalem seeking Jesus.

                    E (46): Jesus listens to the teachers and
                    asks questions.

                    E' (47): All are amazed at Jesus' understanding
                    and answers.

                D' (48): Parents have sought Jesus anxiously.

            C' (49): Jesus' matter-of-fact reply.

        B' (50): Parents do not understand what Jesus said.

    A' (51): Jesus and parents return to Nazareth;
    Jesus is obedient.

Here again Luke has chosen the tenfold chiastic structure (A-E // E'-A'), utilizing the features of intensification to create a helical movement from the extremities (A-A') toward the center (E-E').

A → A': Departure; Jesus is disobedient →
   Return; Jesus is obedient.

B → B': Parents' lack of knowledge of Jesus' whereabouts →
   Parents' lack of understanding of Jesus' "saying."

C → C': Parents travel on, unconcerned →
   Jesus expresses surprise at their concern [as in B-B', "lack of knowledge" is heightened to a "lack of understanding"].

D → D': Parents seek Jesus →
   Parents have sought him anxiously.

E → E': Jesus listens and questions →
   Jesus amazes the teachers with his understanding
   and his answers.

Luke, no less than Matthew and Mark, demonstrates a remarkable talent for employing chiasmus, in order to draw the reader's attention progressively toward his principal theme. Thus the focus of the first passage, 1:7-25, is the person and work of the Forerunner; of the second, 1:28-38b, the exchange between Mary and Gabriel; of the third, 1:68-79, the Covenant between God and his people; and of the fourth, 2:42-51, Jesus' knowledge and understanding as superior to that of the elders of Israel. In each case Luke uses a double focus, E → E', which expresses movement from promise to fulfillment: from a description of John to fulfillment of his mission; from Mary's perplexed question to Gabriel's self-fulfilling prophecy; from the promised Covenant to its realization; and from Jesus as pupil to Jesus as teacher.

For Luke as for other biblical authors, the "rhetorical helix" is a conscious literary device that highlights the writer's chief concern and thereby enables the reader to focus directly on the "literal meaning" of the passage in question.

B. Matthean Structure and The Sermon on the Mount

Few passages in the New Testament have proven more resistant to literary analysis than Matthew's version of Jesus' inaugural sermon. Since the early patristic period, biblical scholars have attempted to find a coherent pattern in the structure of chapters 5 through 7. No consensus has been reached, although the impression persists that "of all the sermons or discourses of Jesus recorded in Matthew, the Sermon on the Mount is by far the most structured."[13]

Some interpreters have seen the opening Beatitudes as programmatic for the Sermon itself or for the Gospel as a whole. Yet debate continues over the very number of Beatitudes. Are there seven, including only vv. 3-9, thereby relegating vv. 10-12 to a separate category concerning the persecuted, as an introduction to the sayings on salt and light? Or are there nine, arranged in triads and concluding with v. 11 or perhaps 12?[14] And do the Beatitudes serve as a sort of table of contents, in either direct or inverse order, that offers a clue as to the overall structure of the Gospel?[15] Without entering into the debate here, we should simply note that Matthew has produced a work whose individual units are often presented in a tight chiastic or parallel pattern, while an overall parallelism is less clearly present. This holds true for the Sermon on the Mount as it does for the Gospel as a whole.

Some light, certainly, can be shed on the problem of the Sermon by examining the structure of surrounding passages. The following outline indicates that the author relied on chiasmus more than most interpreters have been aware.

1:1-17. The genealogy of Christ: three periods of fourteen generations, framed by inverted elements (Jesus Christ → David → Abraham // Abraham → David → the Christ).

1:18-25.

A (18a): The birth of Jesus.

    B (18b): Mary, betrothed to Joseph, conceives by the Holy Spirit.

        C (19): Joseph resolves to divorce Mary.

            D (20): Angelic announcement of the birth of the child, conceived by the Holy Spirit.

                E (21): Jesus = Savior of his people.

D' (22f): Prophetic announcement of the birth of
Emmanuel, "God with us."

C' (24): Joseph accepts Mary as his wife.

B' (25a): Joseph has no sexual relations with Mary prior to
the child's birth.[16]

A' (25b): The naming of Jesus.

2:1-12

A (1): The wise men come to Jerusalem.

B (2): The wise men come to worship the child.

C (3f): Herod troubled, seeks the birthplace of the Christ.

D (5f): Herod learns that the birthplace is Bethlehem.

E (7): Herod ascertains the time the star appeared.

D' (8-9a): Herod sends the wise men to search for the
birthplace in Bethlehem.

C' (9b-10): The wise men rejoice, finding the birthplace of
the Christ.

B' (11): The wise men find the child, worship him and offer
gifts.

A' (12): The wise men return to their own country.

2:13-23 [three units: the flight into Egypt, the massacre of the innocents, and
the return to Nazareth, in A:B:A' format, linked by the theme of "fulfillment
of prophecy"].

2:13-15

A (13a): The angel sends Joseph, Mary and Jesus to Egypt.

B (13b): Herod seeks to kill the child.

B' (14-15a): Herod himself dies.

A' (15b): God's Son called out of Egypt.

2:16-18 (The massacre)

A : Then Herod, when he saw that he had been *tricked*
by the wise men,

B : was in a *furious rage*,

C : and he sent and killed all the male *children*
in Bethlehem and in all that region

   D : who were *two years* old or *under,*

      E : according to the time which he had *ascertained*
from the wise men.

         F : Then was fulfilled what was spoken by
the prophet Jeremiah:

      E' : "A *voice* was *heard* in Ramah,

   D' : *wailing* and loud *lamentation,*

  C' : Rachel weeping for her *children;*

 B' : she *refused* to be *consoled,*

A' : because they were *no more.*"[17]

2:19-23

A (19): Joseph in Egypt.

   B (20): Joseph, Mary and Jesus commanded to return to Israel.

   B' (21-22): Joseph, Mary and Jesus return to Israel.

A' (23): Joseph dwells in Nazareth in order that the child might be
called a "Nazarene."

3:1-4:17 [two originally independent units (3:1-17; 4:1-17) worked together
into a chiastic pattern]

A (3:1f): John → "Repent, for the Kingdom of heaven is at hand."

   B (3:3): Isaiah's prophecy concerning John.

      C (3:4-6): John in the wilderness.

         D (3:7-10): Pharisees and Sadducees come
to be baptized.

            E (3:11ab): Jesus is mightier than John.

               F (3:11c): "He will baptize you with
the Holy Spirit and with fire."

            E' (3:12): Jesus will execute final judgment.

         D' (3:13-17): Jesus comes to be baptized.

      C' (4:1-11): Jesus in the wilderness.

   B' (4:12-16): Isaiah's prophecy concerning Jesus.

A' (4:17): Jesus → "Repent, for the Kingdom of heaven is at hand."

4:18-22

1 As he [Jesus] walked by the Sea of Galilee,

2   he saw two brothers,

3   Simon who is called Peter

4   and Andrew his brother,

5   casting a net into the sea;

6   for they were fishermen.

7   and he said to them,

["Follow me, and I will make you fishers of men."]

8   Immediately they left their nets

9   and followed him.

1 And going on from there

2   he saw two other brothers,

3   James the son of Zebedee

4   and John his brother,

5   in the boat with Zebedee their father,

6   mending their nets,

7   and he called them.

8   Immediately they left the boat and their father,

9   and followed him.[18]

4:23-25

   A (23abc): Jesus teaches and preaches in Galilee.
      B (23d): Jesus heals every disease and infirmity.
         C (24a): Jesus' fame spreads throughout all Syria.
      B' (24bc): Jesus heals every disease and infirmity of the afflicted, demoniacs, epileptics and paralytics.
   A' (25): Jesus' universal mission.[19]

5:1-8:1 [The Sermon on the Mount]

8:2-4

A : And behold, a leper came to him and knelt before
   (lit.: worshiped) him,

   B : saying, "Lord, if you will, you can make me clean."

      C : And he [Jesus] stretched out his hand and touched him

         D : saying, "I will; be clean."

         D' : And immediately his leprosy was cleansed.

      C' : And Jesus said to him, "See that you say
      nothing to anyone;

   B' : but go, show yourself to the priest,

A' : and offer the gift that Moses commanded, for a proof
   to the people."[20]

8:5-13

A (5f): The servant is paralyzed "in terrible distress."

   B (7): Jesus promises to heal the servant.

      C (8): The humble faith of the Gentile centurion.

         D (9): The Gentile's faith.

            E (10): "Not even in Israel have I found such faith."

         D' (11): The Gentiles' destiny.

      C' (12): Judgment upon the unbelieving Jews.

   B' (13ab): Jesus declares the servant healed.

A' (13c): The servant is healed immediately.

8:14-17

A (14): Peter's mother-in-law is infirm, diseased.

   B (15): Jesus heals with a touch.

      C (16a): Multitudes come to be healed.

   B' (16b): Jesus heals with a word.

A' (17): "He took our infirmities and bore our diseases."

8:18-23

A (18): Jesus intends to board the boat to cross the Lake.

   B (19): Scribe: "I will follow you."

      C (20a): Care for basic needs ("foxes have holes").

         D (20b): "The Son of Man has nowhere to lay his head".

      C' (21): Care for basic needs ("bury my father").

   B' (22): Jesus: "Follow me."

A' (23): Jesus boards the boat to cross the Lake.[21]

8:24-27

A (24ab): Winds and sea threaten the disciples.

   B (24c): Jesus is asleep.

      C (25): The disciples' fear before the elements.

         D (26a): Jesus – "Why are you afraid, O men of little faith!"

      C' (26b): Jesus' authority over the elements.

   B' (26c): A great calm comes over the sea.

A' (27): Winds and sea obey Jesus.[22]

8:28-9:1

A (28a): Jesus crosses the Lake.

   B (28b): Jesus comes to Gadarene country.

      C (28cd): Two demoniacs meet Jesus.

         D (29): The demoniacs react with fear.

            E (30): The herd of swine is feeding.

               F (31): The demons beg to enter the swine.

                  G (32a): Jesus sends them: "Go."[23]

               F' (32b): The demons enter the swine.

            E' (32c): The herd of swine perishes.

         D' (33): The herdsmen react with fear.

      C' (34a): All the people of the city meet Jesus.

   B' (34b): The Gadarenes beg Jesus to leave their country.

A' (9:1): Jesus crosses the Lake again.

9:2-8

A (2): Jesus' authority to forgive the paralytic's sins.

    B (3): Scribes accuse Jesus of blasphemy.

        C (4f): Physical healing will confirm Jesus' authority to forgive sins.

    B' (6f): Jesus refutes the accusation of blasphemy by healing the paralytic.

A' (8): The crowds glorify God for Jesus' authority.

9:9-13

[V. 9: anacrusis, introduces 10-13].[24]

A (10): Jesus invites sinners to table.

    B (11): The legalistic Pharisees protest.

        C (12): Jesus comes for those who recognize their sickness (sinfulness).

    B' (13a): God prefers mercy shown towards sinners to the sacrifices of the "just."

A' (13b): Jesus came to call sinners.[25]

9:14-17 [an independent saying followed by two examples]

Then the disciples of John came to [Jesus], saying,
    "Why do we and the Pharisees *fast*
but your disciples do not *fast*?"

And Jesus said to them,
    "can the wedding guests *mourn*
as long as the *bridegroom* is with them?
The days will come when the *bridegroom* will be taken away from them,
and then they will *fast*."[26]

A : No one puts a piece of unshrunk cloth

    B : on an old garment,

        C : for the patch tears away

    B' : from the garment,

A' : and a worse tear is made.

A : Neither do they put new wine into old skins,

    B : else burst

        C : the skins

            D : and the wine is spilled,

        C' : and the skins

    B' : are destroyed,

A' : but they put new wine in new wine-skins, and both are preserved.[27]

From this point in the Gospel, chiastic structures are mixed with other examples of parallelism and straight narrative. The two healings recounted in 9:18-26, for example, are taken over from Mark and represent Mark's tendency to conflate separate units of the tradition by situating one within another which frames it.[28] As these healings appear in Matthew, they are best read as a simple A:B:A' tricolon. In the rest of the chapter, the ingenuity needed to detect chiasmus is enough to disprove its presence altogether. In fact, the tightly structured examples of chiasmus that lead up to the Sermon on the Mount are matched only in isolated passages throughout the rest of the Gospel, as in 14:22ff and 16:13ff. Curiously, Matthew does not abandon chiasmus outright after the Sermon; he merely allows it to deteriorate, to unravel, as it were, to the point where its presence in a given pericope can at times be neither proven nor disproven.

In major sections of discourse, however, Matthew clearly reverts to chiastic structures, again in order to draw the reader's attention to the central elements of Jesus' message. Lund has analyzed several key examples of discourse material, particularly the Missionary Discourse in 10:5-11:1, and the denunciation of the Scribes and Pharisees in 23:1-39. There is no need to reproduce his findings, since the interested reader should study them in the context of his accompanying exegetical comments.[29] Our concern at this point is with the Sermon on the Mount itself and the presence of chiastic elements within it.

Recent analysis of the Sermon[30] has continued a trend that places major weight on the relationship between Jesus and the Mosaic Law. The affirmations of 5:17-19 are taken as programmatic of the whole: Jesus' purpose is to declare himself either a "new Moses," giver of a new Torah, or to set forth for his followers both the enduring importance of Jewish legal and ritual prescriptions and the imperatives of the "greater righteousness" which is demanded of them.

While this approach is sound, it tends to draw attention away from another more fundamental purpose of Jesus' Sermon: *to chart for his followers the way that leads to the Kingdom of Heaven.* Repeatedly Jesus focuses his message on the attitude of heart, summed up in the "Golden Rule" of 7:12, that alone leads to life. This is an attitude of humble trust and unwavering faithfulness towards Jesus' person and his message, one that stands in utter contrast to the ostentation and hypocrisy of the Pharisees and enables the true disciple to withstand both temptation and persecution (7:24-27). It is the attitude of those who "seek first the Kingdom of God and his righteousness" (6:33).

Thus the Beatitudes open with the promise of blessing to those who are poor in spirit, "for theirs is the Kingdom of Heaven," an assurance repeated in the eighth Beatitude concerning those who are persecuted for the sake of justice or righteousness.[31] Those who "relax" (neglect or nullify, λυση) the least precept of the Law will be called "least" in the Kingdom of heaven, whereas those who perform them and teach them scrupulously will be acclaimed there as "great" (5:19). Accordingly, the Kingdom is open only to those who hear the word and do it (7:21). Yet to them is given assurance that if they indeed seek first the Kingdom, all of their other earthly needs will be met (6:33). Therefore their archetypal prayer beseeches the Father to establish the Kingdom in their midst, that they might be granted true nourishment, forgiveness, and preservation from evil in the age to come (6:9-13).

Apart from these few direct references, many other statements confirm that the main thrust of Jesus' message in this section is to spell out conditions which enable one to enter the Kingdom. If the disciples are encouraged to endure persecution, to love their enemies, to avoid hypocrisy in acts of piety, and to seek their treasure beyond this life, it is for the sake of their "reward in heaven" (5:12,46; 6:1f,5,16,19f). If Jesus warns them with rather heavy-handed images to seek reconciliation with one another (5:23-26), to discipline their passions in the most rigorous way (5:27-30), and to preserve their treasure of faith from defilement and abuse (7:6), it is to urge them to aspire toward that degree of perfection which alone renders them worthy of the Kingdom. Yet if he likewise assures them, with images of compassion and consolation, that they need have no fear of want (6:30), that God responds to every request, opens to all who knock, and provides good things to all who ask (7:7-11), it is to provide encouragement for those who choose the rigorous, narrow way that leads to life (7:13f).

There are those who find in the Sermon on the Mount only Law without Grace, instruction in *what* to do with no indication as to how to do it. Such a reading is possible only through the lens of theological presuppositions drawn from sources other than the New Testament. As many recent commentators have noted, the Sermon from beginning to end is a proclamation of Grace.[32] It is, nonetheless, a demanding Grace, one that requires hard choices and unremitting faithfulness to the "perfection" to which Christ's disciples are called. Neither an "interim-ethic" (A. Schweitzer), nor a mere ideal, the ethic of the Sermon is one to be lived — here in the present with an eye to the future. It may be, as some have affirmed,[33] that the Sermon communicates a christology more than it does a moral code. Nevertheless, its chief function in the teaching of the Matthean Jesus is to indicate to his disciples, both present and future, the way into the Kingdom of Heaven.

What, then, can we conclude about the overall structure of the Sermon? The wide variety of attempts to outline its structure is clear indication of the difficulty the interpreter runs into in taking on the task. Nevertheless, an underlying chiastic pattern does appear, although no consensus has been reached as to its precise shape.

Nils Lund, once again, broke ground in this area with an analysis that was subsequently taken up and improved by John Welch.[34] Its major sections, according to Welch's scheme, are as follows:

X : Introduction: Multitudes, mountain, teaching (4:25-5:2).[35]

    Y : Observations on the Nature and Function of the Church (5:2-19).

    Z :The Higher Quality of Christian Righteousness: It is Higher than that of Jew or Gentile (5:17-18, 20-47).

    Z' :The Higher Quality of Christian Righteousness: It is Perfection according to the Golden Rule (5:48-7:12).

    Y' : Observations on the Nature and Function of the Church (7:13-27).

X' : Conclusion: Teaching, mountain, multitudes (7:28-8:1).

This analysis is in many ways quite plausible. Its weakest point is Lund's displacement of 5:17-18 to a position between vv. 19 and 20, thereby making of it an introduction to section Z.[36] Otherwise, he asserts, vv. 17-18 cannot be considered part of the original text. Even with the rearrangement, however, Lund considers v. 18 to be a gloss. This is a frequently expressed view, and in light of the following "antitheses" (5:21ff: "You have heard it said... / but I say to you..."), it is probably accurate. Full weight must be given, nonetheless, to the fact that there is no textual evidence whatsoever for displacing 5:17, however much such a rearrangement may make sense to the modern reader.

Another difficulty with Lund's analysis, as Welch notes, is that the central affirmations of his chiastic patterns carry so little weight. They do not, on the whole, represent the conceptual focus, the center towards which the helical movement would normally progress. Therefore Welch resorts to another scheme, suggesting that "the Sermon elaborates each of the eight beatitudes,[37] taking them one by one in the reverse order from that in which they are initially introduced."[38] While this provides interesting correspondences, it is not without problems.[39] Then again, attempts to determine the shape of the Sermon through what is technically known as "structural analysis" have produced such needlessly complicated results as to be of little value either for the exegete or for the general reader.[40] Is there then no solution to the question? What in fact is the "shape" of the Sermon on the Mount?

However significant various objections to Lund's analysis may be, he has cracked the code, as it were, and has conclusively demonstrated that chiasmus determines the organization of the entire Sermon as well as of many of its individual units. Three of these smaller units represent the same kind of focusing, helical movement we have found elsewhere. In Lund's' literal translation, they are as follows:

5:10-12

A : Blessed are they that have been *persecuted*
    for righteousness sake,
  B : *For* theirs is the kingdom of *heaven*.
    C : *Blessed* are ye,
        D : When they shall *reproach* you,
           E : And *persecute*,
        D': And shall *say* all manner of *evil* against you
        falsely for my sake.
    C': Rejoice and be exceeding *glad*,
  B' *For* great is your reward in *heaven*.
A': For thus *persecuted* they the prophets that were before you.

Here the key theme of the inclusion — persecution — is repeated at the center, with intensification marked by a shift from third to second person as well as by heightened descriptive phrases in the second ("prime") strophe.

A → A': The persecuted righteous →
    The persecuting authorities.

B → B': *Theirs* is the Kingdom →
    Great is *your* reward in heaven.

C → C': Blessed are you →
    Rejoice and be glad.

D → D': They shall reproach you →
    They shall say all manner of evil against you.

E: The central focus is on the reality of persecution experienced *now* by Jesus' own followers.

6:7-9a

A : And in praying use not vain repetitions, as the Gentiles do,

    B : for they think that by their much speaking

        C : they shall be heard.

            D : Be not therefore like unto them.

        C': For your heavenly Father knoweth what things
            ye have need of,

    B': before ye ask him.

A': After this manner therefore pray ye:

This introduction to the Lord's Prayer moves by antitheses from a denunciation of the vain repetitions practiced by the Gentiles to a command to pray with the terse petitions Jesus himself formulates. Since God knows our needs before we ask, these most basic of requests are adequate for all prayer, both personal (6:6, singular προσευχη) and communal (6:5, plural προσευχησθε).

A → A': Gentile prayer →
    The disciples' prayer.

B → B': Vain repetitions →
    Terseness in prayer.

C → C': Gentile misunderstanding →
God's omniscience.

D: The central admonition: be not like the Gentiles.

7:4-5
Or how wilt thou say [anacrusis]

To thy brother,
Let me *cast out* the mote
Out of thine eye;
And behold,
The beam is
In thine own eye?
Thou hypocrite, *cast out* first
Out of thine own eye
The beam;
And then shalt thou see clearly
Out of the eye
To *cast out* the mote
Of thy brother.

The repetition of the penultimate terms in the thematic center (*cast out*) is a feature that occurs elsewhere in Matthew's chiastic patterns (5:10-12; 6:1-17). In this particular example, brief phrases sweep about the central idea: only the hypocrite judges others without first judging himself. Focusing is provided by the principle of conclusion rather than by intensification or specification: whereas the first strophe describes the attitude of the hypocrite, the second instructs the disciple how to avoid such hypocrisy by reference to the central motif: cast out *first* the mote in your own eye!

Recognition of concentric parallelism in these individual units, however, does not answer the question regarding the Sermon as a whole. Is the entire passage, 5:1-8:1, arranged chiastically, and if so, what precisely is its principle of organization?

Recently Jack Dean Kingsbury revived a theory of Günther Bornkamm,[41] according to which the Lord's Prayer (6:9-13) constitutes the conceptual center of the Sermon. Bornkamm perhaps went too far in suggesting that the Prayer provides the organizational

principles which determine the structure of the Sermon as a whole
(and specifically, of 6:19-7:12). But his insight regarding its central
position seems to have led Kingsbury to what is perhaps the simplest
and most adequate analysis to date, one that recognizes an overall
chiastic pattern in the Sermon yet avoids any attempt to force individual units into a grand scheme.[42] According to his analysis, the
Sermon is arranged as follows.

[5:1-2 and 7:28-8:1 frame the five major sections]

> A (5:3-16): Introduction: On Those who Practice the
> Greater Righteousness.
>> B (5:17-48): On Practicing the Greater Righteousness
>> Toward the Neighbor.
>>> C (6:1-18): On Practicing the Greater Righteousness
>>> Before God.
>> B' (6:19-7:12): On Practicing the Greater Righteousness
>> in Other Areas of Life.
> A' (7:13-27): Conclusion: Injunctions on Practicing
> the Greater Righteousness.[43]

This outline confirms that the major theme of the Sermon is the
disciple's practice of a righteousness greater than that manifested by
those who profess to abide by the Mosaic Law: "Unless your righteousness exceeds that of the Scribes and Pharisees, you will never
enter the Kingdom of Heaven" (5:20). It confirms as well that the
whole purpose of seeking and manifesting that "greater righteousness" is to enter eternal life by the "narrow gate" which alone leads
to it (7:13f).

This arrangement also suggests that Bornkamm and others are
on the mark in situating the Lord's Prayer at the very heart of the
Sermon.[44] The central portion (C) consists of three interrelated cultic
themes: almsgiving, prayer and fasting. The opening verse (6:1) is a
general admonition to avoid self-serving ostentation when practicing acts of "righteousness" or "piety."[45] Almsgiving, prayer, and to
a degree even fasting were public as well as private acts in the
Judaism of Jesus' day, representing charity, worship and repentance.
Jesus' admonition, then, is not directed against public worship and
accompanying cultic acts as such, but rather against the hypocrisy
of those who "preach but do not practice," who "do all their deeds
to be seen by men," and by their misuse of authority "shut the
Kingdom of Heaven against men" (23:3-13).

Matthew achieves a striking effect in this central section with his use of parallelism. Jan Lambrecht has convincingly argued that the three counsels on almsgiving (vv. 2-4), on prayer (vv. 5-6) and on fasting (vv. 16-18) originally constituted a "three-strophe exhortation" that Matthew found in his special source.[46] Into this source material he has introduced his own reworking of the (hypothetical) "Q" version of the Lord's Prayer, with its prologue and epilogue (6:7-16). The close relation of the three units to one another, both formally and materially, seems to confirm Lambrecht's arguments. In addition, however, it should be noted that Matthew has arranged these units, together with the introductory warning of 6:1, in a chiastic pattern that condemns the Pharisees' practice of praying for public consumption.

A (1): Beware of practicing your righteousness before men
   in order to be *seen by them;* for then you will have no *reward*
   from *your Father* who is in heaven.

B (2): Thus when you give alms,/
   sound no trumpet before you, as the *hypocrites* do in the
   synagogues and in the streets that they *may be praised by men.*/
   Truly, I say to you, they have their reward.

C (3f): But when you give alms,/
   do not let your left hand know what your right hand
   is doing, so that your alms may be *in secret;*/
   and your Father who sees in secret will reward you.

D (5): And when you pray,/
   you must not be like the hypocrites, for they love
   to stand and pray in the synagogues and at the
   street corners, that they *may be seen by men.*/
   Truly, I say to you, they have their reward.

C' (6): But when you pray,/
   go into your room and shut the door and pray to
   your Father who is *in secret;*/
   and your Father who sees in secret will reward you.

B' (16): And when you fast,/
   do not look dismal, like the *hypocrites,* for they disfigure
   their faces that their fasting *may be seen by men.*/
   Truly, I say to you, they have their reward.

A' (17): But when you fast,/
   anoint your head and wash your face, that your fasting
   may not be *seen by men* but by *your Father* who is in secret;/
   and your Father who sees in secret will *reward* you.

Two overlapping principles of structuring are apparent here. The primary and original pattern, which Matthew found in his special source, consists of a "negative triptych" followed by a matching "positive triptych."[47] In addition, Matthew has imposed upon this pattern a second one that stresses particular key terms:

A → A': seen by them / your Father / reward →
seen by men / your Father / reward.

B → B': hypocrites / may be praised by men / reward →
hypocrites / may be seen by men / reward.

C → C': in secret / and your Father who sees in secret will reward
you (both elements are repeated).

D : The central focus on prayer is a synthesis of the foregoing,
criticizing the hypocrisy of those who seek the reward of
men's praise and thereby forfeit the reward of God.

The repetition of terms and themes throughout these units might seem to argue against the presence of such a chiastic structure. The conclusion of B and B', for example, appears in D as well;[48] and the motif of "the Father in secret" occurs in C, C' and A'. Would Matthew have purposely ordered his material in this way, considering that he intended in any case to insert 6:7-15 as an expansion on the unit concerning prayer?

This example raises an important question we shall have occasion to deal with in more depth later on: *Just how conscious was the biblical author of his use of chiasmus?* Is every example of the form to be reckoned as a carefully and intentionally crafted literary product? Or is chiasmus — the phenomenon of concentric parallelism — such a fundamental "structure" in human thought and perception that an author can employ its principles unconsciously, spontaneously, as a modern writer would exploit the laws of narrative prose without deliberately reflecting on the precise way his creation unfolds? Although Matthew clearly makes intentional use of chiasmus in the major sections of his Gospel that we have already examined, this passage, as much as the units of chapter 9 noted earlier, suggests that it was simply a matter of second nature for him to write according to the laws of concentric parallelism. Both consciously and instinctively, as it were, he wrote "chiastically."[49]

This leads finally to the section Matthew has inserted into his source material, 6:7-15. He signals its independence from the other units by shifting the diatribe from the Jews to the Gentiles. The ostentation described in the "three-strophe exhortation" is clearly that of the Pharisees: those who give alms, pray and fast in the synagogues and streets with the chief aim of receiving praise from men. In vv. 7-8, Jesus condemns the "empty phrases" of the Gentiles and affirms that "your Father knows what you need before you ask him." Then follows the model prayer with its specifically communal (ecclesial) emphasis upon the first person plural: "*Our* Father...give *us.*" It concludes with an elaboration of Mark 11:25.

Mk 11:25,
And whenever you stand praying, forgive, if you have anything against any one; so that your Father also who is in heaven may forgive you your trespasses.

Mt 6:14-15,
For if you forgive men their trespasses, your heavenly Father also will forgive you; but if you do not forgive men their trespasses, neither will your Father forgive your trespasses.[50]

The question that concerns us is whether the Lord's Prayer, like so many other key passages of the First Gospel, is structured chiastically. Although the underlying "Q" material (cf. Lk 11:2-4) was not so arranged, it seems at least possible that Matthew did shape the received tradition into the familiar pattern of concentric parallelism.

As it is usually analyzed, the Prayer appears to be divided into four sections: an introductory address ("Our Father in heaven"); three "thou petitions" ("sanctify thy Name," "cause thy Kingdom to come," "cause thy will to be done as in heaven so also on earth"); four "we petitions" ("our bread for tomorrow give us today," "and forgive us our debts as we have forgiven[51] our debtors," "and lead us not into temptation," "but deliver us from evil"); and a final doxology which is clearly secondary, that is, it did not belong to the original text as Matthew composed it.

Several remarks should be made about this scheme. First, it is not really accurate to distinguish the "thou" petitions from the "we" petitions as is usually done. Each petition of the Prayer in fact concerns "us." If Jesus' disciples are to pray that God sanctify his Name, establish his Kingdom and bring all things under his will, it is for *their* sake and the sake of *their* salvation. There is no discontinuity, then, between these first three petitions and those that follow, whether the nourishment, forgiveness and protection demanded are granted for the present (as conditions for discipleship) or the future (as blessings of life in the Kingdom).

As for the formal arrangement of the Prayer, I would tentatively suggest another scheme that seems plausible but remains admittedly hypothetical. (The determining factor, of course, is the "literal sense" of the passage: what Matthew as author intended, and behind him, what Jesus intended, insofar as the Prayer in its present form may be attributed to him.)[52] Taking account of the two ὡς clauses, 10c and 12b, it appears that Matthew divides the Prayer into four sections as follows:

1 Our Father in heaven,
       sanctify thy Name.

2 Let thy Kingdom come,
       let thy will be done
       as in heaven, so also on earth.

3 Our bread of tomorrow give us today,
       and forgive us our debts
       as we have forgiven our debtors.

4 And lead us not into temptation,
       but deliver us from the Evil One.

The first section concerns God's person, borne and revealed by the Name. Its significance for the disciples lies in the address "Father," *Pater*, which reflects Jesus' own Aramaic expression *Abba*. They, like the Son, may call upon God with the familiar and intimate term that expresses their filial relationship to him.

The second section speaks of God's initiative in ushering in the eschaton, the new age of the Kingdom, in which his reign will be established over all creation and his will exercised without restraint upon the earth as well as in heaven. The final clause, "as in heaven so also on earth," marks a comparison paralleled in the following section, where the emphasis lies on the needs of those who await the coming of the Kingdom. The disciple who begs God to forgive his debts — both material and spiritual — justifies his request on grounds of his own prior forgiveness of those who have sinned against him.[53] The communal, ecclesial aspect is expressed once again by the first person plural: "as we have (already!) forgiven our debtors." Jesus' disciples can pray that God's will be done on earth only insofar as they have already submitted themselves to the divine will. Similarly, they can pray for the forgiveness of their own sins only insofar as they have already granted forgiveness to those indebted to them. Such is the meaning of other sections of the Great

Sermon (5:23f, 43-45; 6:15) and of a number of Jesus' parables (e.g., 5:25f; 18:21-35; 25:31-46).[54]

This leads finally to the fourth section, in which the "temptation" most likely refers to the apocalyptic trials to be suffered by Jesus' disciples before the advent of the Kingdom in power. It has been argued that this is not the usual meaning of πειρασμος in Matthew. The emphasis throughout the Prayer, however, coupled with the final complementary petition, makes it probable that Matthew understood this expression in light of the persecution already experienced by his community and their conviction that the last days were upon them (cf. 24:1-44).

If we are correct in understanding the Lord's Prayer as essentially "eschatological," not only in its "thou" but also in its "we" petitions, this implies that the two most difficult images in the Prayer are also to be understood in light of the "last things": "our bread for tomorrow" (τον αρτον ημων τον επιουσιον), and "deliver us from evil" or "from the Evil One" (ρυσαι ημας απο του πονηρου).

Luke understood the rare and problematic adjective *epiousios* in the temporal sense of "daily" or "for the coming day" (το καθ' ημεραν, a typical Lukan expression, 11:3). This suggests that to his mind the image underlying this petition was that of the Manna in the wilderness, "bread" gathered each day for the next day's provision (Ex 16:4-5). It could, therefore, mean simply divinely provided daily nourishment.

Matthew's formula, on the other hand, suggests a contrast between επιουσιον and σημερον, as though some incongruity exists in requesting *for today* our *bread epiousion*. If the adjective *epiousion* were to be translated simply "daily," then it would seem redundant to place the stress Matthew does on the term "today." On the other hand, the formulation of the petition is thoroughly comprehensible if we understand *epiousion* in the sense of "substantial" or even "supersubstantial" (επι–ουσιος). Then Jesus would be instructing his disciples to pray for "bread to come," that is, the "bread" of the messianic banquet, to be enjoyed by those who eagerly await the coming of the Kingdom.

This line of reasoning, of course, is hypothetical, and to many exegetes it is highly suspect. It may be called the "metaphysical" interpretation of the αρτον επιουσιον, which became so prominent in early patristic tradition. Nevertheless, it should not be rejected out of hand, primarily because of the eschatological tone of the entire Prayer and the tension noted between τον αρτον ημων τον επιουσιον and δος ημιν σημερον. Given these factors, the most plausible translation of the petition would be, "Our bread of tomorrow give us today," implying our "supersubstantial bread of the Kingdom," the equivalent of the Johannine "true Bread from heaven given for the life of the world" (Jn 6:32f). If Matthew and his readers understood the request in this way, then it would have referred not to "daily bread" in the sense of daily sustenance, but to the *eucharistic bread* that serves as a foretaste of the messianic banquet.

Finally, the eschatological context of the Prayer suggests that the concluding expression του πονηρου does not refer to some abstract concept of evil as opposed to virtue or goodness; it refers rather to the embodiment of evil in the person of Satan, the devil. This is confirmed by the parallelism of themes between the penultimate and ultimate petitions of the Prayer: to be delivered from temptation is to be preserved from the influence of the Tempter himself. Thus the Prayer begins with a petition that the Father glorify his Name, and closes with what amounts to an antithetical petition that the disciples be preserved from the power of the Evil One. Although this reading may seem to imply an uncharacteristic dualism between God and Satan, the apocalyptic context in which the Gospel was written — imminent trials and temptations prior to inauguration of God's Kingdom — suggests that Matthew's readers understood the image of του πονηρου in just this way.

If these reflections on the various elements of the Prayer are accurate, they point to the following arrangement.

A : Our Father in heaven,
  sanctify thy Name.
  B : Thy Kingdom come,
    C : thy will be done
      as in heaven, so also on earth.
      D : Our bread for tomorrow give us today.
    C' : And forgive us our debts
      as we have forgiven our debtors.
  B' : And lead us not into temptation,
A' : but deliver us from the Evil One.

A → A': antithesis: Our Father / the Evil One.

B → B': The "age to come" / the "present age."

C → C': The divine will / the human will.

D: The focus would then be upon the "bread" that nourishes for eternal life, partaken of in the Christian eucharist.

The question remains whether Matthew and his readers could have understood the Prayer in this way. This interpretation, once again, is plausible but hypothetical. Given the eschatological tone of the Great Sermon (entrance into the Kingdom of God), however, together with the imminence or reality of persecution "in the last times" (ch. 24) and the significance of the eucharistic meal for Matthew's community as a means of forgiveness that permits entry into the heavenly Kingdom (26:26-29),[55] it remains at the very least an interesting possibility.

C. Markan Structure and the "Little Apocalypse"

The healing of blind Bartimaeus, which we analyzed earlier (Mk 10:46ff), offers an excellent example of Mark's use of chiasmus. We have noted that similar literary patterns occur elsewhere in his Gospel — in the transfiguration scene, for example, or the walking on the water. Furthermore, we have pointed out several passages in Matthew's Gospel that indicate how this evangelist took up material from his Markan *Vorlage* and, by adding an element of description or dialogue, transformed the account into a superbly balanced chiastic arrangement. In this present section, our concern is to demonstrate that Mark's use of chiasmus is as refined as Matthew's and even more pervasive. In fact it is no exaggeration to say that the entire Second Gospel is structured according to the principles of concentric parallelism.

We begin with a complete outline of the Gospel in order to demonstrate the structuring of its individual units. Then we turn to an evaluation of several conflicting theories concerning its overall arrangement. Finally we look somewhat more closely at a major section of Markan dialogue, the so-called "little apocalypse" (13:1-37). The fact that chiastic patterns occur throughout the various sections of his Gospel vindicates Mark as a highly sophisticated, rather than "primitive" or "naive," literary figure, and provides as well important insight into his theology.

To appreciate the helical movement of the Gospel, the reader should work through each outlined section twice: from beginning to end in accordance with its narrative flow; and spirally, from A to A' to B to B', etc., concluding with the central element.

A Chiastic Outline of Mark's Gospel:

1:1-15, *Prologue: Beginning of the Good News.*

A (1): Beginning of the Gospel of Jesus Christ.

    B (2f): John the Baptist comes to prepare the "way" (= the Gospel).

        C (4): John appears in the wilderness.

            D (5): The people confess their sins.

                E (6): John clothed in camel's hair (as the prophet Elijah).

                    F (7): One mightier than John is to come.

                        G (8a): "I have baptized you with water,

                        G' (8b): but he will baptize you with the Holy Spirit."

                    F' (9): Jesus comes and is baptized.

                E' (10): Jesus "clothed" in the Holy Spirit (as the eschatological prophet).

            D' (11): The heavenly voice "confesses" the Son.

        C' (12f): Jesus is driven into the wilderness.[56]

    B' (14): Jesus comes to preach the Gospel (= the Way: 10:52; Acts 9:2).

A' (15): "Repent and believe in the Gospel."[57]

1:16-2:14, *Call of the first disciples, first healings.*

A (16-20): Jesus calls the first four disciples ("Follow me").

    B (21f): Jesus teaches in the synagogue.

        C (23-27): Jesus heals a man with an unclean spirit (they all marvelled).

            D (28): Jesus' fame spreads everywhere.

                E (29-31): Jesus heals Peter's mother-in-law with a touch ("the fever left her").

> F (32-34): Jesus heals and casts out demons (evening).
>
> G (35): Jesus rises early to pray.
>
> F′ (36-39): Jesus preaches and casts out demons (morning).
>
> E′ (40-44): Jesus heals a leper with a touch and a word ("the leprosy left him").
>
> D′ (45): Jesus' fame spreads throughout town and country.
>
> C′ (2:1-12): Jesus heals a paralytic ("they all were amazed and glorified God").
>
> B′ (13): Jesus teaches beside the sea.
>
> A′ (14): Jesus calls Levi ("Follow me").

2:15-3:6, *Conflicts with Pharisees.*

> A (15-17): Pharisees take offense at Jesus.
>
> B (18-22): Jesus defies a tradition about fasting.
>
> C (23-30): "The Son of Man is Lord of the sabbath."
>
> B′ (3:1-5): Jesus defies a tradition about healing.
>
> A′ (6): Pharisees plot to destroy Jesus.

3:7-19a, *Jesus heals, names the Twelve.*

> A (7a): Jesus withdraws with his disciples.
>
> B (7b-8): A crowd comes to Jesus.
>
> C (9f): Jesus in public.
>
> D (11): Unclean spirits confess Jesus as "Son of God."
>
> C′ (12): Jesus in secret.
>
> B′ (13): The disciples come to Jesus.
>
> A′ (14-19a): Jesus appoints the twelve disciples.

3:19b-35, *Jesus rejected by family and authorities.*

> A (19b-21): Jesus' family[58] attempts to seize him.
>
> B (22): Scribes blaspheme, ascribing Jesus' power to Beelzebul (Satan).

C (23-25): Satan does not cast out Satan.

D (26): Satan is coming to an end.

C' (27): Jesus has bound (cast out) Satan.

B' (28-30): Scribes blaspheme against the Holy Spirit.

A' (31-35): Jesus' family is excluded from the circle of disciples.[59]

4:1-36, *Teaching in parables.*[60]

A (1): Jesus in the boat on the sea.

B (2): Jesus teaches with many parables.

C (3-9): The parable of the sower and seed.

D (10-13): Jesus reveals the secret of the Kingdom.

E (14-20): Interpretation of the parable of the sower.

D' (21-25): Jesus (the "Lamp"[61]) brings to light the secret of the Kingdom.

C' (26-32): Parables of the sower and seed.

B' (33f): Jesus teaches with many parables, but explains all to his disciples.

A' (35f): Jesus in the boat crosses the sea.

4:37-41, *Calming the storm.*[62]

A (37): The wind and sea threaten the disciples.

B (38): Jesus is calmly asleep; the disciples are afraid.

C (39a): Jesus rebukes the wind and calms the sea.

B' (39b-40): A great calm ensues; Jesus rebukes the disciples for being afraid.

A' (41): The wind and sea obey Jesus.

5:1-20, *Healing of a Gentile demoniac.*[63]

A (1): Jesus and the disciples cross the sea.

B (2-4): An unclean spirit possesses the man.

C (5): The man is on the hills (εν τοις ορεσιν).

D (6f): The man questions Jesus.

E (8): Jesus exorcizes the unclean spirit.

D′ (9f): Jesus questions the man.

C′ (11-13a): The swine are on the hill (προς τω ορει).

B′ (13bc): Unclean spirits come out of the man.

A′ (13d): The swine drown in the sea.

A (14): The herdsmen tell; the people come.

B (15): Jesus presents the man healed.

C (16f): The people beg Jesus to leave their country.

B′ (18f): Jesus sends the man on mission.

A′ (20): The man tells; all marvel.

5:21-6:1, *Healing of two Jewish women.*[64]

A (21): Jesus returns to Jewish territory.

B (22-24a): Jesus is asked to heal a child by the laying on of hands.[65]

C (35): Some come from the ruler's house: "your daughter is dead."

D (36): "Do not fear, only believe."

C′ (37-40): They come to the ruler's house: "the child is not dead but sleeping."

B′ (41-43): Jesus takes the child by the hand and heals her.

A′ (6:1): Jesus returns to his own country.

A (24b-26): The woman suffers from a flow of blood.

B (27): The woman acts (she touches Jesus' garment).

C (28): The woman's faith.

D (29): *Immediately* she knows in her body that she is healed.

D′ (30): *Immediately* Jesus knows that power has gone forth from him.

C′ (31f): The disciples' incredulity.

B′ (33): The woman confesses (she tells all).

A′ (34): The woman is healed of her disease.

6:2-6, *Jesus' own people take offense at him.*

   A (2a): Jesus teaches in the synagogue.

      B (2b): Many are astonished at Jesus' teaching and works.

         C (2cd): What mighty works he does!

            D (3ab): Jesus' own family is present.

               E (3c): Jesus' family is scandalized by him.

            D' (4): Jesus has no honor among his own family.

         C' (5): He could do no mighty work there.[66]

      B' (6a): Jesus is amazed at their unbelief.

   A' (6b): Jesus teaches in the villages.

6:7-13, *Jesus sends out the Twelve.*

   A (7): The Twelve receive authority over unclean spirits.

      B (8f): Conditions for their journey.

         C (10): Remain in the same place.

      B' (11): Conditions for leaving.

   A' (12f): The Twelve cast out demons.

6:14-29, *The death of John the Baptist.*

   A (14a): Herod "heard of it" (Jesus).

      B (14b-16): Herod had John beheaded.

         C (17-22a): The girl pleases Herod and his guests.

            D (22b-23): Herod's offer.

               E (24): Ask for the head of John the baptizer.

            D' (25): The girl's request.

         C' (26): The girl saddens Herod; he keeps his word
            because of the guests.

      B' (27f): Herod has John beheaded.

   A' (29): John's disciples "heard of it" (John).

6:30-46, *Feeding the five thousand.*

A (30-31a): Jesus and the disciples go off to find rest.

   B (31b-33): *All* are seeking Jesus and the disciples.

      C (34): Jesus teaches the people.

         D (35f): Disciples: "Send them away."

            E (37f): The disciples provide five loaves and two fish.

         D′ (39f): Jesus: "Command them to sit down."

      C′ (41): Jesus feeds the people.

   B′ (42-44): *All* eat and are satisfied.

A′ (45f): Jesus dismisses the disciples and crowd, and goes off to pray.

6:47-53, *Jesus walks on the water.*

A (47): Sea — land.

   B (48a): The wind was against them; they were distressed.

      C (48b-49): Thinking Jesus is a ghost, the disciples cry out.

         D (50a): They all saw him and were afraid.[67]

      C′ (50bc): Jesus reveals himself: "It is I, have no fear."

   B′ (51f): The wind ceased; their hearts were hardened.

A′ (53): Sea — land.[68]

6:54-56 [*An independent summary unit on healings; cf. 1:32-34; 3:7-12.*]

7:1-23, *Traditions of men.*

A (1f): Pharisees: unwashed hands defile a man.

   B (3-5): Tradition of the elders: external things defile.

      C (6f): Pharisees teach as doctrine precepts of men.

         D (8): "You leave the commandment of God and hold fast the tradition of men."

      C′ (9-13): Pharisees make void the word of God through their tradition.

   B′ (14-19): Jesus: nothing external defiles.

A′ (20-23): Jesus: evil things from within defile a man.

7:24-31, *Healing of the Syrophoenician woman's daughter.*

A (24a): Jesus goes to the region of Tyre and Sidon.
  B (24bc): Jesus is found in a house.
    C (25): The daughter is possessed by an unclean spirit.
      D (26): The Syrophoenician woman begs from Jesus.
        E (27): Jesus came to serve "children" (Jews), not "dogs" (Gentiles).
      D' (28): "Dogs" (the woman) beg from "children" (Jesus).
    C' (29): The daughter is healed from demon-possession.
  B' (30): The woman finds her daughter in her house.
A' (31): Jesus returns from the region of Tyre and Sidon.

7:32-37, *Healing of a deaf and dumb man.*

A (32a): A deaf and dumb man is brought to Jesus.
  B (32b): They *beseech* him to lay his hand on the man.
    C (33): Jesus touches the man's ears and tongue.
      D (34): Jesus commands, "Ephphatha, be opened."
    C' (35): The man's ears are opened, tongue loosed.
  B' (36): Jesus *charges* them to tell no one.
A' (37): Jesus heals even the deaf and dumb.

8:1-10a, *Feeding the four thousand.*

A (1ab): Jesus calls the disciples to him.
  B (1c-3): The crowd is hungry.
    C (4f): Seven loaves.
      D (6a): Jesus commands the crowd to sit down (posture of discipleship?).
    C' (6b-7): Seven loaves and a few fish.
  B' (8f): The crowd of 4000 eats and is satisfied.
A' (10a [Gk: 9b]): Jesus sends the crowd away.[69]

8:10-13, *Demand for a sign.*

A (10): Jesus enters the boat and departs.

B (11): The Pharisees seek a sign.

C (12a): "Why does this generation seek a sign?"

B' (12b): No sign shall be given.

A' (13): Jesus enters the boat again and departs.

8:14-21, *True and false bread.*

[This is a summary passage, structured in antithetical parallelism, which allows Jesus to question and correct the disciples' misunderstanding about the (eucharistic?) significance of the bread: Jesus' dominion over the sea (4:35-41; 6:45-52) is linked to his power to multiply loaves (6:30-44; 8:1-9), as God's power over the waters of the Red Sea (Ex 14:21f) is linked to his feeding of the Israelites in the wilderness (Ex 16:13-15).]

8:22-26, *Healing of the blind man of Bethsaida.*[70]

A (22): The blind man is brought from the village.

B (23abc): Jesus lays hands on him.

C (23d): "Do you see anything?"

C' (24): "I see men...like trees walking."

B' (25abc): Jesus lays hands on him again.

A' (25d-26): The man, seeing, is admonished not to enter the village.

8:27-30, *Peter's confession.*[71]

A (27): "Who do men say that I am?"

B (28): "John the Baptist, Elijah, a prophet."

A' (29a): "Who do you say that I am?"

B' (29b): "You are the Christ (Messiah)."

C (30): The charge to remain silent.

8:31-9:1, *The suffering of the Son of Man.*

A (31-32a): The Son of Man must suffer.

B (32b-33): The rebuke by Peter, who will deny him.

C (34): "Take up his cross and follow me."

C′ (35-37): "Lose his life for my sake and the gospel's."

B′ (38): Whoever denies the Son of Man will be denied by him.

A′ (9:1): The Son of Man will come in the Kingdom and with power (cf. 14:62).

9:2-10, *The Transfiguration.*

A (2f): Ascending the mountain; transfiguration.

    B (4-6): Jesus is with Moses and Elijah.

        C (7): The divine voice: "This is my beloved Son."

    B′ (8): Jesus is alone.

A′ (9f): Descending the mountain; resurrection.

9:11-13, *Elijah has come.*

A (11): Why must Elijah come first?

    B (12a): Elijah comes first to restore all things.

        C (12b): The Son of Man must suffer many things.

    B′ (13a): Elijah has already come (John the Baptist).

A′ (13bc): He came to fulfill Scripture.

9:14-29, *Healing of the epileptic boy.*

A (14-17): The boy is possessed by a dumb spirit.

    B (18f): The disciples cannot heal him.

        C (20): The spirit convulses the boy.

            D (21-22a): The possession.

                E (22b): The father's doubt.

                    F (23): "All things are possible to him who believes."

                E′ (24): The father's belief.

            D′ (25): The exorcism.

        C′ (26f): The spirit convulses the boy again and comes out.

    B′ (28): Why could the disciples not heal him?

A′ (29): The spirit is driven out by prayer.[72]

9:30 [*A transitional verse: through Galilee*].

9:31-32, *The second passion prediction.*

A : Jesus teaches the disciples.
  B : Jesus' betrayal.
    C : He will be killed...
    C': After he is killed...
  B': Jesus' resurrection.
A': The disciples do not understand Jesus' teaching.

9:33-50 [*Disparate sayings from a pre-Markan source*].

10:1 [*A transitional verse: through Judea and beyond the Jordan*].

10:2-9, *On marriage and divorce.*

A (2): Is divorce lawful?
  B (3): The law of Moses.
    C (4): Moses allowed divorce.
      D (5): "Because of the hardness of your hearts."
    C' (6-8a): Scripture prohibits divorce.
  B' (8b): The new law of Jesus.
A' (9): Divorce is not lawful.

10:10-12, *On divorce and adultery* [*an independent saying*].

A (10): The setting: in the house.
B (11): Divorce wife – remarry – adultery.
B' (12): Divorce husband – remarry – adultery.

10:13-16, *Children and the Kingdom.*

A (13): The disciples reject the children.
  B (14): Children receive the Kingdom.
  B' (15): Only those who are like children will enter
    the Kingdom.
A' (16): Jesus embraces and blesses the children.

10:17-22, *The rich man.*

A (17a): The rich man runs up (eagerly).

  B (17bc): The man's hopeful question.

    C (18): The man venerates Jesus.

      D (19): The commandments.

      D' (20): The man has obeyed the commandments.

    C' (21a): Jesus loves the man.

  B' (21bcd): Jesus' disappointing answer.

A' (22): The rich man goes away sorrowfully.

10:23-31, *Riches and the Kingdom.*

A (23-24a): How hard for the wealthy (the "first") to enter the Kingdom.

  B (24b-25): The impediment of acquired wealth.

    C (26): "Who can be saved?"

      D (27) : "All things are possible with God."

    C' (28): We shall be saved.

  B' (29f): The blessings of voluntary poverty.

A' (31): "Many that are first will be last, and the last first."

10:32-45, *Jesus' baptism of death.*

A (32-34): The Son of Man will die and rise.[73]

  B (35-37): James and John request to be first in glory.

    C (38): The humility of Jesus.

      D (39a): The reply of James and John.

        E (39b-40): They will share Jesus' "baptism."

      D' (41): The reaction of the other disciples.

    C' (42-43a): The humility of the disciples.

  B' (43b-44): He who would be first must be last.

A' (45): The Son of Man came to give his life as a ransom.

10:46-52, *Healing of blind Bartimaeus.*[74]

A (46): Bartimaeus is sitting in darkness.

  B (47): He seeks healing from Jesus.

    C (48): The people rebuke and silence him.

      D (49a): Jesus stops and calls Bartimaeus.

        E (49b): The people: "Take heart, arise, he is calling you."

      D' (50): Bartimaeus leaps up and comes to Jesus.

    C' (51): Jesus accepts him and encourages him to speak.

  B' (52a): Jesus heals him.

A' (52b): Bartimaeus receives his sight and follows Jesus.

11:1-10, *Jesus' entry into Jerusalem.*

A (1-2a): The disciples are sent into the village.

  B (2bc): The disciples are to bring the colt ("sat," εκαθισεν).

    C (3): "Why are you doing this?" (τι ποιειτε).

      D (4): The disciples find and untie the colt.

    C' (5f): "Why are you untying...?" (τι ποιειτε).

  B' (7): The disciples bring the colt ("sat," εκαθισεν).

A' (8-10): Jesus enters into the city.

11:11, *Jesus inspects the temple.*

A : And he entered Jerusalem, and went into the temple;

  B : and when he had looked around at everything,

  B': the hour being already late,

A': he went out to Bethany with the Twelve.[75]

11:12-14, *Jesus curses the fig tree.*

A (12): Jesus desires to eat from the tree.

  B (13a): He looks for figs.

  B' (13b): He finds nothing but leaves.

A' (14): Jesus curses the tree.

11:15-19, *The cleansing of the temple.*

A (15a): They enter the city.

    B (15b): Jesus manifests his authority.

        C (15c): Those who defile the temple.

            D (16): Jesus prevents anyone from carrying
                anything through the temple.[76]

        C' (17): Those who defile the temple.

    B' (18): Chief priests and scribes fear Jesus' authority.

A' (19): They go out of the city.

11:20-25 [*Disparate sayings from a pre-Markan source*].[77]

11:27-33, *The question of Jesus' authority.*

A (27f): "By what authority...?"

    B (29): Jesus poses a loaded question.

        C (30): "John's baptism: from heaven or from men?"

    B' (31-33a): They refuse to answer Jesus' question.

A' (33b): "I will not tell you by what authority...".

12:1-12, *Parable of the vineyard and the tenants.*

A (1a): Jesus speaks a parable.

    B (1b-e): Description of the Vineyard (Israel).

        C (2): The master sends a servant to the tenants.

            D (3): The tenants beat the servant.

                E (4f): The tenants beat and kill the servants.

                    F (6): The master sends his "beloved son."

                E' (7): The tenants plot to kill the son.

            D' (8): The tenants kill the son and cast him out.

        C' (9): The master will come to destroy the tenants.

    B' (10f): Description of the Stone (Jesus).

A' (12): Jesus' parable is spoken against the authorities.

12:13-17, *Paying taxes to Caesar.*

A (13): Religious leaders seek to entrap Jesus.

   B (14abc): Jesus teaches "the way of God."

      C (14d): "Is it lawful to pay taxes to Caesar?"

         D (15a): "Should we or should we not (pay them)?"

            E (15b): "Why do you put me to the test?"[78]

         D' (15c-16a): "Bring me a denarius."

      C' (16bc): The image on the coin is Caesar's.

   B' (17ab): "Render ... to God the things that are God's."

A' (17c): Religious leaders are amazed at Jesus.

12:18-27, *Question about the resurrection.*

A (18): The Sadducees say there is no resurrection.

   B (19-22): The wife and her husbands died.

      C (23): In the resurrection, whose wife will she be?

         D (24): "You know neither Scripture nor the power of God."

      C' (25): In the resurrection there will be no giving or taking in marriage.

   B' (26): Abraham, Isaac and Jacob died.

A' (27): "God is the God of the living" (hence, there is a resurrection).

12:28-34, *The Great Commandment.*

A (28a): Jesus' adversaries argue with him.

   B (28bc): The scribe perceives the truth of Jesus' answers.

      C (29-31): The Great Commandment.

         D (32a): "You are right, Teacher."

      C' (32b-33): The Great Commandment.

   B' (34ab): The scribe is not far from the Kingdom of God.

A' (34c): Jesus' adversaries dare not ask him any questions.

12:35-37, *Question about David's son.*

A (35a): Jesus taught in the temple.
  B (35b): "How is the Christ the son of David?"
    C (36): The messianic quotation.
  B' (37ab): "How is he his son?"
A' (37c): The crowd heard Jesus gladly.

12:38-40, *Denouncing the scribes.*

A (38a): Beware of the scribes.
  B (38b-40b): Description of the scribes.
A' (40c): They will receive the greater condemnation.

[A certain parallelism may be implied in 38b-40b]:

A : who like to go about in long robes [false piety]
  B : and to have salutations in the market places [elicit acclaim]
    C : and the best seats in the synagogues [false pride]
    C' : and the places of honor at feasts [false pride]
  B': who devour widows' houses [elicit financial support]
A': and for a pretense make long prayers [false piety]

12:41-44, *The widow's offering.*

A (41f): The poverty of riches.
  B (43): The widow makes the greatest offering.
A' (44): The riches of poverty.

13:1-31, *Apocalyptic warnings.*[79]

A (1f): The temple will pass away.
  B (3f): The sign to announce the End.
    C (5f): False Christs.
      D (7f): Sufferings of the last days.
        E (9): You will suffer and bear witness.
          F (10): "Yet the Gospel must first be preached
            to all nations."

E′ (11-13): You will suffer and bear witness
by the Holy Spirit.

D′ (14-20): Sufferings of the last days shortened
for the elect.

C′ (21-23): False Christs, false prophets.

B′ (24-27): The End, with the coming of the Son of Man.

A′ (28-31): Jesus′ words will not pass away.

13:32-37, *Watch!*
[V. 32: an independent saying, introducing vv. 33ff]

A (33a): Jesus to four disciples (13:3): "Take heed, watch;

B (33b): for you do not know when the time (καιρος) will come.

C (34): ...commands the doorkeeper to watch.

C′ (35a): Watch, therefore,

B′ (35b-36): for you do not know when the master (κυριος)
will come.

A′ (37): And what I say to you I say to all: Watch."

14:1-2 [*Transitional passage introducing the Passion Narrative*].

14:3-9, *Jesus anointed by a woman at Bethany.*

A (3): The act of anointing.

B (4): The anointing appears to be a waste.

C (5): The poor.

D (6): "She has done a beautiful thing to me."

C′ (7): The poor.

B′ (8): The anointing is to prepare Jesus′ burial.

A′ (9): Proclaiming the act of anointing.

14:10-11, *Judas prepares the betrayal.*

A (10): Judas goes to betray Jesus.

B (11ab): The chief priests offer him money.

A′ (11c): Judas seeks an opportunity to betray Jesus.

14:12-16, *Preparing the Passover.*

A (12): The disciples want to prepare the Passover.

    B (13f): The sign is given.

        C (15): The large upper room.

    B′ (16ab): The sign is fulfilled.

A′ (16c): The disciples prepare the Passover.

14:17-26, *The Lord's Supper.*

A (17): The beginning of the feast.

    B (18): Jesus eats now with his betrayer.

        C (19f): Bread.

            D (21): The Son of Man and his betrayer.

        C′ (22-24): Bread.

    B′ (25): Jesus will not drink again until the Kingdom.

A′ (26): The close of the feast.

14:27-42, *Jesus' prayer in the garden.*

A (27f): "After I am raised up, I will go...."

    B (29-31): Peter's denial is foretold.

        C (32f): Jesus with the disciples is distressed.

            D (34): The disciples are to watch.

                E (35): Jesus prays.

                    F (36): Jesus' temptation.

                        G (37): "Simon, ...could you not watch one hour?"

                    F′ (38): The disciple's temptation.

                E′ (39): Jesus prays in the same words.

            D′ (40): The disciples are asleep.

        C′ (41a): Jesus is distressed with the disciples.

    B′ (41bc): Judas' betrayal is fulfilled.

A′ (42): "Rise up, let us go...."

14:43-50, *Jesus' betrayal and arrest.*

A (43): Judas comes to Jesus.
  B (44): "Seize him."
    C (45): Judas betrays with a kiss.
      D (46): "And they ... seized him."
    C' (47): Another disciple strikes with a sword.
  B' (48f): "You did not seize me."
A' (50): They all forsake and flee from Jesus.

14:51-52, *The young man who fled.*

A : And a young man *followed* him [Jesus],
  B : with nothing but a *linen cloth* about his body;
    C : and they seized him,[80]
  B': but he left the *linen cloth*
A': and *ran away* naked.

14:53 [*Transitional verse: Jesus is led to the high priest*].

14:54-65, *Jesus before the council.*

A (54): Peter is welcomed by the guards.
  B (55): The council seeks to put Jesus to death.
    C (56-59): Testimony of the false witnesses.
      D (60ab): High priest's question: "Have you
        no answer?"
        E (61a): Jesus is silent about himself.
          F (61b): The high priest's unwitting confession:
            "Christ, Son of the Blessed" (cf. 15:9,18).
        E' (62): Jesus proclaims himself.
      D' (63): High priest's question: "Why do we still
        need witnesses?"
    C' (64ab): Accusation of the high priest.
  B' (64c): The council condemns Jesus to death.
A' (65): Jesus is beaten by the guards.

14:66-72, *Peter's denial.*

A (66f): Peter warms himself.
  B (68): Peter's statement of denial.
    C (69): The maid to the bystanders.
      D (70a): "But again he denied it."
    C' (70bc): The bystanders to Peter.
  B' (71): Peter's stronger statement of denial.
A' (72): Peter breaks down and weeps.[81]

15:1-15, *Jesus before Pilate.*

A (1): Jesus is delivered to Pilate.
  B (2-5): Pilate questions Jesus (King of the Jews).
    C (6f): Barabbas the murderer.
      D (8): Pilate acquiesces to the crowd.
        E (9): Pilate's unwitting confession: "King of the Jews" (cf. 14:61b).
      D' (10): Pilate acquiesces to the chief priests.
    C' (11): Barabbas to be released.
  B' (12-14): Pilate questions the people (King of the Jews).
A' (15): Jesus is delivered to be crucified.

15:16-20, *The soldiers mock Jesus.*

A (16): The soldiers lead Jesus away.
  B (17a): They clothe him in the purple cloak.
    C (17b): They place a crown of thorns on his head.
      D (18): The soldiers' unwitting confession: "Hail, King of the Jews" (cf 14:61b; 15:9).
    C' (19): They strike him on the head.
  B' (20ab): They strip him of the purple cloak.
A' (20c): They lead him away to crucify him.[82]

15:21-39, *The crucifixion.*

A (21): Simon of Cyrene carries Jesus' cross.

B (22): The Place of a Skull.

C (23): Wine mingled with myrrh.

D (24): They crucified Him.

E (25f): Third hour: crucifixion of the King of the Jews.

F (27): Two robbers crucified with him.[83]

G (29f): "Come down from the cross!"

H (31): "He saved others; he cannot save himself."

G' (32ab): "Come down now from the cross."

F' (32c): The two robbers revile him.

E' (33): Sixth to Ninth hour: darkness over the earth.

D' (34f): "My God, why hast thou forsaken me?"

C' (36): A sponge full of vinegar.

B' (37f): The death of Jesus.

A' (39): The centurion confesses Jesus as Son of God.

15:40-41, *The faithful women. [Forms an inclusion with 15:47-16:1]*

A : Women disciples.

B : They followed him,

B': They ministered to him.

A': Many other women disciples.

15:42-46, *Jesus is buried.*

A (42f): Joseph requests Jesus' body.

B (44): Pilate wonders if Jesus is dead.

B' (45): Pilate confirms that Jesus is dead.

A' (46): Joseph buries Jesus' body.

15:47-16:1, *The faithful women [Forms an inclusion with 15:40-41].*[84]

16:2-8, *The empty tomb.*

A (2f): The women come to the tomb, saying to each other, "Who will roll away the stone?"

B (4f): The angelic presence.

C (6): The resurrection announcement.

B' (7): The angelic commission.

A' (8): The women flee from the tomb and say nothing to anyone.

16:9-20, *Appearances of the Risen Christ* [*secondary ending*].

A (9-11): The Lord's appearance, Mary's proclamation.

B (12f): The risen Lord appears "in another form" (εν ετερα μορφη).

C (14): Unbelief and hardness of heart.

D (15f): Proclamation - faith - baptism - salvation.

C' (17f): Belief and wondrous signs.

B' (19): The risen Lord becomes the ascended (glorified) Lord.

A' (20): The disciples' proclamation, the Lord's accompaniment.

The consistent use of concentric parallelism throughout the Gospel leaves little doubt that Mark himself is the primary composer of its chiastically structured units, even though certain elements of the tradition may have been concentrically ordered when it reached him (for example, the feeding of the four thousand). Those brief sections that are not so arranged include heterogeneous elements from some pre-Markan source (9:33-50; 11:20-25), geographic or chronological markers (e.g., 10:1; 14:1f), and stereotyped summary statements of Jesus' miraculous healing power (6:54-56; cf. 1:32-34; 3:7-12).[85] Other longer passages of Markan composition that are not formally chiastic fall out of the usual pattern because of their content. In 8:14-21, for example, a modified antithetical parallelism contrasts the disciples' obtuse concern for bread with, on the one hand, Jesus' metaphorical allusion to the "leaven of the Pharisees," and, on the other, references to the ultimate revelatory and eucharistic significance of the feedings in the wilderness.

If Mark has created such an elaborate design within individual units, we can reasonably infer that the entire Gospel is ordered according to similar principles. For nearly two decades, scholars sensitive to the chiastic "shape" of Mark's composition have tried to discern within it an overall pattern or system of organization. To my knowledge, no one has worked out the structure of individual units as they are presented here. Others have recognized the chiastic arrangement of certain of these passages,[86] but only recently have theories been advanced about the structure of the Gospel as a whole. The results of these attempts have been mixed. Nevertheless, a certain consensus has emerged that locates the "hinge" or conceptual center of the Gospel in chapters 8-9, either with Peter's confession or with the transfiguration scene.

Representative of the second view is a study by M. Philip Scott[87] that took as its starting point the apparent parallelism between 3:33 and 12:35. The question, "Who is my mother...?" Scott sees as parallel to another, "How is Christ David's son?"; and the two, with other parallel elements, pivot around the affirmation made by the heavenly voice at the transfiguration, "This is my Son, listen to him." The overall scheme he sees as follows:[88]

A (1:2) An angel witnesses to his coming
    B (1:11) You are my Son
        C (2:7) Who can forgive sins ει μη εις ο θεος
            D (3:29) The guilt of the scribes
                E (3:33) Who is my mother...?
                    F (3:35) The primacy of doing God's will
                        G (4:40) Who is this that the winds ...
                        obey him?
                            H (6:3) Jesus is called the son of Mary
                              I (8:27) Who do you say that I am?
                                J (8:31) Prophecy of betrayal,
                                passion, resurrection
                                  K (9:7) This is my Son:
                                  listen to him
                              J' (9:30) Prophecy of betrayal,
                                passion, resurrection
                            I' (10:18) Why call me good? ...
                            ει μη εις ο θεος
                        H' (10:47) Jesus is called Son of David
                      G' (11:28) By what authority do you do
                      these things?

F′ (12:30) The primacy of God's
commandment of love

E′ (12:37) How is Christ David's Son?

D′ (12:40) A judgment on the scribes

C′ (14:61) Are you the Christ the Son of the Blessed?

B′ (15:39) Truly, this man was the Son of God

A′ (16:6) An angel witnesses to his going

While Fr. Scott has drawn a number of interesting parallels, his analysis poses serious problems. The "angellos" of A refers to John the Baptist as the messianic forerunner, whereas the "young man" in the tomb (A′) is a true angelic witness, more closely related to the νεανισκος of 14:51 than to the Baptist. The true parallel to B is not B′ but K, the nearly identical declaration at the transfiguration. C then balances with I′ more evidently than with the high priest's question of 14:61. The connection between E and E′ seems far more tenuous than Fr. Scott believes it to be, particularly as regards the supposed parallel between 3:35 and 12:28. The question of Jesus' authority raised in G and G′ is one that his disciples and adversaries raise repeatedly throughout the Gospel (1:22,27; 11:33; plus other less direct allusions such as Jesus' teaching that confounds the Jewish authorities, eg., ch. 12). Whether the identification of Jesus as son of Mary ("and brother of...") in H can be said to stand parallel to the messianic title "Son of David" in H′ is highly debatable in light of 12:35ff. Jesus' question and Peter's affirmation, "You are the Messiah" (I), can be connected with 10:18, "No one is good but God alone" (I′), by only the most tortuous reasoning. Certainly 8:31 (J) finds more than a distant echo in 9:30 (J′); but where then in the chiastic framework are we to situate 10:32, the third, last and most complete of the three passion predictions that without question stand in parallel relation to one another?

Objections such as these can be answered to some degree, but their cumulative weight speaks against this arrangement. Fr. Scott has nevertheless spelled out his arguments, and the method by which he proceeded, clearly and usefully. His stress upon the role of questions in Markan arrangement is to the point, and his analysis of the architectonic structure of the Gospel (finding 5,375 words before and 5,376 words after the central affirmation of 9:7) is, to say the least, intriguing.[89] And given the subjective element inherent in any analysis of chiasmus in an ancient writing, it is quite likely that he or others could level similar objections against many of the parallels we have proposed above. As we shall point out in further detail, however, the real issue is not precisely which phrases balance which, or how many words stand to one side or the other of a central theme. The real issue is whether or not the author both thought and composed concentrically, "helically," achieving his aim through generalized use of the literary technique we refer to and define as "chiasmus."

Other attempts to discern the outline of the Second Gospel also locate both the thematic and the structural center at the transfiguration scene.[90] Another approach pays less attention to symmetry than to the development of thought. Peter Ellis, for example, sees the Gospel divided into three (rather than the usual two) major parts, preceded by a prologue. Each major part is itself divided into three sub-sections, reflecting Mark's preference for triadic arrangement.[91] In an unpublished outline worked out for his students, Ellis noted that the sub-sections typically begin with an introductory summary, followed by a brief passage concerning the apostles, and move on to a chiastically structured narrative complex or teaching unit. The following outline is based upon his work and differs from it only insofar as individual sections conform to the chiastic analysis of the Gospel given above.[92]

The Structure of Mark's Gospel

Prologue: 1:1-15, The beginning of the Good News

Part I (1:16-8:30), Jesus' Credentials and the Arrival of the Kingdom
    Section A (1:16-3:6), Jesus' Popularity and the Jew's Opposition
    Section B (3:7-6:6), Jesus Is Rejected By His Own
    Section C (6:7-8:30), Who Is Jesus? Peter's Response

Part II (8:31-10:52), The Suffering Son of Man and Discipleship
    Section A (8:31-9:29), Suffering and Discipleship
    Section B (9:30-10:31), Characteristics and Rewards of Discipleship
    Section C (10:32-10:52), Suffering and Discipleship

Part III (11:1-16:8), The Last Seven Days and the Resurrection
    Section A (11:1-13:37), From the Coming of Jesus to Jerusalem
    in triumph to the Coming of the Son of Man in Glory
    Section B (14:1-16:1), The Passion, Death and Burial
    of the Son of Man
    Section C (16:2-8), The Resurrection of Jesus

Ellis defends the placement of Peter's confession, 8:27-30, on several grounds. Most commentators attach it to what follows, since the passage 8:27-33, including the mutual rebuke between Jesus and Peter, almost certainly stood as a unit in pre-Gospel tradition. Nevertheless, Ellis notes the inclusion Mark has created between 6:14-16 and 8:28 (John the Baptist, Elijah, a prophet) and concludes that the confession itself serves as the end of the first Part of the Gospel. In addition, he observes that "the triadic pattern of 8:31-10:52 is perhaps the most clear-cut triadic pattern in the whole gospel," with sections A and C clearly linked by the theme of suffering and discipleship.[93] The passage, then, must begin with the first passion prediction, 8:31f, rather than with the messianic confession.

If we attempt to work out the chiastic structuring within individual sections of Mark's Gospel, we meet with any number of problems and frustrations. For example, 1:16-3:19 is concentrically arranged around a parallel series of healings and teachings:

A (1:16-20): Jesus calls the first disciples.

    B (1:21-28): An unclean spirit confesses Jesus as the "Holy One of God."

        C (1:29-31): Jesus heals Peter's mother-in-law on the sabbath.

            D (1:32-2:12): various healings.

            D' (2:13-28): various teachings.

        C' (3:1-6): Jesus heals a man with a withered hand on the sabbath.

    B' (3:7-12): Unclean spirits confess Jesus as the "Son of God."

A' (3:13-19): Jesus calls the twelve disciples.

So far so good. When we attempt to continue the pattern, however, we find it necessary to begin not with 3:20, but to backtrack and take up 3:7-12 as the first element in a chiasmus that concludes with 6:29.

A (3:7-12): The crowd hears of Jesus (v. 8).

    B (3:13-19a): Jesus calls the Twelve.

        C (3:19b-35): Jesus is opposed by his family.

            D (5:1-20): Jesus heals a Gentile man.

            D' (5:21-6:1): Jesus heals two Jewish women.

        C' (6:2-6): Jesus' house and kin take offense at him.

    B' (6:7-13): Jesus sends out the Twelve.

A' (6:14-29): Herod hears of Jesus (vv. 14, 16).

Although at first glance this fits together very neatly, it does so at the intolerable cost of omitting from the outline the entire fourth chapter. While a case might possibly be made for considering the section on the parables (4:1-34[6]) to be an interpolation into Mark's original composition, the same cannot be said for the calming of the storm (4:35[7]-41). A similar situation arises with an analysis of 5:21-9:29, a passage that overlaps 3:7-6:29, and likewise omits a key passage, namely the healing of the blind man of Bethsaida, 8:22-26. Since this last unit clearly forms an inclusion with the healing of blind Bartimaeus (10:46-52), it would seem at best farfetched to claim that 8:22-26 is an interpolation into the original chiastic unit.

A (5:21-6:1): Jesus heals two women (involving touch).

  B (6:2-6): Jesus' family takes offense at him.

    C (6:7-13): Conditions for the disciples' mission.

      D (6:14-29): John was killed (Jesus identified as John, Elijah or a prophet).

        E (6:30-46): Feeding of the 5000: bread.

          F (6:47-53): Walking on the water (the disciples do not understand about the bread).

            G (6:54-56): Jesus heals all.

              H (7:1-13): Unfaithful Pharisees.

                I (7:14-23): "He declared all foods clean."

              H' (7:24-31): A faithful pagan woman.

            G' (7:32-37): Jesus heals all, even the deaf and dumb.

          F' (8:1-10): Feeding the 4000 (bread).

        E' (8:11-21): Leaven of the Pharisees (with reference to the Feedings).

      D' (8:27-33): Jesus will be killed (Jesus identified as John, Elijah, a prophet).

    C' (8:34-38): Conditions for discipleship.

  B' (9:1-13): The Father proclaims Jesus to be "my beloved Son" (Jesus' true family).

A' (9:14-29): Jesus heals a child (involving touch).

What is of particular interest here is the unevenness in the quality of the various parallels. Some are clear and undeniable, whether or not they were originally intended to fill their present position in this passage: C-C', D-D', G-G'. Others offer apparent but debatable parallels: A-A', B-B', H-H'. The remainder (E-E', F-F'), with their various allusions to bread, do parallel one another; yet a far clearer balance would be achieved between E and F', and F and E', thereby paralleling on the one hand the two feedings, and on the other the two accounts — each occurring on the water — of the disciples' misunderstanding regarding the multiplication of loaves.

Several different conclusions could be drawn from this kind of analysis. It could indicate, for example, that the two omitted passages, 4:1-41 and 8:22-26, were in fact later additions to sections that Mark had originally arranged in a chiastic pattern. Again, however, this is highly unlikely. It could also indicate that Mark received certain large blocks of material in chiastic form and inserted into them these two passages as he composed (or compiled) his Gospel. But this seems equally unlikely, given the fact that the two are also structured chiastically, and that there is no evidence whatever that their literary history was any different from that of their context.[94] A third conclusion might be that chiasmus as such is a chimera: that apparent parallels are merely random repetitions of a limited number of themes and key words, and that any quest for a grand chiastic design is futile. To reach this conclusion, however, we would have to dismiss the overwhelming evidence to the contrary, evidence presented not only here, but in a growing number of scholarly studies that examine biblical writings from a literary-critical point of view. Even if some parallels are more tenuous and less convincing than others, chiasmus is an established literary device that can not be reasonably denied. Perhaps the surest proof of that fact lies in the difficulty one encounters with trying to force into a chiastic pattern a passage that was not so composed. Whether we choose a poem or a page from a telephone book, if a literary unit was not originally structured according to the principles of concentric parallelism, there is no way it can be made to conform to a chiastic pattern.

There is, however, another conclusion suggested by the evidence presented above. If larger sections — "macro-units" — overlap one another, yet chiasmus is still evident, this suggests that the author was working less from a tightly structured outline than from *an acquired sense for balance and heightening* as he produced his literary work. His overall plan is evident; yet the unfolding of that plan step by step is far from evident, as shown by the significant divergence in the various outlines of the Gospel that have been proposed. The laws governing micro-units of tradition are, as we have seen, relatively fixed and clear-cut. This is not the case with larger passages. Repetition of key words can be mixed with balanced themes, in longer or shorter parallel sections, to create a chiastic effect. While an author will write according to a preconceived plan, he may very well flesh out that plan by using traditional elements already structured in parallelism as well as by composing new elements that are similarly structured. Quite naturally he would extend these same principles of composition to larger units, and he would do so at times with conscious design, at times "instinctively" or intuitively. It appears that Mark did both. This would explain why chiasmus seems so evident throughout his Gospel, yet why an overall chiastic plan is so elusive. It would explain as well why in sections such as we have just outlined, chiastically shaped units overlap and even exclude major units from the basic pattern.

However valid this assessment may be, it should not obscure the fact that Mark, like most biblical authors, is fully aware of the structure he gives to his writing. On the macro-level, this is perhaps most evident in the Passion Narrative. The one element that seems to fall out of the chiastic pattern in 14:1-16:8 is the uniquely Markan account of the young man who fled naked at the time of Jesus' arrest (14:51f). Whether we are to see here a veiled image of the evangelist himself, or a parallel to the "young man" who announces the resurrection to the women at the tomb, or even a prefiguration of the buried Christ (the linen cloth!), it is a singular piece whose place within the Gospel is still to be clearly assessed.[95] The last three chapters of the Gospel can be outlined as follows:

A (14:1f): The Passover Feast (Resurrection theme).

    B (14:3-9): A woman comes to anoint Jesus.

        C (14:10f): Judas the betrayer.

            D (14:12-16): Paschal lambs are sacrificed (preparation for the Passover).

                E (14:17-26): Jesus foretells a disciple's betrayal.[96]

                    F (14:27-31): Peter will deny Jesus.

                        G (14:32-42): Jesus' agony in the garden.

                            H (14:43-50): Judas betrays Jesus.

                              I (14:53-65): Interrogation by the high priest.

                                J (14:66-72): Peter's denial.

I' (15:1-5): Interrogation by Pilate.

H' (15:6-15): The people betray Jesus.

G' (15:16-38): Jesus' agony on the cross.

F' (15:39): The centurion confesses Jesus.

E' (15:40f): The faithful women remain at the foot of the cross.

D' (15:42-46): Jesus is buried (preparation for the Resurrection).

C' (15:47): Faithful women at the tomb.

B' (16:1-4): Women come to anoint Jesus.

A' (16:5-8): The Resurrection (Passover theme).

The chiastic structure of this section reveals with unusual clarity Mark's primary concern. His focus is upon the contrast between the disciples, who will betray, deny and desert Jesus, and the faithful women, who will remain at the foot of the cross and then come to the tomb in order to complete the prescribed burial rites.

The theme of the disciples' incomprehension and weakness, introduced in chapter 4 and carried throughout the Gospel with increasing intensity, is given its most forceful and poignant expression in the narrative of Jesus' suffering and death. This is the ugly and painful truth that underlies the Good News of Jesus' life, death and resurrection: those closest to him will fall away and deny him, whereas only demons and a Gentile centurion will confess him to be Son of God. Even the women will desert him at the end (16:8). His own people, family, disciples, and faithful friends will finally abandon him. Yet it is only through their desertion that the Gospel will come to the nations. The Risen One — who in Mark's expression remains always "the Crucified One" (ο εσταυρωμενος, 16:6) — will go before his disciples into Galilee, in order that through his presence and their proclamation, the Good News might be preached to the entire world.

The longer ending of Mark is certainly secondary, but its author well understood the implications for mission expressed in the paradoxical conclusion Mark gave to his writing. The disciples who once betrayed and abandoned their Lord will become his indispensable agents, through whom the Good News will come "to the whole creation" (16:15).

In the final analysis, it does not really matter if scholars disagree as to the precise divisions and parallel interrelationships in the

Gospel. By studying each of their suggested outlines the reader gains fresh insight into the intricacies of Mark's composition. Perhaps there is a definitive pattern that will someday be recovered, to prove once and for all that the evangelist first created an elaborate plan and then followed it to the letter, although that seems highly unlikely. The essential point, nevertheless, is already established by the various analyses that have been proposed: Mark unquestionably relied on the principles of chiasmus to work out the various sections of his Gospel, and in some measure he applied those principles to the structuring of the Gospel as a whole.

To conclude this section we should take a brief look at an especially important example of Markan dialogue: the so-called "little apocalypse" (13:1-37). This chapter, filled with dire warnings about the tribulations to be endured before the End, is often referred to today as a Markan "farewell discourse."[97] This is something of a misnomer, however. True farewell discourses, such as John 14-16 and the intertestamental "Testaments of the Twelve Patriarchs," have as a major theme the consolation of those to be left behind, together with moral exhortations and prophecies concerning the future of the community. They take as their model Jacob's final words to his sons recorded in Genesis 49 and, to a lesser degree, Moses' final discourse in Deuteronomy 32. While Mark 13 includes end-time prophecies of persecution and apostasy, it is noticeably short on consolation.[98] Nor does it include the kinds of exhortations that are typical of the genre. Rather, the single theme "Watch!" is underscored to prepare the disciples for the *parousia* or coming of the Son of Man as world-judge. This is not to deny that significant parallels of style and content exist between Mark 13 and Deut 32.[99] The designation "farewell discourse," however, should not obscure the main point of the Markan apocalypse: that no one, "not even the Son, but only the Father" can tell the day and hour when the Son of Man will return (13:32f).[100] Therefore Jesus confines himself to a single basic exhortation, addressed to the disciples and through them (in the words of Mark) to the Church: "Watch." Be filled with an eager yet discerning anticipation in the face of persecution and other trials. For despite the many tribulations that will cause suffering for all peoples, the elect who remain faithful will be saved.

The most obvious structural pattern of the chapter is the A:B:A' arrangement by which vv. 5-23 and 28-37 frame the independent saying on the coming of the Son of Man, vv. 24-27. A closer reading, however, suggests that there are at least four separate units that make up the chapter. Within 28-37 there are distinct elements that possess their own inner organization. Clearly vv. 28-31 are set apart by the double theme of "signs of the times" and the enduring quality of Jesus' prophetic words. V. 32 reverts to the idea that the time of Christ's coming is unknowable. In the closing verses, Mark takes up a parable from traditional material and reshapes it to fit his overall theme of watchfulness. As with the parable of the fig tree in v. 28, traditional elements are adapted throughout this portion of the chapter in order to convey the evangelist's message (note the similarity, in concept as well as in expression, of 13:28 to 11:12ff; of 13:30 to 9:1; and of 13:31 to Mt 5:18).

Turning to the first section of the "little apocalypse," 13:1-23, we should recall the outline given earlier that located the chiastic center at v. 10: "Yet[101] the Gospel must first be preached to all nations." It is remarkable that commentators who appreciate the chiastic arrangement of Mark's composition have overlooked this point,[102] since it bears directly on the interpretation of the entire passage. In the first place, the chiastic format includes vv. 1-5a as an integral part of the chapter's opening segment, vv. 1-31. Although it is possible to break that segment down into its various components (1-5a, 5b-23, 24-27, 28-31), as Mark has worked these (received?) elements together, the foretelling of the destruction of the temple sets the tone and provides the key for an interpretation of the entire segment and, indeed, for the chapter as a whole. Read chiastically, the theme of the temple's destruction and the accompanying tribulations provides the setting in which the disciples are called to "watch" for the coming of the Son of Man. As the following outline indicates, Mark makes particularly effective use of the heightening technique as he moves from the initial prophecy to the closing exhortation.

A → A': The temple will pass away →
Jesus' words will not pass away.

B → B': The sign to announce the End →
The End itself, with the coming of the
Son of Man.

C → C': False Christs →
False Christs and false prophets
working wonders.

D → D': Sufferings of the last days (wars, natural disasters, persecutions, sacrilege) → Sufferings of the last days shortened for the sake of the elect.

E → E': The disciples will suffer and bear witness → They will suffer and bear witness by the Holy Spirit who speaks through them.

F: "But first the Gospel must be preached to all nations."

V. 32: "No one knows the hour..."

A → A': The disciples are to take heed and watch → *All* are commanded to "Watch!"

B → B': You do not know when the *time* (καιρος) will come → You do not know when the *Lord* (κυριος) will come.

C → C: The doorkeeper must watch → *You* must watch.

In the first segment, the helical movement leads from Jesus' prophecy concerning the coming destruction, through various signs announcing the End, and on to the sufferings to be endured by the disciples because of the witness they are called to bear, a witness ultimately rendered by the Holy Spirit. And the whole is given meaning by the central theme, which justifies the disciples' watchful endurance in the face of persecution: the Gospel must be preached to the Gentiles. Like Paul (Romans 11), Mark believed that God would provide an interim between the resurrection and the parousia, in order for the nations to receive the message of salvation. The trials and tribulations in the period just prior to and during the siege of Jerusalem (68-70 A.D.) are inevitable; but the disciples will be empowered to bear appropriate witness, before the authorities and by implication before the nations, by the Spirit who speaks through them.

This primary apostolic vocation, however, can only be realized insofar as the disciples (of every generation) persevere in their hope and expectation of the parousia. The quality of "watchfulness" quickly became a cornerstone of monastic spirituality within a Church that lost its martyr's fervor once Constantine became the champion of Christianity. What the desert dwellers and other monastics preserved, however, is nothing other than the vivid sense of anticipation to which Jesus summons all those who stand at the brink of the "last days." Proclamation of the good news is ultimately proclamation of the most ancient Christian conviction, expressed by Paul (Phil 4:5) and the prophet John (Rev 22:20), as well as by Mark: "the Lord is near." The "little Apocalypse," then, appropriately concludes with an exhortation to "watch ... lest he come suddenly and find you asleep."

D. The Parables of Jesus

In his study of chiasmus in the New Testament, John Welch includes "A Note on the Parables."[103] He offers a sample of four of Jesus' parabolic stories, together with a perceptive analysis of the way chiastic structuring sets in relief the chief theme of each passage. In this concluding section on Synoptic dialogue we want simply to reproduce his findings, then take them one step further by illustrating the helical movement that carries the thread of meaning from the extremities to the center.

(a) *Matthew 13:24-30, the parable of the wheat and tares*

   A (24): A man sowed good seed in his field.

      B (25): The enemy comes and sows tares.

         C (26f): *Crisis*: Bad fruit is discovered among the good and the servants doubt the master.

      B' (28f): The enemy is exposed and the tares left to grow.

   A' (30): The good seed is ultimately harvested safely.

Professor Welch's analysis shows that the central theme is not — as is usually supposed — "the master's decision to allow the wheat and the tares to grow side by side until the day of judgment." The crisis or critical focus is rather upon the *doubt* expressed by the servants. This is the turning point of the entire story, leading to the resolution symbolized by the successful harvest. Each parable, in fact, focuses about such a crisis, reflecting actual situations within the circle of Jesus' disciples and, beyond them, within the apostolic community in which the Gospel was produced. The helical movement of this parable can be illustrated as follows:

   A → A': From the sowing of the seed to the successful harvest and burning of the tares.

   B → B': From the enemy's initial activity to his exposure by the householder.

   C : The conceptual center is the "crisis" precipitated by the enemy's actions, which sow dissention and doubt regarding the master's motives.

The tares, in the context of Matthew's Gospel, most likely symbolize false teachers within the Christian community. The crisis reflected — again from Matthew's perspective — is the presence within the church of these disruptive elements. The servants' doubt ("How then has it weeds?") expresses bewilderment that God would allow such destructive influences within the community of believers. Resolution occurs through the householder's wise decision to permit good and evil elements to coexist, with the assurance that the latter will receive their just recompense at the last judgment.

(b) *Matthew 25:1-13, the parable of the ten bridesmaids*

A (1): Ten bridesmaids went forth to meet the bridegroom.

   B (2-4): Five were foolish and took no oil, five were wise.

      C (5): They all slumber and sleep.

         D (6): *Crisis*: At midnight there is a cry:
         "The bridegroom is coming!"

      C' (7): They all arise and trim their lamps.

   B' (8f): Five ask for oil and the wise five send them to buy.

A' (10-12): The bridegroom comes forth and receives only those who were ready.

Epilogue: "Watch, therefore, for you know neither the day nor the hour [when the Son of Man will come]."

Welch concludes this analysis with the remark, "The second half of the parable is a foregone conclusion once the first half has been laid out." True, but it is more than that. The "foregone conclusion" in II represents clear intensification or focusing relative to I. This can be illustrated once again by reading from the extremities toward the center.

A → A': From the bridesmaids' desire to meet the bridegroom, to the meeting itself and its consummation, including judgment upon those who were unprepared.

B → B': From the actions of the bridesmaids, to the decisive consequences of their actions.

C → C': From the period of waiting (sleep), to the moment of rising to meet the bridegroom.

D : The moment of "crisis" that illustrates the point of the parable: the bridegroom comes at an unforeseeable moment; therefore be constantly on the watch.

(c) *Luke 14:16-24, the parable of the great banquet*

A (16): Many are bidden to a great banquet.

    B (17): "Come, all things are ready."

        C (18-20): Antagonism: excuses are given for not coming.

          D (21ab): *Crisis*: The master is angry.

        C' (21c): Antagonism resolved: others invited.

    B' (22-23): "There is still room / let the house be filled."

A' (24): "None of those invited shall taste my banquet."

The entire parable turns on the theme of the master's anger. Jesus came first to the house of Israel, yet he was rejected by his own people. The Jews, invited by God to the messianic banquet, refused the invitation, and the spokesmen for the master are ordered to bring in the Gentiles. This familiar theme that runs throughout the New Testament writings is adapted in the present parable to address those who, like the five foolish bridesmaids, allow other priorities to interfere in their concern for "the last things." The excuses are legitimate only within the framework of present historical and social life. Once the bridegroom appears, once the table is prepared for the banquet of the Kingdom, there can be only one priority. Those invited must choose to abandon every concern and possession or they will find the invitation rescinded. At the last hour, a man must be willing to leave his bride to discover a greater joy. Otherwise he incurs the master's wrath and loses everything.

Note again how the theme of judgment serves as the critical focus of the story:

A → A': From the invitation extended to many, to the
      judgment pronounced because of their refusal.

B → B': From preparation for those originally invited,
      to the new invitation to fill the house
      with others.

C → C': From the initial antagonism, to its resolution.

D : The master's wrath.

From the initial invitation to the final judgment, from the initial preparation to the command to fill the house, from the lame excuses to their consequences with the bringing in of others: the movement of the whole leads both to and from the central idea, which is the master's reaction to the refusal of those first invited. Luke's readers would have detected a double meaning to this story: an explanation for the Jews' attitude toward Jesus, and a parabolic illustration of Jesus' command, comprehensible only in an eschatological framework, to "let the dead bury their own dead" (Lk 9:60).

(d) *Luke 15:11-32, the parable of the two sons*

Welch's analysis of the chiastic structuring of this story shows indisputably that its usual title, "the prodigal son," is a misnomer. Here Jesus' contrast between the two sons is analogous to Paul's distinction drawn between the two covenants of the earthly and heavenly Jerusalem, represented respectively by Hagar and Sarah (Gal 4:21ff). The critical center of this parable is less a "crisis" in the accepted sense than a revelation: the father manifests his faithful love for the prodigal by running to meet and embrace him.

A (11f): One son takes his inheritance; conversation
between father and son.

   B (13-16): One son goes out; his conduct.

      C (17): The well-being of the father's servants recalled
("I am perishing").

         D (18f): I will say, "I have sinned."

            E (20): The father runs to meet his son and
is compassionate.

         D' (21): The son says, "I have sinned."

      C' (22-24): The father instructs the servants to make well;
the lost is found.

   B' (25-30): One son refuses to go in; his conduct.

A' (31f): One son promised his inheritance; conversation
between father and son.

This parable, like so many others, can be read as an allusion both to the attitude of Jews and Gentiles to Jesus' message, and to the reaction of some within the Christian community to others whose conduct seems to violate conditions for acceptable ecclesial living. In the parable of the great banquet, the respectable citizens first invited are replaced by the disreputable who accept the invitation. In this present story, the second, respectable son refuses to participate in the banquet, ceding his place to the reprobate who has behaved like a pagan. Whether the reader understands the tension to be between Jew and Gentile, or between various factions within the local church, the chief point is clear: repentance brings an unexpected and unqualified outpouring of love and compassion from the Father.

The intensification evident here is built upon contrast. While the behavior of the prodigal seems far more reprehensible than that of the elder son, it is in fact the latter whose conduct and attitude draw the sternest condemnation.

A → A': From the first son, who demands his inheritance
unjustifiably, to the second, who jeopardizes
his privileged place by refusing to rejoice
in his brother's return.

B → B': From the moral debauchery of the younger son,
to the arrogant self-justification of the elder.

C → C': From the younger son's self-inflicted suffering,
to his restitution through the father's compassion.

D → D': From the son's decision to repent, to the actual
repentance.

E : The love of the father that accepts the son's
repentance and readmits him into the communion
of his family.

By discerning the concentric movement of this parable, the reader is able to grasp its true focus: not the repentance of the younger son (which, after all, was based on expediency: his belly was empty), nor the fact that a greater inheritance is promised to the elder ("All that is mine is yours!"), but the love of the father, who bestows everything he possesses upon *both* sons equally. To Luke's readers, this parable would express in different imagery Jesus' assurance, expressed in Matthew's Gospel (chs. 20-21), that the workers of the eleventh hour would receive the same recompense as those who struggled from the first hour; that the son who refuses to follow his father's orders, yet later obeys, likewise receives his reward; in other words, that the Gentiles who repent, despite their former conduct, are promised the same blessings of life in the Kingdom as the children of Abraham. If an allusion is in fact intended here to Jews and Gentiles, then the parable illustrates still another point: that the Jews, like the elder son, possess the *future promise* of the Kingdom, whereas the former pagans, because of their repentance, enter *already* into the banquet hall and partake of the feast *now*.[104]

Welch's most important contribution in analyzing the chiastic structure of these passages is to show how each one focuses about a crisis. That critical turning point is the alpha and omega of the whole, the source and end of the parable's meaning. Through the use of concentric parallelism, these simple yet penetrating stories draw the reader's attention to the heart of Jesus' message: the ultimate sense in God's plan (Mt 13:26f), the command to watchfulness (Mt 25:6), the threat of judgment (Lk 14:21), but also the Father's all-forgiving love (Lk 15:20).

It is perhaps significant that the terms "parable" and "parabola" are derived from the same Greek expression for "juxtaposition" with implied parallelism. Like the geometric figure, the chiastically shaped parable juxtaposes elements in a curve, proceeding from a central point. While the extremities reflect each other as mirror images, they never meet; rather, each extends to infinity. In chiastic patterns, strophe I and strophe II are dissimilar as well as similar. The movement from the initial element to its "prime" reflection (e.g., from A to A') is almost invariably one of heightening. This means that II is never a simple repetition of I, but rather complements it by taking it a step further. Yet the elements of both I and II derive their ultimate meaning from the "parabolic center."

We have seen how frequently and with what effect this juxtaposition of parallel members, distinguished by the heightening effect and focusing about the conceptual center, is used by the first three evangelists. The Fourth Gospel, as we shall find in the next chapter, offers a still more striking example of this remarkable literary technique. There both individual passages and the work as a whole exhibit a tightly woven chiastic pattern. The overall effect, perhaps more than with the Synoptic Gospels, is to convey to the reader the truth that the whole equals more than the sum of its parts, and it must be read accordingly if it is to be properly understood.

ENDNOTES

[1]We cannot discuss here the form and redaction history of the elements that make up the infancy narrative. This has been admirably treated by R. E. Brown, *The Birth of the Messiah. A Commentary on the Infancy Narratives in Matthew and Luke* (New York: Doubleday, 1977) p. 233ff; and J.A. Fitzmyer, *The Gospel According to Luke I-IX* (New York: Doubleday, 1981) p. 303ff. For a partial analysis of the structure of this section, see C.H. Talbert, *Reading Luke. A Literary and Theological Commentary on the Third Gospel* (New York: Crossroad, 1982), p.15ff; and for Lukan studies in general, his important monograph *Literary Patterns, Theological Themes and the Genre of Luke-Acts* (Missoula: Scholars Press, 1974).

[2]See the table presented by Fitzmyer, *Luke*, p. 313f.

[3]The 26th ed. of the Nestle Greek NT renders all of the angel's announcement in verse form, vv. 13b-17. This obscures the chiastic pattern of the passage as a whole.

[4]It could be argued that Jesus' virginal conception is heightened relative to John's natural conception, despite Elizabeth's advanced age. In the present context, however, nothing has yet been said about the virginal character of Mary's conceiving. The parallels should be taken as they appear in their immediate context, without reading in those themes that are expressed further on, even in the same passage.

[5]*Luke I-IX*, p. 315.

[6]Fitzmyer discusses the various theories as to the referent in the two sections, *Luke I-IX*, p. 377f. Brown, *The Birth of the Messiah*, p. 383, rejects Vanhoye's analysis of the Benedictus and adds a further criticism of "the general theory of chiastic patterns" analyzed by Vanhoye and I. de la Potterie.

[7]See Talbert, *Reading Luke*, p. 28

[8]This arrangement is found in Bullinger's *The Companion Bible*, (Grand Rapids, MI: Zondervan, reprinted 1964, 1974), p. 1434. I am grateful to Dr. Frederick Harm, formerly of Concordia Lutheran Seminary, St Louis, MO, for having pointed this out to me.

[9]The *RSV* rendering of this obscure phrase seems to be correct. For suggestions as to the meaning of ανατολη, see Fitzmyer, Luke I-IX, p. 387f.

[10]The variant reading επεσκεψατο in v. 78 is probably the result of assimilation to v. 68. There is a shift in interest from the first to the second half of the canticle represented by the change from aorist to future.

[11]Mention should be made as well of the recent analysis of the "Magnificat," made by S. Terrien, *Till the Heart Sings. A Biblical Theology of Manhood & Womanhood* (Philadelphia: Fortress, 1985), p. 147. Considering this piece to be "an entire Biblical theology in miniature, viewed from the perspective of a woman," Terrien breaks it down into four strophes (vv. 46-48; 49-50; 51-53; and 54-55). As my student Nancy Holloway demonstrated in a recent seminar on chiasmus (March 1990), the last three strophes possess their own chiastic format: A = 49; B =50; C = 51; D = 52; C' = 53; B' = 54; and A' = 55. Following Terrien's translation: inclusion (A-A') = God's great deeds and God's eternal promise; B-B' = inversion of "his womblike compassion" toward all and specifically toward "his slave boy Israel"; C-C' = God's power against the proud and on behalf of the poor. The focus (D) is upon the overthrow of the mighty and the exaltation of the humble (v. 52). This analysis of the poem's structure

reinforces the argument that only vv. 46-48 represent words of Mary, whereas the final seven verses can most appropriately be read as a song by Israel, praising Yahweh for his gracious deliverance and salvation (confirmed by vv. 54f). The "Magnificat," therefore, seems to be a composite piece, including an original hymn of Mary (1:46-48) to which Luke has appended an Israelite celebration of victory (1:49-55).

[12]"Sonship, Wisdom, Infancy: Luke 2:41-51a," *NTS* 24 (1978), p. 317-354, quoted in Talbert, *Reading Luke*, p. 37.

[13]John Welch, "Chiasmus in the New Testament," p. 235. This is certainly an overstatement, as we shall see.

[14]Dale C. Allison, Jr., "The Structure of the Sermon on the Mount," *JBL* 106/3 (1987), p. 423-445, has convincingly demonstrated the presence of triadic structures in the Sermon. According to his analysis, there are nine Beatitudes (3 x 3). See his outline, p. 437f, and note 17, p. 429. Nils Lund (*Chiasmus in the New Testament*, p. 250), followed by John Welch (*ibid.*, p. 235) and many others, holds to seven Beatitudes. As Lund notes, the matter has been discussed since at least the days of St. Augustine.

[15]See Allison's evaluation of various theories on this topic, *ibid.*, p. 424f, n. 8.

[16]The original purpose of this statement was to affirm that Mary conceived by the power of the Holy Spirit and bore her child wholly apart from normal human means of reproduction. It stressed the divine, miraculous nature of the conception rather than, for example, Mary's perpetual virginity.

[17]A subtle parallelism appears to be operative here, contrasting the violent massacre with the anguished lament of Rachel (Jer 31:15) that prophetically announces Herod's act. A → A' (Herod deprived of information → Rachel deprived of her children); B → B' (Herod's rage → Rachel's grief); C → C' (Jerusalem's children → Rachel's children [Israel's exiled northern tribes]); D → D' (the massacre of infants → commensurate lamentation); E → E' (voice of the wise men → voice in Ramah); F (the focal affirmation: fulfillment of prophecy). To those who remain skeptical about the very existence of chiasmus in the NT, these parallels will appear tenuous at best. They assume substance only when taken in the context of the whole Gospel.

[18]Here again we find an example of step-parallelism with a focus about Jesus' command (anacrusis): "Follow me...". Intensification occurs in the movement from the final versets of the first strophe to the close of the unit: Peter and Andrew leave their nets to follow Jesus, while James and John leave their entire means of livelihood (the boat) as well as family relationships (their father). They thus exemplify Jesus' characterization of the true disciple, Mt 19:29.

[19]The principles of intensification and specification are especially apparent in this unit. A → A' (Jesus' mission in Galilee → Jesus' mission to the Jews and Gentiles); B → B' (Jesus heals every disease → Jesus heals every disease of mind, body and spirit); C (centering about his fame that spreads beyond Palestine and into the Gentile world).

[20]The chiastic structuring of this passage becomes apparent only when consideration is given to its location in the Gospel and the tension Matthew preserves between the abiding significance of Jewish institutions (5:17-19) and the radical newness of Jesus' demands (5:21-48; 9:16f). It follows immediately upon the Sermon on the Mount, illustrating Jesus' adherence to Jewish legal and ritual prescriptions, and yet it serves to contrast the divine authority and power by which Jesus heals

with the relatively impotent means prescribed by Jewish ritual law for the cleansing of "leprosy" (not Hansen's disease, but a variety of eruptive skin ailments). The parallelism is as follows: A → A' (worship offered to Jesus → offering made according to Mosaic Law); B → B' (faith in Jesus' power to heal → conformity to Jewish ritual practice); C → C' (Jesus' healing miracle → prohibition to declare the miracle); D → D' (Jesus' expressed will to replace Jewish ritual healing → the miracle accomplished by his word and gesture).

[21]The central theme of this pericope is the contrast (C:D:C') between the demands of daily life (shelter, burying the dead) and the radical demands of discipleship. Those who follow Jesus, like the Son of Man himself, will have nowhere to lay their head. Their daily needs and obligations will be trivial compared with the conditions and responsibilities they must assume in following their Lord.

[22]The parallel between B and B' lies in the image of Jesus calmly asleep in the boat, and that of the calm that descends over the water.

[23]As with Jesus' command to Peter to "Come" and meet him on the waters of the Lake, here the command to the demons highlights Jesus' authority and power to effect his word (cf. 9:2-8).

[24]V. 9 is an independent unit with no perceptible parallel structure other than the contrast between the tax collector (who is by definition a sinner) sitting at the toll booth and his rising up to follow Jesus. The passage centers about the name, Matthew: Ματθαιον λεγομενον. It serves to introduce the following unit in which Jesus welcomes recognized sinners to share table fellowship with himself and the disciples.

[25]Lund, Chiasmus in the New Testament, p. 309, points out Matthew's way of creating inverted parallelism (which Lund terms chiasmus) here by adding comments to the quotation from Hosea (6:6): "Mercy I desire / And not sacrifice. // For I came not to call the righteous (who sacrifice), / But sinners (who need mercy)." This is another example of the "hysteron-proteron" reversal.

[26]The parallelism in Jesus' reply is still clearer in the Greek, where "bridegroom" (νυμφιος) occurs at the end of each central line: mourn → bridegroom → bridegroom → fast.

[27]Lund's translation, ibid., p. 311, rendering the Greek literally to illustrate the parallelism.

[28]This is the so-called Schachteltechnik or "bracketing," as in Mk 3:21-35 (22-30); and 5:21-43 (25-34).

[29]See N. Lund, Chiasmus in the New Testament, chs. 13-15; as well as his article, "The Influence of Chiasmus upon the Structure of the Gospel According to Matthew," ATR 13/4 (1931), p. 405-433. Daniel Patte, The Gospel According to Matthew. A Structural Commentary on Matthew's Faith (Philadelphia: Fortress, 1987) offers numerous examples of chiasmus in Matthew yet omits Lund's name altogether in his lengthy bibliography. See especially his table of "narrative oppositions" on chs. 5-7, p. 407f.

[30]In addition to D. Allison's article cited above and its bibliographical references, see Jan Lambrecht, The Sermon on the Mount. Proclamation and Exhortation (Wilmington, DE: Glazier, 1985), who presents a valuable comparison of the Matthean and Lukan versions of the Sermon.

[31]The envelope effect created by reference to the Kingdom in the first and eighth

Beatitudes suggests that the true number of Beatitudes is eight, not seven or nine. This is reinforced by the fact that, unlike the others, the final blessing (5:11) is expressed in the second rather than the third person. In this regard it is more like the Lukan Beatitudes, which express the actual state of affairs of the poor, the mournful, the hungry and the persecuted whom Jesus addresses directly with assurance that in the Kingdom their misery will turn to joy (Lk 6:21-23). Expressed in the third person and somewhat "spiritualized," Matthew's Beatitudes represent not so much the present condition of the addressees (disciples or the crowd) as the qualities, attitudes and virtues they are to acquire if they are to follow Jesus faithfully.

[32]See Robert A. Guelich, "The Matthean Beatitudes: Entrance Requirements or Eschatological Blessings?", *JBL* 95 (1976), p. 415-434, who decides for "eschatological blessings"; and his survey of interpretations of the Sermon, "Interpreting the Sermon on the Mount," *Int* 41/1 (1987), p. 117-130. D. Allison's remarks on the purpose of 6:25-34 and 7:7-11, which "function to ease the burden of the Sermon on the Mount," are relevant here; see his art. "Structure," p. 434-439.

[33]See, for example, J.D. Kingsbury, *Matthew: Structure, Christology, Kingdom* (Philadelphia: Fortress, 1975).

[34]Lund, *Chiasmus in the New Testament*, p. 240ff; Welch, "Chiasmus in the New Testament," p. 235f.

[35]The chiastic structure of 4:23-25, worked out above, shows that v. 25 in fact belongs with the preceding pericope, although the three verses serve as an introduction to the Sermon.

[36]Lund, *ibid.*, p. 254.

[37]In his revision of Lund's outline, Welch accepts *seven* Beatitudes (vv. 3-9) and groups vv. 10-12 in a separate unit that describes "the true prophets."

[38]*Ibid.*, p. 236.

[39]This theory in a somewhat different form was first put forth by Austin Farrer in 1966, and Prof. Welch acknowledges its limitations. D. Allison argues that such correspondences or presumed parallels throughout the Sermon may often be due to random repetition of vocabulary from a common store, "Structure," p. 427-429.

[40]A case in point is Andrej Kodjak's *A Structural Analysis of the Sermon on the Mount* (Berlin/New York: Mouton de Gruyter, 1986).

[41]Bornkamm, "*Der Aufbau der Bergpredigt*," *NTS* 24 (1978), p. 419-432. See as well Ulrich Luz, *Das Evangelium nach Matthäus* (Neukirchen: Neukirchener Verlag, 1985), vol. I *ad loc.*

[42]Kingsbury's initial work in this area appeared in *Matthew: Structure, Christology, Kingdom* and was continued in *Matthew as Story* (Philadelphia: Fortress, 1986). See especially his article, "The Place, Structure, and Meaning of the Sermon on the Mount Within Matthew," *Int* 41/2 (1987), p. 131-143. This last work is the source for the following arrangement.

[43]Art. cit., p. 136.

[44]This remains true despite certain valid criticisms leveled against Bornkamm's theory: see D. Allison, "Structure," p. 424-429; and J. Lambrecht, *Sermon*, p. 155-164.

[45]The *RSV* renders την δικαιοσυνην in 6:1 as "piety." While this accurately

reflects the cultic context of the passage, it obscures its relationship with the rest of the Sermon, which focuses upon "practicing the greater righteousness."

[46]An expansion of the two-source hypothesis, we recall, holds that Matthew and Luke each had access to a third body of material in addition to Mark and "Q," designated respectively "M" and "L." For Lambrecht's analysis, see *Sermon*, p. 122-125.

[47]Lambrecht, *Sermon*, p. 122f.

[48]Yet as we have just seen, a similar repetition of B:B' in the thematic center occurs in 7:4-5 (cf. 5:11-12).

[49]Only on re-reading this paragraph after I finished writing it did I realize that it, too, falls into an A:B:C:B':A' pattern (each letter representing a single sentence), whose focus is the central "conclusion" regarding "fundamental structures of human thought and perception." This was unintentional and uncontrived. Is it merely an interesting coincidence? The more likely answer, that we are dealing in the phenomenon of chiasmus with some form of unconscious "intuited" structure (a "deep-structure"), is one we will have to consider later on.

[50]Mk 11:26, read by a number of important manuscripts, is almost certainly a scribal gloss based on Mt 7:15. For Matthew's use of Mark in composing the Prayer, see M.D. Goulder, "The Composition of the Lord's Prayer," *JTS* 14 (1963), p. 32-45. Goulder holds that Luke's version of the Prayer was derived from Matthew, whose Gospel Luke had before him, and that the Prayer was in essence first composed by Matthew on the basis of Markan and other tradition, particularly Jesus' prayer in the Garden of Gethsemane.

[51]The aorist αφηκαμεν represents an Aramaism and is better translated as a perfect: "as we have (already) forgiven."

[52]A comparison of the Matthean and Lukan versions of the Lord's Prayer makes it evident that neither stems directly from Jesus. Both are literary compositions of the respective evangelists; and Goulder, *art. cit.*, offers considerable evidence for attributing the original composition to Matthew, while concluding that Luke shortened this version and turned some of its Aramaisms into better Greek. His evidence does not warrant the conclusion, however, that Jesus did not teach such a prayer to his disciples, at least in its general outline.

[53]The Lukan parallel reads και αφες ημιν τας αμαρτιας ημων (11:4), a Lukan "improvement" that accurately expresses the meaning of the Matthean τα οφειληματα.

[54]This last example of the final judgment (Mt 25:31ff) is usually interpreted as referring to acts of charity exercised for or withheld from those in need. Its meaning is broader than that and, like all of Jesus' parables, concerns ultimately the whole range of conditions that determine human relationships. The image of refusing to feed the hungry and clothe the naked can apply equally to those who refuse to grant forgiveness, and excuse their refusal by some form of self-justification.

[55]Matthew alone among the evangelists (and Paul) records that the cup symbolizes Jesus' blood "poured out for many for the forgiveness of sins," and continues with Jesus' affirmation, "I shall not drink again ... until that day when I drink it new *with you* in my Father's Kingdom" (cf. Mk 14:25; Lk 22:16-18).

[56]For the concentric structure and flow of 1:12f, see above on the Temptation

of Christ, II.1.B.

[57]While 1:1 serves as a title or heading for the entire Gospel, it also functions as the opening element of an inclusion that closes with Jesus' proclamation of the Good News. Throughout this initial unit Mark uses parallelism, with intensification, to depict Jesus as "one mightier" than John.

[58]The expression οι παρ' αυτου refers not to "friends," but to members of Jesus' family.

[59]A-A' reflect misunderstanding on the part of Jesus' family; cf. 6:4.

[60]On the structure of this passage, see G. Fay, "Introduction to Incomprehension: The Literary Structure of Mark 4:1-34," *CBQ* 51 (1989), p. 65-81, who modifies an outline proposed by J. Dewey, *Markan Public Debate: Literary Technique, Concentric Structure, and Theology in Mark 2:1-3:6* (Chico, CA: Scholars Press, 1980), p. 150f. Fay's detailed outline on p. 81 repays close study. It offers an excellent example of the way chiasmus can be present in even the smallest literary units.

[61]That Jesus himself is the "lamp" is clear from the active voice of the verb ερχεται. The major translations (*RSV, NEB, NKJV*, etc.) miss this point by assimilating the passage to its counterpart in Mt 5:15.

[62]Here the boat obviously represents the Church. While this identification may be less apparent in other passages, Mark's readers would hardly have mistaken this most ancient of Christian symbols.

[63]It appears that 5:1-13 was originally a separate unit, subsequently augmented by 5:14-20, in order to fit Mark's scheme of discipleship and mission. Both sections bear the stamp of Markan composition. The original piece, an *exorcism* story, ended with the destruction of the swine (spirits) in the sea: the whole is framed by 5:1 (θαλασσης) and 5:13 (θαλασση). The second part, a *mission* story, includes proclamation by the herdsmen and the sending of the man on mission throughout the Decapolis, thus making of him the first witness to the Gentiles.

[64]This section offers the clearest example in the Gospel, of Mark's technique of "bracketing": conflating two stories by enveloping one within the other.

[65]Mk 5:24b-34 is a separate unit, treated below.

[66]Is the startling qualification, "except that he laid his hands upon a few sick people and healed them," an example of supposed Markan "naiveté"? Or is it further evidence of the author's remarkable literary skill, making his point by juxtaposing apparent contradictions?

[67]The central focus of this passage (D) again stresses the Markan theme of the disciples' incomprehension.

[68]Another analysis would include 6:45-56 in a single unit, with the A:A' inclusion composed of 6:45f (boat-crowd-pray) and 6:54-56 (boat-crowd-healings). As we shall see, Mark is capable of overlapping elements of juxtaposed chiastic units (6:30-46; 6:45-56; see below on 1:16-3:19 and 3:7-6:29).

[69]The chiastic structuring of this passage tends to confirm the opinion that it served as a model for the feeding of the 5000 (6:30-46) and hence is the more original form of this tradition (see on this whole question, R. Fowler's literary-critical study: *Loaves and Fishes. The Function of the Feeding Stories in the Gospel of Mark* [Chico, CA: Scholars Press, 1981]). That the two feedings are doublets can hardly be doubted.

This passage is less tightly structured than 6:30ff. Here the focus is upon Jesus' command to the people to sit; there, upon the elements of bread and fish. Here the envelope includes Jesus' call and the dismissal (A-A'); there, "to find rest" is paralleled with "to pray." Here the focus is uniquely on the feeding; there, a parallelism is created between teaching (C) and feeding (C'). Yet while the account of the 5000 is more tightly and elaborately structured, with additional balancing elements, it looses intensification relative to the account of the 4000. In the latter there is a marked heightening evident from I to II, creating once again a helical pattern: A → A' (calling the twelve disciples → dismissal of the 4000); B → B' (hunger → eating to the full); C → C' (seven loaves → seven loaves plus a few fish); D (Jesus' command). The focus is less on the "elements" (as in 6:37f) than on Jesus' authority, implying his ability to satisfy the most basic needs of those who follow him. In both passages, eucharistic overtones are unmistakable.

[70]This passage forms an inclusion with the healing of blind Bartimaeus, 10:46-52.

[71]See II.1.A, above. Although the Markan form of Peter's confession follows the basic A:B:A':B':C pattern discussed above, it can also be read chiastically: A = popular proclamation of Jesus; B = popular identification of Jesus; C = Jesus elicits the messianic confession ("Who do *you* say...?"); B' = Peter's identification of Jesus; A' = the command not to proclaim Jesus. The point is not that we must choose between one arrangement or the other, but that the composition is characterized by *both* incremental direct parallelism (A:B:A':B':C) and concentricity (A:B:C:B':A').

[72]Here is an especially clear example of the helical effect, moving incrementally (i.e., with heightening or intensification) from I (A-E) to II (E'-A'), and from the extremities toward the center, while focusing on the theme Mark wishes to underscore at this point in his Gospel narrative: all things are possible to those who believe.

[73]This begins a third geographic transition: toward Jerusalem.

[74]See II.1.E above.

[75]The parallelism here is between geographical (A - A') and temporal (B - B') references.

[76]This crucial gesture was to stop traffic through the Gentile court. That traffic effectively impeded the worshipers from praying and thereby frustrated the true purpose of the temple as the House of God.

[77]Cf. 9:33-50. Note that the reader can pass directly from 11:19 to 11:27 with no break in continuity (v. 26 is secondary).

[78]The verb πειραζετε implies "tempt": "Why do you tempt me?" There is perhaps a conscious intent on the author's part to link this passage with 1:13, and to imply that the Jew's question is demonic. This might explain the connection (otherwise unclear) between D and D'. From C to D the thought moves from what is legal to what is obligatory: if indeed it is legal to pay taxes, should we do so, thereby honoring a worldly authority and, implicitly, the imperial cult? By posing the question, they seek to align Jesus either with those who accepted to pay the tax (Pharisees and Herodians) or with those who refused to do so (the Zealots). By requesting a coin Jesus makes the issue concrete: the coin symbolizes the reality of the fallen world in which they live, a world in which it is possible and necessary to distinguish between exterior loyalty to the state and interior faithfulness to God.

[79]We discuss this passage in detail further on.

[80]As they just seized Jesus, 14:46.

[81]The intensification from line to line in this passage is especially pronounced. A (Peter's concern for himself) → A' (Peter's recognition of the enormity of his act); B (his first denial) → B' (invoking a curse on himself, he denies Jesus all the more vehemently); C (the maid addresses the bystanders) → C' (the bystanders accuse Peter directly [they, and not he, speak the truth: αληθως εξ αυτων ει]); all focusing upon the central denial of v. 70. Again the "helix" is evident, a spiraling movement with intensification toward the central element: A → A' → B → B' → C → C' → D.

[82]If there remains any doubt that Mark's chiastic structuring is in many instances intentional and a conscious literary device that serves his proclamation, it should be dispelled by the fact that "confession" of Jesus — by the Chief Priest, Pilate and the soldiers — constitutes the central focus of each pericope: 14:61b; 15:9; 15:18. Even the thieves crucified with Jesus will make an ironic "negative confession" that serves as the focus of 15:21-39 (Jesus *does* save others through his own self-sacrifice).

[83]V. 28 is secondary.

[84]The purpose of the inclusion is to stress the faithful presence of the women at Jesus' crucifixion and at his burial, implying that only they — and not the disciples — were present at both.

[85]This is not to say that only brief, non-chiastic passages derive from pre-Markan sources. A large if indeterminable amount of Mark's witness is undoubtedly based on oral — and perhaps even written — tradition that had come down to him. This analysis, however, confirms the view that Mark is a genuine author, who has taken received tradition and thoroughly reworked it to produce a "gospel" which makes its proclamation chiefly through the use of chiasmus.

[86]Joanna Dewey sparked particular interest in this area back in 1973 with her article "The Literary Structure of the Controversy Stories in Mark," *JBL* 92 (1973), p. 394-401. See also her *Markan Public Debate;* and Peter Ellis, "Patterns and Structures of Mark's Gospel," in *Biblical Studies in Contemporary Thought*, ed. M. Ward (Burlington, VT: The Trinity College Biblical Institute, 1975), p. 88-103. A major, if not entirely satisfactory, contribution in this area has been made by Rudolf Pesch, *Das Markusevangelium, Teil I* (Freiburg im B.: Herder, 1976). Pesch underrates Mark's contribution as an author, attributing the section 3:7-6:56 to a pre-Markan source where it was already structured in a chiastic pattern. The tendency to see Mark as a mere compiler is especially marked in Pesch's second volume, which deals with the passion narrative. For useful summaries and analyses of recent studies on Markan composition, see P. Achtemeier, *Mark* (Philadelphia: Fortress, 1986), ch. 3-4; and F.J. Matera, *What Are They Saying About Mark?* (New York: Paulist, 1987), ch. 4.

[87]"Chiastic Structure: A Key to the Interpretation of Mark's Gospel," *BTB* 15/1 (1985), p. 17-26.

[88]A more complete and precise rendering of the Gospel chiasmus according to Scott's analysis is given at the close of the article, p. 25. The outline given here, from "chart 3," p. 18, gives a clearer idea of the parallels and their content.

[89]This "stichometric" breakdown of Mark represents an improvement over a similar analysis made by Pesch that omits from consideration ch. 13. See P. Achtemeier, *Mark*, p 37f.

[90]In *The Message and Method of Mark*, A. Stock takes up a suggestion by B. Standaert (*L'Evangile selon Marc: Composition et genre littéraire* [Brugge: Sint Andriesabdij, 1978]) that Mark is structured according to a fivefold pattern: I (1:2-13) =

"Wilderness"; II (1:14-8:26) = "Galilee"; III (8:27-10:32 [*sic.*, read 10:52]) = "The Way"; IV (11:1-15:41) = "Jerusalem"; V (15:42-16:8) = "The Tomb"; (see esp. pp. 25-31). The various geographic markers in the Gospel support this division. Standaert also locates the "center" at the transfiguration. See as well the interesting analysis of Laurence F.X. Brett, "Suggestions for an Analysis of Mark's Arrangement," in C.S. Mann, *Mark. A New Translation With Introduction and Commentary* (New York: Doubleday, 1986), p. 174-190.

[91]P. Ellis, "Patterns and Structures of Mark's Gospel."

[92]I am most grateful to Professor Ellis for sharing with me this outline and other extensive notes.

[93]"Patterns and Structures of Mark's Gospel," p. 101.

[94]Rudolph Pesch and others have argued that Mark did receive units of tradition that were already shaped chiastically. While this may be true with some individual pericopae, it seems implausible on the scale of larger units, given the consistency with which Mark uses chiasmus throughout his work. In the fullest sense Mark is the *author* of his Gospel, and concentric parallelism is his preferred literary technique.

[95]See A. Stock's discussion on this figure, *The Method and Message of Mark*, p. 373-375.

[96]Note the parallelism between E and E': E (the Last Supper with the pouring of "blood"; και οψιας γενομενης, 14:17) → E' (the Crucifixion with the shedding of blood; και ηδη οψιας γενομενης, 15:42).

[97]For example, W. Harrington, *Mark* (Wilmington, DE: Glazier, 1979), p. 193; A. Stock, *The Method and Message of Mark*, p. 321ff.

[98]Even the promise of the gathering of the elect, v. 27, is set in a context of judgment, when the created order will come to a violent end.

[99]As Fr. Stock points out, p. 323f.

[100]The suggestion has often been made that the Markan apocalypse so strongly stresses that the time of the parousia is unknowable because, as in 2 Thess 2, members of Mark's community were proclaiming that the parousia had already occurred. See the illuminating discussion on the matter of the parousia in P. Achtemeier, *Mark*, ch. 12.

[101]The και clearly has adversative force.

[102]See J. Lambrecht, *Die Redaktion der Markus-Apokalypse: Literarische Analyse und Strukturuntersuchung* (Rome: Biblical Institute, 1967), who is followed in essentials by B. Standaert, *L'Evangile selon Marc. Composition et genre littéraire*; W. Harrington, *Mark*; and A. Stock, *The Method and Message of Mark*.

[103]Welch, *Chiasmus in Antiquity*, p. 237-239.

[104]See Robert J. Shirock, "The Growth of the Kingdom in Light of Israel's Rejection of Jesus: Structure and Theology in Luke 13:1-35," *NovT* 35/1 (1993), 15-29. Shirock argues that Luke 13:1-35 is chiastic, with the two Kingdom parables (18f and 20f) forming "a strong centerpiece with a forceful message," p. 24. His persuasive analysis leads him to conclude that in Luke "we meet a literary craftsman, not a careless compiler of traditions," p. 29.

3. THE GOSPEL OF JOHN

A. Gospel Structure: The 'Gerhard Hypothesis'

Commentators usually divide the Fourth Gospel into two major sections, the "Book of Signs" (chs. 1-12) and the "Book of Glory" (chs. 13-21), including a Prologue (1:1-18) and an Epilogue (ch. 21). Conventional wisdom in the field of Johannine studies holds as well several theories which, with minor variations, have been accepted as indisputable: (1) the Prologue was originally an independent piece — perhaps an early liturgical hymn — that was taken up and rewritten to serve as an introduction to the entire Gospel; (2) the apparent disorder in chronological sequence from the end of ch. 4 to the beginning of ch. 7 is due to an inadvertent displacement of materials and requires rearrangement to recover the author's original sequence; (3) the Farewell Discourse originally ended with Jesus' charge in 14:31b, so that chs. 15-17 represent secondary additions; (4) chapter 21 is an appendix, the original Gospel having ended with 20:30f; and (5) the Gospel is the product not of a single hand but of a school, including the original evangelist (responsible for the underlying oral proclamation), the author(s) proper of the earliest version of the work, and at least one "final redactor," who rearranged and added materials to produce the Gospel as we have it today.[1]

Raymond Brown has led the field in recent discussions of this issue and his overall contribution to Johannine studies leaves us all greatly in his debt. His monumental commentary had the rare virtue of drawing together and synthesizing the work of preceding generations, while at the same time charting new directions for New Testament scholarship as a whole. Nevertheless, in the wake of his research something of a bifurcation has occurred in the area of

Johannine studies. While the main stream of interpreters continues to probe for evidence of multiple underlying traditions and multiple authorship, a small minority has concentrated on the literary structure of the Fourth Gospel, and particularly on the chiastic patterns that recur throughout. Their conclusions point to the unity of composition that characterizes the Gospel, suggesting that a single hand was in fact responsible for shaping Johannine tradition into its present form.

Unfortunately these orientations have tended to polarize, as if they were mutually exclusive. Brown represents something of an exception in that he readily acknowledges the presence of chiasmus in both small isolated units and larger sections;[2] yet his chief interest is with the underlying stages in the process of Gospel composition. In recent years, Talbert,[3] Malatesta,[4] Di Marco,[5] Welch,[6] Ellis,[7] Staley,[8] Culpepper,[9] and many others[10] have concentrated rather on the actual literary shape of John's narrative. Their efforts have demonstrated that a major portion, and perhaps the whole of the Gospel, is structured chiastically. If this is the case, however, it would seem to undermine the current theory of Gospel composition worked out by Brown and others. For it is highly unlikely that a literary work could reflect an intricate, overall chiastic pattern and still be the product of many different hands.

Here we find a classic example of the potential conflict between two very different approaches to biblical interpretation: form and redaction history on the one hand, and literary criticism on the other. The question is, are these two approaches in fact mutually exclusive? Or can they complement one another so as to throw new and valuable light on the matter of Gospel composition?

Perhaps it is not out of place for me to mention in this connection something of my own experience. For years I taught my students in courses on the Fourth Gospel that the Prologue and Epilogue were not a part of the original composition, and that the displacement theory, developed by Bauer and Bultmann and elaborated by their disciples, offered the most likely solution to the problem of *aporeia* (difficulties or inconsistencies) that occur with respect to chronological sequence. Because 20:30f clearly ended the narrative, and found a weak repetition in 21:25, and the entire twenty-first chapter served as an apology for the roles of Peter and the Beloved Disciple in the Johannine community, I accepted — and taught — that the last chapter was indeed an appendix. I raised similar questions about chs. 15-17 of the Farewell Discourses, as well as about apparently independent units such as 12:44-50; 3:16-21; and (why not?) 6:51c-58. The effect of this approach was to convey to my students the impression that much of the Gospel was "secondary," and therefore possessed of a degree of authority and theological value comparable to that of the pericope of the adulterous woman in 7:53-8:11 (a passage which is unquestionably secondary). That my students should have drawn such a conclusion is of course my fault, not that of redaction criticism. Nonetheless, I mention this experience because I have found that it has been shared by a good many colleagues who have themselves recently come to appreciate the role of chiasmus in the Fourth Gospel. It has probably been shared as well by a number of the readers of this book.

My particular interest in chiasmus came with reading Peter Ellis's *The Genius of John*. While I was aware that chiastic structuring appeared in the Old and New Testaments, it seemed more like a literary peculiarity than the key to what was to become for me a wholly new way of reading the one evangelist whom the ancient Church canonized as "the Theologian." Reading the Gospel in a new way, according to its chiastic pattern, I am teaching it differently as well. Yet this does not mean reverting to an ultra-conservative insistence upon the absolute unity of authorship, any more than it means denying the presence of underlying elements of oral and possibly written tradition out of which the whole work was constructed. While the discovery of the chiastic "shape" of John's Gospel certainly modifies some long-standing opinions about the process of its composition, it does not at all vitiate the findings of form and redaction criticism. Those sciences remain indispensable for explaining the way originally independent units of tradition were produced and gathered within the Johannine communities, and worked into successive stages of the Gospel. What the chiastic structure does make clear, however, is that the so-called "final redactor" is in reality the true *author* of the work. It is he who took received tradition (perhaps already in primitive gospel form) and, using the principles of concentric parallelism, reshaped it into what is arguably the theological and literary masterpiece of the Church's canon.

John Welch follows the lead of Charles Talbert, who divides the Book of Signs into two sections, each structured chiastically: (1) 1:19-5:47, with the focus upon 3:22-36 (D) and 4:1-42 (D'), both of which concern "ritual and life"; and (2) 6:1-12:50, whose central theme parallels "the Jews reaction to Abraham, God and the Devil"

(8:31-47 = F) with "Jesus' reaction to the Devil, God and Abraham" (8:48-59 = F'). Talbert also demonstrated the presence of chiastic arrangements in the Book of Glory. In Welch's presentation they are as follows:

A : The hour of departing to the Father and Jesus' love
    for his own (13:1)

    B : Inspired by the Devil, Judas is to betray Jesus (2)

        C : Jesus' knowledge of the betrayal (3)

            D : Jesus rises from supper, lays aside his garments
                and begins to wash their feet (4-5)

                E : Peter objects, but will understand later (6-11)

            D' : When he has washed their feet, has taken up
                his garments, he resumes his place at the table[11]

        C' : Jesus' knowledge of the betrayal (18-26)

    B' : Inspired by Satan, Judas goes out to betray Jesus (26-30)

A' : Now is the time of glorification and Jesus' going away,
    love for one another and by Jesus (31-35).

A : Peter claims that he can follow Jesus now (13:36-38)

    B : Let not your hearts be troubled (14:1-7)

        C : Philip asks a question. Jesus' answer: My words are
            the Father's (8-14)

            D : If you love me, keep my commandments (15-21)

        C' : Judas asks a question. Jesus' answer: My word
            is the Father's (22-27)

    B' : Let not your hearts be troubled (27-30)

A' : Jesus follows the Father's commandment
    and goes forth (20-31).

A : The unity of Jesus, the disciples and the Father (15:1-17)

    B : The sufferings of the disciples in the world (15:18-16:3)

        C : The Comforter to give all truth (16:4-15)

            D : The Little While (16:16-22)

        C' : The Father to give all truth (16:23-31)

    B' : The tribulation of the disciples in the world (16:32-33)

A' : The unity of Jesus, the disciples and the Father (17:1-26).[12]

This arrangement clearly corresponds to the distribution of themes throughout the Farewell Discourse and can be verified by glancing at any English translation. Detection of the chiastic patterns throughout the Gospel, and particularly in chapters 13-17, provides a simple answer to a question that has long plagued Johannine scholars: why is the Gospel so repetitious? Why do the same themes recur, in nearly identical terms, in section after section of the author's narrative? The answer is that he did not write "narrative" *per se*. He composed his work chiastically, using repetition to reinforce key elements of his message.

As we noted in the first part of this study, Welch concludes that the whole of John's Gospel lacks a single, coherent chiastic structure. This was certainly the prevailing opinion among Johannine scholars, until publication in 1984 of Peter Ellis's "composition-critical commentary on the Fourth Gospel." His title, *The Genius of John*, pays tribute in the first instance to the evangelist and his extraordinary literary as well as theological skills. But it acknowledges implicitly the contribution of John Gerhard, S.J., whose doctoral dissertation produced compelling evidence that the whole of the Fourth Gospel is in fact chiastically arranged.[13] Working closely with Gerhard, Ellis took up and further developed this thesis. He showed that the entire work is organized according to the pattern A:B:C:B':A', a pattern that defines the whole and every subsection as well. The Gospel, in other words, is composed of five major sections, each of which is itself composed of five subsections. And within those subsections, individual units tend also to follow the fivefold A:B:C:B':A' format. In addition, the entire work is divided into 21 "sequences," that correspond only roughly to its 21 chapters.[14] According to the 'Gerhard hypothesis,' the Gospel is organized as follows:

A: Part I (1:19-4:3)
   B: Part II (4:4-6:15)
      C: Part III (6:16-21)
   B': Part IV (6:22-12:11)
A': Part V (12:12-21:25)

A : Seq. 1 (1:19-51)
　B : Seq. 2 (2:1-12)
　　C : Seq. 3 (2:13-25)
　　　D : Seq. 4 (3:1-21)
　　　　E : Seq. 5 (3:22-4:3)
　　　　　F : Seq. 6 (4:4-38)
　　　　　　G : Seq. 7 (4:39-45)
　　　　　　　H : Seq. 8 (4:46-52)
　　　　　　　　I : Seq. 9 (5:1-47)
　　　　　　　　　J : Seq. 10 (6:1-15)
　　　　　　　　　　K : Seq. 11 (6:16-21)
　　　　　　　　　J' : Seq. 12 (6:22-72)
　　　　　　　　I' : Seq. 13 (7:1-8:58)
　　　　　　　H' : Seq. 14 (9:1-10:21)
　　　　　　G' : Seq. 15 (10:22-39)
　　　　　F' : Seq. 16 (10:40-12:11)
　　　　E' : Seq. 17 (12:12-50)
　　　D' : Seq. 18 (chs. 13-17)
　　C' : Seq. 19 (chs. 18-19)
　B' : Seq. 20 (20:1-18)
A' : Seq. 21 (20:19-21:25)

The conceptual center of the Fourth Gospel, accordingly, is the episode of Christ walking on the water, 6:16-21. As with Mark, only in clearer fashion, John situates this account in such a way as to make of it a proclamation of the "New Exodus," which recapitulates and fulfills the first Exodus under the leadership of Moses. By flanking this central panel with sequences 10 and 12, the multiplication of bread and the "bread of life" discourse, the author supplies the whole with eucharistic significance. This fundamental paschal motif, then, serves as the core of the evangelist's proclamation, about which the rest of the Gospel develops in concentric circles.

It is disappointing that Ellis's book has not received a wider audience. Reviews of his study in scholarly journals have usually pointed to the unequal length of parallel subsections. Sequence 18, for example, comprises John 13:1-17:26, including the Last Supper, Farewell Discourses, and High Priestly Prayer, while its parallel in sequence 4 consists only of the relatively brief discourse with Nicodemus, 3:1-21. This fact is supposed to be a major argument against the book's chief premise. Criticism has also been leveled at the entire literary approach to biblical interpretation, with the claim that those who seek out chiastic patterns in a given text simply cut up the narrative in arbitrary ways to suit their preconceived hypotheses. And the fact that Talbert's analysis does not entirely correspond to that of Gerhard and Ellis would be proof to some that the entire quest for chiastic structures is fanciful.

Nevertheless, we have already found ample indication that parallels are established on the basis of verbal and thematic repetitions, irrespective of the length of the corresponding elements. And the evidence accumulated over the years to confirm the existence of chiasmus as a literary device is too overwhelming simply to be dismissed out of hand. As for the divergences between Talbert and Ellis, for example, they can easily be explained by the flexibility inherent in any longer set of chiastically balanced units, and by the fact that such units often overlap one another (as we have found in the Gospel of Mark). In the case of sequences 4 and 18 of John's Gospel, it should be noted that these two sections comprise the first and last discourses, in which thematic parallels and the principle of inclusion are unmistakable. From the similar nighttime settings to the common themes of eternal life, discipleship, love, good and evil deeds, Jesus as true/truth, Jesus' ascension, the world, water, and the Spirit, the two sections are as closely reflective of one another as the bread of life discourse is of the feeding of the five thousand that precedes it.

Resolution of the question in the reader's mind will come only through fresh study of the Gospel in the light of the 'Gerhard hypothesis.' To facilitate that study, I have included in Appendix II a graphic representation of Gerhard's thesis, worked out by Mrs. Judy Ellis.

In the remainder of this chapter we examine several individual sections of the Fourth Gospel that offer particularly interesting examples of chiasmus. It should become evident that the five theories outlined above, concerning the composition of the Gospel, need to be either thoroughly revised or discarded altogether.

B. The Prologue

In the first part of this study we pointed out that the chiastic center of the Gospel Prologue (1:1-18) is the affirmation in vv. 12-13, "But to all who received him [Jesus], who believed in his name, he gave power to become children of God; who were born, not of blood nor of the will of the flesh nor of the will of man, but of God."

This point, argued by M.E. Boismard in the early 1950s,[15] has not met with general acceptance, even among those who recognize the chiastic shape of the passage. P. Borgen, for example, proposes this structure:[16]

A (1-2): The Word and God.

B (3): All things made by Him.

C (4f): The light of all men.

C' (6-9): The witness of the light.

B' (10-13): The creation rejects the creator.

A' (14-18): The Word reveals God in the flesh.

Gerhard's analysis, which respects far better the balance of concepts in the prologue, demonstrates that the A:B:C:B':A' pattern is operative here as well as in the rest of the Gospel.

A (1-8): *Through the pre-existing Word*, all things *came to be*.

B (9-11): The true light is *rejected* by his own.

C (12f): To all who believe, power is given to become children of God.

B' (14): The Word become flesh is *accepted* by those who beheld his glory.

A' (15-18): *Through Jesus Christ*, grace and truth *came to be*.[17]

Once again, it would be misleading to say, for example, that Borgen is "wrong" and Ellis (Gerhard) is "right." The characteristics of chiasmus are such that different divisions are possible, each representing different facets of the composition. Ellis's presentation, nonetheless, does reflect the principal themes of the whole, a fact borne out by extended analysis. If we press the search for parallels somewhat further, the following structure emerges.

A (1f): The Word with God

   B (3): His role in creation

      C (4f): He gave life and light to men

         D (6-8): The witness of the Baptist

            E (9-11): The Word came into the world

               F (12f): Believers become children of God

            E' (14): The Word became incarnate

         D' (15): The witness of the Baptist

      C' (16): He gave grace upon grace to men

   B' (17): His role in the "new creation"

A' (18): The Son in the Father.[18]

Within these parallel elements, further correspondences can be found:

1:1-2,

A : In the beginning was the Word

   B : and the Word was with God,

   B' : and the Word was God.

A' : He was in the beginning with God.

1:4-5, [an example of run-on parallelism]

In him / *life* was //

   And the *life* was / the *light* of men //

   And the *light* shines / in the *darkness* //

and the *darkness* / has not overcome it. //

1:6 [anacrusis, introducing vv. 7-8]
There was a man sent from God, whose name was John.

1:7-8,

A : He came for a *witness*,

   B : to bear witness to the *light*,

      C : that all might believe through him.

   B' : He was not the *light*,

A' : but [he came] to bear *witness* to the light.[19]

1:9-11,

    A : The *true light*

        B : that enlightens *everyone*

            C : was *coming* into the world.

                D : He was in the *world*

                    E : and the world was made through him,

                D' : yet the *world* knew him not.

            C' : He *came* to his own home,

        B' : and *his own people*

    A' : *received* him *not.*

1:12-13,

    A : But to all who received him,

        B : who believed in his name,

            C : he gave power to become children of God;

        B' : who were born, not of blood nor of the will of the flesh
           nor of the will of man,

    A' : but [were born] of God.[20]

1:14,

    A : And the Word became flesh

        B : and dwelt among us [εσκηνωσεν]

            C : and we have beheld his glory,

        B' : glory as of the only Son from the Father,

    A' : full of grace and truth.[21]

1:15,

    A : John *bore witness* to him

        B : and cried out, saying,

    A' : "This was he of whom *I said,*

    A : He who comes *after me*

        B : ranks before me

    A' : for he was *before me.*[22]

1:16-18,

A : And from his *fullness*

    B : have we all received,

A' : *grace* upon *grace.*

A : For the Law was *given through* Moses

    B : grace and truth

A' : *came through* Jesus Christ.

A : *No one* has ever *seen God;*

    B : the only Son,

    B' : who is in the bosom of the Father,

A' : *he* has *made him known.*[23]

The principle of intensification appears throughout the Prologue, from strophe I to strophe II. It confirms that the primary theme
of the passage is *soteriological:* salvation is bestowed upon those who
receive the revelation accorded by the divine Word and "believe in
his name."

A → A': From the unity of the Word with God,
      to the revelation accorded by the Son,
      "who is in the bosom of the Father."[24]

B → B': From the work of the Logos in creating the world,
      to his revelatory ("truth") and saving ("grace") work
      in the "new creation."

C → C': From the gift of light and life, to the gift
      of abundant saving grace.

D → D': From the Baptist's vocation to bear witness,
      to the witness itself (with heightening from v. 8
      to v. 15b of the theme of John's subordination to Jesus).

E → E': From the coming of the Word into the world,
      to his incarnation in human flesh that
      manifests grace, truth and glory.

F: The focus is upon the results of the revealing,
      saving work of the Word/Son: adoption of believers
      as "children of God."

The heightening effect is not only forward, from I to II. It is also helical, moving with increasing intensity from A → A' (affirmation of the divine origin of the Word/Son), to B:C → B':C' (his work in creation and human life), to D → D' (the Baptist's witness and subordination to him),[25] to E → E' (the affirmation that the Word came into the hostile world through incarnation), and concluding with F, the purpose of this entire movement, namely the salvation of those who believe.

In addition to demonstrating that the Prologue is structured as a chiastic pentacolon, Fr. Gerhard has argued as well that it functions as a virtual outline, or table of contents, for the twenty one Gospel sequences. The following is his outline, with minor changes.

Part I (1:19-4:3):

In the beginning was the Word, and the Word was with God,
   and the Word was God. He was in the beginning with God;

[// 1:19-51, Jesus in relation to John]

all things were made through him, and without him
   was not anything made (that was made).

[// 2:1-12, Jesus makes wine]

In him was life, and the life was the light of men.

[// 2:13-25, Jesus challenged by men; "Destroy this temple and I will raise it up"]

The light shines in the darkness, and the darkness
   has not overcome it.

[// 3:1-21, Jesus illumines Nicodemus's darkness]

There was a man sent from God, whose name was John ...
   [he] came to bear witness to the light.

[// 3:22-4:3, John's final witness]

Part II (4:4-6:15):

The true light

[// 4:4-38, Jesus enlightens the Samaritan woman]

that enlightens every man

[// 4:39-45, the Samaritan men believe]

was coming into the world.

[// 4:46-54, the official believes]

> He was in the world, and the world was made through him,
> yet the world knew him not.

[// 5:1-47, the Jews do not believe]

> He came to his own home, and his own people received him not.

[// 6:1-15, Jesus feeds the people, then flees when they misunderstand his mission and try to take him by force to make him king]

Part III (6:16-21):

> But to all who received him, who believed in his name, he gave
> power to become children of God; who were born ... of God.

[// 6:16-21, Jesus is received "gladly" by the disciples into the boat]

Part IV (6:22-12:11):

> And the Word became flesh

[// 6:22-71, discourse on Jesus' "flesh"]

> and dwelt (lit., "tabernacled") among us

[// 7:1-8:59, the Feast of Tabernacles]

> and we have beheld his glory,

[// 9:1-10:21, the man healed of blindness]

> glory as of the only Son from the Father,

[// 10:22-39, Jesus affirms he is the Son of God]

> full of grace and truth.

[// 10:40-12:11, Jesus exercises love and fidelity to the family of Bethany (cf. Heb. *chesed, emeth*)]

Part V (12:12-21:25):

> John bore witness to him, and cried, "This was he of whom I said,
> 'He who comes after me ranks before me, for he was before me.' "

[// 12:12-50, Jesus is acclaimed by the crowd, that hails the one who comes]

> And from his fullness have we all received, grace upon grace.

[// 13:1-17:26, Jesus promises to send the Spirit]

For the law was given through Moses;

[// 18:1-19:42, Jesus, through suffering and death, ends and fulfills the Mosaic law]

grace and truth came through Jesus Christ.

[// 20:1-18, Jesus is resurrected, shows kindness and fidelity to his own family, Mary and his brothers]

No one has ever seen God; the only Son, who is in the bosom
of the Father, he has made him known.

[// 20:19-21:25, Jesus makes himself known, through his glorious hands and side, as God (cf. Thomas' confession, 20:28)]

A few of these parallels appear forced. Yet taken in light of the overall structure of the Gospel, they seem to confirm Gerhard's conviction that "the order of words and ideas in the Prologue follows the order of words and ideas in the Gospel."

What is not clear is whether the Prologue was first composed as an outline for the work as a whole, or whether it represents a synthesis of Johannine theology, modeled upon the Gospel and therefore composed afterwards. That question may never be satisfactorily answered. What has been conclusively demonstrated, however, is the total interconnectedness of one with the other. In light of this comparison, it seems hardly likely that the Prologue was, as many hold, an originally independent hymn, taken up at a secondary stage of composition and added, with various modifications, as an (artificial) introduction. Whatever the sequence of composition, the Prologue is without question an original and integral part of Johannine theology and proclamation.

C. John 6 and
The 'Displacement Theory'

If John Gerhard's analysis of the chiastic structuring of the Fourth Gospel is correct, it implicitly does away with the various "displacement" theories advanced to explain many of the chronological and geographical *aporeia* that have long troubled Johannine scholars.

The most flagrant of those inconsistencies occurs from the close of ch. 4 to the beginning of ch. 7. In 4:54, the author declares that the healing of the official's son "was the second sign that Jesus did when he had come from Judea to Galilee." Ch. 5 opens with the assertion that Jesus went up to "a feast of the Jews" in Jerusalem. There he remained until, at the beginning of ch. 6, he "went to the other side of the Sea of Galilee," followed by the crowd that had witnessed his signs. Explicit mention is made in 6:4 that "the Passover, the feast of the Jews, was at hand." In ch. 7, Jesus is still in Galilee, but the time is now that of the Jewish feast of Tabernacles. Jesus goes up secretly to Jerusalem, then he begins teaching publicly in the temple. In an ensuing dispute with the authorities he declares, "I did one work, and you all marvel at it!" (7:21). As v. 23 confirms, this "work" to which Jesus alludes is the healing recounted in 5:1ff.[26]

Two interrelated problems appear here: the abrupt change of location in ch. 6, and the wide separation between the healing of ch. 5 and Jesus' reference to it in ch. 7. As Bultmann and many others have noted, if we simply reverse the order of chs. 5 and 6, the problems are resolved. Then both geographic and chronological sequence are respected, and the allusion to the "work" in ch. 7 clearly refers to the healing at the pool.

It is ironic that the displacement theory, created out of concern to preserve a sense of continuity in time and place from chapter to chapter, should have been advanced by a scholar such as Bultmann, who otherwise shows little interest in the "historicity" of the Fourth Gospel. Be that as it may, the issue of the apparent *aporeia* in this section is a serious one and calls for a solution.

Such a solution is easily attainable if we alter our presuppositions regarding the author's intentions. Bultmann would have been the first to insist that the evangelists wrote theology, not history. While an historical grounding for the "Christ-event" is indispensable, its truth transcends the confines of history. It is this fact that led Bultmann to an existential approach to the Christian message, particularly as it appears in the Gospel of John. While the author of the Gospel was sensitive to chronological sequence, his chief purpose was to convey the meaning of Jesus' person and works. Consequently, he frequently subordinated concern for historical accuracy to the greater concern for proclaiming the Good News. Because he found in chiasmus the most suitable literary tool for conveying his message, he was often obliged to modify chronological sequence to fit the chiastic structure, even if it meant creating the sort of inconsistencies that admittedly abound throughout his writing.[27]

The triptych that constitutes ch. 6 of the Gospel is set off by an inclusion: 6:1 ("After this Jesus went to the other side of the Sea of Galilee") and 7:1 ("And after this Jesus went about in Galilee"). The chapter itself is an enclosed unit, consisting of the feeding of the five thousand (6:1-15), the walking on the water (6:16-21), and the bread of life discourse (6:22-71). The only sequence in the Gospel to have no parallel is the second of these, which Gerhard identifies as the conceptual center of the entire work. Several details appear in this account that substantiate the theory that it represents a "new Exodus."

In the Synoptic version of the narrative (Mk 6:45-52 // Mt 14:22-33), Jesus compels the disciples to enter the boat, then he dismisses the crowd and goes off into the hills to pray. Perceiving that the disciples have been struggling against the wind and waves, Jesus draws near to them upon the water and, according to Mark, intends to pass them by. There follows the disciples' reaction, together with Jesus' statement, "Take heart, it is I; have no fear." Whereas Mark concludes the episode with the disciples' incomprehension, Matthew shows them worshiping Jesus and confessing, "Truly you are the Son of God."

This traditional story remains largely intact in John's treatment. The few changes he makes to it, however, are significant. In the first place, he eliminates Jesus' word, "Take heart," leaving only the divine name (εγω ειμι) and the revelatory indicator "be not afraid" (μη φοβεισθε).[28] This strengthens the affirmation, as does elimination of the disciples' initial reaction. While Mark and Matthew concentrate on this latter aspect, John is more interested in the person of Jesus himself. Who is this man who even walks upon the waters? The answer lies in his self-designation: it is he who bears divine authority and power, who "turns the seas into dry land" and provides "through the paths of the seas" a safe passage for those who are faithful to him. With this recognition, the disciples are "glad" (ηθελον) to receive him into the boat: they earnestly desire to receive him and to be led by him to their destination.

The final Johannine touch consists of the statement, "and immediately the boat was at the land to which they were going." To Mark and Matthew, the crossing occurs in quite ordinary fashion: "And when they had crossed over...." To John, the crossing itself is as miraculous as the walking on the water. For the very purpose of the episode in his Gospel is to depict Jesus as God himself, who leads his people (the boat, once again, represents the Church) through the turbulent waters and on to the other shore. The Exodus motif is patent.

The two panels that flank this episode continue the Exodus theme. Each one uses eucharistic language, whose effect is to create a paschal atmosphere. In the multiplication of bread, eucharistic language describes Jesus' gestures, as it does in the Synoptic accounts: Jesus "took" the loaves, "gave thanks" (ευχαριστησας), "distributed them," and they "ate their fill" (ενεπλησθησαν). On the basis of this "sign," the people confess Jesus to be the eschatological prophet who would inaugurate the Kingdom on earth. Here again, John has taken up and modified an element of ancient tradition in such a way as to draw out its paschal implications.

What is unique in his version is the complement to this episode. Following the central account of the New Exodus, the evangelist offers an interpretation of the feeding of the multitude that focuses upon Jesus' person as the source of eternal life. Whereas Moses in the wilderness provided the people with bread from heaven, Jesus himself is the true Bread from heaven, come down to give life to the world (6:32f).

The eucharistic interpretation of this chapter, accepted since early patristic times, has often been called into question. G. Bornkamm began the most recent wave of discussion on this question with an article published in 1956.[29] There, as well as in his graduate seminars at the Ruprecht-Karl Universität in Heidelberg, he argued that 6:51c-58 is a secondary addition to the original discourse, whose purpose is to create eucharistic imagery out of a passage that originally referred only to the "bread" of Jesus' teaching. Pointing out that the accent in vv. 51c-58 shifts from "bread" to "flesh," he held that the secondary nature of the passage becomes evident when it is compared with 6:63, Jesus' assertion that "the flesh is of no avail." To his mind, it scarcely seems possible to reconcile such a statement with the declaration of 6:55, "my flesh is food indeed, and my blood is drink."

The debate over these verses continues. Too little attention, however, has been paid to two points. First, the evangelist consistently presents Jesus as building image upon image to convey his message. At Cana, water becomes wine (2:9ff); at Jacob's well, "a prophet" becomes "the Messiah" (4:19, 30); at the Sheep Gate Jesus appears as a thaumaturge, then "makes himself equal with God" (5:15-18); in Jerusalem he is identified by the crowd as "the Messiah"

(7:27,31,41), then he reveals himself to be Son of Man and Son of God (8:19,28, etc.), declaring that he has "come forth from God" (8:42); and finally he affirms that he is "one" with God (10:30). There is nothing inconsistent, then, with the heightened shift in imagery from "bread" to "flesh" in 6:51; in fact it conforms to a typical Johannine pattern of teaching.

In the second place, the statement in 6:63 is an independent saying that has no direct connection with 6:51-58. The contrast between spirit and flesh in v. 63 refers to strength and weakness, a common Semitic theme found throughout the Old Testament (cf. esp. Isa 31:3). Whereas the explicitly eucharistic imagery of 6:51-58 may have been introduced into the bread of life discourse at a secondary stage in its oral transmission, it stands in its present context as an integral element which is indispensable to the evangelist's presentation of Jesus' teaching. Remove it, and the meaning of the entire discourse is changed; for the parallel would then be lost between the eucharistic language describing Jesus' distribution of the bread in 6:11f, and the interpretation of Jesus' words as "the bread which comes down from heaven, that a person may eat of it and not die" (6:50). Only the following verses, 51-58, make clear the fact that the bread referred to previously is indeed the "bread of his flesh."

It is a commonplace that 6:51-58 is the Johannine equivalent of the "words of institution," spoken by Jesus, according to Synoptic tradition, at the Last Supper. This view is substantiated, however, only by the fact that 6:51-58 stands in parallel to the eucharistic gestures of 6:11. Those gestures, together with these words, reproduce in the framework of the Fourth Gospel what occurred in the upper room on the night of Jesus' betrayal: "He took bread, and blessed, and broke it, and gave it to them, saying, 'This is my body'" (Mk 14:22). The A:B:A' structure of John 6, therefore, confirms the eucharistic character of the whole: from physical bread to spiritual bread, in the context of the Exodus experience.

The fact that 6:51-58 belongs in its present context is also apparent from the chiastic structure of 6:43-58. Ellis presents this section as follows:

A (6:43-50): Jesus answered them, "Do not murmur among yourselves. No one can come to me unless the *Father* who sent me draws him; and *I will raise him up at the last day*. It is written in the prophets, 'And they shall all be taught by God.' Every one who has heard and learned from the *Father* comes to me. Not that any one has seen the *Father* except him who is from God; he has seen the *Father*. Truly, truly, I say to you, he who believes has *eternal life*. I am the bread of life. *Your fathers* ate the manna in the wilderness, and they *died*. *This is the bread which comes down from heaven, that a man may eat of it and not die*.

B (51): "I am the *living* bread which came down from heaven; if any one *eats* of this bread, he will *live for ever*; and the bread which I shall give for the *life* of the world is my *flesh*."

C (52): The Jews then disputed among themselves, saying, "How can this man give us his flesh to eat?"

B' (53): So Jesus said to them, "Truly, truly I say to you, unless you *eat* the *flesh* of the Son of man and drink his blood, *you have no life in you*;

A' (54-58): he who *eats* my flesh and drinks my blood *has eternal life*, and *I will raise him up at the last day*. For my flesh is food indeed, and my blood is drink indeed. He who *eats* my flesh and drinks my blood abides in me and I in him. As the living *Father* sent me, and I live because of the *Father*, so he who *eats* me will live because of me. *This is the bread which came down from heaven, not such as the fathers ate and died; he who eats this bread will live for ever*.

As we have discovered elsewhere, chiastic structures often overlap one another. This is the case in John 6; for the bread of life discourse also divides neatly into two chiastic strophes, vv. 35-47, and 48-58.[30]

A (35): I am the bread of life; he who comes to me shall not hunger,
and he who believes in me shall never thirst.

B (36): But I said to you that you have seen me and
yet do not believe.

C (37): All that the Father gives me will come to me;
and him who comes to me I will not cast out.

D (38): For I have come down from heaven, not to do
my own will, but the will of him who sent me;

E (39f): and this is the will of him who sent me, that I
should lose nothing of all that he has given me,
but raise it up at the last day. For this is the will
of my Father, that every one who sees the Son
and believes in him should have eternal life; and
I will raise him up at the last day.[31]

F (41a): The Jews then murmured at him,

    G (41b): because he said, "I am the bread
    which came down from heaven."

       H (42a): They said, "Is not this Jesus,
       the son of Joseph, whose father
       and mother we know?

    G' (42b): How does he now say,
    'I have come down from heaven'?"

F' (43): Jesus answered them, "Do not
    murmur among yourselves.

E' (44): No one can come to me unless the Father
    who sent me draws him; and I will raise him
    up at the last day.

D' (45a): It is written in the prophets, 'And they shall all
    be taught by God.'[32]

C' (45b): Every one who has heard and learned
    from the Father comes to me.

B' (46): Not that any one has seen the Father except him
    who is from God; he has seen the Father.

A' (47): Truly, truly I say to you, he who believes has eternal life.

A → A': life / come to me →
    believe in me / life.

B → B': they have seen Jesus →
    Jesus alone has seen the Father.

C → C': comes to me →
    comes to me.

D → D': the will of God →
    taught by God (concerning his will).

E → E': Father saves all / raise him up at the last day →
    Father draws all / raise him up at the last day.

F → F': The Jews murmured →
    Do not murmur.

G → G': I came down from heaven →
    I have come down from heaven.

H: The people's hostility and misunderstanding.

The focus throughout this first section is upon the hostility manifested toward Jesus by his own people, expressed in their rhetorical question, "Is not this the son of Joseph...?" Behind the question is an implicit denial of the truth Jesus expresses throughout: his Father is God, from whom he has come and to whom he will return.

The truly decisive argument for the unity of ch. 6 and the place of 6:51c-58 within its present context, however, is the fact that vv. 48-58 are likewise structured according to an elaborate chiastic pattern, with v. 53 as the central focus.

A (48): "I am the bread of life.

B (49): Your fathers ate the manna in the wilderness,
and they died.

C (50a): This is the bread which comes down from heaven,

D (50b): that a man may eat of it and not die.

E (51a): I am the living bread which came
down from heaven;

F (51b): if any one eats of this bread,
he will live for ever;

G (51c): and the bread which I shall give
for the life of the world is my flesh."

H (52): The Jews then disputed among
themselves, saying, "How can this
man give us his flesh to eat?"

I (53): So Jesus said to them,
"Truly, truly I say to you,
unless you eat the flesh of
the Son of Man and drink his
blood, you have no life in you;

H' (54): he who eats my flesh and
drinks my blood has eternal life,
and I will raise him up
at the last day.

G' (55): For my flesh is food indeed,
and my blood is drink indeed.

F' (56): He who eats my flesh and drinks
my blood abides in me, and I in him.

E' (57ab): As the living Father sent me,
and I live because of the Father,

D' (57c): so he who eats me will live because of me.

C' (58a): This is the bread which came down from heaven,

B' (58b): not such as the fathers ate and died;

A' (58c): he who eats this bread will live forever."

Here, too, intensification and the helical movement are evident:

A → A': Jesus as the bread of life →
This bread confers eternal life.

B → B': The fathers ate manna →
They did not eat the true heavenly bread.

C → C': The bread of life comes down from heaven →
This bread came in the person of Jesus.

D → D': He who eats of it will not die →
He who eats of it will have [eternal] life.

E → E': Jesus is the living bread from heaven →
Jesus lives because of the living Father.

F → F': He who eats this bread will live forever →
Eating and drinking leads to mutual indwelling
between Jesus and the believer.

G → G': The bread is Jesus' flesh →
Jesus flesh is true food, his blood is true drink.

H → H': The Jews' question about eating flesh →
Jesus' answer: to consume his flesh and blood gives eternal life.

I: Eating the flesh and drinking the blood of the Son of Man.

This entire passage displays a spiral movement—with heightening through intensification — from the source of the bread and its life-giving properties, to identification of the bread with Jesus' own flesh, to Jesus' response to the Jews that he is the source of resurrection and eternal life, to the culminating affirmation of 6:53. The fathers ate manna in the wilderness and died; "the Jews" rely on the law of Moses and their traditions — and they too will die. For only those who consume the flesh and blood of the Son of Man (the unique usage of the christological title in this section) will obtain life in themselves.

Whatever elements of this passage may have circulated in the form of oral tradition prior to the Gospel's composition, it is clear from this analysis that 6:51c-58 is an integral and inseparable part of the whole. While that conclusion could be supported on exegetical grounds, the chiastic structure of the larger section, 6:48-58, makes the conclusion inescapable. This is still further evidence that traditional exegetical method needs to be complemented by an analysis of literary structures and the author's technique of composition.

Moving outward from the central sequences included in ch. 6, we find another significant parallel between chs. 5 and 7. The reason the healing of the paralytic is referred to only in 7:21-23 is not because of some displacement of chapters. It is because the chiastic structure naturally balances sequence 9 (5:1-47) with sequence 13 (7:1-8:58).

The arrangement of chapters four through seven, then, is to be explained on the model of concentric circles, whose focal point is the walking on the water. These various factors would seem to eliminate once and for all the need for a "displacement" theory applied to the early portions of John's Gospel. The same holds true for the apparently problematic sequences in the Farewell Discourse.

D. The Farewell Discourse and Spirit-Paraclete Logia

Early in this chapter we noted Talbert's analysis of the chiastic structuring of John 13:1-35; 13:36-14:31; and 15:1-17:26. According to Gerhard's theory, chs. 13-17 represent sequence 18, which stands parallel to sequence 4, comprising 3:1-21. Ellis presents the parallel structure of the Farewell Discourse as follows:[33]

> A (13:1-32): The footwashing and Judas the traitor. Jesus speaks about the arrival of *his hour*, about *love* unto the end, about the *mission of the apostles*, and about *his glorification*.
>
> B (13:33-14:31): Jesus speaks about *his going away, the Counselor*, his love commandment, dwelling places in heaven, *asking in his name*, and *his gift of peace*.
>
> C (15:1-25): The true vine and the false vine. During the time of the gap, the disciples must remain in Jesus as the branch remains in the vine. Despite the hatred and persecution of the world, the disciples will produce much fruit as long as they remain in Jesus.
>
> B' (15:26-16:33): Jesus speaks about *his going away, the Counselor, asking in his name*, and *his gift of peace*.
>
> A' (17:1-26): Jesus prays for the Church. He speaks about the arrival of *his hour, his glorification*, the *mission of the apostles*, and the *love* that he prays may be in those who believe in him.

Each of these five sections is itself chiastically structured according to the same A:B:C:B':A' model.

A (13:1): The *hour* has arrived.

B (13:2-11): All are *clean* except *one*.

C (13:12-17): The footwashing as an example
for the apostles.

B' (13:18-27): Jesus singles out the *one* who is not *clean*.

A' (13:28-32): Judas' departure sets in motion the *hour* of Jesus'
death and glorification.

A (13:33-14:4): Jesus speaks about his *going away*, about *his love
commandment*, and about *dwelling places* in heaven.

B (14:5-14): Jesus speaks of himself as "the way, and the truth
and the *life*," and says, "*I am in the Father....*"

C (14:15-17): Jesus will ask the Father, and he will give
another Counselor.

B' (14:18-20): Jesus says, "You see me as one who has *life*.
On that day you will know that *I am in my Father...*"

A' (14:21-31): Jesus speaks about *his love commandment*, about him
and the Father making a *dwelling place* with him who loves,
and about his *going away*.

A (15:1-6): The *true* vine, i.e., the true Israel.

B (15:7-10): This is my *commandment* that you *love* one another.

C (15:11): These things I have spoken to you,
that my joy may be in you.

B' (15:12-17): This *I command you*, to *love* one another.

A' (15:18-25): The *false* vine, i.e., the synagogue.

A (15:26-16:4): *The time* of persecution *is coming*.

B (16:5-15): I am *going to him who sent me*.

C (16:16-22): A little while, and you will see me no more.

B' (16:23-30): I am leaving the world and *going to the Father*.

A' (16:31-33): *The time* of persecution *is coming*.

A (17:1-5): Jesus prays to the Father to glorify him with the *glory* he had *before the world was made.*

B (17:6-8): Jesus speaks about his apostles,
to whom he has given the Father's word.

C (17:9-13): Jesus prays for his apostles.

B' (17:14-19): Jesus again prays for his apostles,
to whom he has given the Father's word.

A' (17:20-26): Jesus prays for all believers and concludes by speaking about the *glory* the Father gave him *before the foundation of the world.*

This analysis clearly corresponds to the movement of thought throughout the sequence. As we have found elsewhere, however, it is possible to detect still other chiastic patterns within this overall framework. Raymond Brown, for example, pointed out the chiastic shape of 15:7-17,[34] as Edward Malatesta did for the "high priestly prayer" of ch. 17.[35] The following divisions show that the Discourse proper, beginning with 13:33 and concluding with 16:33, can be broken down into chiastic units that do not always correspond to the Gerhard/Ellis analysis. This does not call their conclusions into question; it merely illustrates once again how one chiastic passage can overlap or be contained within another (tr. *RSV*).

13:32-14:31,
[13:32 is an independent saying on reciprocal glorification between the Father and the Son that introduces the entire discourse.]

A (13:33-36): "Little children, yet a little while I am with you. You will seek me; and as I said to the Jews so now I say to you, 'Where I am going you cannot come.' *A new commandment I give to you,* that you love one another; *even as I have loved you, that you also love one another.* By this all men will know that you are my disciples, if you have love for one another." Simon Peter said to him, "Lord, where are you going?" Jesus answered, "*Where I am going* you cannot follow now; but *you shall follow afterward."*

B (13:37f): Peter said to him, "Lord, why cannot I follow you now? I will lay down my life for you." Jesus answered, "Will you lay down your life for me? Truly, truly, *I say to you,* the cock will not crow, till *you have denied me* three times."

C (14:1-3): "*Let not your hearts be troubled;* believe in God, *believe also in me.* In my Father's house are many rooms; if it were not so, would I have told you that *I go* to prepare a place for you? And when *I go* and prepare a place for you, *I will come again and will take you to myself,* that where I am you may be also."

D (14:4-7): "And you know the way where I am going." Thomas said to him, "Lord, we do not know where you are going; how can we know *the way?*" Jesus said to him, "I am the way, and the truth, and the life; no one comes to the Father, but by me. *If you had known me, you would have known my Father also;* henceforth you know him and have seen him."

E (14:8): Philip said to him, "Lord *show us the Father* and we shall be satisfied."

F (14:9-11): Jesus said to him, "Have I been with you so long, and yet you do not know me Philip? *He who has seen me has seen the Father;* how can you say, '*Show us the Father*'? Do you not believe that *I am in the Father* and the Father in me? The words that I say to you I do not speak on my own authority; but the Father who dwells in me does his works. Believe me that I am in the Father and the Father in me; or else believe me for the sake of the works themselves."

G (14:12): "Truly, truly, I say to you, he who believes in me will also do the works that I do; and greater works than these will he do, because *I go to the Father.*"

H (14:13-14): "Whatever you ask in my name, I will do it, that the Father may be glorified in the Son; if you ask anything in my name, I will do it."

G' (14:18-19): "I will not leave you
desolate; *I will come to you.* Yet a
little while, and the world will see
me no more, but you will see me;
because I live, you will live also."

F' (14:20-21): "In that day you will know that
I am in my Father, and you in me, and I in
you. He who has my commandments and
keeps them, he it is who loves me; and *he
who loves me will be loved by my Father*, and
I will love him and *manifest myself to him.*"

E' (14:22): Judas (not Iscariot) said to him, "Lord,
how is it that you will *manifest yourself* to us,
and not to the world?"

D' (14:23-24): Jesus answered him, "*If a man loves me,*
he will keep my word, and my Father will love
him, and *we will come to him* and make our home
with him. He who does not love me does not keep
my words; and the word which you hear is *not
mine but the Father's* who sent me."

C' (14:27-28): "Peace I leave with you; my peace I give to
you; not as the world gives do I give to you. *Let not
your hearts be troubled,* neither let them be afraid. You
have heard me say to you, '*I go away, and I will come to
you.*' If you loved me, you would have rejoiced because
I go to the Father; for the Father is greater than I."

B' (14:29-30): "And now *I have told you before it takes place,*
so that when it does take place, *you may believe.* I will no
longer talk much with you, for *the ruler of this world is
coming.* He has no power over me;

A' (14:31): but *I do as the Father has commanded me,* so that the world
may know that *I love the Father.* Rise, *let us go* hence.

The parallels between I and II are thematic rather than verbal.
Key ideas (Father-Son, love, knowledge, mutual indwelling) are
so often repeated, that the divisions inevitably appear somewhat
arbitrary. As the following schema indicates, however, the correspondences are sufficient to show that the author composed
this section chiastically.

A → A': Disciples commanded to obey and love one another / Je-
sus goes, Peter will go [to suffering and death] →
Jesus commanded to obey and love the Father /
Jesus and disciples go forth [to his suffering and death].

B → B': Jesus foretells Peter's denial / (implied influence of Satan?) →
Jesus foretells the disciples' belief / Satan is coming.

C → C': Consolation: Jesus will come again to receive his disciples
/ Believe in me →
Peace and consolation: Jesus will come again / Love me.

D → D': The disciples come to the Father through
their knowledge of Jesus →
The Father will come to the disciples through
their love for Jesus.

E → E': A disciple's question: show us the Father →
A disciple's question: manifest yourself.

F → F': The Son in the Father / the Father in the Son →
The Son in the Father / the disciples in the Son.

G → G': Ascension →
Parousia.

H: The Father glorified in the Son.

Many of the lapidary statements of the Farewell Discourse,
connected only by a single link-word or familiar theme, must have
circulated in the oral tradition of the Johannine communities long
before they were incorporated into the Gospel. Parallels with the
First Epistle of John, as with the rest of the Gospel, indicate that the
same teaching existed in several variant forms (e.g., repeated references to the commandment to love Jesus, God, and one another;
repeated assurance that whatever they ask will be granted; repeated
allusions to persecution). In Mark, the equivalent of the Farewell
Discourse is ch. 13, the "little apocalypse;" in Luke, it is a disparate
collection of sayings that appear in other contexts in the Synoptic
parallels; and in Matthew the discourse is omitted altogether.
Clearly, the Johannine writer constructed these three chapters, 14-16,
basing them upon elements of Jesus' teaching from various occasions during his ministry, as well as upon sayings uttered in the
upper room and transmitted by those present. As they appear in the
Gospel, the sayings have been reshaped to reflect the evangelist's
own language and style; and they have to some degree been recast
so as to speak to critical problems within his community: Jesus'
apparent abandonment of his disciples, and their consequent
anxiety in the face of persecution.[36]

The reader should have noticed that *two passages are omitted* from the above arrangement of 13:33-14:33, namely *the two Spirit-Paraclete sayings*, 14:15-17, and 25-26. In the following outline of chiastic units in chs. 15 and 16, the other three Spirit-logia (15:26f; 16:7-11 and 12-15) likewise fall out. We shall discuss the reason for this in a moment. For the present, we should simply note the way the last two chapters of discourse employ the familiar device of concentric parallelism.

15:1-6,

> A (15:1-2): "I am the true vine, and my Father is the vinedresser. Every branch of mine that *bears no fruit, he takes away,* and every branch that does bear fruit *he prunes,* that it may bear more fruit."
>
> B (15:3-4): "You are already made clean by the word which I have spoken to you. *Abide in me, and I in you.* As the branch cannot *bear fruit* by itself, unless it abides in the vine, neither can you, *unless you abide in me.*"
>
> C (15:5a): "I am the vine, you are the branches."
>
> B' (15:5bc): "He who *abides in me, and I in him,* he it is that *bears much fruit,* for *apart from me you can do nothing.*"
>
> A' (15:6): "If a man does not abide in me, he is *cast forth as a branch* and withers; and the branches are gathered, *thrown into the fire and burned.*"

A → A': Bear fruit or be pruned →
Abide in Jesus or be pruned and burned.

B → B': Abide in Jesus to bear fruit →
Abide in Jesus to bear much fruit.

C: Jesus is the vine, the disciples are the branches.

15:7-17,

> A (15:7-9): "If you *abide* in me, and my words *abide* in you *ask whatever you will, and it shall be done for you.* By this my *Father* is glorified, *that you bear much fruit,* and so prove to be my disciples. As the Father has loved me, so have I loved you; *abide in my love.*"

B (15:10): *"If you keep my commandments,* you will *abide in my love,* just as I have kept *my Father's* commandments and abide in his love."

    C (15:11): "These things I have spoken to you, that my joy may be in you, and that your joy may be full."

B' (15:12-15): "This is *my commandment,* that you *love one another* as I have loved you. Greater love has no man than this, that a man lay down his life for his friends. You are my friends *if you do what I command you.* No longer do I call you servants, for the servant does not know what his master is doing; but I have called you friends, for all that I have heard from *my Father* I have made known to you."

A' (15:16-17): "You did not choose me, but I chose you and appointed you that you should *go and bear fruit* and that *your fruit should abide;* so that *whatever you ask the Father in my name, he may give it to you.* This I command you, to *love one another."*

A → A': Abide in me to bear fruit of love / ask and it shall be done for you →
Your fruit of love should abide / ask, and the Father will give it to you.

B → B': Keep my commandments / abide in my love →
Keep my commandment / love one another.

C: Joy.

15:18-25,

A (15:18-19): "If the world *hates you,* know that it has *hated me* before it *hated you.* If you were of the world, the world would love its own; but because you are not of the world, but I chose you out of the world, therefore the world hates you."

B (15:20): "Remember the word that I said to you, 'A servant is not greater than his master.' If *they persecuted me, they will persecute you;* if they kept my word, they will keep yours also."

    C (15:21): "But all this they will do to you on my account, because they do not know him who sent me."

B′ (15:22): "If I had not come and spoken to them, they would not have sin; but now *they have no excuse for their sin*."

A′ (15:23-25): "He who *hates me hates my Father* also. If I had not done among them the works which no one else did, they would not have sin; but now they have seen and *hated both me and my Father*. It is to fulfill the word that is written in their law, 'They hated me without a cause.'"

A → A′:   The world hates me and you →
The world hates me and my Father.

B → B′:   The world's sin (persecution of believers) →
The world has no excuse for its sin.

C: The world sins because it does not know God.

16:1-33,

A (16:1): "I have said all this to you *to keep you from falling away*."

B (16:2-4a): "*They will put you out* of the synagogues; indeed, *the hour is coming* when whoever *kills you* will think he is offering service to God. And they will do this because they have not known the *Father*, nor me. But *I have said these things to you*, that *when their hour comes you may remember* that I told you of them."

C (16:4b-6): "I did not *say these things to you* from the beginning, because I was with you. But now *I am going to him* who sent me; yet *none of you asks me*, 'Where are you going?' But because I have said these things to you, *sorrow* has filled your hearts."

D (16:16-19): "*A little while, and you will see me no more; again a little while, and you will see me*." Some of his disciples said to one another, "What is this that he says to us, 'A little while, and you will not see me, and again a little while, and you will see me'; and, 'because *I go to the Father*'?" They said, "What does he mean by '*a little while*'? We do not know what he means." Jesus knew that they wanted to ask him; so he said to them, "Is this what you are asking yourselves, what I meant by saying, '*A little while, and you will not see me, and again a little while, and you will see me*'?"

E (16:20-21): *"Truly, truly, I say to you, you will weep and lament,* but the world will rejoice; you will be sorrowful, but *your sorrow will turn to joy.* When a woman is in travail she has sorrow, because her hour has come; but when she is delivered of the child, she no longer remembers the anguish, for *joy* that a child is born into the world."

  F (16:22): "So you have sorrow now, but I will see you again and your hearts will rejoice, and no one will take your joy from you."

E' (16:23-24): "In that day you will ask nothing of me. *Truly, truly, I say to you,* if you ask anything of the Father, he will give it to you in my name. Hitherto you have asked nothing in my name; ask, and you will receive, that *your joy may be full."*

D' (16:25-28): "I have said this to you in figures; *the hour is coming* when I shall no longer speak to you in figures but tell you plainly of the Father. In that day you will ask in my name; and I do not say to you that I shall pray the Father for you; for the Father himself loves you, because you have loved me and have *believed that I came from the Father. I came from the Father and have come into the world; again, I am leaving the world and going to the Father."*

C' (16:29-30): His disciples said, "Ah, now you are speaking plainly, not in any figure! Now we know that you know all things, and need *none to question you;* by this *we believe* that *you came from God."*

B' (16:31-33b): Jesus answered them, "Do you now *believe? The hour is coming,* indeed it has come, *when you will be scattered,* every man to his home, and will leave me alone; yet I am not alone, for the Father is with me. *I have said this to you, that in me you may have peace.* In the world you have *tribulation;*

A' (16:33c): but *be of good cheer,* I have overcome the world."

A → A': Jesus' words of assurance →
Jesus' (stronger) word of assurance.[37]

B → B': Jesus prophesies the hour of persecution →
Jesus prophesies the hour of persecution to give them peace.

C → C': Jesus says he is going to God / disciples sorrow →
Jesus came from God / disciples believe.

D → D': Jesus soon going to the Father / ascension —
parousia →
Jesus soon going to the Father / incarnation —
ascension.

E → E': Your sorrow will turn to joy →
Your joy will be full.

F: Your joy will be everlasting.

The principle of intensification or heightening is unmistakable in these passages from chs. 15 and 16. The heart of the message is again expressed by the central element. Whether it contains a warning (15:21) or a promise (15:5a,11; 16:22), that element summarizes and provides meaning to the entire unit. Although this is less clear in ch. 14,[38] the same principles appear to be operative there as elsewhere.

Once again, the Spirit-Paraclete passages are omitted from the overall chiastic pattern. Gerhard and Ellis divide ch. 14 in such a way as to place the first of these passages at the center of 13:33-14:31. This was certainly the evangelist's intention, as shown by the structure of the Discourse as a whole. Yet once we work down to smaller chiastic units, those five passages appear to be extraneous. Each one represents something of an intrusion into its context, and the thought moves smoothly from verse to verse when they are omitted. Again this is more true of chs. 15 and 16 than of 14. The first Spirit saying, 14:15-17, begins with a theme found elsewhere in somewhat different form (cf. 15:10; 1 Jn 5:3), "If you love me, you will keep my commandments." Its effect in this context is to provide the conditions whereby Jesus' following promise is fulfilled: he will "come to you," not through his word (as in 14:23), nor through his return in glory (14:3,18(?), 28; 16:16ff), but through the presence of the Holy Spirit within the believing community. The second passage, 14:25-26, functions in a similar way. Here the Spirit will "remind" the disciples of Jesus' assurances and recall for them all of Jesus' teachings. The Paraclete will thus serve as a "Comforter," to reassure the disciples that Jesus' word will be fulfilled. It is well integrated into its context, since the very next word is "Peace!" In fact, if it were not for the greater independence that characterizes the Spirit-Paraclete logia in chs. 15-16, there would be no good reason to suggest that these first two passages might be interpolations.[39]

Turning to 15:26f, we find that this unit interrupts the sequence of thought from 15:18-25 to 16:1-4. There the theme is that of the world's hatred directed against the disciples, together with Jesus' consoling word that the disciples' suffering is because of the world's prior hatred of the Father and the Son. The saying in 15:26f, however, deals with the double witness to be offered by the Spirit and the disciples, a theme that occurs nowhere else in the Discourse.

From 15:18 through 16:4, and from 16:16 to the end of the chapter, concern is with the disciples' sense of abandonment and Jesus' assurance that despite their suffering they will be vindicated: their sorrow will turn to joy and their anxiety to peace, because Jesus has "overcome the world." If the third Spirit logion intrudes with the theme of mission, the fourth (16:7-11) introduces the theme of judgment accomplished by the Paraclete. And the final passage (16:12-14) describes the work of the Spirit of Truth, who will guide the disciples into all truth and reveal to them "the things to come." Here the Spirit acts not so much to recall or remind the disciples of Jesus' teachings during his earthly ministry (14:26), as to reveal to them the word of the risen and glorified Lord: "He will take what is mine and declare it to you." The forensic role of the Paraclete in 16:7-11 is juxtaposed with the revelatory function of the Spirit of Truth in 16:13-15. Since the risen Jesus serves as a "heavenly Paraclete" in 1 John 2:1,[40] it is reasonable to conjecture that the two figures were originally independent in early Johannine tradition, and became fused into one in light of the experience of Pentecost (Jn 20:22). Yet there is no doubt that both titles, "Paraclete" and "Spirit of Truth," refer in the Gospel to the Holy Spirit, as is clear from 14:16f and 14:26.

Whatever the origin of the five sayings, they effectively solve the *problem of Jesus' absence* by affirming that he and his word are present within the church community through the presence of the Spirit-Paraclete. The forensic role of intercession and judgment, originally ascribed to Jesus as the "heavenly Paraclete," was transferred to the Spirit, to produce the image of the "earthly Paraclete," who defends the faithful by "convicting" the world of sin, righteousness and judgment (16:8). This function combined with the revelatory or teaching role of the Spirit described variously in 16:13ff and 14:26[41] to produce the figure of the Spirit-Paraclete of ch. 14, where this divine presence "comforts" the faithful by dwelling within them and actualizing Jesus' words in their midst. This is further indication that ch. 14, including the Spirit logia, is later than chs. 15-16, and is based upon material such as they contain.

This partial reconstruction of the Spirit-Paraclete logia, and of the Discourse as a whole, is admittedly hypothetical.[42] We need not pursue the question here, except to point out the interesting fact that each Spirit logion is itself chiastic in shape. Again, this is more evident in chs. 15-16 than in ch. 14. Nevertheless, even in ch. 14 the form of the saying suggests that it was originally an independent unit that was reworked to fit into its present context. The precise shape of each logion appears more clearly in the Greek.

14:15-17,

A : εαν αγαπατε με, τας εντολας τας εμας τηρησετε

   B : καγω ερωτησω τον πατερα και αλλον παρακλητον δωσει
      υμιν, ινα μεθ' υμων εις τον αιωνα η,

   C : το πνευμα της αληθειας,

   B': ο ο κοσμος ου δυναται λαβειν, οτι ου θεωρει αυτο
      ουδε γινωσκει.

A': υμεις γινωσκετε αυτο, οτι παρ' υμιν μενει και εν υμιν εσται.

A: If you love me, you will keep my commandments.

   B: And I will pray the Father, and he will give you
      another Paraclete, to be with you forever,

   C: the Spirit of Truth,

   B': whom the world cannot receive because
      it neither sees him nor knows him;

A': you know him, for he dwells with you and will be in you.

A → A': To love Jesus is to keep his commandments
         [= to dwell in him, 14:21; 15:10] →
         To know the Spirit is to dwell in and with him.

B → B': You will receive the Spirit →
         The world will not receive the Spirit.

C: As the one who represents Jesus and recalls
         his teaching, the "Paraclete" is identified as
         the "Spirit of Truth."

14:25-26,

> A: ταυτα λελαληκα υμιν παρ᾽ υμιν μενων
>> B: ο δε παρακλητος, το πνευμα το αγιον,
>>> C: ο πεμψει ο πατηρ εν τω ονοματι μου,
>> B′: εκεινος υμας διδαξει παντα
> A′: και υπομνησει υμας παντα α ειπον υμιν.[43]

> A: These things I have spoken to you, while I am still with you.
>> B: But the Paraclete, the Holy Spirit,
>>> C: whom the Father will send in my name,
>> B′: he will teach you all things,
> A′: and bring to your remembrance all that I have said to you.

> A → A′: Jesus has taught the disciples →
>   The Spirit will teach the disciples.
> B → B′: The (teaching) Spirit →
>   He (εκεινος) will teach them "all things."
> C: The Spirit is sent by the Father in Jesus' name.

As tenuous as the parallels are, they do appear to have been consciously forged into concentric patterns. The other three logia are unquestionably chiastic.

15:26,

> A: οταν ελθη ο παρακλητος
>> B: ον εγω πεμψω υμιν παρα του πατρος,
>>> C: το πνευμα της αληθειας
>> B′: ο παρα του πατρος εκπορευεται,
> A′: εκεινος μαρτυρησει περι εμου.[44]

> A: When the Paraclete comes,
>> B: whom I shall send to you from the Father,
>>> C: the Spirit of Truth
>> B′ who proceeds from the Father,
> A′ He will bear witness to me.

A → A': The Spirit will come →
The Spirit will bear witness when he comes.
B → B': The Spirit is sent from the Father →
The Spirit proceeds from the Father.
C: He is the "Spirit of Truth" [the source of true witness].

16:7,

A: συμφερει υμιν ινα εγω απελθω.

B: εαν γαρ μη απελθω,

C: ο παρακλητος ουκ ελευσεται προς υμας

B': εαν δε πορευθω,

A': πεμψω αυτον προς υμας.[45]

A: It is to your advantage that I go away.

B: For if I do not go away,

C: the Paraclete will not come to you;

B': but if I go,

A': I will send him to you.

A → A': Jesus will depart →
Jesus will depart to send the Spirit.
B → B': If I do not go →
If I go.
C: Unless Jesus departs, the Spirit will not come.

[Vv. 8-11 are parallel statements detailing the forensic work of the Spirit as "Paraclete."]

16:12-14,

A: ετι πολλα εχω υμιν λεγειν, αλλ' ου δυνασθε βασταζειν αρτι

B: οταν δε ελθη εκεινος, το πνευμα της αληθειας,

C: οδηγησει υμας εν τη αληθεια παση

D: ου γαρ λαλησει αφ' εαυτου,

D': αλλ' οσα ακουσει λαλησει

C': και τα ερχομενα αναγγελει υμιν.

B': εκεινος εμε δοξασει,

A': οτι εκ του εμου λημψεται και αναγγελει υμιν.[46]

A: I have yet many things to say to you,
   but you cannot bear them now.

B: When the Spirit of Truth comes,

C: he will guide you into all the truth;

D: for he will not speak on his own authority,

D': but whatever he hears he will speak,

C': and he will declare to you the things that are to come.

B': He will glorify me,

A': for he will take what is mine and declare it to you.

A → A': Jesus' teaching cannot be borne now →
   Jesus' teaching will be given by the Spirit then.

B → B': The Spirit of Truth will come →
   He will come to glorify Jesus.

C → C': The Spirit will guide you →
   The Spirit will announce to you.

D → D': The Spirit will not speak of/from himself →
   The Spirit will speak of/from Jesus.

The structure of these passages, once again, suggests that they circulated in some independent form among the Johannine communities prior to their incorporation into the Gospel. They interrupt the sequence of thought of the Discourse, they possess their own "shape" distinct from that of their contexts, and they contain the only references in these chapters to the Spirit and his work. In addition, the image they offer of the "person" of the Spirit — a "hypostatic" image, in patristic language — is very different from the picture of

Spirit given elsewhere in the Gospel. Outside of the Farewell Discourse, Spirit appears rather as a divine power, that bestows authority upon Jesus (1:32f; 3:34), or acts as the source of spiritual regeneration for the believer (3:5f; 4:24; 6:63; 7:38f; 20:22).

There is no basic incompatibility between these two images of Spirit, within and outside of the Discourse. Nevertheless, this difference — coupled with evidence that the Spirit-Paraclete logia were intentionally given chiastic form — strongly suggests that these sayings existed independently in pre-Gospel tradition. If so, then we may conclude that they were inserted by the evangelist into the Discourse, in order to address the crisis occasioned by Jesus' delayed return. The disciples, and later members of the Johannine communities, face apparent abandonment by their Lord and very real persecution at the hands of hostile Jewish authorities. The Spirit-Paraclete sayings serve to assure them that Jesus' promise to return to his own followers is fulfilled through the presence among them of the Holy Spirit. Assuming the forensic role of Jesus, the Spirit as Paraclete will convict the "world" of sin and unrighteousness. As Spirit of Truth, he will call to remembrance Jesus' former teachings and serve as the vehicle for his further teaching regarding "things to come" (16:13f). This complex theme, however, is unique to these five passages. If they were removed — as they can be, without disturbing the flow of thought — the disciples' hope would rest not upon the presence and activity of the Spirit, but upon the living memory of Jesus' teachings and the promise of his future coming in glory. *The Spirit-Paraclete logia, in other words, provide an immediate and definitive solution to the "problem" of the delayed parousia.*

E. John 21: The Gospel Conclusion

The final chapter of St John's Gospel is considered by the vast majority of commentators to be secondary. It is, they hold, the product of a "final redactor" or editor, who also inserted passages such as the "eucharistic" text 6:51c-58, and perhaps the Prologue as well. If the chiastic structure of these passages demonstrates beyond reasonable doubt that they were composed as part of the original Gospel, can the same be said of chapter 21?

Elsewhere we have demonstrated that the usual objections to the authenticity of ch. 21 — based on apparent inconsistencies between it and the rest of the work — do not stand up to scrutiny. In fact, it can be shown that the final chapter completes in numerous ways themes of the preceding sections of the Gospel that otherwise would be left "hanging," wanting for resolution.[47] Without repeating that evidence, we can note what appears to be the decisive argument for the authenticity of ch. 21. This is based, once again, on the concentric structure of Johannine prose. Peter Ellis demonstrated that ch. 21 together with 20:19-31 make up the final "sequence" of the Gospel, sequence 21. He also showed that significant thematic and verbal parallels link this sequence with sequence 1 (1:19-51). Taking this analysis somewhat further, we can demonstrate that the two passages, sequences 1 and 21, in fact constitute a perfect example of inverted parallelism, with all the familiar characteristics of focusing or intensification from one parallel line to its prime complement. The paradigm is as follows:

A : (1:19-28) John the Baptist as witness

   B : (1:29-34) John bears witness to Jesus

      C : (1:35-39) Jesus to two disciples: "Come and see!"
         (theme: to follow Jesus)

         D : (1:40-42) Jesus calls Peter

            E : (1:43-46) In Galilee: Jesus calls five disciples,
               including Nathanael

               F : (1:47-49) Nathanael's confession
                  (Son of God / King of Israel)

                  G : (1:50f) The disciples will see greater
                     things: angels descending and
                     ascending on the Son of Man

                  G': (20:19-23) The disciples see the risen
                     Lord who bestows the Holy Spirit

               F': (20:24-31) Thomas' confession (Lord / God)

               E': (21:1-14) In Galilee: Jesus appears to five (?)[48]
                 disciples, including Nathanael

            D': (21:15-17) Jesus rehabilitates Peter

         C': (21:18f) Jesus to Peter: "Follow me!"
           (theme: to follow Jesus to death)

   B': (21:20-23) Jesus bears witness to the Beloved Disciple

A': (21:24) The Beloved Disciple as witness.

The parallels can also be illustrated by the following outline:

A : John the Baptist as witness →
A': The Beloved Disciple as witness

B : John the Baptist bears witness to Jesus →
B': Jesus bears witness to the Beloved Disciple

C : Jesus summons two unnamed disciples: "Come and see!" →
C': Jesus summons Peter: "Follow me!"

D : Jesus calls Peter →
D': Jesus rehabilitates Peter

E : Jesus calls the disciples (Galilee, Nathanael) →
E': Jesus appears to the disciples (Galilee, Nathanael)

F : Nathanael's confession (Son of God / King of Israel) →
F': Thomas' confession (Lord / God)

G : The disciples shall see greater things →
G': The disciples see the risen Lord.

Again the sense of the passage unfolds in a progressive spiral, from the extremities (A:A') toward the center (G:G'). From the dual witness of John the Baptist and the Beloved Disciple, the flow of meaning develops the theme of witness, the command to discipleship, the call and rehabilitation of the chief disciple. Progressing through the double confession, by Nathanael and by Thomas, its main focus is upon the disciples' direct experience of Jesus: seeing, they believe.

Yet within this spiraling movement, there is a heightening or increment from one line to the next, as the reader is drawn toward the primary affirmation of the two sequences: the disciple's belief is ultimately grounded in their personal experience, their vision, of the Resurrected Lord.

There is no question that John 20:19-29 (30-31) is an original and integral part of the evangelist's composition. Analysis of the Gospel into sequences, however, demonstrates that ch. 21, as much as

20:19ff, finds both verbal and thematic parallels in 1:19-51. It is inconceivable that a redactor could have created such intricate parallelism beginning with 21:1, even if he had been aware of such parallelism throughout the rest of the Gospel. The structural correspondence between the two segments, sequences 1 and 21, thus confirms that John 21 itself is an original and integral part of the composition, a genuine "conclusion" to themes introduced in chapter one.[49]

F. Addendum: The Book of Revelation

The "revelation of Jesus Christ" to John, the seer of Patmos, should almost certainly be attributed to someone other than the author of the Fourth Gospel. Nevertheless, Church tradition, coupled with internal evidence concerning vocabulary, syntax and theological ideas, support the "Johannine" character of Revelation, and we may therefore consider it under the present chapter.[50]

With virtually all other New Testament writings, Revelation contains many examples of simple inverted parallelism, such as

A: who opens and no one shall shut, /
B: who shuts and no one opens. //
(Rev 3:7)

Examples of authentic chiasmus can be found throughout the writing as well. Rev 9:17d-18, for example — describing the seer's vision of destroying horses — reads in translation like repetitious prose: "...and fire and smoke and sulphur issued from their mouths. By these three plagues a third of mankind was killed, by the fire and smoke and sulphur issuing from their mouths" (*RSV*). The original Greek text, however, is structured as a chiastic octacolon, with four parallel couplets (A-D // D'-A') centering about the key element (E).

A : εκ των στοματων αυτων

  B : εκπορευεται

    C : πυρ και καπνος και Θειον.

      D : απο των τριων πληγων τουτων

        E : απεκτανθησαν

      D': το τριτον των ανθρωπων,

    C': εκ του πυρος και του καπνου και του θειου

  B': του εκπορευομενου

A': εκ των στοματων αυτων.

A : Out of their mouths

   B : came forth

      C : fire and smoke and sulphur.

         D : By these *three* plagues

         E : was killed

         D': a *third* of mankind,

      C': by the fire and the smoke and the sulphur

   B': coming forth

A': out of their mouths.

The nightmare vision depicts the afflictions caused by the locust-horses, emissaries from hell, as apocalyptic counterparts to the plagues of Egypt. These three plagues (fire, smoke and sulphur), coming forth from the horses' mouths, kill a third of humankind. The parallelism, as the Greek text makes clear, focuses upon the murderous outcome of the beasts' mission: ἀπεκτάνθησαν.

A further example appears with a literal translation of Rev 14:9b-11.

A : (a) If anyone worships the beast and its image

    (b) and receives a mark

    (c) on his forehead or on his hand,

   B : he also shall drink of the wine of the wrath of God poured unmixed into the cup of his anger

      C : and he shall be tormented with fire and sulphur

         D : before holy angels

         D': and before the Lamb.

      C': And the smoke of their torment

   B': into the ages of ages rises up and does not cease day or night

A': (a) [for] the worshipers of the Beast and his image

    (b) and whoever receives the mark

    (c) of his name.

The relationship between each line of strophe I (and its prime complement in strophe II (D'-A') can be indicated schematically as follows:

A → A': The place of the mark (the head, the hand) →
The meaning of the mark (the Name of the Beast).

B → B': The content of the punishment →
The duration of the punishment.

C → C': The torment (future tense) →
The torment (present tense).

D → D': In the presence of the angels →
In the presence of the Lamb.

Notice the change from singular to plural and from future to present as the passage moves from strophe I to strophe II. The helical movement is evident with the intensification or heightening from the first line of each couplet to its prime complement. A → A: Those who bear the mark of the beast on the forehead or the hand are bearers of its Name: their identity is one with his, just as "Christians" bear the Name of the one with whom they identify in faith, love and obedience. B → B': Those who so identify with the beast will drink the cup of God's wrath; their punishment will endure forever. C → C': The future torment of "fire and sulphur" becomes a present reality ("realized eschatology"?), symbolized by the eternally rising smoke (cf. 9:17), a foul incense that represents the very opposite of the prayer of the saints (Ps. 140/141:2). The entire passage then focuses on the parallelism between D and D', with intensification or heightening evident in the contrast between "angels" and "the Lamb."

As a final example, we can note the vision of the New Jerusalem in Rev 21:1-4 (*RSV*).

A : Then I saw a new heaven and a new earth; for the first heaven
and the first earth had passed away, and the sea was no more.

B : And I saw the holy city, new Jerusalem, coming down
out of heaven from God, prepared as a bride adorned
for her husband;

C : and I heard a loud voice from the throne saying,
"Behold, the dwelling of God is with men.

C': He will dwell with them, and they shall be his people,
and God himself will be with them;

B': he will wipe away every tear from their eyes, and death
shall be no more, neither shall there be mourning
nor crying nor pain any more,

A': for the former things have passed away."

A → A': The first heaven and earth have passed away →
All former things have passed away.

B → B': New Jerusalem — joy (wedding feast) →
New existence — joy (no more death or suffering).

C → C': God's dwelling place is with humanity →
They will be his people(s); he will be "God with them."
[Notice the inversion in C'.]

These several examples from the Book of Revelation could easily be multiplied. They suffice to indicate, however, that as with other New Testament writings, detection of chiastic patterns can be of significant aid to the exegete insofar as they focus directly upon the major theme the author seeks to communicate.

Thanks to the spiraling or "helical" movement inherent in concentric parallelism, the reader is drawn step by step into the progressively "heightened" theme of the passage. From the inclusion (A:A') inward, the flow of thought intensifies, revealing progressively nuances of meaning that come to fullest expression at the "center," whether that center is a single line or a couplet. This helical structure, from Genesis to Revelation, illustrates as few other rhetorical devices can, how theological meaning comes to expression through literary form.

Returning to the five points mentioned at the beginning of this chapter, we can propose alternative solutions to various questions of Johannine interpretation that are suggested by the Gospel's structure.

(1) The chiastic shape of the Prologue, together with the insight of Gerhard and others that the passage serves as a virtual table of contents for the entire work, shows conclusively that it was not a secondary addition to the "Gospel proper" (1:19ff). While it may have been composed after the evangelist had completed his major literary effort, it is an integral and indispensable part of the entire work. The conjecture that the Prologue was originally an independent, perhaps even pre- or non-Christian, hymn with no direct relation to Johannine teaching, appears therefore to be untenable.

(2) The chiastic structure of the Gospel as a whole explains, far more satisfactorily than any displacement theory, the sequence of events related in chs. 4-7. While *aporeia* exist, they can be adequately explained as the result of the evangelist's efforts to integrate many

different elements of tradition into the overall composition, while providing the entire work with a consistent chiastic format. At the very least, it is clear that the sequence from the healing of ch. 5, through the triptych of ch. 6, and on to the allusion to the healing in ch. 7, is to be explained on the basis of the evangelist's artistry, and not as the haphazard result of an accident or carelessness.

(3) Chiasmus in the Farewell Discourse — however tenuous the structure may at times appear — also confirms that the flow of thought from ch. 14 through chs. 15-16 represents the thought of the evangelist and does not reflect some accident of transmission. While the conclusion to ch. 14 seems to lead directly to 18:1, and preclude the possibility of two further chapters of discourse plus a lengthy prayer, it, too, can be readily explained on the basis of structure. At the beginning of the unit (13:33), Jesus has predicted that Peter would indeed "go" where Jesus is going, namely to suffering and death. Balanced with this is Jesus' command to the disciples to "go forth," so that he might accomplish his mission by assuming his own suffering and death. Therefore, 14:31 is to be understood not in relation to 15:1ff (from which it is structurally distinct), but rather in relation to 13:33-36, its chiastic parallel.

(4) The Gerhard/Ellis analysis of the Gospel shows that ch. 21 is an original and integral part of the overall composition. If it be objected that the close of that chapter merely repeats 20:30f, then we can point to the "double ending" of the first Johannine epistle: 1 John 5:13, followed by vv. 14-21. Paul was partial to double endings as well, as evidenced by Rom 15:33ff (whatever the literary history of ch. 16); Phil 4:20ff; cf. 2 Thess 3:16f; and 1 Tim 6:16ff. The real argument for the original place of John 21 within the Fourth Gospel, however, is the parallel created between it and sequence 1 (1:19-51). Juxtaposing sequences 1 and 21, as Ellis has demonstrated,[51] makes strikingly clear the parallels, both verbal and conceptual, that exist between the two sections.[52] And our own analysis, given above, shows that sequences 1 and 21 form a single, perfectly balanced and highly intricate concentric pattern. Evidence of the chiastic structuring of the Gospel, then, puts the burden of proof for the inauthenticity or secondary character of ch. 21 squarely on the shoulders of those who consider it to be an "appendix."

(5) This leaves us with the question whether the Gospel was produced by a single hand or by a "school," including an original evangelist and one or more editors or redactors. The chiastic shape

of the Gospel suggests that this is perhaps a false question, in that it presents deceptive alternatives. There is no question that the work was composed on the basis of disparate units of tradition, including Jesus' own teachings together with kerygmatic and didactic elements which originated in the "post-Easter" Johannine community. Yet there can no longer be any question either that one principal author composed the Gospel in its present chiastic form. Whether we label him the "evangelist" or the "final redactor," his work was far more than that of mere compilation and editing.

Once again, it is the chiastic structure of the Fourth Gospel that reveals its author to be a figure of extraordinary literary creativity, theological vision, and spiritual depth. His skill at expressing the truths of his faith through consummate literary expression is sufficient in itself to justify the Church's veneration of him as "the Theologian."

ENDNOTES

[1]The most important discussion of the growth of the Fourth Gospel is still Raymond Brown's *The Community of the Beloved Disciple* (New York: Paulist, 1979), that complements the introduction to his two volume commentary in the Anchor Bible series, *The Gospel According to John* (New York: Doubleday, 1966 and 1970). See as well his *The Churches the Apostles Left Behind* (New York: Paulist, 1984), chs. 6-7. A more recent treatment of this question is by Urban C. von Wahlde, *The Earliest Version of John's Gospel. Recovering the Gospel of Signs* (Wilmington, DE: Glazier, 1989). This is an important study of the "earliest edition" of the Fourth Gospel, but it gives no consideration to studies by Malatesta, Talbert, Ellis or others who have analyzed the chiastic structure of the Gospel. See however Prof. von Wahlde's relatively positive review of Ellis's *The Genius of John*, in *BTB* XVI/1 (1986), 31-32.

[2]See his remarks on 6:36-40 (p. 276); 15:7-17 (p. 667); 16:16-33 (p. 728); 18:28-19:16a (p. 858f); and 19:16b-42 (p. 910f), in his two-volume commentary. Fr. Brown's analysis of chiasmus and its implications for an evangelist's theology is not restricted to the Fourth Gospel. See his perceptive article, "The Resurrection in Matthew (27:62-28:20)," *Worship* 64/2 (1990), p. 157-170.

[3]C. Talbert, "Artistry and Theology: An Analysis of the Architecture of John 1:19-5:47," *CBQ* 32 (1970) p. 341ff., and especially his *Reading John. A Literary and Theological Commentary on the Fourth Gospel and the Johannine Epistles* (NY: Crossroad, 1992).

[4]E. Malatesta, "The Literary Structure of John 17," *Bib* 52 (1971), p. 190ff.

[5]A. Di Marco, *Il Chiasmo nella Bibbia*, German translation, "*Der Chiasmus in der Bibel. 3 Teil*," *LingBibl* 39 (1978), p. 69ff.

[6]J. Welch, *Chiasmus in Antiquity*, p. 239ff.

[7]P.F. Ellis, *The Genius of John*.

[8]J. Staley, "The Structure of John's Prologue: Its Implications for the Gospel's Narrative Structure," *CBQ* 48 (1986), p. 241ff.

[9]R.A. Culpepper, "The Pivot of John's Prologue," *NTS* 27 (1980), p. 1-31.

[10]I. de la Potterie, *The Hour of Jesus* (New York: Alba House, 1989), p. 22-25, for example, discusses the chiastic form of the Johannine passion narrative, 18:12-19:42.

[11]Vv. 12-17 (omitted in Welch's text).

[12]J. Welch, *Chiasmus in Antiquity*, p. 240-42.

[13]John J. Gerhard, S.J., *The Literary Unity and the Compositional Method of the Fourth Gospel*, dated March 25, 1981, but completed the preceding December.

[14]It should be remembered that the division of the Bible into chapters was made only in 1226 by Stephen Langton, Archbishop of Canterbury (versification is attributed to the Dominican scholar Santes Pagninus, 1528).

[15]M.E. Boismard, *Le prologue de S. Jean* (Paris: Cerf, 1953).

[16]Peder Borgen, "Targumic Character of the Prologue of John," *NTS* 16 (1970), p. 291-293; discussed by Welch, *Chiasmus in Antiquity*, p. 239f.

[17]Ellis, *The Genius of John*, p. 20.

[18]This is essentially Boismard's analysis, *Le prologue de S. Jean*, p. 106ff. This "parabolic" structure reflects the movement of the descending-ascending Son of Man: cf. the inverted parallelism of 16:28, "I came from the Father / and have come into the world; // again I am leaving the world / and going to the Father."

[19]For this arrangement and for others in this section, I owe special thanks to Michael Breck.

[20]This rendering simply follows the *RSV*, although it does some violence to the parallels as they appear in the Greek original. A similar arrangement can be found in the fine study by R.A. Culpepper, "The Pivot of John's Prologue." Culpepper also locates the focus of the prologue in v. 12b, "he gave them power to become children of God." His analysis better respects the Greek word order (12a: οσοι ... ελαβον αυτον // 12c: τοις πιστευουσιν) and certainly reflects the evangelist's main theme. He then finds a thematic contrast between v. 11 and v. 13: "his own (Israel)" // "his own (believers)." The remainder of his schema (p. 16) conforms to Boismard's analysis.

[21]The parallelism here is thematic rather than verbal. A → A': The Word becomes flesh for the express purpose of revealing "grace and truth" (as 1:17b). B → B': his making his abode among us evokes by the verb εσκηνωσεν theophanies of the Old Covenant (cf. the "shekinah"), whose glory merely foreshadowed that of the "only Son from the Father." (The preposition παρα in B' perhaps echoes the thought of incarnation expressed in B: he must come from the Father in order to dwell among us.) The focus is upon our perception of his glory, in contrast to those who are not "born of God."

[22]In the first triplet, the focus is upon the verb κεκραγεν, signaling a word of revelation in Johannine tradition (cf. 7:28,37; 12:44, etc.). In the second, the "before-after" motif of A:A' is heightened in B by a shift from chronology to status.

[23]It is interesting, but probably coincidental, that the Prologue begins and ends with an A:B:B':A' pattern. Similar variety in patterns appears throughout the individual units of the Gospel. The fivefold structure holds consistently on the level

of macro-units, less often on that of micro-units.

[24]Technical terms in v. 18 include μονογενης ("unique" Son, implying as in the older translations, "only-begotten") and ο ων (the divine name revealed to Moses on Sinai, Ex 3:14, LXX: Εγω ειμι ο ων). The (original) reading μονογενης Θεος implies a heightening relative to 1:1f, θεος ην ο λογος: whereas the Logos is "oriented towards (προς) God" and likened to him (the anarthrous θεος), the "Only Son" is designated "God" by these two expressions that serve as christological titles in Johannine theology (cf. 1:14; 3:16, 18; and the self-designation εγω ειμι). For a somewhat different, recent interpretation of this passage, that argues for the reading μον. υιος, see Theodore P. Letis, "The Gnostic Influences on the Text of the Fourth Gospel: John 1:18 in the Egyptian Manuscripts," *The Bulletin of the Institute for Reformation Biblical Studies* (Fort Wayne, Ind.), 1:1 (1989), p. 4-7.

[25]This important theme runs throughout the first part of the Gospel and almost certainly reflects tension between members of the Johannine community and disciples of John the Baptist, who recognized in their own master the awaited messiah or prophet from God (cf. Acts 19:1ff, which shows that groups of itinerant Baptist disciples were present in Ephesus during Paul's ministry in that area).

[26]See R. Brown, *The Gospel According to John I-XII*, p. 312.

[27]Other aporias include the conclusion of ch. 14 and its relation to chs. 15-17; the inconsistencies in Jesus' statements regarding where he is going, 13:36 and 16:5; and a further inconsistency between 12:36 and 12:44ff. Furthermore, there is a frequent shift in terminology (from Pharisees, scribes, etc. to "the Jews"; from "signs" to "works"). The chiastic shape of the Gospel, of course, does not explain all of these; they are to be explained rather as remnants of primitive tradition that have been woven into the Gospel in its final form.

[28]This latter phrase is omitted by sy[c]. As we have noted, it is a recognized "formula of revelation" throughout the Old Testament and in earliest Christian tradition, and is certainly original. See L. Köhler, "Die Offenbarungsformel 'Fürchte dich nicht' im Alten Testament," *STZ* (1919), p. 33ff.

[29]"Die Eucharistische Rede im Johannes-Evangelium," *ZNW* 47 (1956), p. 161-169.

[30]Paul Gächter, "Die Form der eucharistischen Rede Jesu," *ZKT* 59 (1935), p. 419-441, demonstrated this division with his analysis of the rhythmic patterns in the discourse. He did not, however, consider its overall chiastic structure. Talbert, *Reading John*, p. 134-139, proposes a similar analysis of the first of these passages, but includes v. 48 as an inclusion with v. 35a, "I am the bread of life." His center (F – F') is then vv. 39-40. This obliges him, however, to include all of vv. 41-43 (our F:G:H:G':F') into E'. It also obscures the more obvious parallels in his analysis of the following passage, 6:49-58.

[31]Vv. 39 and 40 are variants of the same theme. Although they seem to destroy the chiastic symmetry, in fact they balance very well with v. 44 (E'). Both parallel elements (E:E') concern the Father's will to save those whom he draws to the Son, that the Son might "raise them up at the last day."

[32]The parallelism between D and D' concerns "doing the Father's will." Jesus has come down from heaven for this purpose; those who are taught by the prophets are in fact taught by the Father himself (who speaks through the prophets) to do his will.

[33]*The Genius of John*, p. 210. See Talbert's reworking of these sections in *Reading John*, pp. 200ff.

[34]*The Gospel According to John*, II, p. 667f.

[35]"The Literary Structure of John 17."

[36]This widely accepted point does not mean that the teaching of Jesus in the Farewell Discourse – or elsewhere in the Gospel – is simply the product of post-Easter reflection by members of the Johannine community and the evangelist in particular. The author was unquestionably convinced that the risen Lord continues to address the Church through the inspirational activity of the Spirit of Truth (see below on 16:13f), of whom he, the evangelist, was a principal spokesman.

[37]In A, Jesus' motive in telling the disciples of coming persecutions and of his absence is "to keep you from falling away." In A', his word of encouragement, "Be of good cheer," ties in with the theme of rejoicing, and is reinforced by his assurance that he has "overcome the world."

[38]This would seem to reinforce the widespread view that ch. 14 is the "final version" of the Farewell Discourse, composed by the evangelist from pre-existing units of tradition such as found in chs. 15-16. Presumably those originally independent units were preserved in tighter chiastic form to facilitate memorization and transmission.

[39]Hans Windisch, "Die fünf johanneische Parakletsprüche," *Festgabe für A. Jülicher*, Tübingen, 1927, p. 110-137; ET: *The Spirit-Paraclete in the Fourth Gospel* (Philadelphia: Fortress, 1968), p. 1-26, was the first to put forth detailed arguments for the independence of these logia. His thesis has not received wide acceptance. It falters especially in its assertion that the Paraclete sayings were of pre-Christian origin and were taken up by the Gospel writer with the effect of transforming the image of the Spirit from an impersonal force to a personal, abiding presence. Paul, too, knew of the "personal" aspect of the Spirit (1 Cor 2:10f; Rom 8:26f); that is no Johannine invention. This fact, however, does not invalidate Windisch's argument that the Spirit-Paraclete logia were originally independent units of tradition which were taken up and reshaped by the evangelist.

[40]Cf. Rom 8:27,34, where Paul describes both the Spirit and Christ as heavenly intercessors.

[41]A similar dual role is attributed to the Spirit in Mk 13:11.

[42]It can, however, be further substantiated by a closer examination of the Discourse. The relevant evidence will appear in the second volume of our study *The Spirit of Truth*, to be published by St. Vladimir's Seminary Press, Crestwood, NY.

[43]Read εγω with v. 27, to produce an inverted parallelism:
εγω ειρηνην αφιημι υμιν,
ειρηνην την εμην διδωμι υμιν.

[44]V. 27 is an expansion of the original saying, to link the witness to be borne by the disciples with that of the Spirit.

[45]Note the repetition of απελθω in A-B, and of προς υμας in C-A'. Against P[66], the parallelism shows B'-A' to be original.

[46]Like 14:15 and 14:25, 16:12 is a preliminary observation that introduces the reference to the Spirit. V. 15 should probably be eliminated (with P[66]) as an addition based on 17:10, τα εμα παντα σα εστιν / και τα σα εμα. Note the inversion from D

to D', and the repetition of αναγγελει υμιν in C'-A'.

[47]J. Breck, "John 21: Appendix, Epilogue or Conclusion?", *SVTQ* 36/1-2 (1992), pp. 27-49.

[48]See "John 21," p. 37 n. 18, for the number of disciples in this passage.

[49]A great deal of evidence concerning the place of ch. 21 in the overall plan of the Gospel further confirms its authenticity. This is given in detail, together with other examples of Johannine chiasmus, in our article, "John 21: Appendix, Epilogue or Conclusion?"

[50]This section is excerpted from our article "Chiasmus in Revelation," in *The Revelation of John*, (Proceedings of the Orthodox Biblical Society, Leukosia, 26 Sept. - 3 Oct., 1991), Ιερα Αρχιεπισκοπη Κυπρου, 1991, pp. 247-251 (in Greek).

[51]*The Genius of John*, p. 310-312.

[52]See P. F. Ellis, "The Authenticity of John 21," *SVTQ* 36/1-2 (1992), pp. 17-25. Ellis states: "Any one who places Jn 1:19-51 and 21:1-25 in opposite columns will notice immediately the repetition of such names as Simon, Son of John, Jesus, Son of God, Nathanael, and the two unnamed disciples; such places as Cana and Galilee; such expressions as: follow me, who are you, whom you do not know, bear witness, turned and saw following; such words as: remain, word, and wrote. In addition to reechoing so many names, places, expressions, and words, the author reechoes in 21:24 the 'we' of the Prologue (1:14, 16) and the significant description of Jesus, the revealer, being in the 'bosom' (κολπος) of the Father (1:18)."

4. THE PAULINE EPISTLES

A. First Corinthians

Our chief concern thus far has been to demonstrate the presence of chiastic patterns in the gospel narratives and discourses. The letters of the apostle Paul, which predate the gospels, also employ chiasmus both in micro-units and in their overall structure. These patterns have been examined at length by Lund, Welch, Jeremias, Ellis, and many others. Our purpose here is simply to note some of their findings and to offer an occasional analysis of our own.

A. First Corinthians

Paul's penchant for the A:B:A' format has long been observed.[1] In Part I we referred to the triptych formed by 1 Corinthians 12-14, with complementary discussions of spiritual gifts flanking the central theme of love. Nils Lund demonstrated that this global pattern can also be read as a chiastic pentacolon:

A : Introduction: The gifts and those that have them:
the Spirit (11:34b-12:3).

    B : The diversity and unity of the spiritual gifts:
the principle (12:4-30).

        C : The gifts and the graces (12:31-14:1a).

    B': The diversity and unity of the spiritual gifts:
the application (14:1b-36).

A': Conclusion: The leaders and the gifts: the Lord (14:37-40).[2]

While Lund made his point that Paul thought and wrote using the literary technique we have described as concentric parallelism, he was less successful in working out the chiastic outline of the letter as a whole. Peter Ellis divides the letter into five major parts, the first three of which are subdivided according to the A:B:A' model.[3] John Welch finds all of 1 Corinthians to be organized as a chiastic octacolon, whose parts III, IV, IV' and III' comprise smaller units also arranged in the threefold A:B:A' pattern. His major divisions are as follows:

I :   Introduction (1:1-9)

  II :   Divisions in the Church regarding Leadership:
     Resolution in Christ crucified (1:10-2:5)

    III :   Man is led by the Spirit of God (2:6-4:21)

      IV :   Sexual Problems within the Church (5:1-7:40)

      IV':   Idolatry within the Church (8:1-11:34)

    III':   Man is led by the Gifts of the Spirit (12:1-14:40)

  II':   Divisions in the Church regarding Resurrection:
     Resolution in Christ resurrected (15:1-58)

I':   Conclusion (16:1-24).[4]

This arrangement is particularly helpful in balancing the two major theological issues of the epistle, II and II'. The breakdown of individual parts, however, is somewhat less convincing, although it does succeed in demonstrating a harmonious distribution of themes according to chiastic principles.

There can be little question that individual micro-units of 1 Corinthians are elaborately organized in concentric parallelism. Paul's contrast between the "spiritual" and "unspiritual" or "natural" person in 2:14-16 is typical. The following is a literal translation:

A :   But an *unspiritual person* does not receive *the things*
    of the Spirit of God,

  B :   for they are *folly* to him,

    C :   and he is not able to *know* (them)

      D :   because spiritually they are *judged.*

        E :   Now the spiritual person judges all things,

      D':   yet he himself by no one is *judged.*

    C':   "For who has *known* the mind of the Lord

  B':   so as to *instruct* him?"

A':   Now *we* have *the mind* of Christ.

The contrast here is between "them" (natural or unspiritual persons) and "us" (who have the "mind of Christ"). The quotation from Isaiah 40:13, referring to the absolute unknowability of God's mind, is applied to Paul's readers, precisely because they have that "mind of Christ." Despite the moral corruption and liturgical decadence evident in the Corinthian community, the apostle can affirm that they are "spiritual persons," called to discern or judge "all things," just as he can address them as "sanctified in Christ Jesus," and "called to be saints" (1:2). The source of their knowledge, and the authority behind their "judgment," lies in their reception of the divine Spirit, who alone bestows the gift of discernment. A little farther on, in 3:16f, Paul can repeat this theme with a fresh emphasis. The structure appears most clearly in the Greek:

A : ουκ οιδατε οτι ναος θεου εστε

   B : και το πνευμα του θεου οικει εν υμιν;

      C : ει τις τον ναον του θεου φθειρει,

      C': φθειρει τουτον ο θεος

   B': ο γαρ ναος του θεου αγιος εστιν,

A': οιτινες εστε υμεις.

A : Do you not know that *you are* the *temple* of God?

   B : and the *Spirit* of God *dwells* in you?

      C : If anyone *destroys* the temple of *God*,

      C': *God* will *destroy* that person.

   B': For the *temple* of God is *holy*,

A': and *you are* (that *temple*).

A' is an emphatic repetition of A, intensifying by means of the intervening versets the original affirmation, "You are God's temple." B' represents the conclusion to be drawn from B: because the Spirit dwells in you and you are the temple of God, therefore that temple *must* be holy. The parallel is established between the affirmation of B and the exhortation implied by B'. Grounds for the exhortation are then provided by the center: the threat of "destruction" that hangs over the heads of those who fail to preserve the sanctity of their body, which is the temple of God (cf 6:19).[5]

A similar contrast, this time between "physical" and "spiritual" athletes, appears in 9:23-27.

A (23):   I do all things for the sake of the gospel,
          that *I may share* in its blessings (γενωμαι).

  B (24):   Do you not know that in a race all the runners
          compete, but only one receives the prize? So *run*
          that you may *obtain* it.

    C (25a):   Every athlete *exercises self-control* in all things.

      D (25b):   They do it to receive a *perishable* wreath

      D' (25c):   but we an *imperishable* one.

    C' (26):   Therefore I do *not run aimlessly;* I do not box
          as one beating the air.

  B' (27a):   but I *pommel* my body and *subdue* it,

A' (27b):   lest after preaching to others I *myself become*
          disqualified (γενωμαι).

Here again the parallels are both verbal and conceptual:

A → A':   That I may share in the reward →
          That I not be deprived of the reward.

B → B':   General ascetic discipline →
          Paul's ascetic discipline.

C → C':   General self-control and purpose →
          Paul's self-control and purpose.

D → D':   Their perishable reward →
          Our imperishable reward.

As an addition to the number of larger chiastic units discovered by Lund and others, we can point to chapters 10 and 11. Here the conceptual center is the enigmatic statement of 11:10, "a woman ought to have authority (εξουσια, signifying a head covering, a veil) on her head because of the angels." Presumably this reflects the belief that angels are responsible for order (ταξις) within the church. Proper "order" requires that a woman's head be covered, just as a man's be uncovered.[6] However antiquated (and sexist) this entire passage may sound to modern ears, its point is not the subjection of women but the need for all members to respect order, discipline and authority within the Christian community.

A (10:1-13): Spiritual food and drink of Israel.

  B (10:14-22): The Body and Blood of Christ.

    C (10:23-11:1): Eat and drink to the glory of God in the neighbor's house.

      D (11:2): Traditions.

        E (11:3-5): Man prays with his head uncovered, woman with her head covered.

          F (11:6): A woman should veil herself when praying.

            G (11:7-9): Woman created from and for man.

              H (11:10): Woman should cover her head because of the angels.

            G' (11:11f): Interdependence (equality?) of men and women.

          F' (11:13): A woman should not pray with her head uncovered.

        E' (11:14f): Man wears his hair short, woman wears her hair long.

      D' (11:16): Traditions.

    C' (11:17-22): Eat and drink to the glory of God in church.

  B' (11:23-26): The Body and Blood of the Lord.

A' (11:27-34): Spiritual food and drink of the Church.

The link Paul establishes between sacramental communion (A:B // B':A') and proper decorum becomes clear by virtue of the helical movement that culminates in the central affirmation, 11:10. Participation in the body and blood of the Lord, like the obligation for a woman to cover her head during public worship, is a function of the "order" that should govern every aspect of ecclesial life (cf. 14:40).

A → A': The spiritual food and drink of Israel → The spiritual food and drink of the Church.

B → B': Participation in the body and blood of Christ → Institution of the Lord's Supper [i.e., the tradition in which communion is grounded].

C → C': Eating and drinking in the house of the neighbor → Eating and drinking in the Church of God.

D → D': Traditions Paul handed on →
      The specific practice regarding women.

E → E': The practice →
      Its reasons ("nature itself").

F → F': The threat: "Let her be shorn (or) wear a veil" →
      The reasoning: "Judge for yourselves..."

G → G': Subordination of woman to man →
      Interdependence of woman and man.

H: The reason why a woman should cover her head
      while praying is divinely ordained and established.

This larger unit, moreover, is itself composed of chiastically structured elements.[7]

11:2-7,
[V. 2 is an introduction, a further example of anacrusis]
I commend you because you remember me in everything and maintain the traditions even as I have delivered them to you.

A (3): But I want you to understand that the head of every man
      is Christ, the head of a woman is her husband, and the head
      of Christ is God.

B (4): Any man who prays or prophesies with his head
      covered dishonors his head,

C (5a): but any woman who prays or prophesies
      with her head unveiled dishonors her head —

D (5b): it is the same as if her head were shaven.

E (6a): For if a woman will not veil herself,
      then she should cut off her hair;

D' (6b): but if it is disgraceful for a woman
      to be shorn or shaven,

C' (6c): let her wear a veil.

B' (7a): For a man ought not to cover his head,

A' (7b): since he is the image and glory of God;
      but woman is the glory of man.

11:8-12,

A (8): For man was not made from woman, but woman from man.

B (9): Neither was man created for woman,
      but woman for man.

> C (10): That is why a woman ought to have a veil
> on her head, because of the angels.

> B' (11): Nevertheless, in the Lord woman is not independent
> of man nor man of woman;

> A' (12): for as woman was made from man, so man is now born
> of woman. And all things are from God.

11:13-16,

> A (13): Judge for yourselves: is it proper for a woman to pray
> to God with her head uncovered?

> B (14): Does not nature itself teach you that for a man
> to wear long hair is degrading to him,

> C (15a): But if a woman has long hair, it is her pride
> (lit: her glory)?

> B' (15b): For her hair is given to her for a covering.

> A' (16): If any one is disposed to be contentious, we recognize
> no other practice, nor do the churches of God.

Chiastic structuring may indicate that a given passage was originally an independent unit of tradition that circulated alone or in another context in the oral stage of transmission.[8] This is certainly not the case here, since each element constitutes a crucial segment of Paul's overall argument. These passages (and we could point to many others here and elsewhere in the apostle's writings) indicate rather that Paul "thought chiastically," that his process of reasoning was shaped and given expression by the principles of concentric parallelism. Even in the heat of debate he draws upon those principles — not so much as a "literary technique," in any formal sense, but as a spontaneous or intuitive means of creating a conceptual framework to shape his thoughts and defend his position.[9]

There can be little question, however, that Paul consciously and intentionally gave a chiastic structure to the whole of this epistle. That fact, illustrated by the following outline, offers what seems to be irrefutable proof that 1 Corinthians is not a patchwork of answers to various practical questions with no particular order, as many commentators have held. To the contrary, it is as carefully and purposefully crafted as any of the apostle's other writings, including the letter to the Romans.

A (1:1-9):   Opening greetings.

B (1:10-17):   Parties create division [Stephanas named].

C (1:18-2:5):   Christ crucified.

D (2:6-16):   Revelations of the Spirit.

E (3:1-4:21):   Ministries of the apostles.

F (5:1-6:19):   Abuses in the Body (Church).

G (7:1-40):   Women (in the community).

H (8:1-13):   Freedom: the obligation
not to scandalize others.

I (9:1-2):   Paul as an apostle is
free in Christ.

H' (9:3-11:1):   Freedom: the obligation
to serve others.

G' (11:2-16):   Women (in worship).

F' (11:17-34):   Abuses in the Body
(Lord's Supper).

E' (12:1-31a):   Ministries of the people.

D' (14:1-40):   Manifestations of the Spirit.

C' (15:1-58):   Christ resurrected.[10]

B' (16:1-18):   Jerusalem collection creates unity
[Stephanas named].

A' (16:19-24):   Closing greetings.

While this outline offers a clear and easily verifiable analysis of the entire letter, it contains one important peculiarity: the omission of the "hymn to love," 12:31b-13:13. Commentators have often noted the fact that this passage interrupts the flow of thought from ch. 12 to ch. 14, each of which speaks of the practical application of spiritual gifts within the community. It has even been suggested that ch. 13 was an independent hymn designed to depict the love manifested by Jesus Christ, which serves as a paradigm for every relationship between Christians. Couple this with the fact that Paul regards love as a *fruit* of the Spirit rather than as a *charisma* or gift of the Spirit (Gal 5:22), and it appears indeed that 1 Cor 13 is something of an extraneous element within the epistle as a whole.

Nonetheless, there is ample evidence that Paul himself incorporated the passage into its present context. An inclusion is formed by 12:23b and 14:1, "Earnestly desire the higher gifts" // "Earnestly desire the spiritual gifts." The "higher gift," it could be argued, refers not to love, but to *prophecy*, which, with the problem of speaking in tongues, constitutes the subject matter of ch. 14. The transition, however, is provided by 12:31b-14:1a, "And I will show you a still more excellent way: Make love your aim." This reads like an initial interpolation that interrupts the flow from tongues to prophecy in chs. 12-14. It may be supposed, then, that ch. 13 was inserted into this envelope as a sublime example of that "more excellent way."

However that may be, it should be noted that ch. 13 itself displays a chiastic pattern:

A (12:31): Seek the greatest gifts, the greatest way.

   B (13:1-2): Without love I know and understand nothing.

      C (13:3): Without love, no gift has enduring value.

         D (13:4-7): The qualities of love (positive →
           negative → positive).

      C' (13:8-11): Without love, no spiritual gift has
        enduring value.

   B' (13:12): With love I shall know and understand fully.

A' (13:13): The greatest gift/way is love.[11]

The language and style of this passage are recognizably Pauline. Whether it was composed for its present context or taken over from some other source is another and relatively unimportant question. The argument that it represents an interpolation, however, is strongly reinforced by the fact that the chiastic center of the letter as a whole focuses upon the theme of *freedom*. Whether the issue is sexual behavior, food, comportment in worship, or the hope of resurrection, true freedom in Christ necessitates discernment and discipline, that "all things be done decently and in order" (14:40).

B. Romans

While the chiastic units in 1 Corinthians 11 are integral parts of Paul's original argument, the same can not be so easily affirmed of a rather curious passage in Romans 8 that has long puzzled commentators. Vv. 9-11 are arranged as follows in a literal translation:

A: You are not in (the) flesh but in (the) Spirit if indeed (the) Spirit of God dwells in you.

    B: If anyone does not have (the) Spirit of Christ, one does not belong to him (literally: is not of him).

        C: But if Christ is in you [plural], your body is dead because of sin but your spirit is alive because of righteousness.

    B': If the Spirit of him who raised Jesus from the dead dwells in you,

A': he who raised Christ [Jesus] from the dead will make your mortal bodies live through the indwelling of his Spirit in you.

A → A': You are in the Spirit who dwells in you →
You will have life through the indwelling Spirit.

B → B': (antithesis) Does not have the Spirit of Christ →
Does have the Spirit of God.

C: Your body is dead; your spirit is alive.

Here the conceptual or thematic focal point is the (characteristically un-Pauline) body-spirit contrast, based upon the (typically Pauline) antithesis "death through sin / life through righteousness." The peculiar alternating of titles "Spirit of God → Spirit of Christ → Christ → Spirit of (God)" is perhaps to be explained by inclusion and the theme of "indwelling." The "Spirit of God" appears at either end of the passage as the divine power that gives life in the present age to those in whom it dwells. The "Spirit of Christ" (a title that appears only here in Paul[12]), however, is equivalent to "Christ" (as shown by 2 Cor 3:18) and the two are used interchangeably, as are "Jesus Christ," "Christ Jesus," "Christ," and "the Son of God" in Galatians 2:16-21. The significant point is that thanks to the chiastic structuring, C (Rom 8:10) clearly emerges as the pivotal theme about which the other elements are symmetrically arranged by direct (A:A') and antithetical (B:B') parallelism.

The hypothesis that Romans 8:9-11 was originally an independent unit is supported by the antithesis between "body" and "spirit," whereas the surrounding context (8:2-8; 12ff) contrasts "flesh" and "spirit"; and by the fact that vv. 9-11 can be deleted from their context without disturbing the flow of thought from v. 8 to v. 12.

To this should be added the double observation that Rom. 8:9 speaks of being "in the Spirit," whereas 8:1 addresses those who are "in Christ Jesus"; and that the overall theme of vv. 9-11 is rather "Christ / the Spirit of God *in you*," rather than "you in him." The "in you" theme is a common Pauline motif (Gal 2:20; Col 1:27). Nevertheless, it does not fit easily into the present context of Romans 8. For there emphasis is upon the moral obligations of one "set free from the law of sin and death," who is "led by the Spirit of God," having received "the Spirit of sonship." In vv. 9-11, on the other hand, the key element is the *indwelling* of Christ and the Spirit in the believer.

We have here, then, a chiastically structured unit whose theme is life through the indwelling of Christ and the Spirit, life grounded in Christ's resurrection from the dead. This is a *kerygmatic* formulation that has evidently been inserted into a passage which is essentially *hortatory*. The effect is to provide the first part of chapter 8 with a threefold structure of A (vv. 1-8), B (vv. 9-11), A' (vv. 12-17).

Taking the analysis another step, we find that 8:1-17 itself exhibits a chiastic structure when vv. 9-11 are excluded. This further substantiates the independence of these latter three verses.

8:1-17,

> A (1):   We have no condemnation in Christ.
>> B (2):   Freedom in the Spirit.
>>> C (3f):   Son of God / Spirit.
>>>> D (5-7):   To set the mind on the flesh is death.
>>>>> E (8):   Those in the flesh cannot please God.
>>>> D' (12f):   To live according to the flesh is death.
>>> C' (14):   Spirit / sons of God.
>> B' (15f):   Sonship in the Spirit.
> A' (17):   We are fellow heirs with Christ.

A further example of Pauline chiasmus appears in Romans 10:9-10. Jeremias analyzed this passage as a:b:b:a.[13] His conviction that inverted parallelism is the primary feature of chiasmus led him to miss the focal point of this unit, which is the affirmation, "you shall be saved."

A : εαν ομολογησης εν τω στοματι σου κυριον Ιησουν

   B : και πιστευσης εν τη καρδια σου οτι ο θεος αυτον ηγειρεν εκ νεκρων,

      C : σωθηση.

   B': καρδια γαρ πιστευεται εις δικαιοσυνην,

A': στοματι δε ομολογειται εις σωτηριαν.

A : If you confess with your mouth that Jesus is Lord

   B : and believe in your heart that God raised him from the dead,

      C : you will be saved.

   B': For a person believes with the heart and is justified,

A': and confesses with the mouth and is saved.

The characteristic pivot (C) of the passage allows the reader to focus on its primary message: neither our confession nor our faith saves us, but *God's response* bestows on us the gift of salvation. The initiative and the saving power remain his.

As to the shape of the Epistle as a whole, no clear-cut chiastic pattern has yet emerged. A single basic theme is developed throughout the work: less "justification by faith" than "the righteousness of God." The first seven chapters depict essentially the human predicament, together with its solution in Christ. Our inability to obtain righteousness under the Law because of our bondage to sin leads inevitably to death. The righteousness that bestows life is God's free, unmerited gift in Jesus Christ, offered to Jew and Gentile alike. Chapters 9-15 then develop the practical aspects of the life of faith, beginning with the problem of the Jews' rejection of Christ and moving to an exhortation to follow the example of Christ's own righteousness (15:1-13).

Chapter 8 in this scheme represents something of a hinge, in that it demonstrates how true righteousness derives from "life in the Spirit." Through the Spirit, eschatological hope is proleptically realized within the community of faith: those who live "according to the Spirit" obtain adoption as sons of God and share in the ultimate hope that nothing "will be able to separate us from the love of God in Christ Jesus our Lord" (8:39). Moving toward the extremities, Paul's thought in ch. 7 — describing the plight of "one under the law" yet redeemed by Christ, who delivers the believer "from this body of death" — balances with his agonized analysis in chs. 9-11 of the plight of Israel, excluded now from the promises of God, but destined ultimately to be saved once "the full number of the Gentiles come in" (11:25f). Ch 6, "let not sin reign in your mortal bodies" (v. 12), then finds an echo in ch. 12, with its admonition to "present your bodies as a living sacrifice" (v. 1). The moral imperatives of chs. 13-15 in effect detail the responsibilities of those who are "justified by faith" and "have peace with God through our Lord Jesus Christ" (5:1), thus balancing the theoretical discussion of justification (chs. 1-5) with its concrete expression in the "justified life," the life of righteousness.

Viewed in this way, Romans is arguably chiastic. The parallels, however, are too general and tenuous to allow the conclusion that Paul consciously and systematically employed concentric parallelism in its composition. Yet once again it appears that the biblical author has drawn intuitively on the principles of chiasmus, in order to develop doctrinal themes and ethical exhortations into a finely crafted theological treatise.

C. Philippians

An interesting example of the present progress being made in the discovery of chiastic passages in the New Testament is offered by two studies that appeared in the early 1980s. In his section on the Pauline epistles, John Welch concluded that Philippians "contains no overall chiastic structure," and that the few shorter chiastic passages that do occur "are for the most part relatively insignificant and unremarkable."[14] Shortly thereafter, Peter Ellis demonstrated that Philippians, like most of Paul's writings, is structured on the A:B:A' model, and he included a list of parallel phrases from A (1:1-3:1) and A' (4:4-23) that clearly substantiate his claim. Furthermore, he showed that themes and expressions in ch. 3 find such numerous correspondences in the rest of the letter as to undermine the widely accepted hypothesis that Philippians is a composite of two or three originally separate writings.[15]

Chiasmus in Antiquity, edited by Professor Welch, is a remarkable achievement. Its several articles taken together constitute a milestone in modern literary criticism and should be compulsory reading for anyone seriously interested in the "shape" of biblical language. Welch's own dependence on Lund's analysis of Philippians, however, led him to underestimate the role of chiasmus in the letter, and to conclude that its few chiastic sections are "insignificant and unremarkable." One passage in particular, the so-called "Christ-Hymn" of 2:5-11, throws this judgment very much into question.

Ernst Lohmeyer was among the first to speak of Phil 2:5-11 as a christological hymn, organized in two stanzas of three strophes each.[16] The first stanza (vv. 6-8) describes a descending movement, culminating with the phrase, "obedient unto death." The second stanza (vv. 9-11) depicts Christ's ascension and glorification. The entire passage thus reproduces the descending-ascending paradigm which is familiar from the Old Testament[17] and programmatic for the Fourth Gospel: "I came from the Father and have come into the world; again I am leaving the world and going to the Father" (Jn 16:28).

Lohmeyer excises Phil 2:8c, "even death on a cross," because it adds an anomalous fourth line to his third strophe and, more importantly, because it represents what he considers to be a theological interpolation. The original hymn, he maintains, stressed the contrast between Christ's divinity and his death. To the mind of its author, the nature of that death was immaterial. To Paul, however, the cross is "a sign of God's power and wisdom." The phrase, "death on a cross," then, according to Lohmeyer, is to be understood as a paraenetic addition, whose purpose is to encourage the Philippians to accept the possibility of a martyr's death, a death for Christ and in his image.[18]

In an evaluation and criticism of Lohmeyer's analysis, Joachim Jeremias further dissected the passage, dividing it into three strophes of four lines each.[19] To achieve a thematic balance, however, and to correct Lohmeyer's division that artificially separates lines, Jeremias was obliged to treat as Pauline interpolations not only v. 8c, but also the last line of vv. 10 and 11: "in heaven and on earth and under the earth," and "to the glory of God the Father." With minor variations, this analysis has been accepted by a great majority of commentators. Joachim Gnilka[20] attempted to give fuller weight to the "paral-lelismus membrorum" evident in the passage. His arrangement of five strophes of two lines each, however, is achieved only by accepting Jeremias's "additions."

This is not the place to discuss the host of complex theological questions this passage raises.[21] Our purpose is to demonstrate two points: that the conceptual background of the Christ-hymn is to be found chiefly in the Servant Songs of Deutero-Isaiah, especially the fourth song, 52:13-53:12; and that the supposed Pauline additions to the hymn are in fact elements integral to its structure and message.

The link between the humiliated and exalted Servant of God and the crucified and glorified Christ has been made at least since the time of Origen.[22] The theological parallels between the *pais tou theou* and the Son of God are so striking that hardly a Christmas or Easter service in our churches fails to evoke them. Interest in the possible gnostic influences on Pauline christology has led many scholars to minimize this well-established link. In support of it, however, we can add to the theological parallels a literary consideration: the Servant Songs, like the Christ-hymn, were composed according to the laws of chiasmus.

A cursory reading of the Songs — Isaiah 42:1-4; 49:1-6; 50:4-11; and 52:13-53:12 — reveals close affinities between the first two, whereas the third and fourth seem to stand apart both in content and in form. This impression is confirmed once it is recognized that the first two Songs can be read as a single chiastic unit:

A (42:1):   Behold *my servant*, whom I uphold, my chosen,
in whom my soul delights; I have put my Spirit upon him,
he will bring forth justice to the nations.

B (42:2f):   *He will not cry* or lift up his voice, or make it heard
in the street; a bruised reed he will *not break,*
and a dimly burning wick he will *not quench;*
he will faithfully *bring forth justice.*

C (42:4):   *He will not fail or be discouraged* till he has
established justice in the earth; and the coastlands
wait for his law.

D (49:1):   Listen to me, O coastlands, and hearken, you
peoples from afar. *The Lord called me from the womb,*
from the body of my mother he named my name.

E (49:2):   He made my mouth like a sharp sword,
in the shadow of his hand *he hid me;*
he made me a polished arrow, in his quiver
he hid me away.

F (49:3):   And he said to me, "You are my
servant, Israel, in whom I will be glorified."

E′ (49:4):   But I said, "I have labored in vain,
I have spent my strength for nothing and
vanity; yet surely *my right is with the Lord,*
and *my recompense* with my God."

D′ (49:5a):   And now *the Lord* says — who *formed me
from the womb* to be his servant, to bring Jacob back
to him, and that Israel might be gathered to him,

C′ (49:5b):   for I am honored in the eyes of the Lord,
and my *God has become my strength* —

B′ (49:6a):   He says, "It is *too light a thing* that you should
be my servant to *raise up* the tribes of *Jacob* and to
restore the preserved of *Israel;*

A′ (49:6b):   *I will give you as a light to the nations,* that *my salvation*
may reach to the end of the earth.

A → A′:   The Servant will bring forth justice (*mishpat*)
to the nations (the Gentiles) →
The Servant will *become* a light for salvation to the nations,
even to the end of the earth.

B → B': The Servant's mission: the restraint of his method →
The Servant's mission: the breadth of his purpose.

C → C': He will succeed, since God has ordained his mission →
He will succeed, since God is his strength.

D → D': Called/named from the womb to gather the Gentiles →
Formed from the womb to gather Israel.

E → E': God is his protection →
God is his right and recompense.

F: The voice of God: "You are my Servant Israel..."

These parallels are not close enough to justify the conclusion that the two passages originally constituted one song and were simply split apart to appear in their present contexts. As they now stand, there are very different emphases in each. The speaker in 42:1-4 is God, who describes his Servant in the third person. In 49:1-3, the Servant himself describes the universal vocation to which he has been called; and the passage concludes with his quotation of God's words that broaden his vocation to embrace all the nations of the earth. Whether speaking or quoting, the voice throughout the second song is the Servant's. Then again, the Servant in the first song clearly represents personified Israel, bearer of God's Spirit, who is called to summon the nations to faith. In the second song, the Servant is the *new* Israel, personified as a prophetic figure who will glorify Yahweh by reaching out beyond the limits of the Hebrew people, to bring salvation to the Gentiles. In both songs, the mission is the same: to bring "justice" (right faith and conduct) to the nations. Whereas in ch. 42 the Servant seems to represent collective Israel, however, in ch. 49 he is depicted rather as the "collective personality" of God's people. This explains the apparent inconsistency between 49:3 and 49:6a. The Servant is indeed Israel, in whom God will be glorified. But he is distinct from the "old" or former Israel, including both "Jacob" (the original tribal confederation) and the "remnant."

Perhaps the chiastic configuration of these two songs, which is admittedly tenuous, is purely coincidental. The close correspondence between A:A', forming a neat inclusion, together with D:D'("called/formed from the womb"), the link-word "coastlands" in 42:4 and 49:1, and the divine affirmation of F, however, suggest otherwise. Nevertheless, there is too little to go on in this regard to warrant any conclusions about the literary history of these passages.

A different chiastic arrangement appears in the third song, Isa 50:4-11.

A (4-5):

    (a) The Lord God has given me the tongue of those who are taught,

        (b) that I may know how to sustain with a word him
           that is weary.

           (c) Morning by morning he wakens, he wakens my ear

               (d) to hear as those who are taught.

           (c') The Lord God has opened my ear,

        (b') and I was not rebellious,

    (a') I turned not backward.

B (6):

    (a) I gave my back to the smiters, and my cheeks to those
        who pulled out the beard;

        (b) I hid not my face from shame and spitting.

           (c) For the Lord God helps me;

        (b') therefore I have not been confounded;

    (a') therefore I have set my face like a flint, and I know that
        I shall not be put to shame;

C (7): He who vindicates me is near.

B' (8-9):

    (a) Who will contend with me? Let us stand up together.

        (b) Who is my adversary? Let him come near to me.

        (b') Behold, the Lord God helps me; who will declare
           me guilty?

    (a') Behold, all of them will wear out like a garment;
        the moth will eat them up.

A' (10f):

    (a) Who among you fears the Lord and obeys the voice of his Servant,

        (b) who walks in darkness and has no light, yet trusts
           in the name of the Lord and relies upon his God?

           (c) Behold, all you who kindle a fire, who set brands alight!

        (b') Walk by the light of your fire, and by the brands
           which you have kindled!

    (a') This shall you have from my hand: you shall lie down
        in torment.

A → A': The acceptance of the Servant →
   The rebellion of the people.
B → B': The persecution of the Servant →
   The vindication of the Servant.
C: "My vindication is near."

These five elements, that together constitute a chiastic penta-colon, have their own internal parallel structure:

A (4-5):

   a: The servant is equipped for his mission
      b: The servant willingly accepts his mission
         c: The Lord awakens him
            d: The Lord teaches him
         c': The Lord prepares him
      b': The servant did not rebel against his mission
   a': The servant fulfills his mission.

B (6):

   a: The servant accepted persecution (positive)
      b: The servant did not refuse persecution (negative)
         c: "The Lord God helps me"
      b': The servant did not weaken under persecution (neg.)
   a': The servant has defied persecution (pos.).

C (7): God, who vindicates the Servant, is near.
B' (8-9):

   a: None will contend against the servant
      b: The servant's adversary
      b': The servant's advocate
   a': None will defeat the servant.

A' (10-11):

   a: They neither fear nor obey
      b: They walk in darkness
         c: All of them rebel
      b': They walk in their own darkness
   a': They shall receive their reward.

For our purposes the most important passage is the Fourth
Servant Song, 52:13-53:12. Without setting out the entire text, we can
note the parallels as follows:

A (52:13-15): God speaks: exaltation and humiliation
    of his Servant (he shall be exalted, lifted up,
    made very high; he was humbled, disfigured;
    his humiliation will lead to salvation).

  B (53:1-3): The narrator speaks: describes the Servant's
      affliction (no beauty, despised, rejected, a man of sorrows,
      grief, esteemed not).

    C (53:4-6): The purpose of the Servant's suffering:
        vicarious atonement (afflicted by God, he has
        borne our transgressions, our iniquities,
        our chastisement).

  B' (53:7-9): The narrator speaks: describes the Servant's
      affliction (oppressed, slaughtered, stricken, killed,
      buried in shame; yet he is innocent and willingly
      accepts his suffering).

A' (53:10-12): God speaks: humiliation and exaltation
    of his Servant (he was bruised, put to grief, made an
    offering for sin; he shall live, prosper, see the fruit
    of his suffering; by his humiliation and death he bore
    the sins of many and made intercession for the transgressors).[23]

Once more a forward movement is apparent from strophe I to
strophe II. Beginning with an affirmation of the Servant's ultimate
victory through glorification, the passage recounts his descent into
utter humiliation, degradation and death. It concludes with emphasis upon the final exaltation as a reward for the Servant's faithful
obedience to the divine will. From A to A' the heightening effect is
evident in the change in tenses: from the future promise of salvation
to be accomplished through him, to the present realization of that
salvation ("he *bore* the sin of many, and *made* intercession..."). Similarly, from B to B' the narrator passes from a simple description of
the Servant's affliction to the assertion that his suffering is *innocent*
and *voluntary*. The true "conclusion" to the passage, then, is its
conceptual focus in 53:4-6, proclamation of the Lord's grace in
healing our iniquity through the chastisement laid upon the innocent Servant.

A → A': God speaks: exaltation - humiliation: the mighty will
understand (that God will work salvation through his Servant) →
God speaks: humiliation → exaltation: the Servant will share
with the mighty (because his voluntary suffering has already
worked salvation).

B → B': The narrator's description: the Servant bears suffering →
The narrator's description: the Servant bears innocent suffering
voluntarily.

C : Vicarious atonement accomplished through the Servant's
innocent suffering.

Turning now to the Christ-hymn of Philippians 2:5-11, we should
note first of all the remarkable fact that nothing explicit is said here
about the reason for Christ's descent and ascension, humiliation and
exaltation. The purpose of his assuming the "form" and "likeness"
of human existence is not merely to attain universal acclamation as
Kyrios or Lord, expressed in v. 11. Its real purpose, as the surrounding context indicates, is to enable the pre-existent Son of God to
assume the conditions of fallen human life, in order to work out
salvation through an act of uncompromised obedience. Thus v. 7:
"He emptied [εκενωσεν] himself, taking the form of a servant."

This expression of Jesus' "kenotic" obedience could hardly fail
to evoke in the minds of Paul's readers the image of the Suffering
Servant, who gave up his life voluntarily to atone for the sin of the
people.[24] Accordingly, the Christ-hymn of Philippians 2 unfolds in
such a way as to center upon the proclamation of v. 8, "He humbled
himself *unto death, even death on a cross.*" Like the Servant of the Isaiah
prophecy, Jesus Christ descends into total humiliation, suffers an
innocent and voluntary death, and because of his obedience he is
exalted by God through bestowal of the divine name and by universal acclamation. This descending, ascending movement, in the image
of the humiliated and exalted Servant, readily explains why the
passage contains no allusion to resurrection.[25] Its original purpose
was to evoke in the minds of those who read it — or perhaps
chanted it in liturgical antiphony — the voluntary suffering of the
innocent Servant, whose obedience achieves vicarious atonement
for God's people.

The chiastic structuring of the hymn can be indicated as follows:

A : Have this mind among yourselves which is also [yours]
in *Christ Jesus:* who, being in the form of *God,*
did not count it robbery to be *equal to God,*

    B : but emptied himself taking the form of a *servant,* being
born in the likeness of human persons; and being found
in human form, *he humbled himself* becoming obedient

        C : *unto death / death on a cross.*

    B': Therefore God *highly exalted him* and bestowed on him
the name which is above every name, that at the name
of *Jesus* every knee should bow in heaven, and on earth
and under the earth,

A': and every tongue confess that *Jesus Christ* is LORD to the *glory
of God* the Father.

A further breakdown of the passage indicates more clearly the antithetical parallels established between strophe I (descent) and strophe II (ascent).

A : Have this mind among yourselves which is also [yours]
in *Christ Jesus:* who, being in the form of *God,*
did not count it robbery to be *equal to God,*

    B : but emptied himself taking the form of a *servant,*

        C : being born in the likeness [εν ομοιωματι]
of human persons;

            D : and being found in human form

                E : *he humbled himself* becoming obedient

                    F : *unto death* (μεχρι θανατου)

                    F': *death on a cross* (θανατου δε σταυρου)

                E': Therefore God *highly exalted him*

            D': and bestowed upon him the Name which is
above every name,

        C': that at the name [εν τω ονοματι] of *Jesus* every knee
should bow in heaven, and on earth and
under the earth,

    B': and every tongue confess that LORD

A': is *Jesus Christ* to the *glory of God* the Father.

This analysis does not attempt to divide the hymn into lines that correspond to the author's hypothetical poetic structure (two, three or four line strophes). Whether or not such a poetic form was ever intended is a question that may never be satisfactorily answered.[26] What this analysis does show, however, is that the passage reflects a concentric parallelism that focuses attention on the central affirmation of both the fact and the means of Christ's death. Repetition with specification augments the force of the central lines, thereby laying particular stress on Christ's total identification with suffering humanity "even unto the [humiliating and agonizing] death on the cross."

A → A': Christ Jesus - one with God →
Jesus Christ – the glory of God.

B → B': The humbled servant →
The exalted Lord.

C → C': He assumes the likeness of all persons →
He is acclaimed by all creatures.

D → D': He assumes a human form →
He receives a Name above every (human) name.

E → E': Humble obedience →
Divine exaltation.

F → F': The double affirmation (with heightening through specification and inverted parallelism) from death, to the innocent and voluntary death of the cross.

The literary composition of this passage, utilizing the principles of chiasmus and focusing upon the inverted affirmations of F:F', shows that we need to reconsider and probably discard the various theories which would excise certain phrases as Pauline interpolations. In the first place, the parallelism between v. 5 and the conclusion of the hymn (A:A') demonstrates that the passage begins not with the relative pronoun *hos* of v. 6, but with the preceding line that includes the name "Christ Jesus." Inclusion with "Jesus Christ" of v. 11, then, shows that the paraenetic introduction of v. 5, "Have this mind among yourselves...," is an essential part of the entire passage and cannot be treated simply as a bridge between the exhortations of 1:27-2:4, and 2:12ff.

Then again, the parallels established between A:A' (Christ Jesus / Jesus Christ; equal to God / glory of God), as between F:F' (death / death on a cross), indicate that the phrases "even death on a cross" and "to the glory of God the Father" cannot reasonably be excised as secondary additions. Similarly, the qualification of v. 10, "in heaven and on earth and under the earth," should be read as a specification of "every knee," thereby balancing the plural "likeness of (all) persons" in C with the acclamation by (all) creatures in C'.

These factors suggest conclusions that run counter to the usual interpretations regarding both the structure and the meaning of this passage. On the one hand, they show that the "hymn" is integrally woven into its context and serves to ground Paul's call to obedience in the image of the kenotic Christ, who humbly and faithfully accepts the role of servant in order to assume the death of the cross and be exalted as the victorious Lord. In some form the passage may indeed have circulated in the early Church as a christological confessional statement, a prototype of later credal formulations. As it appears in Paul's letter to Philippi, however, it has become his own composition, utilized to offer a sublime model for moral conduct appropriate within the community of believers. Although it clearly and strongly proclaims the death and exaltation of the "crucified God," at Paul's hands it does so less as a christological affirmation than as an ethical model that grounds his overall exhortation.

The fact that interpreters have long sensed the rhythmic flow of the passage, yet have reached no consensus regarding its structure, suggests finally that they may have been questing in the wrong direction. Greek poetic forms rely, as we have seen, upon rhythm, rhyme and meter. This is not the case with Hebrew poetry. If Paul is in fact the author of Phil 2:5-11, and his method of composition is similar to what we have found elsewhere in his epistles, then we would expect him to rely more upon his Hebrew than his Greek heritage in shaping this passage. Rather than continue the frustrating quest for a metrical scheme that is not there, we may simply conclude that the evident rhythm and balance of the lines in this passage are the result of Paul's conscious effort to structure it chiastically. His purpose is to call the fractious Philippians to assume the "mind of Christ," to pattern their own ethical behavior after the innocent Suffering Servant. He does so by drawing upon the christological model of the descending-ascending Son of God, whose sacrificial death climaxed in his exaltation.

Those who assume the mind of Christ may, like Paul himself, be made a sacrificial offering in the image of their Lord (1:29; 2:17). The conviction remains, however, as throughout the Pauline corpus, that those who suffer with Christ will surely be exalted and glorified with him. Therefore the ultimate focus of their behavior, and the ultimate model for their imitation, must be the death *on the cross* of the one whose own suffering and exaltation served "to the glory of God the Father."

D. Ephesians

However we may decide the question of authorship, the theological meditation that has come down to us as a letter from the apostle Paul to the saints "in Ephesus" also displays an adroit use of chiasmus to convey its message. A typical example is the concluding passage of chapter five that treats the relationship between wives and husbands in the context of Christian marriage.

The major commentaries recognize that v. 21, "Submit yourselves to one another out of reverence [lit. 'fear'] for Christ," is an integral part of 5:21-33. The RSV and NKJ, however, set v. 21 apart from the succeeding verses,[27] perhaps regarding it as a statement of the principle of mutual submission that should govern all relations described in the *Haustafel*, including those between children and parents, and masters and slaves (6:1-9). This gives the clear impression that Paul begins his discourse on marriage with the command that wives be *subject* to their husbands, as to the Lord. Little wonder that women — and not only militant feminists — have voiced their dismay at what is apparently a blatant expression of sexism. The participle υποτασσομενοι, however, should be translated "submit" rather than "subject," to convey the sense of a voluntary act, performed out of love rather than by compulsion (cf. 1 Cor 16:16; 1 Pet 5:5). Furthermore, separating vv. 21 and 22 does violence to the Greek, in which vv. 21-23(4) constitute a single sentence. Read correctly, the passage first calls for mutual submission between husband and wife out of love grounded in the "fear of Christ."[28] This submission then works itself out in complementary ways, the wife accepting the husband's authority and the husband loving the wife "as Christ loved the Church and gave himself up for her...". There is no abject "subjection" expected here, but rather a submission in love, that respects "order" (*taxis*) within the family as within the Church community as a whole (cf. 1 Cor 14:40).

Such an understanding, that views the mutual submission of v. 21 as the ground for the conjugal relationships described in vv. 22-33, is confirmed by the intricate structure of the passage. Reading it as a chiastic unit, v. 21 forms an inclusion with v. 33, indicating that the "fear" (φοβηται) shown by the wife towards her husband is properly understood as a function of the "fear" (φοβω) or reverence owed by both husband and wife to Christ.

A (21): Submit yourselves to one another out of reverence
[fear] for Christ:

    B (22-24): Wives, submit yourselves to your husbands, as to
the Lord. For the husband is the head of the wife as Christ
is the head of the Church, his Body, and is himself its
Savior. As the Church submits itself to Christ, so let wives
also submit themselves in all things to their husbands.

        C (25): Husbands, love your wives, as Christ loved
the Church and gave himself up for her,

            D (26): that (ἵνα) he might sanctify her,
having cleansed her by the washing of water
with the Word;

            D' (27): that (ἵνα) he might present the Church
to himself in splendor, without spot or wrinkle
or any such thing, that she might be holy
and without blemish.

        C' (28-30): Even so husbands should love their wives as
their own bodies. He who loves his wife loves himself.
For no man ever hates his own flesh, but nourishes
and cherishes it, as Christ does the Church,
because we are members of his Body.

    B' (31-32): "For this reason a man shall leave his father and
mother and be joined to his wife, and the two shall
become one flesh." This mystery is a profound one,
and I am saying that it refers to Christ and the Church.

A' (33): However, let each one of you love his own wife as
himself, and let the wife respect [fear] her husband.

In addition to the inclusion created by v. 21 and v. 33, the
principle of intensification — a "climactic parallelism" — is evident
from strophe I (A → D) to strophe II (D' → A'):

A → A': Mutual submission (reverence for Christ) →
Mutual submission (love/respect).

B → B': Wives submit to husbands as the Church submits itself to
Christ →
Husbands unite to wives as the Church unites itself to Christ.

C → C': Husbands love your wives as Christ *loved* the Church →
Husbands love your wives as Christ *loves* the Church.

D → D': In order to sanctify the Church →
In order to glorify the Church.[29]

The helical movement thus begins with an exhortation to mutual submission between husband and wife, passes through affirmation of Christ's love for the Church, and culminates with the purpose of Christ's self-offering on behalf of the Church: that he, the Bridegroom, might sanctify his Bride through the "washing of water with the word" (baptism and catechesis?) and glorify her by uniting her to himself in a state of perfection. The covenant-bond of marriage, then, is a paradigm of the eternal covenantal relationship established by Christ with those who unite themselves to him in love.

Seen in this perspective, Christian marriage is not merely a social convention based on some contractual agreement. It is an eschatological image of the bond of mutual devotion and self-sacrifice that unites Christ with members of his Body, the Church; and as such, it is indeed a great and profound "mystery."

ENDNOTES

[1] See especially the commentaries of Jerome Murphy-O'Connor, *1 Corinthians* (Wilmington, DE: Glazier, 1979), and Peter F. Ellis, *Seven Pauline Letters* (Collegeville, MN: The Liturgical Press, 1982). Paul appears to be especially influenced by the *hysteron-proteron* model we examined earlier. See J. Jeremias, "Chiasmus in den Paulusbriefen," *ZNW* 49 (1958), p. 145-156. Jeremias discusses numerous examples of a:b:b':a' inverted parallelism in the Pauline corpus that he considers chiastic (e.g., Col 3:11; 1 Cor 6:13a; 1 Cor 6:13b-14; Rom 2:7-10). [For a good example of the *hysteron-proteron* pattern, see 1 Cor. 1:15-17, which the *RSV* has clarified by translating *hoi men* and *hoi de* respectively as "the latter" and "the former."]

[2] *Chiasmus in the New Testament*, p. 164.

[3] *Seven Pauline Letters*, p. 45f. See also his article, "Salvation Through the Wisdom of the Cross (1 Cor 1:10-4:21)," in *Sin, Salvation, and the Spirit*, Daniel Durken, ed. (Collegeville, MN: Liturgical Press, 1979), p. 324-333, which served as groundwork for his later study.

[4] *Chiasmus in Antiquity*, p. 216f.

[5] Notice the inverted parallelism of C:C'.

[6] This remains the most plausible interpretation of this passage, despite the arguments of T. P. Shoemaker, "Unveiling of Equality: 1 Corinthians 11:2-16," *BTB* 17 (1987), p. 60-63, who translates 11:10, "the woman ought to have liberty over her head."

[7] With minor changes, the following analysis is that of my former student, Esther Juce. By interpreting the chiastic "flow" of these passages, she convincingly demonstrated that the apostle's argument in 1 Cor 11:2-16 is a matter of order, not subordination.

[8] A possible example is the Spirit-Paraclete passages of the Johannine Farewell

Discourse; see the preceding chapter.

[9]This is especially evident in the polemical letter to the Galatians, which is also chiastic. See John Bligh, *Galatians in Greek: A Structural Analysis of Paul's Epistle to the Galatians* (Detroit: Univ. of Detroit Press, 1966).

[10]This key chapter contains a number of chiastic micro-units. See C.E. Hill, "Paul's Understanding of Christ's Kingdom in I Corinthians 15:20-28," *NovT* 30 (1988), p. 297-320, and the revision by J. Lambrecht of Hill's analysis in "Structure and Line of Thought in 1 Cor. 15:23-28," *NovT* 32 (1990), p. 143-151. Other chiastic units in 1 Cor 15 include vv. 35-50, focusing about the statement in v. 42, "So also is it with the resurrection of the dead."

[11]J. Welch, "Chiasmus in the New Testament," p. 215f, following N. Lund, offers a somewhat different analysis of ch. 13, but his divisions depend in part on his paraphrase of the passage.

[12]Cf. Rom 8:2; Gal 4:6; Phil 1:9.

[13]"Chiasmus in den Paulusbriefen," p. 149. Similarly, Charles D. Myers, Jr., "Chiastic Inversion in the Argument of Romans 3-8," *NovT* 35, 1 (1993), p. 32 n. 16. Myers offers an interesting analysis of Paul's use of chiasmus in 3:9-5:19, as well as in the larger unit 3:9-8:39. His argument is not wholly persuasive because of the large number of "broken" patterns he uncovers, where "parallel" lines are out of sequence.

[14]"Chiasmus in the New Testament," p. 226.

[15]*Seven Pauline Letters*, p. 115-138.

[16]*Kyrios Jesus. Eine Untersuchung zu Phil. 2,5-11* (Heidelberg, 1928); and *Der Brief an die Philipper* (Göttingen, 1929), esp. p. 90.

[17]E. Schweizer, *Erniedrigung und Erhöhung bei Jesus und seinen Nachfolgern* (Zürich, 1955), draws a parallel between this depiction of Christ and the humiliation-exaltation of the righteous in Israel.

[18]*Der Brief an die Philipper*, p. 96. Joseph Fitzmyer, "The Aramaic Background of Philippians 2:6-11," *CBQ* 50/3 (1988), p. 470-483, presents a convincing reconstruction of the Aramaic "original" lying behind the hymn. He retains Lohmeyer's basic analysis, however, of eighteen lines divided into two strophes containing three verses of three lines each. This is problematic, as we shall see farther on. While his reconstruction confirms his contention that the passage represents a "rhetorical composition of Jewish-Christian origin," and evidences an underlying Aramaic original, it is less clear that it must be viewed as "pre-Pauline," at least in its present form (p. 483).

[19]"Zur Gedankenführung in den paulinischen Briefen," *Studia Paulina* (ed. J.N. Sevenster) (Haarlem, 1953), p. 152ff; "Zu Phil. 2,7," *NovT* 6 (1963), p. 182ff; and his art. "*pais theou*," *TWNT* V, p. 711ff.

[20]*Der Philipperbrief* (Freiburg, Basel, Wien: Herder, 1980), p. 136f. For a sound evaluation of critical studies on the passage published up to the mid-1960s, see R.P. Martin, *Carmen Christi: Philippians ii,5-11 in Recent Interpretation and in the Setting of Early Christian Worship* (Cambridge, 1967). A. Feuillet, "L'hymne christologique de l'épître aux Philippiens (2,6-11)," in *Christologie paulinienne et tradition biblique* (Paris 1973), p. 83ff, evaluates both modern and patristic interpretations of the hymn.

[21]P. Ellis, *Seven Pauline Letters*, p. 124-130, treats the major issues in his excursus on Phil 2:6-11.

[22]On the patristic commentaries dealing with Phil 2, see Feuillet, "*L'hymne christologique de l'epître aux Philippiens*," p. 92f.

[23]In 53:10 the speaker appears to be the narrator, whereas in the following verses it is God who speaks. Editorial modification of the subject occurs in 52:14, and the text of 53:10-11a shows signs of corruption. I would accept the suggestion of Nabil Hanna, that the original reading of 53:10 was "And I willed," whereby God resumes his declaration from 52:15.

[24]This emphasis alone is enough to tip the balance in favor of a "Servant" christology for the passage rather than an "Adam" christology.

[25]This hymn offers little support for the hypothesis that an "exaltation christology" was developed in the early Church prior to a "resurrection christology." The two simply express different yet complementary facets of the same reality.

[26]Barbara Eckman's study, "A Quantitative Metrical Analysis of the Philippians Hymn" (*NTS* 26 [1980], p. 258-266), is interesting but finally unsatisfying; too many emendations of "anomalous phrases" need to be made to produce the desired result. This and other such attempts simply confirm that the "hymn" does not conform to the laws of Greek metric poetry.

[27]The *RSV* 1971 edition intrudes the subtitle "Wives and Husbands" between Eph 5:21 and 22. In other editions, including the *NRSV*, v. 21 begins a new paragraph.

[28]On this expression, see Heinrich Schlier, *Der Brief an die Epheser* (Düsseldorf: Patmos-Verlag, 1957), p. 252f; and Markus Barth, *Ephesians*, vol 2 (New York: Doubleday, 1974), p. 608-610. Rudolf Schnackenburg, *Der Brief an die Epheser* (Zürich/Neukirchen-Vluyn: Benziger/Neukirchener Verlag, 1982), p. 248-251, compares the Ephesians passage with Phil 2:1-5, where Paul exhorts his readers to humble acceptance of the "same mind" and "same love" out of devotion to Christ.

[29]Notice as well the parallel structure in vv. 22-24, where the pivot or conceptual center is the formula "Christ: Head of the Church." Inverted parallelism also occurs in vv. 28-30.

PART THREE:

THE PERSISTENCE OF CHIASMUS

THE PERSISTENCE
OF CHIASMUS

In an appendix to his study of biblical poetry, James Kugel offers "a brief sampling of some of the parallelistic prayers and songs written in Hebrew during the rabbinic period and on into the Middle Ages."[1] His well-substantiated point is that parallelism on the biblical model persists throughout the centuries in a variety of forms.

When students are first introduced to chiastic structuring in the Bible, they almost immediately raise the question whether the pattern is to be found in extra-biblical sources as well. When I was first asked about this in 1985, I had to admit quite frankly that I had no idea of the answer. An examination of Kugel's examples of parallelism, however, indicated that a chiastic pattern is present in some of the texts he cites, including a ninth century alphabetical acrostic composed by Moses b. Asher. This piece, reflecting themes from the "Song of the Vineyard" from Isaiah 5, is characterized, as Kugel notes, by an "unusual repetitive style."[2] A partial reason for this repetition is that it is structured according to the principles of concentric parallelism. Kugel reproduces P. Kahle's translation of the opening lines, which we can arrange as follows:

A : You planted the stock of a *vine* /
praised it was over all other *vines* //

  B : In the tower of David *it* was planted /
and a cedar from Lebanon was in *its* midst //

    C : The tribes of Jacob are the Lord's *vine* /
and the man of Judah is his favored plant //

    C': The branches of the *vine*, these are the Prophets /
and the tower of David is Mount Zion //

B': *It* was rooted beside mighty waters /
     and [*it*] grew most lofty among the bushes //
A': And that very *vine* stuck its roots /
     and sent forth its sprigs beside mighty waters //

Repetition is evident throughout the poem, as is the heightening effect from verset to verset. Less evident, but equally significant, is the helical movement: A → A' → B → B' → C → C', beginning with the planting and growth of the vine, moving to its location, and concluding with the meaning of its imagery. Even in this fragment, intensification appears not only from verset to verset, but from line to line and strophe to strophe, focusing upon the symbolism expounded in C:C'. The conceptual center or "point" to this portion of the poem is thus the identification of the vine with the Lord's chosen people and, more specifically, with the prophetic witness emanating from the holy city of Jerusalem.

A → A': The vine is planted →
         The vine grows
B → B': Its location (tower of David) / the (lofty) cedar →
         Its location (by mighty waters) / the lofty vine
C → C': Its symbolism (Jacob / Judah) →
         Its symbolism (Prophets / Mt. Zion).[3]

If this analysis is accurate, then it suggests one of two possibilities. Either the author resorted to concentric parallelism in conscious imitation of biblical patterns familiar to him, or he (consciously or unconsciously) drew upon a literary technique common in his own day. The former possibility seems excluded, since the chiastic pattern is so "loose"; although it is present, it is clearly subordinated to other features such as the repetition of key expressions (vine, tower of David, mighty waters) and the heightening effect from verset to verset. This leaves the intriguing possibility that in the ninth century chiasmus was still employed as a literary device with the same characteristics and purpose it had during the biblical period.

Reflection such as this led naturally to the question whether chiasmus "persists" in Christian literature as well. The examples given in this third part of our study show that chiastic structuring on the helical model in fact appears from the post-apostolic period down to at least the end of the nineteenth century, particularly but not exclusively in liturgical hymns. In secular writings it can be found in a variety of forms from every age, including the carefully crafted pieces of today's newspaper columnists.

1. BACKGROUND

A s background to these examples, we should note briefly the presence of concentric parallelism in intertestamental Jewish literature as well as in writings of the New Testament Apocrypha and the Apostolic Fathers. This is virtually virgin territory and requires much broader and more systematic study than has been done to date. The examples given here are of uneven quality: some are obviously chiastic, others are debatably so. Taken together, they nevertheless substantiate the claim that shortly before and after the time of Christ chiastic parallelism was employed in a variety of extra-biblical Jewish and Christian writings.

a) The Dead Sea Scrolls

T he passage 1 QS 3:13-4:26, from the Scroll known as the Rule of the Community, reflects a "spirit-dualism" that we have discussed in detail elsewhere.[4] The subject is the origin and influence within the community and the world of twin spirits, the Spirit of Truth and the Spirit of Perversity. The passage itself is composite. It is introduced by a statement of conditions for entering the Qumran fellowship, which is structured in a simple A:B:A' parallelism.

> A: It is through the *Spirit of true counsel* concerning the ways of man that all *his sins shall be expiated* (atoned for) that he may contemplate the light of life.
> B: He shall be cleansed from all his sins by the *Spirit of holiness* (Holy Spirit) uniting him to his truth.
> A': *His iniquity shall be expiated* (atoned for) by the *Spirit of uprightness and humility.*

The spirit-passage itself seems to incorporate two incompatible traditions. On the one hand there appears a metaphysical dualism influenced by teachings of Iranian origin (1 QS 3:13-21a, 3:25b-4:14). According to this tradition, twin spirits, one good and the other evil, reign over two separate camps of human beings: the righteous and the wicked respectively.[5] The passage begins with an introductory address (3:13-17a) to the "Master" or "Instructor" concerning the influence of the two spirits in determining human ethical behavior. It continues in an A:B:A' pattern, as follows.

> A: (3:17b-21a) introduces the two Spirits of Truth and Perversity, stipulating their origin in light or darkness and their dominion over two separate camps or classes of people.
>
> B: (3:25b-4:1) affirms God's creation of both Spirits according to his plan — he loves the Spirit of Truth and detests the "ways" and "counsel" of the Spirit of Perversity.
>
> A': (4:2-14) describes the "ways" of the two Spirits and their manifestation in the works of "the sons of light" and "the sons of darkness."

A parallel but contrasting theme is spelled out in the second major section, 1 QS 4:15-26. Key terms indicating the chiastic parallels can be given as follows:[6]

> A: (4:15-16a) humanity's inheritance in the spirits.
>
> B: (16b-18a) God has established the spirits in equal parts; they will not walk together.
>
> C: (18b-19a) God has fixed an end to Perversity; it will be destroyed at his "visitation."
>
> D: (19b-23a) Truth will come forth forever;
>
> a :   God in his truth will pour out his
>
> b :   Spirit of Truth for purification;
>
> a':   The upright will know God's truth.[7]
>
> C':   (23b) all Perversity will be destroyed, put to shame.
>
> B':   (23c-25a) until now the spirits walk together in the human heart; God has established them in equal parts.
>
> A':   (25b-26) humanity's inheritance in the spirits.

A rough parallelism seems to be operative as well in some of the Thanksgiving Hymns (1 QH) of the Dead Sea community. Hymn 11 can be set out as follows:[8]

> A: I thank Thee, O Lord, for Thou hast *upheld me* by Thy strength. Thou hast shed Thy Holy Spirit upon me that I may *not stumble.*
>
> B: Thou hast *strengthened* me before the battles of *wickedness...* Thou hast made me like a strong tower, a high wall...

C: Thou hast [established my mouth] in Thy *Covenant* ...
for the *lying lips* shall be dumb.

D: For Thou wilt *condemn* in Judgement all those
who *assail* me, *distinguishing* through me
between the *just* and the wicked.

E: *Thou knowest the whole intent of a creature*...Thou
hast established my heart...directing my steps...

E': *Thou knowest the inclination of Thy servant* ...
I have not ... sought refuge in my own strength.

D': I have no fleshly refuge... Thou wilt bring *salvation*
to flower ... *providing refuge* in (Thy) strength.

C': Thou hast appointed me for Thy *Covenant*,
and I have clung to *Thy truth*.

B': Thou hast *lifted* my horn above those who insult me,
and those who *attack* me...

A': Thou hast *succoured my soul*, O my God, and hast lifted
my horn on high ... (Thou) wilt *establish my feet*
[upon level ground forever].

While a certain tenuous parallelism is evident here, it is not nearly as complete as in the selection from 1 QS. The question whether 1 QH in fact includes examples of chiasmus is complicated by the fragmentary state of the text. But at best the parallels are thematic rather than verbal, and can arguably be explained as simple and random repetition of key ideas.

A liturgical fragment, categorized under "Hymns for the Sabbath Day,"[9] displays a more obvious parallelism:

A: Give thanks...[*Bless*] His holy Name *unceasingly*

B: ...all the *angels* of the holy firmament ... [above] the *heavens*,

C: the *earth* and all its deep places,

B': the great [*Abyss*] and *Abaddon* and the *waters* and all that is
[in them].

A': [Let] all His creatures [*bless* Him] *unceasingly* for *everlasting*
[ages. Amen! Amen!]

Here the ceaseless blessing of God is offered by all his creatures: in heaven, on earth and under the earth (cf. Phil 2:10). The focus appears to be on "the earth," and praise offered by humankind.

b) Old Testament Apocrypha

Typical Hebrew parallelism is evident throughout the apocryphal or deutero-canonical work known as Ecclesiasticus or Jesus ben Sirach, and is unmistakable even with a casual reading. Of other intertestamental Jewish writings we could mention, interesting examples appear in 3 Maccabees, Psalm 151, and the Prayer of Manasseh.[10]

The so-called Third Book of the Maccabees is in fact an account of the struggles of Egyptian Jews under Ptolemy IV Philopator at the end of the third century B.C. The work describes Ptolemy's attempt to enter the Holy of Holies of the Jerusalem temple, and his successful expulsion through the prayers of the high priest Simon. The entire work is structured chiastically.[11]

A: Ptolemy threatens to desecrate the temple [1:1-29]

    B: Simon's prayer of intercession (divine intervention) [2:1-24]

        C: Ptolemy's cruel treatment of the Jews [2:25-4:13]

            D: Thwarting the registration (divine intervention) [4:14-21]

        C': Ptolemy's cruel treatment of the Jews [5:1-51]

    B': Eleazar's prayer of intercession (divine intervention) [6:1-29]

A': Ptolemy delivers and defends the Jews [6:30-7:23].

The holy intercessors of the persecuted Jews, Simon and Eleazar, find their prayers answered. Divine intervention, a theme repeated throughout the book, takes its most striking and significant form with the miracle that prevents the Jews from submitting to official registration, torture and death (D).

The Septuagint version of Psalm 151 appears as follows in the *NRSV:*

1. I was small among my brothers, and the youngest
   in my father's house; I tended my father's sheep.

2. My hands made a harp; my fingers fashioned a lyre.

3. And who will tell my Lord? The Lord himself;
   it is he who hears.

4. It was he who sent his messenger and took me from
   my father's sheep, and anointed me with his anointing oil.

5. My brothers were handsome and tall, but the Lord was not pleased with them.

6. I went out to meet the Philistine, and he cursed me by his idols.

7. But I drew his own sword; I beheaded him, and took away disgrace from the people of Israel.

This passage reads more like narrative prose than like the poetry we associate with the psalter. Its poetic flow, however, appears once we set its themes in chiastic parallelism:

A : (v. 1)   The humility of David in his father's house →
A': (v. 7)   The greatness of his victory among the sons of Israel

B : (v. 2)   David the musician →
B': (v. 6)   David the warrior

C : (v. 3)   The Lord himself chooses David →
C': (v. 5)   The Lord rejects David's brothers

D: (v. 4)   David's anointing
    και ηρεν με / εκ των προβατων / του πατρος μου //
    και εχρισεν με / εν τω ελαιω / της χρισεως αυτου. //

Without reproducing the entire text of the Prayer of Manasseh, we can indicate its chiastic flow by the following outline:[12]

A : (v.1-4)   Praise of God as Lord over heaven and earth →
A': (v.15)   Praise of God by those in heaven and on earth

B : (v. 5-7a)   God's mercy on the suffering repentant sinner →
B': (v. 13e-14)   God's mercy on the unworthy repentant sinner

C : (v. 7b)   God's promised forgiveness →
C': (v. 13a-d)   Manasseh's petition for forgiveness

D : (v. 8)   Manasseh acknowledges himself to be a sinner →
D': (v. 11f)   Manasseh acknowledges his sins and transgressions

E : (v. 9)   The multitude of Manasseh's sins →
E': (v. 10)   The burden of Manasseh's sins.

c) New Testament Apocrypha

Third century Egyptian Christianity produced the *Pistis Sophia*, a gnostic gospel that purports to relate instructions of the risen Christ to his disciples. This curious work contains numerous passages that exhibit some form of parallelism. The following examples represent a random sampling:

> A: But Mary Magdalene and John, the maiden [*sic*], will
> *surpass all my disciples* and all men who shall receive
> mysteries in the *Ineffable*,
>
> > B: they will be on my right hand and on my left,
> >
> > > C: and I am they and they are I,
> >
> > B': and they will be equal with you in all things,
> > save that your thrones will surpass theirs,
>
> A': and my own throne will *surpass yours* and those of all men
> who shall find the word of the *Ineffable* (ch.96).[13]

A:A' form an inclusion as indicated by the italic type. Heightening is suggested in A', in that Christ's throne will surpass every other, both of the disciples and of the favored Mary (Magdalene) and John the Virgin (παρθενος). The parallel between B and B' reflects the Synoptic Gospel affirmation that the disciples will sit on thrones in the Kingdom of God to judge the twelve tribes of Israel (Mt 19:28). Even though Mary and John will sit at Jesus' side in glory, the thrones of the disciples will surpass theirs. The central focus of the passage presents the typical gnostic teaching of mystical union between Christ and his chosen, one in which total identity exists between the two: "I am they and they are I."

Another example, from ch. 61 of the *Pistis Sophia*, concerns the union of the child Jesus with the Spirit.

[Mary declares to the risen (Jesus)]:

> A: When you were small, before the *Spirit* had come upon you,
> while you were with Joseph in a vineyard, the Spirit came
> from on high and *came to me* in my house,
>
> > B: *resembling you*, and I did not recognize him, and I thought
> > that it was you. And the Spirit said to me: Where is Jesus,
> > my brother, that I may meet him?
> >
> > > C: When he said this to me, I was perplexed and thought
> > > that it was a ghost come to tempt me. And I seized him
> > > and *bound him to the foot of the bed* which is in my house,

> D: until *I went out to you both,* to you and Joseph
> in the field and found you in the vineyard,
> while *Joseph* was fencing in the vineyard.
>
> E: Now it came to pass that, when *you heard* me
> speak the word to Joseph,
>
> F: you understood the word, and were glad
>
> E': *and said:* Where is he, that I may see him?
> For I await him in this place.
>
> D': And it came to pass that, when *Joseph* heard you
> say these words, he was perplexed, and *we went
> up together,*
>
> C': entered the house, and found the Spirit *bound to the bed.*
>
> B': And we looked at you and him and found that
> *you resembled him,*
>
> A': and when *he* who was bound to the bed was freed,
> he embraced you and *kissed you,* and you kissed him
> and *you both became one.*[14]

The passage concludes with the familiar gnostic theme of union, this time between Christ and the Spirit. The central focus, however, is the affirmation by Mary that her son heard the word she spoke, understood it and was glad. As E:E' declare, the word addressed by Mary to Joseph was in fact intended for the child Jesus, who "in this place" was waiting for the coming of his brother-Spirit.

There is growing evidence that chiasmus was a literary device used extensively in the apocryphal and pseudepigraphical writings of the early centuries A.D. One of my former students, Nicolae Roddy, has analyzed the chiastic structure of the Protevangelium of James.[15] By eliminating interpolated material in the latter half of the work, he finds the whole composition — a second century panegyric to the Virgin Mary — to center about Mary's miraculous birth, her presentation in the temple, and her espousal to Joseph. Preliminary study indicates that this central passage itself represents the concentric parallelism so familiar from the Hebrew and Christian Scriptures.

d) The Apostolic Fathers

The conditions under which St. Ignatius of Antioch composed his extant letters hardly provided the time and serenity needed for formal composition. Nevertheless, there appear throughout his writings passages that do reflect chiastic patterns. Again we offer a few random selections:

Ephesians 8.2 (inverted parallelism)

> They who are carnal cannot do spiritual things,
> neither can they who are spiritual do carnal things,
>
> just as faith is incapable of the deeds of infidelity,
> and infidelity of the deeds of faith.[16]

Ephesians 7.2 (a creedal fragment)

> A: There is one Physician:
>   B: both flesh and spirit,
>   C: begotten and unbegotten,
>   D: in man, God,
>   D': in death, true life,
>   C': both from Mary and from God,
>   B': first passible and then impassible,
> A': Jesus Christ our Lord.[17]

Magnesians 13.1-2 (concentric prose exhortation)

> A: Be diligent therefore to be confirmed in the ordinances
>   of the Lord and the Apostles, *in order that* "you may *prosper*
>   in all things whatsoever ye do" *in the flesh and in the spirit*,
>   B: in faith and *love*, in the *Son* and the *Father* and the Spirit,
>   at the beginning and at the end,
>   C: together with your revered *bishop* and with
>   your *presbytery*, that aptly woven spiritual crown,
>   and with the godly *deacons*.
>   C': Be subject to the *bishop* and to *one another*,
>   B': even as Jesus Christ was *subject* to the Father,
>   and the Apostles were *subject* to *Christ* and to the *Father*,
> A': *in order that* there may be a *union* both of *flesh and of spirit*.[18]

The most poignant and moving account of an early Christian martyrdom is that of the aged Polycarp, bishop of Smyrna, that took place in 155 or 156. This is the oldest example of the genre we possess. It takes the form of a letter from the church in Smyrna to the church in Philomelium, and among other interesting characteristics, it attests to the veneration of martyrs' relics already by the mid-second century. Chapter 14 describes Polycarp bound to the stake "as a noble ram out of a great flock, for an oblation, a whole burnt offering made ready and acceptable to God."[19] The old man lifts his eyes to heaven and offers the following prayer. This passage has been the object of numerous studies because of its obvious liturgical ring and its reflection of mid-second century theology.[20]

A: Lord, God almighty, Father of *your beloved* and blessed *Child Jesus Christ* (ο του αγαπητου και ευλογητου παιδος σου Ιησου Χριστου), *through whom* we have received full knowledge of you, the God of angels and powers and all creation, and of the race (γενους) of the righteous who live before you:

   B: *I bless you*

      C: that you have found me *worthy* of this day and hour

         D: to receive (του λαβειν με) a portion among the number of the *martyrs* in the *cup of your Christ*

            E: for resurrection to eternal life both of body and soul in the incorruption of the Holy Spirit;

         D': among whom may I be received (προσδεχθειην) before you today as a rich and acceptable *sacrifice*,

      C': just as you *prepared beforehand* and made manifest and fulfilled (it), O unlying and true God.

   B': For this reason and for all things *I* also praise, *bless* and glorify you

A': through the eternal and heavenly High Priest, Jesus Christ, *your beloved Child* (Ιησου Χριστου, αγαπητου σου παιδος) *through whom* to you, with himself and the Holy Spirit, be glory both now and into the ages to come. Amen.

A → A': Revelation from God to the righteous through Christ → Doxology to God from the righteous through Christ.

B → B': Polycarp: I bless you → Polycarp: I praise, bless and glorify you.

C → C': Election (you have found me worthy) →
Predestination (you prepared beforehand).

D → D': Polycarp a martyr →
Polycarp a sacrifice.

E: Central focus on the resurrection of body and soul.

One final example needs to be mentioned among the writings attributed to the Apostolic Fathers. Chapters 9 and 10 of the Didachê or Teaching of the Twelve Apostles, have generally been thought to represent parallel prayers, the first concerning the eucharist proper, the second giving the thanksgiving to be offered at the conclusion of the meal.[21] In a seminar paper entitled "Chiasmus in Jewish Meal Blessings and Some Christian Anaphoras," (Spring, 1990) my student Walter Ray demonstrated that these two chapters are woven together in a tight A:B:C:B'A' pattern, with B and C containing internal chiasms. The focus of the entire passage is on the parallelism of 10:3, "thou gavest food and drink to men for their enjoyment...and to us thou didst grant spiritual food and drink."

Furthermore, Ray convincingly grounded both the structure and the content of other early Christian anaphoras in ancient Jewish meal blessings: the anaphora of *Addai and Mari;* the *Liturgy of St. John Chrysostom* (in which the anaphora balances the anamnesis with the epiklesis, and the whole focuses on the celebrant's declaration: "Thine own of Thine own, we offer unto Thee, on behalf of all and for all;" and the people's response: "We praise Thee, We bless Thee, We give thanks unto Thee, O Lord; and we pray unto Thee, O our God"); and the canon of the ancient *Roman Mass*, the central focus of which is the institution narrative, flanked by the two petitions requesting God to accept this offering.

Other examples of chiastic patterns, given below, further demonstrate the persistence of this literary form, from apostolic times to the present, and in secular as well as religious compositions.

2. "PHOS HILARON" ("O Gladsome Light")

An ancient example we should discuss in some detail is the early Christian hymn known as the *Phôs hilaron* — from the office of the Lucernarium [λυχνικον] — commonly translated "O Gladsome Light." Dating perhaps as far back as the early second century, this praise to Christ, as the joyful or radiant Light, is still sung at every Vespers service in the Eastern Orthodox Church. Its origins, according to Gregory Dix, lie in the ancient Jewish practice of lighting and blessing a lamp at the evening meals of Friday and Saturday, to mark the beginning and end of the Sabbath.[22] The traditional Jewish evening service preserves elements that support this opinion. Its opening benedictions, preceding the Shema, are composed in such a way as to suggest a concentric flow:[23]

Asher bid'varo (b. Ber. 11b)

A : *Blessed art Thou, O Lord* our God, King of the universe, *who* at Thy word *bringest on the evening twilight,*

    B : with wisdom *openest* the gates of the heavens, and with understanding *changest* times and *variest* the seasons, and *arrangest* the stars in their watches in the sky, according to Thy will.

        C : *Thou createst day and night;*

            D : Thou rollest away the *light* from before the *darkness* / and the *darkness* from before the *light* //

        C': *Thou makest* the *day* to pass *and* the *night* to approach, and dividest the day from the night, the Lord of hosts is Thy name;

    B': a God living and enduring continually, mayest Thou *reign over us* for ever and ever.

A': *Blessed art Thou, O Lord, who bringest on the evening twilight.*

A → A':   Blessing God who brings on the evening twilight →
          Blessing God who brings on the evening twilight.

B → B':   God reigns over his creation →
          May God reign over his people.

C → C':   God creates day and night →
          God creates day and night.

D: God brings light out of darkness.

Ahavath olam (b. Ber. 11b)

A :   With everlasting love Thou hast *loved* the house of *Israel*,
      Thy people;

   B :   a *Law* and commandments, statutes and judgments
      hast *Thou taught us.*

      C :   Therefore, O Lord our God, when we lie down and
      when we rise up we will *meditate* on Thy statutes;

         D :   yea, we will rejoice in the words of Thy Law /
      and in Thy commandments for ever / /

      C':   for they are our life and the length of our days,
      and we will *meditate* on them day and night.

   B':   And mayest Thou never take away *Thy love from us.*

A':   Blessed art Thou, O Lord, who *lovest Thy people Israel.*

A → A':   God has loved his people Israel →
          God loves his people Israel.

B → B':   God taught his Law (the expression of his love) →
          Take not Thy love (Thy Law) from us.

C → C':   We will meditate on Thy statutes →
          We will meditate on them as the source of our life.

D: We will rejoice in Thy Law / In Thy commandments *forever.*

It is this ritual in its pre-Christian Jewish form that was presumably taken over by the Church as a blessing of the evening lamp. Recently, Robert Taft has called this widely accepted view into question, arguing that "the Christian lucernarium is a baptized pagan rite."[24] Parallels with the above benedictions nevertheless point in favor of the more traditional understanding. However the matter may be decided, the following hymn stood as a primary element of the Jerusalem vesperal service from at least the fourth century.[25]

To stress the importance of the central element, we revert to the use of numbers for each verset:

2: Φως ιλαρον αγιας δοξης, αθανατου Πατρος, ουρανιου, αγιου, μακαρος Ιησου Χριστε,

    1: ελθοντες επι την ηλιου δυσιν, ιδοντες φως εσπερινον, υμνουμεν

        0: Πατερα, Υιον και Αγιον Πνευμα· Θεον.

    1': αξιον σε εν πασι καιροις υμνεισθαι φωναις αισιαις,

2': Υιε Θεου, ζωην ο διδους, δι' ο ο κοσμος σε δοξαζει.

2: *O Gladsome Light* of the holy *glory* of the immortal, heavenly, holy Father: blessed *Jesus Christ,*

    1: Having come to the setting of the sun and beheld the light of *evening, we hymn*

        0: *Father, Son and Holy Spirit:* **God!**

    1': Thou art worthy to be *hymned at all times* with voices of praise,[26]

2': *O Son of God,* giver of *life,* therefore the cosmos *glorifies* Thee.

From 2 to 2' there occurs a heightening from Christ as the reflection of the glory of the immortal Father, to glorification of Christ himself as Son of God and Giver of Life. The contrast from 1 to 1' is between the immediate hymning of praise to the Trinity at the vesperal service, and the hymning of Christ's praise "at all times," thereby ascribing to the Son of God the same adoration due in Christian worship to the other divine Persons of the Godhead. This implicit affirmation of the consubstantiality of the Son with the Father and the Spirit (*homoousios*) then leads to the central motif: the trinitarian confession of Father, Son and Holy Spirit as God.

The chiastic structuring of this passage serves to affirm the most basic element of the orthodox creeds worked out from the second through the fourth centuries: Jesus Christ, the Son of God, who embodies both the glory and the life-giving power of the Father, is himself God. As one of the Holy Trinity, he is worthy to receive — from the Church and from the cosmos as a whole — the same adoration and praise that are due to the Father and the Holy Spirit.[27]

3. KATAXIOSON
("Vouchsafe, O Lord")

A nother early Christian liturgical prayer, of still more obscure origin, also displays a chiastic shape. Designated by its opening words, Καταξιωσον Κυριε ("Vouchsafe, O Lord"), it appears in the Byzantine tradition at the close of the Lesser Doxology as well as independently in the Vespers service, where it precedes the Litany of Supplication. There it occupies a central place, marking the transition from one day to the next, from the day past to the day to come.[28]

The origins of this prayer have been located in Book VIII of the "Apostolic Constitutions," a fourth century Syrian document that preserves an ancient form of the Antiochene Liturgy.[29] It is essentially a composite of scriptural verses, drawn particularly from the Psalms (33:22; 119:12; 138:8), that concludes with a traditional doxology to the Holy Trinity. In its present form it seems to derive from Palestinian monasticism. According to the testimony of John Moschus (d. ca. 619), it was a familiar element of the Palestinian monastic office by the early seventh century.[30] The text that appears in the Greek *horologion* (*Book of the Hours*) can be arranged chiastically as follows:

Καταξιωσον, Κυριε, εν τη νυκτι ταυτη, αναμαρτητους φυλαχθηναι ημας.

2: Ευλογητος ει Κυριε, ο Θεος των πατερων ημων και αινετον και δεδοξασμενον το ονομα σου εις τους αιωνας. Αμην.

    1: Γενοιτο, Κυριε, το ελεος σου εφ' ημας, καθαπερ ηλπισαμεν επι σε.

        0: Ευλογητος ει Κυριε, διδαξον με τα δικαιωματα σου. Ευλογητος ει Δεσποτα, συνετισον με τα δικαιωματα σου. Ευλογητος ει Αγιε, φωτισον με τοις δικαιωμασι σου.

    1': Κυριε, το ελεος σου εις τον αιωνα, τα εργα των χειρων σου μη παριδης.

2': Σοι πρεπει αινος, σοι πρεπει υμνος, σοι δοξα πρεπει, τω Πατρι και τω Υιω και τω Αγιω Πνευματι, νυν και αει και εις τους αιωνας των αιωνων. Αμην.

[Anacrusis:] Vouchsafe, O Lord, to keep us this night without sin.

2: Blessed art Thou, O Lord, the *God* of our fathers, and *praised* and *glorified* is Thy Name forever. Amen.

  1: Let *Thy mercy, O Lord,* be upon *us,* as we have hoped in Thee.

    0: Blessed art Thou, O Lord: teach me Thy statutes;
    Blessed art Thou, O Master, let me understand
    Thy statutes;
    Blessed art Thou, O Holy One, enlighten me with
    Thy statutes.

  1': *O Lord, Thy mercy* is for ever; do not turn away from the *works of Thy hands.*

2': To Thee belongs *praise,* to Thee belongs worship, to Thee belongs *glory,* to the *Father* and to the *Son* and to the *Holy Spirit,* now and ever and unto ages of ages. Amen.

Here again the principle of intensification, from 2 to 2' to 1 to 1' to the threefold central benediction, is evident.

2 → 2': Opening doxology: God praised and glorified →
Closing doxology: the Holy Trinity praised and glorified.

1 → 1': The Lord's mercy upon us →
The Lord's mercy upon us (who are the work of his hands).

0: The threefold benediction, moving incrementally from "Lord" to "Master" to "Holy One."

This threefold designation, "Lord – Master – Holy One," appears as well in the prayers of introduction to the Byzantine office: "O All holy Trinity, have mercy on us. Lord, forgive us our sins. Master, pardon our transgressions. Holy One, visit and heal our infirmities, for thy Name's sake." Popular piety has often understood these designations as referring respectively to the three persons of the Trinity: Father, Son and Holy Spirit. The original intention of "Vouchsafe" seems rather to have focused on the intensification implied by the verbs: teach – understand – enlighten. That a trinitarian allusion cannot be altogether discounted, however, is indicated by the fact that this prayer concludes the Lesser Doxology, also structured chiastically, and forms a parallel with the Doxology's earlier references to Father, Son and Holy Spirit. The following is a literal translation.

4: Glory to God in the highest and on earth peace, good will
to all people. We *hymn* you, we bless you, we worship you,
we *glorify* you, we give thanks to you for your great *glory*.

3: Lord, King, heavenly *God*, Father almighty; *Lord*,
only-begotten *Son* Jesus Christ; and the *Holy Spirit*.

2: *Lord God*, Lamb of God, Son of the Father, who *takes
away the sin of the world*, have *mercy* on us,
you who take away the *sins* of the world.

1: *Receive our prayer*, you who sit at the right hand
of the Father, and have mercy on us.

0: For you alone are Holy, you alone are Lord, Jesus
Christ, to the glory of God the Father. Amen.

1': Every evening *we bless you*, and *praise* your Name
for ever, even to the ages of ages.

2': O Lord, you have been our refuge from generation to
generation. I said: Lord, have *mercy* on me; heal my
soul, for *I have sinned* against you. Lord, to you I have
fled: teach me to do your will, for *you are my God*. For
from you is the source of life; in your light we see light.
Grant, O Lord, in this night, to keep us without *sin*.

3': Blessed are you, *O Lord, God* of our fathers, and praised
and glorified is your name for ever. Amen. Let your mercy,
O Lord, be upon us, as we have hoped in you. Blessed are
you, *Lord:* teach me your statutes. Blessed are you, *Master:*
enlighten me by your statutes. Blessed are you, *Holy One*,
illumine me by your statutes.

4': Lord, your mercy endures forever, do not reject the works of
your hands. To you is due praise, to you is due a *hymn*, to you
is due *glory*, to the Father and to the Son and to the Holy Spirit,
now and forever, and to the ages of ages. Amen.

The parallels in the Doxology as a whole are less apparent and
more tenuous than in the concluding portion, "Vouchsafe" ("Grant,
O Lord"). The movement, however, seems to follow the same concentric pattern. Thus:

4 → 4': Opening praise and glorification →
Closing praise and glorification.

3 → 3': God as Lord → Son → Holy Spirit →
God as Lord → Master → Holy One.

2 → 2': Lord God, sin, mercy →
Lord, God, sin, mercy.

1 → 1': Our prayer for mercy →
Our prayer of blessing and praise.

0: The central focus attributes to Jesus Christ the divine
attribute Holy and the divine title Lord, "to the glory
of God the Father" (cf. Phil 2:11).

Hypothetical as the reconstruction of the entire Doxology may
be, there can be no doubt that the prayer "Vouchsafe, O Lord," was
deliberately composed in accordance with the principles of concentric parallelism. A primitive version of the Doxology appears in ch.
7 of the Apostolic Constitutions, but without this final prayer.[31] This
has led specialists in the field of liturgics to conclude that "Vouchsafe" originally circulated independently of the Doxology, finding
a fixed place in the vesperal office sometime before the end of the
sixth century.

If this is true, it raises a perplexing question. In the Doxology
proper, an intentional balance seems to have been created between
1 and 1', and between 2 and 2'. How then could the *Kataxioson* have
been integrated into a previously existing composition, so as to
expand the parallelism to 3:3' and 4:4'? The tight chiastic structure
of the *Kataxioson* clearly indicates that the prayer circulated as an
independent unit and became attached to the Doxology only at a
secondary stage of composition. This means that the Lesser Doxology would have had to be restructured so as to create parallelism
throughout the entire composite piece. This, however, seems unlikely since the first half of the Lesser Doxology is virtually identical
to the (presumably) more primitive Great Doxology (which incorporated a truncated version of *Kataxioson*). The history of these
doxological texts and their relation to the *Kataxioson* remain an
enigma. Its solution would go far toward helping us understand
how one chiastic unit can be integrated into another so as to preserve
concentric parallelism throughout the whole.

4. ROMANOS THE MELODIST: KONTAKIA

The liturgical hymns of St. Romanos "the Melodist" (ο μελωδός) further indicate that during the sixth century A.D., chiasmus was a familiar and widely used technique of literary composition.

Although he is relatively unknown in the West, Romanos easily ranks among the most outstanding of Christian poets. His "kontakia," or metrical sermonic hymns, immediately established this converted Jew from Emesa (Syria) as one of the leading theologians of his day.[32] A few examples from "On the Nativity I (Mary and the Magi)"[33] will suffice to illustrate his use of concentric parallelism.

The *Prooimion* or introduction to this series of hymns celebrating Christ's birth is still sung today in Orthodox (Byzantine rite) churches, and is alone referred to as the "kontakion" of the feast. It is composed on an A:B:C:B':A' model, where A' expresses the antinomy of the "Newborn babe" who is "God before time."

A: The Virgin today *gives birth* to the *superessential One*,

    B: And the *earth proffers* the cave to the unapproachable One.

        C: Angels with the shepherds sing songs of praise;

    B': The Magi, with the *star to guide* pursue their way.

A': For us there has been born a *newborn babe*, the *God* before time.

A → A': The birth in the flesh of the God beyond nature →
The birth in time of the God beyond time.

B → B': The role of the earth (to offer a cave) →
The role of the heavens (a star to guide).

C: The central theme unites the voices of humble shepherds
with those of the angelic chorus, to offer praise to God
born in the flesh.

Many of the following strophes are structured according to a similar chiastic pattern. In each instance the strophe concludes with repetition of the fundamental mystery, "A newborn babe, the God before time."

Strophe 1:

A: Bethlehem opened Eden, *come let us behold*. We have found joy in *this* hidden *place*, *come* let us seize the pleasures of Paradise within the cave.

   B: There appeared an *unwatered root* which sprouted *forgiveness*.

      C: There was found an undug well from which David once yearned to drink.

   B': And there the *Virgin brought forth* an infant who at once *quenched their thirst*, that of Adam and of David.

A': *Come*, then, *let us hasten* to *this place* where there has been born a newborn babe, the God before time.

A → A': Let us come to this Paradise within the cave →
Let us come to visit the babe who is God.

B → B': An unwatered root has sprouted forgiveness →
A Virgin has borne a child who quenched thirst.

C: The well (of Bethlehem, 1 Chr 11:17-19) from which David yearned to drink is a typological image of the Virgin (the "undug" well), who bears the Water of Life.[34]

Particularly significant here is the heightening effect from strophe I to II: from "the pleasures of Paradise" to the newborn babe, who is the eternal God; and from the unwatered root that sprouts forgiveness, to the Virgin's child who quenches thirst. Reference to Adam as well as to David in B' serves to heighten the conceptual center, by proclaiming that the water issuing from the virginal source quenches the thirst for forgiveness in humankind as a whole.

Further examples are offered by strophes 4 and 5, which include a dialogue between Mary and the Magi.

Strophe 4

A: While she was pondering these things in secret, and entreating *Him* who has knowledge of all secret things,

   B: She hears the Magi who are *seeking the child*.

      C: Straightway, the maiden called out to them: "Who are you?"

         D: And they to her: "Who art thou

           E: Who hast produced and brought forth such an One?

D′:   Who, thy father? Who, thy mother?

C′:   For thou hast become the mother and nurse
of a fatherless son.

B′:   It was *His* star that we saw when we came to *behold*

A′:   a newborn babe, the *God* before time."

A → A′:   The secret things →
The ultimate mystery.

B → B′:   The Magi seek the child →
The Magi behold the child.

C → C′:   Mary's question: puzzlement →
The Magi's response: wonder.

D → D′:   The Magi's question →
The Magi's questions.

E: Mary has brought forth God in the flesh.

Strophe 5

A: "Clearly did Balaam reveal to us the meaning of the words
which were *prophesied*,[35]

B: Saying that a *star* would rise up,

C: A *star* which would *dim* all prophecies and divinations,

D: A star to destroy the parables of the wise,
their teachings and their enigmas.

C′:   A *star* much *brighter* than this star which just appeared,

B′:   for He is the maker of *stars*

A′:   About whom it was *written:* 'From Jacob shall rise up
a newborn babe, the God before time'."

A → A′:   The prophecy of the Davidic King →
The prophecy of God in the flesh.

B → B′:   The prophetic star →
The Creator of the stars.

C → C′:   A Star that dims prophecies →
A Star brighter than the guiding star.

D: That Star will destroy the false wisdom of "the wise."

In each of these passages, as in many more we could cite, the author makes conscious use of chiasmus to draw the reader's attention step by step toward the conceptual center. The heightening effect and helical movement appear here, just as they do in Scripture. Must we conclude that Romanos learned this technique from the Bible itself, that he has merely taken over a pattern of composition he detected in the biblical texts? Far more likely is the alternative possibility that he is adapting a technique of literary composition which flourished in the Mediterranean world of his day. This is confirmed by the fact that his near contemporary, St. John of Sinai, also drew on principles of chiasmus to construct a spiritual classic that has inspired generations of monastics and laypersons alike.

5. JOHN OF SINAI: "THE LADDER OF DIVINE ASCENT"

S t. John Climacus (ca. 570-649) is the author of a highly popular ascetic work that deals with the acquisition of monastic virtues leading to ἀπαθεια or "passionlessness." Called *The Ladder of Divine Ascent*,[36] the work is divided into thirty chapters, to correspond to the age of Christ at the beginning of his public ministry.

Several attempts have been made in recent years to analyze the structure of the *Ladder*.[37] In 1972, Guerric Couilleau published an analysis of the work that recognized its system of "parallel oppositions," that is, concentric parallelism or chiasmus.[38] Building on this and subsequent studies, Richard Lawrence proposed an outline for the *Ladder* that divides the thirty chapters into three subgroupings: Repentance (chs. 1-6), Mourning (chs. 7-24), and Humility (chs. 25-30).[39]

I. *Repentance*

    1. Renunciation of Life

        2. Detachment

           3. Exile

           4. Obedience

        5. Penance

    6. Remembrance of Death

II. *Mourning*

    7. Mourning

        8. Anger

        9. Malice

        10. Slander

        11. Talkativeness

        12. Falsehood

           13. Despondency

14. Gluttony
15. Lust
16. Avarice
17. Poverty
18. Insensitivity
19. Sleep
20. Alertness
21. Fear
22. Vainglory
23. Pride
24. Meekness

III. *Humility*

25. Humility
26. Discernment
   Summary of Preceding
27. Stillness
28. Pure Prayer
29. Apatheia
30. Agape (Love)

As the outline indicates, the meditations on Repentance and Humility flank the central portion on Mourning like wings that lift and transform soul-destroying vices into saving virtues. Each part is itself structured chiastically, and the whole focuses on the struggle against Lust. As Fr. Lawrence points out, the pivotal role played by this passage concerning the ultimate temptation of the flesh is underscored by Climacus himself: "This is the fifteenth reward of victory. He who has earned it while still alive has died and been resurrected. From now on he has a taste of the immortality to come."[40]

Once the penitent has passed beyond the "rung" of lust, the bodily passions are more readily subjected to the spirit's quest for true virtue, which culminates in passionlessness and love. By detecting the concentric flow of this remarkable ascetic work, Fr. Lawrence has offered an indispensable key to its interpretation. The force of Climacus' work, and its enduring appeal as a guide to the spiritual life, lies once again in the author's deft use of chiasmus.

6. CLEMENCE OF BARKING: "LIFE OF ST. CATHERINE"

Byzantine tradition is not alone in preserving chiastic structures down to the Middle Ages. A twelfth century "Life of Saint Catherine," by Clemence of Barking[41] contains several passages that display a similar concentric, helical "shape." The original Old French version reveals the pattern more clearly, and is reproduced here from MacBain's critical edition.[42]

According to the Catherine legend, the Alexandrian saint found herself engaged in debate with fifty rhetors, summoned by the Emperor Maxentius (d. 312) to refute her Christian beliefs. Catherine had defied the Emperor's command to offer sacrifices to pagan idols. Recognized by him to be of noble birth because of her exceptional beauty and eloquence, she became the spokeswoman for the persecuted Christians of Alexandria. Through her impassioned yet well-reasoned witness, all fifty of the orators were converted to Christianity, only to endure the "baptism of flames."

The first selection consists of the chief rhetor's angry reply to Catherine's profession of faith in the God-man, Jesus Christ. It begins with a typical introductory statement (anacrusis), then continues in an A:B:C:D:E:D':C':B':A' pattern.

(Vv. 781-804)
Car li respunt par mult grant ire,
Car a peine li sout que dire:

A: *'Par fei, fait il, par ço te pruis*
      Qu'en tes diz verté nen truis.
      Se il est tel cum tu nus diz,
      E Deu e hume e a Deu fiz,
      Cument pot le fil Deu murir
      Ne nun mortel la mort suffrir?

B: *Murir ne puet pas par dreiture*
      Quant nun mortele est sa nature.

C: *Se hume fud, dunc est mortel*
      E nient a nun mortel uel.

D: *Murir ne pot se il fu Deus*
    Ne revivre se fud mortels.

 E: *Cument puet hume veintre mort?*

D': *E se Deu murut ço fut tort.*

C': *Mortel ne puet mort eschiver*
     Ne nun mortel la mort user.

B': *Cuntre nature te desleies,*
     C'ors de raisun te forveies.

A': *Deu u hume granter le puis,*
     Kar d'ambure le dreit nen truis.
     L'un u l'altre estre l'estuet,
     Car l'un e l'altre estre ne puet.'

He replied to her with great anger, for he hardly knew what to say to her:

A: "In faith, he said, I prove it to you thus that in your words
    I find no truth. If he is such as you tell us, *both God and man*
    and son of God, how can the son of God die, or an immortal
    suffer death?

 B: Die he cannot rightfully when immortal is his *nature.*

  C: If he was man, then he is *mortal* and in no way equal
      to an *immortal.*

   D: *Die* he cannot if he was *God*, nor live again
       if he was mortal.

    E: How can a man conquer death?

   D': And if *God died*, this was wrong.

  C': A *mortal* cannot avoid death, nor an *immortal* death
       undergo.

 B': Against *nature* you are unleashing yourself,
      since from the path of reason you are straying.

A': *God or man* I can allow, but in both together *I find no truth.*
     One or the other it must be, for one and the other it cannot be.

A → A': No truth that he is both God and man →
         No truth that he can be both God and man.

B → B': God's nature is immortal →
         Catherine argues against God's nature.

C → C': He was mortal and not immortal →
Only a mortal, and not an immortal is subject to death.

D → D': God can not die →
God must not die.

E: The central affirmation of Christian faith: a (God-)man
has conquered death.

In her response, Catherine argues from Christ's manifestation in creation and human life, to his resurrection in the flesh, focusing her witness on the mystery of the God-man.

(Vv. 823-874)

A: *Or esguardez ses criatures*
E lur estres e lur natures,
Kar par els purras saveir
Le suen nun disable poeir.

B: *En tutes mustre sa poissance;*
Il sul est a tuz sustenance.

C: *Des qu'il tute rien fist de nient*
E tute rien par sei maintient
E sur tute rien est poissant
E tut ad fait a sun talant,
Ne pot cil dunc hume devenir,
Ki tut puet faire a sun plaisir?

D: *E ne pot il faire de sei*
Ço qu'il fist de mei e de tei?

E: *Par poesté, nient par nature,*
Devint li faitres criature.
Hume devint a tuz mustrable,
Kar en sei fud Deu nun veable.

F: *Se huem ne fust ne poust murir,*
E se Deus, ne poust revesquir.

G: *Briefment te dirrai ci la sume:*
L'ume fu en Deu et Deu en l'ume.

F': *Le fiz Deu en charn mort suffri*
E la char en Deu revesqui.

E': *Ne pot il sei resusciter*
Ki mortels morz fist relever,
Li quel erent mort par nature
E par destresce de dreiture?

D': *Leprus e desvez esmunda,*
     Enferms e avoegles sana.

C': *Se tu ne creis que Jhesu Crist*
     Ses miracles el mund feist,
     Crei sevels nun que el nun Jhesu
     Unt plusurs eu ceste vertu.

B': *Plusurs par lui morz raviverent*
     E par sun nun enferms sanerent.

A': *Bien deit estre cil Deu creu*
     Ki dune as suens tele vertu.
     Mult est la vertu grande en sei
     Quant hume l'ad tele par sa fei.
     Bien la puet cil en sei mustrer
     Ki as altres la puet duner.

A: Now behold *his creatures* and their beings and their natures,
    for through them you will be able to know his ineffable *power*.

B: In all he shows his *might;* he alone is to all things *sustenance*.

C: Since he *made all things from nought* and maintains them
    by himself and is *powerful* over all things and has made
    everything according to his own will, can he not then
    become man?

D: And can he not *make* of himself what he made
    of *me* and of *you?*

E: By might, not by *nature*, did the *Creator become
    a creature*. Man he became, demonstrable to all,
    for in himself he was God invisible.

F: If he had not been *man*, he could not have
    died, and if not *God*, he could not have *risen*.

G: In a word I shall tell you here the
    whole story: the man was in God
    and God in the man.

F': The son of God suffered *death* in the *flesh*,
    and in the flesh *rose* again in *God*.

E': Could he not *resuscitate himself* who as a mortal
    raised the dead who had died as was meet
    and right and by the constraint of *nature?*

D': Lepers and lunatics he *cleansed*, the infirm
    and blind he *cured*.

C': If you do not believe that Jesus Christ *performed*
these miracles in the world, believe at least that
in the name of Jesus many have had this *power*.

B': Many through him have *restored life* to the dead,
and by his name have *cured* the infirm.

A': This God truly deserves to be believed in, who gives such
power to his people. This *power* is great in itself when man
can have it by faith. Well can he show it in himself who
is able to give it to *others*.

A → A': God's power manifest in his creatures →
God's power given to his creatures.

B → B': God shows his might and sustains all things →
God raises the dead and cures the infirm.

C → C': Christ's creative power →
Christ's miraculous power given to men.

D → D': He makes himself man →
As man he cleanses and cures.

E → E': Incarnation (contrary to nature) →
Resurrection (contrary to nature).

F → F': Death and resurrection of the God-man →
Death and resurrection of God-in-the-flesh.

G: Man and God united in a single person.

The passage concludes with the following declaration of Christ's
power over death, a power that proves that he was indeed both man
and God, human and divine.

A : *Ci te pruis jo apertement*
Que Jhesu est Deu veirement.

B : *Car bien seit l'um, si Deu ne fust,*
Que ço pas faire ne poust;

C : *E bien set l'um que hume fu Jhesu;*
Ore est Deu e huem par vertu.

B': *E se Jhesu la mort senti,*
Par fei, pur ço mort nel venqui.

A': *La mort n'ocist pas Jhesu Crist,*
Mais Jhesu en sei mort ocist.

A: Here I prove to you clearly that Jesus is God.

    B: For it is well known that, if he were not God,
he could not do this [i.e., raise the dead, raise himself,
grant others power over death].

        C: And it is well known that Jesus was a man. Now he
is God and man by his intrinsic power [*par vertu*].

    B': And if Jesus felt death, that in no way means that death
conquered him.

A': Death did not kill Jesus Christ, but Jesus in himself
killed death.

Here the movement is somewhat different. Parallelism has given way to a spiraling argument which proceeds in its proof from what is known (Jesus accomplished these things; he was a man) to the inevitable conclusion that he must be both God and man. While the passage can be read as straightforward narrative, its inner flow nevertheless remains concentric:

A → A': Jesus is God →
As God, Jesus has conquered death.

B → B': Were he not God, he could not "do this" →
Were he not God, he would have been conquered by death.

C: The central affirmation provides the link between what is
known about Jesus (he performed miracles, gave miraculous
power to others) and what is to be deduced (he is God): he is
both God and man by his *intrinsic power*.

Examples of this kind abound in the work, but one further passage will suffice to illustrate our point. The central section includes an encounter between Catherine and Maxentius' Queen, in which Clemence of Barking has elaborated upon the original legend by stressing the tension between passionate romantic love and unalloyed devotion to God. The Queen has had a dream in which Catherine set a glorious crown upon her head. The Queen comes to the saint in prison and expresses to her both her love for her pagan husband and her desire for deeper knowledge of God. Catherine responds by contrasting the treacherous and ephemeral love of a man with the eternal love promised by God to "his friends." The entire passage focuses upon the vainglory of the rich and powerful: today clothed in magnificent raiment, tomorrow lying in the corruption of death.

(Vv. 1631-1660)
Vers la reine est dunc turnee;
Bonement l'ad recunfortee.

    A: Reine, fait ele, bele amie,
        Mun Deu a ses noces t'envie.
        Seiez dame de fort curage,
        Ne dutez terrien ultrage,
        Car n'est pas digne ceste peine,
        Ne ceste grant dulur mundeine,
        De la joie de pareis,
        Que Deus pramet a ses amis.
    B: Ne dutez pas l'empereur,
        N'aiez mais desir de s'amur.
        S'amur est fraille e decevable,
        E sa poesté trespassable.
        C: De sa vie est si nun certein,
            S'il est oi, ne set si ert demein.
            D: S'il ui reluist en sa purprine,
                Ne set se demein iert vermine.
        C': Tel est le seir rei apelé,
            Ki l'endemein est enterré.
    B': Tels est la poesté humeine,
        Ci n'ad nule joie certeine.
        Dame reine, pur ço pri,
        Ne dutez cest mortel mari.
        Sa poissance ne deis duter,
        Ne s'amur guaires desirer.
  A': Mais met en lui tut tun desir,
        Ki dampner te puet e guarir,
        Ki pur cestes muables peines
        Nus dunrad les joies certeines.

[Anacrusis:] Toward the Queen she then turned; in a kindly manner she comforted her.

    A : "Queen, she said, fair friend, my God invites you to his wedding. Be a lady of strong courage, *fear not any earthly calamity*, for such *pain* and such worldly suffering is not worthy of the *joy of paradise* which God promises to his friends.

B : *Fear not the emperor*, desire no longer *his love*. *His love* is frail
and unreliable, and his *power ephemeral.*

C: He is so uncertain of his life, if he is *here today*,
he does not know if he will still be here *tomorrow*.

D: If today he is resplendent in his purple,
he knows not if tomorrow he may be worms.

C′: One is called king in the *evening* who
the *next day* is buried.

B′: Such is *human power*, here there is no joy that is certain,
Lady Queen, for this reason I implore you: *fear not
this mortal husband*. His *power* you must *not fear*,
nor even *his love* desire.

A′: But in him place all your desire who has the *power to damn
or save* you, for in return for these transitory *pains*,
he will give us the *joys which are certain.*

A → A′: Fear not earthly suffering; God promises the joy of paradise →
Fear him who can damn or save; God will give eternal joys.

B → B′: Fear not the emperor, desire not his love →
Fear not your mortal husband, desire not his love.

C → C′: Here today, gone tomorrow →
A king in the evening, the next day a corpse.

D: The emperor's destiny: from earthly splendor to death
and corruption.

Read as plain narrative, the passage would seem to focus upon the transitoriness of earthly suffering, relative to the promised joys of paradise. In this case, Catherine's purpose would be to comfort the Queen and confirm her in her decision to seek the love of God rather than the love of her husband. Read "chiastically," however, a different theme emerges: that of the futility of human power and glory. The passage is concerned to speak more of Maxentius than of the Queen. And it makes its point by the concentric movement from consolation amidst earthly suffering, through a double admonition neither to fear human power nor to desire human love, to insistence upon the wholly ephemeral nature of human power and glory that end inevitably in the grave.

These several examples from Clemence of Barking's *Life of Saint Catherine* display the essential features of chiastic structuring we have found elsewhere: a helical movement, bounded by the "envelope effect" (inclusion), that proceeds in conceptual sweeps about a central theme. The poetic beauty of the composition is further heightened by the fact that the couplets rhyme. This feature is lost with a literal translation into English. Nevertheless, even the reader who is unfamiliar with Old French can sense the power expressed by the central affirmations:

> *Cument puet hume veintre mort?*
>
> *Briefment te dirrai ci la sume:*
> *L'ume fu en Deu e Deu en l'ume.*
>
> *S'il ui reluist en sa purprine,*
> *Ne set se demein iert vermine...*

7. RUSSIAN RELIGIOUS POETRY: "DUKHOVNYE STIKHI"

For nearly three centuries much of Eastern Christendom lay under the rubble of the Byzantine empire, following the sack of Constantinople by the Turks in 1453. Orthodox piety continued to flourish, however, particularly in Russia. In addition to iconography and liturgical poetry, the period saw the spread of popular religious songs known as "dukhovnye stikhi" or "spiritual verses."

One of the most popular of these songs is entitled the "Saturday of St. Dimitri." In his introduction to the genre, D. Obolensky notes that this piece refers to the battle of Kulikovo (1380), "in which the Russians, led by Prince Dimitri of Moscow, defeated the Tatars. It has been described as a 'perfect short story in verse.' "[43] It also reflects the same concentric parallelism we have found elsewhere. As an oral composition, it reinforces the theory that chiastic principles were in some sense "intuited." Rather than working from a tight outline that imposed a concentric structure on the work, the author or composer gave expression to his/her ideas and sentiments through a more or less *unconscious* use of chiasmus. The following is Prof. Obolensky's translation.

A: On the vigil of the *Saturday of St Dimitri*, in the holy cathedral of the Assumption, Saint Cyprian was celebrating the Liturgy;

 B: at this Liturgy *Prince Dimitri* was *present*, with his Orthodox *Princess Evdokiya*, with his princes and boyars, and his glorious generals.

  C: It was just before the singing of 'It is meet'[44] that Prince Dimitri ceased to pray; he leant against a pillar: Prince Dimitri was rapt in contemplation, his spiritual eyes were opened, and he beheld a marvellous *vision:* he sees not the *candles burning* before the icons nor the *gems sparkling* on the gold *casings of the images*, he hears not the sacred chanting:

D: he sees the open plain, the open plain of Kulikovo.
The plain is strewn with corpses of Christians and
Tatars: the Christians glimmer like candles, and
the Tatars are like black pitch. Over the plain of
Kulikovo walks the *most holy Mother of God*, ... and
behind her come the *Apostles* of the Lord, the holy
archangels and angels, with brightly burning candles.

E: They are *chanting the requiem* over the relics
of the Orthodox [warriors]; the most holy
Mother of God censes them, and crowns
descend from Heaven upon *the dead*.

F: The most holy Mother of God inquired:
'And where is Prince Dimitri?'

E': The Apostle Peter answered her: 'Prince
Dimitri is in the city of Moscow, in the holy
cathedral of the Assumption; he is *attending
the Liturgy* with his Princess Evdokiya, with
his *princes* and *boyars*, and his *glorious generals*.'

D': The *most holy Mother of God* said: 'Prince Dimitri
is not in his place: he shall lead the throngs
of *martyrs*, and his princess shall be in *my train*.'

C': Then the *vision* faded. The *candles* began to *burn*
in the church, ... the *gems* began to *sparkle* on the
casings of the images:

B': *Prince Dimitri* came to himself, and he wept tears;
he spoke these words: 'Ah, the hour of my *death* is
at hand, it seems; soon I shall be lying in my tomb,
and *my princess* will become a *nun*.'

A': And in memory of the marvellous vision he instituted
the *Saturday of St Dimitri*.

A → A': Saturday of St. Dimitri / Saturday of St. Dimitri.

B → B': Dimitri and Evdokiya present in life →
Dimitri destined to die; Evdokiya destined for the convent.

C → C': The vision comes: candles, sparkling gems,
casings of images →
The vision ends: candles, sparkling gems, casings of images.

D → D': The Mother of God with her train (Apostles, angels) →
The Mother of God: Dimitri will lead her train; Evdokiya will
be in her train.

E → E': Requiem →
Liturgy.

F: The focal point is the question posed to the Apostle Peter by the
Mother of God: "Where is Prince Dimitri?"

From early Byzantine hymnography, through French romantic
poetry, and on to pious Russian folk-songs, literature produced
throughout medieval Europe displays the same fundamental chiastic "shape" characteristic of ancient Semitic writings. For reasons yet
to be explained, that "shape" crosses historical, cultural and linguistic boundaries with ease. As the following sections illustrate,
it can be found as well in contemporary writings, both religious
and secular.

8. CHIASMUS IN 19th CENTURY RELIGIOUS LITERATURE

We turn now to a few randomly selected examples of poetry and popular hymnography from the nineteenth century that also display a concentric parallelism. In each case the author has made use of the principles of chiasmus to compose his work. And in several cases at least, it appears that he has done so *unconsciously*, drawing as it were upon an intuited form or structure that is as elemental a mode of human communication as narrative development or the language of myth.

The French poet Paul Verlaine (1844-1896) published his well known "Poèmes saturniens" in 1866. Imbued with a profound, if confused and negative, spiritual vision, this collection includes what is perhaps his most famous and popular piece, "Chanson d'automne," or "Autumn Song." It is a masterpiece of discreet images, worked with exquisite precision into an a:a:b:c:c:b rhyme scheme. Interpreters tend to read it literally, fixing upon its "nature" imagery, with the sighing of the autumnal breeze that transports the poet "here and there" in a vapid reverie. But in so doing they miss its distinctively spiritual content. As the A:B:A' structure indicates, the poem is in fact a meditation on the meaning of a man's life in the autumn of his years: as the hour of his death approaches, he finds that memory is no guarantee of immortality, and he ends his life in hopeless acquiescence, a dead leaf blown about by the wind.

> *Les sanglots longs*
> *Des violons*
> *De l'automne*
> *Blessent mon coeur*
> *D'une langueur*
> *Monotone.*[45]
>
> *Tout suffocant*
> *Et blême, quand*
> *Sonne l'heure,*
> *Je me souviens*
> *Des jours anciens,*
> *Et je pleure.*

> *Et je m'en vais*
> *Au vent mauvais*
> *Qui m'emporte*
> *Deçà, delà,*
> *Pareil à la*
> *Feuille morte.*[46]

A rough translation of this poetic gem — that gives the general meaning, but with no hint of its literary beauty and rhythmic precision — would be as follows:

> The drawn out sobbing
> Of autumn's violins
> Wounds my heart
> With a dreary lassitude.
>
> Oppressed and wan
> When the Hour strikes,
> I remember days past,
> And I weep.
>
> And I depart
> On an ill wind,
> Blown here and there
> Like a dead leaf.

In strophe I (A), the autumn breeze evokes the mournful notes of a violin that lull the poet into a "dreary lassitude" both in and over the "fall" of his life. The same theme reappears in strophe III (A'), when the wind turns bad and carries him off to a meaningless end of death with no distinction and no direction. The focus, or conceptual center, is expressed by the middle strophe (B). As the hour of his death draws on, the poet reaches into the well of memory but finds there nothing to sustain him. "Oppressed" and "wan," he faces that hour with a numbing sense of loss, since nothing of the past retains meaning for the present moment. Finally, devoid of hope, he echoes the wind with his own weeping.

The author's use of inclusion is apparent even when the poem is read literally: the images of the first strophe are taken up and heightened in the final strophe.[47] The mournful breeze that at first wounded the poet's heart becomes an ill wind that tosses him to and fro like a dead leaf. It is the concentric flow of the composition, however, that reveals the deeper meaning of Verlaine's images. For the primary focus of the work is upon the decisive Hour that evokes memories of days past, a recollection that offers neither meaning nor consolation in the face of death.

As pessimistic as this reading of "Chanson d'automne" may be, it does seem to correspond to Verlaine's vision, particularly at this stage in his life. The poem stands as a fitting epitaph to his early, troubled years, prior to his return to the Catholic faith of his childhood. Once that return was made, he produced some of the finest mystical poetry in Western literary tradition, despite his lingering depression and frequent moral lapses. In his *Sagesse* (1881), he created a dialogue between himself and Christ. This time, the tears he shed were tears of ecstatic joy. The torment never left his soul, but the profound sense of loss and of meaninglessness, expressed in *Chanson d'automne*, had at this point in his life been superseded by a vision of grace. Now Verlaine portrays Christ as the source of love and peace, who evokes within him both devotion and fear. The "dreary lassitude" has given way to "dread at being called" because of his unworthiness, a dread nevertheless outweighed by hope and longing.

"I am in *ecstasy* and in *terror* of *being chosen*.
I am unworthy, but I know Thy leniency.
Ah, what *struggle* — yet what *desire!* And *here I am*,

Filled with a humble *prayer*, even though an inner *tumult*
Dims the hope Thy voice reveals within me.
And I *long* for Thee, with *trembling*."

— "Poor soul," Christ replies, "you have understood!"

(*Dialogue mystique*, VIII)

A definite concentric movement characterizes as well a number of pieces from the old English Hymnal.[48] E. Caswall's translation of Prudentius' fourth century "*O sola magnarum urbium*"[49] can be arranged as follows:

A : *Bethlehem*, of noblest cities
None can once with thee compare;
Thou alone the *Lord* from heaven
Didst for us incarnate bear.

B : Fairer than the sun at morning
Was the *star* that told his birth;
To the lands their *God announcing*,
Hid beneath a form of *earth*.

C : By its lambent beauty guided
See the eastern kings appear;
See them bend, their gifts to offer,
Gifts of incense, gold and myrrh.

B': Solemn things of mystic meaning:
Incense doth the God disclose,
Gold a royal child proclaimeth,
Myrrh a future *tomb* foreshows.

A': *Holy Jesu*, in thy brightness
To the *Gentile world* displayed,
With the Father and the Spirit
Endless praise to thee be paid.

A → A': Jesus, the incarnate Lord, born into the Jewish world
(Bethlehem) →
Jesus, praised with the Father and the Spirit, revealed
to the Gentile world (the magi).

B → B': The star announces God, born in the earth (a cavern) →
Incense and gold disclose God, myrrh foretells his burial
in the earth.

C : The star, the eastern kings, the offered gifts.

A more interesting form of composition appears in a hymn to the Saints by J. Montgomery (d. 1854).[50] Here the concentric movement is complemented by inversion.

A : Palms of glory, raiment bright,
Crowns that never fade away,
Gird and deck the *Saints in light*,
Priests, and kings, and conquerors they.

B : Yet the conquerors bring their palms
To the *Lamb* amidst the *throne*,
And proclaim in joyful psalms
Victory through *his Cross* alone.

C : Kings for harps their crowns resign,
Crying, as they strike the chords,
'Take the kingdom, it is thine,
King of kings, and Lord of lords.'

> B':   Round the *altar* priests confess,
> If their robes are white as snow,
> 'Twas the *Saviour's* righteousness,
> And *his Blood*, that made them so.

> A':   They were *mortal too like us;*
> Ah! when we like them must die,
> May our souls translated thus
> *Triumph, reign, and shine* on high.

> A → A':   The Saints are priests, kings, conquerors →
> May we mortals triumph (as conquerors), reign (as kings), and
> shine (as priests).

> B → B':   Conquerors around the throne proclaim the Lamb's sacri-
> fice (the Cross) →
> Priests around the altar confess the Savior's sacrifice (his
> Blood).

> C :   The Lamb and Savior is King of kings and Lord of lords.

The last line of the first strophe, "Priests, and kings, and conquerors," is inverted in the final line of the hymn, to create an inclusion:
conquerors triumph, kings reign, and priests shine. This final order
in turn reflects the order of the intervening strophes, describing
respectively "conquerors," "kings," and "priests." Special emphasis
is laid on the central strophe (C) by the parallelism created between
the kingly saints who exchange their crowns for harps, and their
confession of the Lord who is "King of kings." This confessional
affirmation serves to focus the entire hymn on the One whose
sacrifice offers the saints the possibility to reign with him as priests,
kings and conquerors.

Even such a popular processional hymn as "Onward Christian
Soldiers,"[51] attributed to S. Baring-Gould (d. 1924), shows some
evidence of chiastic structure.

> A :   *Onward Christian soldiers,*
> Marching as to war,
> With the Cross of Jesus
> Going on before.
> *Christ the royal Master*
> Leads against the foe;
> Forward into battle,
> See his banners go!

B : As the sign of triumph
Satan's legions flee;
On then, Christian soldiers
On to victory.
Hell's foundations quiver
At the shout of praise;
Brothers, lift your voices,
Loud your anthems raise.

    C : Like a mighty army
    Moves the Church of God;
    Brothers, we are treading
    Where the saints have trod;
    We are not divided,
    All one body we,
    One in hope and doctrine,
    One in charity.

B': Crowns and thrones may perish,
Kingdoms rise and wane,
But the Church of Jesus
Constant will remain;
Gates of hell can never
'Gainst that Church *prevail;*
We have Christ's own promise,
And that cannot fail.

A': *Onward, then, ye people,*
Join our happy throng,
Blend with ours your voices
In the triumph song;
Glory, laud, and honour
Unto *Christ the King;*
his through countless ages
Men and angels sing.

A → A': Onward to wage war with Christ the royal Master →
Onward to proclaim the victory of Christ the King.

B → B': By the Church's praise Satan/Hell are vanquished →
By Christ's promise the gates of Hell will not prevail.

C: Focus upon the unity of the Church militant and the Church
triumphant, in faith, hope and love.

The first strophe is a call to Christian people to engage in battle with the foe (Satan and his legions). It is complemented and heightened in the final strophe by a similar call addressed to *all* peoples, to join with the victorious members of Christ's army, and, with the communion of saints (Men and Angels), to sing unending praises to Christ the King. The second and fourth strophes then address specifically the object of their struggle: Satan and his legions, and the domain of Hell. Heightening from B to B' is marked by the contrast between the initial triumph of v. 2 and the declaration of v. 4 (recalling Matthew 16:16ff) that the Church of Christ will remain forever victorious, since the "gates of hell" shall never prevail against it. The movement of the whole is both toward and away from v. 3, with its evocation of the universal Church that unites in one Body those who share a common hope, doctrine and charity: the Pauline virtues of faith, hope and love (1 Cor 13:13).

Although the concentric flow is not as evident as in many of the biblical passages we have examined, it undeniably exists in popular hymns such as these. The question remains whether their authors made conscious use of chiastic principles in composing them, or whether their structure reflects an unconscious, "intuited" mode of communication. In our final example from 19th century hymnography, the frequency and complexity of the parallel patterns suggests that the composer consciously and intentionally structured his verse to reflect a double movement: forward, according to common narrative development, and concentric, with its focus upon a conceptual or thematic center. Thereby he has produced modern liturgical hymns that exhibit all the characteristics of authentic chiasmus.

The composer in question is W.J. Sparrow Simpson, the librettist for Sir John Stainer's well-known oratorio, "The Crucifixion."[52] At least four major hymns from this composition display some form of concentric parallelism. The least complicated is the hymn entitled "The Mystery of Intercession," structured according to a simple A:B:B':A' inversion.[53]

A : Jesus, the Crucified, pleads for me,
      While He is nailed to the shameful tree,
      Scorned and forsaken, derided and curst,
      See how His enemies do their worst!
      Yet, in the midst of the *torture and shame*,
      Jesus, the Crucified, breathes my name!
      Wonder of Wonders, oh! how can it be?
      Jesus, the Crucified, pleads for me!

    B : *Lord, I have left Thee*, I have denied.
        Followed the world in my selfish pride;
        Lord, I have joined in the hateful cry,
        Slay Him, away with Him, crucify.
        Lord, I have done it, oh! ask me not how;
        Woven the thorns for Thy tortured Brow!
        Yet in His pity so boundless and free,
        Jesus, the Crucified, pleads for me!

    B': *Though thou hast left Me* and wandered away,
        Chosen the darkness instead of the day;
        Though thou art covered with many a stain,
        Though thou hast wounded Me oft and again,
        Though thou hast followed thy wayward will;
        Yet in My pity, I love thee still.
        Wonder of wonders it ever must be!
        Jesus, the Crucified, pleads for me.

A': Jesus is *dying*, in agony sore,
      Jesus is *suffering* more and more,
      Jesus is bowed with the weight of His woe,
      Jesus is faint with each bitter throe,
      Jesus is bearing it all in my stead,
      Pity Incarnate for me has bled;
      Wonder of wonders it ever must be!
      Jesus, the Crucified, pleads for me.

A → A': Jesus tortured and shamed pleads for me →
        Jesus suffering and dying pleads for me.

B → B': I have abandoned Thee →
        Thou hast abandoned Me.

Repeated theme: Jesus, despite all, intercedes for me.

A similar inversion appears in the "Litany of the Passion,"
moving from "love" to "disgrace" to "agony."

A :   Holy Jesu, by *Thy Passion*,
      By the woes which none can share,
      Borne in more than kingly fashion,
      By Thy *love* beyond compare:
      Crucified, I turn to Thee,
      Son of Mary, plead for me.

  B :   By Thy look so sweet and lowly,
        While they *smote Thee on the Face*,
        By Thy patience, calm and holy,
        In the midst of keen *disgrace*:
        Crucified, I turn to Thee,
        Son of Mary, plead for me.

    C :   By the path of sorrows dreary,
          By the Cross, Thy dreadful load,
          By the pain, when, faint and weary,
          Thou didst sink upon the road:
          Crucified, I turn to Thee,
          Son of Mary, plead for me.

    C': By the treachery and trial,
         By the blows and sore distress,
         By desertion and denial,
         By Thine awful loneliness:
         Crucified, I turn to Thee,
         Son of Mary, plead for me.

  B': By the hour of condemnation,
       By the *blood which trickled down*,
       When for us and our salvation,
       Thou didst wear the *robe and crown*:
       Crucified, I turn to Thee,
       Son of Mary, plead for me.

A': By the Spirit which could render
     Love for hate and good for ill,
     By the mercy, sweet and tender,
     Poured upon *Thy murderers* still:
     Crucified, I turn to Thee,
     Son of Mary, plead for me.

A → A': In love he bears his passion →
In love he forgives his murderers.

B → B': Disgrace through blows →
Disgrace through beatings, robe and crown.

C → C': Agony through carrying the Cross →
Agony through desertion and denial.

In each of these hymns the parallelism could be unintentional, reflecting a chance repetition of themes. When considered in the light of the entire composition, however, there seems little doubt that the librettist resorted intentionally to concentric parallelism. The complexity and balance of the next two hymns bear out that impression. In "The Mystery of the Divine Humiliation," the helical movement carries the theme from an inclusion, which affirms the God-manhood of him who bears the Cross of Sorrow, through condescension and voluntary suffering, to the central affirmation that God has surrendered his divine power to assume not only mortal weakness but even the scorn of those he has come to save.

A : Cross of Jesus, Cross of Sorrow,
Where the blood of Christ was shed,
Perfect man on thee was tortured,
Perfect God on thee has bled,

B : Here the *King* of all the ages,
Throned in light ere worlds could be,
Robed in mortal flesh is dying,
Crucified by sin for me.

C : O mysterious *condescending!*
O abandonment sublime!
Very God Himself is bearing
All the *sufferings* of time!

D : Evermore for human failure
By *His Passion* we can plead;
God has borne all mortal *anguish,*
Surely *He will know our need.*

E : This — all human thought surpassing —
This is earth's most awful hour,
God has taken *mortal weakness!*
God has *laid aside His Power!*

E':   Once the *Lord* of brilliant seraphs,
        Winged with Love to do His Will,
        Now the *scorn* of all *His creatures,*
        And the aim of every *ill.*

D':   Up in heaven, sublimest glory
        Circled round Him from the first;
        But *the earth finds none to serve Him,*
        None to quench *His raging thirst.*

C':   Who shall fathom that *descending,*
        From the rainbow-circled throne,
        Down to earth's most base profaning,
        Dying desolate alone.

B':   From the *"Holy,* Holy, Holy,
        We adore Thee, O *Most High,"*
        Down to earth's blaspheming voices
        And the shout of *"Crucify!"*

A':   Cross of Jesus, Cross of Sorrow,
        Where the Blood of Christ was shed,
        Perfect man on thee was tortured,
        Perfect God on thee has bled!

A → A':   Inclusion.

B → B'   Eternal King crucified →
             Holy, Most High God crucified.

C → C':   He con*descends* to bear all sufferings →
             He *descends* to die desolate, alone.

D → D':   By his Passion he bears our anguish and knows our need →
             In his Passion we forsake him in his anguish and need
             (raging thirst).

E → E':   God freely accepts to assume our mortal weakness →
             God freely accepts the scorn of all his creatures.

As in the case of Psalm 8, which we examined in Part I, verbal agreement between the first and last strophes suggests more than mere repetition. The simple device of ending strophe 1 (A) with a comma, and strophe 10 (A') with an exclamation point, indicates that a heightening and focusing is implied in light of the entire semantic context. The opening profession of Jesus as perfect man and perfect God, slain on the "Cross of sorrow," takes on new depth and power as the reader (hearer) moves strophe by strophe through Jesus' voluntary condescension, abasement and rejection, to the final "shout of Crucify" (B'). While the repetition serves on one level to frame the hymn, its real purpose is to heighten the "Mystery of the divine Humiliation," by asserting that the one who suffered rejection, tortures and death is none other than perfect man and perfect God.

The final example is a true chiasmus, structured according to the familiar A:B:C:B':A' pattern. It is the final hymn of the composition, "to be sung by the Choir and Congregation," and is entitled "For the Love of Jesus."

A : *All for Jesus* — all for Jesus.
    This our *song* shall ever be;
    For we have no hope, nor Saviour,
    If we have not *hope in Thee*.

    B : All for Jesus — *Thou wilt give us*
        Strength to serve Thee, hour by hour;
        None can move us from Thy presence,
        While we trust *Thy love* and power.

        C : All for Jesus — at Thine *altar*
            Thou wilt give us sweet content;
            There, dear Lord, we shall receive Thee
            In the solemn *Sacrament*.

    B': All for Jesus — *Thou hast loved us;*
        All for Jesus — Thou hast died;
        All for Jesus — *Thou art with us;*
        All for Jesus Crucified.

A': *All for Jesus* — all for Jesus,
    This the Church's *song* must be;
    Till, at last, her sons are gathered,
    One in love, and *one in Thee*.

A → A': Our song: All for Jesus, source of hope →
        The Church's song: All for Jesus, source of unity.

B → B': Jesus' loving presence gives us strength to serve →
        Jesus' loving presence enables us to give him *all*.

C: We receive his presence in the solemn Sacrament (the Eucharist).

The parallels in each of these hymns tend to be more thematic than verbal, although verbal repetitions frequently occur. The consistency with which the patterns emerge, together with the heightening and focusing effect they achieve, lead to the inescapable conclusion that the author drew consciously and intentionally upon the principles of chiasmus to convey his message. The fact that most songs of any type and origin are composed using inclusion and repetition by no means minimizes the significance of these examples. To a greater or lesser degree, each one given here displays the structure we have referred to as the "rhetorical helix," the spiraling effect that leads both inward toward and outward from the theme situated at the center of the composition.

9. CHIASMUS TODAY

A quest for chiastic structures in contemporary literature produces some remarkable finds. Of the many examples we could offer to demonstrate the persistence of this ancient rhetorical pattern down to the present day, one of the most striking appeared in the form of a syndicated column by the noted commentator Ellen Goodman of the *Boston Globe*, on Friday, June 22, 1990. This is not a religious work; yet its concentric parallelism is so clear as to make it a fitting conclusion to the present study of chiastic patterns. The author, by the way, was not at all aware of the chiastic shape she gave to this piece.[54]

"Medical Research Ignores Women"

A : This is a story that begins with *white male rats*. No, it is not a political fantasy created by those who regard "white male rats" as redundant. The subject here is *science* and sex.

   B : It turns out that most of the basic *research* that teaches us what is good and bad for human beings begins with rodents of the male persuasion. Their female counterparts are usually excluded because of what might be called "raging hormonal imbalance." *Their female physiology is more complex.*

      C : I didn't come across this information through personal experience. I have never seen a *female rodent* with PMS, let alone hot flashes. Nor have I ever worried that they were *denied equal employment opportunities as research subjects.*

         D : Rather, the tale of the white male rat was reiterated at the *congressional hearings* of the House Subcommittee on Health and the Environment this week. These creatures were a small if furry part of the larger saga. In research, *female humans* are also *excluded from most studies* done on "people."

E :   The pills women swallow, the diets that we
      follow, the exercises we adhere to — the
      health plan that is *prescribed for us* — are for
      the most part based on *research done on a
      thoroughly male model*. Remember the
      cholesterol study? Its 4,000 subjects were men.
      Remember the smoking study? The 15,000
      subjects were men. How about the aspirin
      study? Its 22,000 doctors were all male.

F :   The end result is that *women* with heart
      disease — the *number one killer* of women
      — and all sorts of ills are by and large
      treated as if they were men. And while this
      experience might be refreshing in a pay-
      check, it could be dangerous in a checkup.

G :   The hearings that brought the tale
      of the *neglected females* of two species
      to the public consciousness were
      called because of a government study
      pushed by the congressional women's
      caucus. The study showed that *the
      National Institutes of Health had failed to
      fulfill its own four-year policy to include
      women in clinical trials*. The scientists
      who planned, proposed and funded
      research had paid little more attention
      to it than a smoker pays to a warning
      on a cigarette pack.

H :   But it turns out that the exclusion
      of women as subjects for research
      is only one piece of a profoundly
      skewed research program. Not
      only are men studied more, so are
      their health problems. Diseases
      like ovarian cancer and
      osteoporosis remain second-class
      subjects. Even breast cancer,
      which kills 40,000 women a year,
      gets only $17 million for basic
      research.

G':   All in all, *about 13 percent of NIH's $5.7*
      billion budget goes to study the health
      risks of the half of the population that is fe-
      male. While every woman in America
      will go through menopause, hormone
      treatment has little priority in terms of
      federal dollars. While every woman
      ages, the latest study — entitled "Nor-
      mal Human Aging" — has *no data*
      about women at all.

F':   "I've had a theory that *you fund what you*
      fear," says Rep. Patricia Schroeder, who
      along with Reps. Olympia Snowe of
      Maine and Henry Waxman of California
      has kept a spotlight on this issue. "When
      you have a *male-dominated group* of
      researchers they are more worried about
      prostate cancer than breast cancer."

E':   The fund-what-you-fear bias in health
      research goes straight through the medical
      system. After all, *who decides* what we should
      study, what is important and who is
      important? The dearth of female researchers,
      female reviewers, female doctors and
      administrators at NIH has directly resulted in
      a *dearth of research on women's health issues.*

D':   But conversely, the *rise of women* in medical and
      policy-making positions in the rest of the world
      has put these issues in the public eye. This
      summer, the *congressional women's caucus*
      will be presenting a health package that *calls*
      for more research.

C':   In fairness, medical science is not all that different
      from any other *business in America* that is *just beginning*
      to adjust to women. There is the dual notion that
      you can either treat women just like men or
      exclude them altogether.

B':   According to the rat theory, many *researchers* lament
      that including women with all *their peculiar plumbing*
      is too complicated, and too expensive.

A':   But in the long run, *research* that is only valid for half the hu-
      man species is no bargain. So the next time you pop a pill,
      or follow the doctor's orders, check carefully for the telltale
      paw prints of the *white male rats*.

A → A':   White male rats, the subject is science →
          Scientific research limited to white male rats.

B → B':   Research excludes female rats because of their
          complex physiology →
          Researchers exclude women because of their
          peculiar plumbing.

C → C':   Female rodents denied equal employment opportunities →
          Women denied equal opportunities by American business
          and medicine.

D → D':   Congressional hearings: women excluded from studies →
          Congressional women's caucus: women call for more research.

E → E':   Men prescribe for women: research done on male model →
          Men decide for women: dearth of research on female model.

F → F':   Medical care determined by male model →
          Medical research determined by male concerns.

G → G':   NIH neglects women →
          NIH effectively ignores women.

H: Thematic focus = Sexism in medical research.

Each parallel section of the above text constitutes a separate
paragraph, with the exception of B'-A'. This suggests that the writer,
although making no conscious effort to create balance and concentric
symmetry, nevertheless "sensed" or intuited a chiastic movement or
flow as she composed her column.

This spiral movement, coupled with the heightening or focusing
effect, confirms the "persistence of chiasmus" in Christian, Jewish
and secular literature through the Middle Ages and down to modern
times. As far as we know, however, there has been no conscious
effort to teach these compositional features in schools or universities.
This is evident from the fact that biblical scholars have only recently
rediscovered the chiastic form and begun to understand its significance for exegesis and hermeneutics.

The question remains, then, as to just *why* chiasmus has persisted
throughout the centuries. A great deal more research needs to be

done in this area, but one plausible explanation emerges from the many different examples we have considered in this chapter. Concentric parallelism, it seems, like narrative and myth, represents what specialists term a "deep structure," a mode of communication with definite rules and linguistic relations that appears at all times in all cultures, and in all forms of literature, both religious and profane. If this is so, it would imply that Homer was not necessarily under the direct influence of the Semites, nor was Clemence of Barking merely imitating the Byzantines, when they composed their works on the chiastic model. Concentric parallelism, in fact, is a universal form that finds analogues beyond the realm of literature, even within the physical world. It is this universal aspect of the phenomenon, together with its implications for the interpretation of biblical passages, that we want to explore finally under the guise of a Conclusion.

ENDNOTES

[1] *The Idea of Biblical Poetry*, p. 305ff.

[2] *Ibid.*, p. 313.

[3] The principle of concentric parallelism appears to be operative as well in other examples given by Kugel. See especially the "Rabbinic Benediction" (p. 307f) that moves from strophe I (the old temple) to strophe II (the new Temple), and spirally from atonement to eternal love, from animal sacrifices to songs of praise, and from the former offering to the future offering.

[4] J. Breck, *Spirit of Truth*, vol. I, "The Origins of Johannine Pneumatology" (Crestwood, NY: St. Vladimir's Seminary Press, 1991), p. 125-140.

[5] Verses 21b-25a constitute an interpolation, whose purpose is to show how evil can dwell even in the hearts of the righteous members of the covenantal fellowship. See *Spirit of Truth*, p. 127.

[6] For the text, see A.R.C. Leaney, *The Rule of Qumran and Its Meaning* (Philadelphia: Westminster Press, 1966).

[7] This is a clear allusion to the priestly oracle, Ezek 36:24, analyzed above.

[8] Translation by G. Vermes, *The Dead Sea Scrolls in English* (London: Penguin, 1968), p. 173ff.

[9] Vermes, p. 205.

[10] This last piece is considered deutero-canonical by the Eastern Orthodox Churches and is a fixed element of their service of Great Compline. It is included in the *NRSV Apocrypha*. See for each of these three texts *The New Oxford Annotated Bible*

with the Apocrypha (New York: Oxford University Press, 1991).

[11]This analysis I included in my contribution of the notes and introduction to 3 Maccabees for the *New Oxford Annotated Bible (Apocrypha)*, p. 285ff. It is reproduced here with the kind permission of the editors.

[12]*NRSV Apocrypha*, p. 281f.

[13]E. Hennecke, *New Testament Apocrypha*, vol. I, "Gospels and Related Writings" (London: Lutterworth, 1963), p. 256f.

[14]*Ibid*, p. 403f.

[15]English translation in E. Hennecke, *ibid.*, p. 370ff. Roddy's study, "The Form and Function of the Protoevangelium of James," appeared in *Coptic Church Review*, 14/2 (1993), pp. 35-45.

[16]Translation by Kirsopp Lake, *The Apostolic Fathers* vol. I (London: Heinemann / New York: Harvard University Press, 1959), p. 183. The Greek text is provided.

[17]Translation by R.M. Grant, in J. Sparks (ed.), *The Apostolic Fathers* (Nashville, TN: Thomas Nelson, 1978), p. 79f.

[18]Translation by Kirsopp Lake, *The Apostolic Fathers*, p. 209f.

[19]Translation by Kirsopp Lake, *The Apostolic Fathers*, vol II, p. 331f. The rendering of the prayer is my own.

[20]See Th. Camelot, *Lettres, Martyre de Polycarpe* in *Sources Chrétiennes 10* (Paris: Cerf, 1969), p. 202-207.

[21]See W. Rordorf, A. Tuilier, *La Doctrine des Douze Apôtres (Didachê), Sources Chrétiennes 248* (Paris: Cerf, 1978), p. 175-183.

[22]Dom Gregory Dix, *The Shape of the Liturgy* (London: Dacre Press, 1945/1964), p. 87.

[23]Taken from A. Philips, *Prayer Book for the New Year* (revised) (New York: Hebrew Publishing Co., 1931), p. 24.

[24]Robert Taft, S.J., *The Liturgy of the Hours in East and West* (Collegeville, MN: The Liturgical Press, 1986), p. 37f.

[25]Taft (p. 38) quotes St. Basil the Great, *On the Holy Spirit* (29/73): "It seemed fitting to our fathers not to receive the gift of the evening light in silence, but to give thanks immediately upon its appearance. We cannot say who was the father of the words of the thanksgiving for the light. But the people utter the ancient formula, and those that say 'We praise you Father, Son and Holy Spirit of [sic] God' were never thought impious by anyone." Thus by the latter third of the fourth century the hymn was regarded as an "ancient formula."

[26]Or, "with worthy titles."

[27]The cosmic aspect of this adoration is expressed as well in the ancient Christ-hymns of Phil 2:10f and Col 1:15-20. Hippolytus preserves a late second or early third century prayer of the lamp-lighting, performed by the deacon during an evening meal: "We give thanks to Thee, O Lord, through Thy Son Jesus Christ our Lord, through whom Thou has enlightened us, by revealing to us the incorruptible light. Having spent the whole day and come to the beginning of the night, being filled with the light of day which Thou hast created for our satisfaction, and since

now, by Thy grace, we are not deprived of the evening light (*non egemus luce vesperi*), we praise and glorify Thee by Thy Son Jesus Christ our Lord, through whom are due unto Thee glory, power and honor, together with the Holy Spirit, now and forever, and unto ages of ages. Amen" ("Apostolic Tradition," 25; in B. Botte, *Hippolyte de Rome. La Tradition Apostolique, Sources Chrétiennes* [Paris: Cerf, 1968], p. 100).

[28]This transitional position in Eastern Orthodox tradition is especially evident during Great Lent, when at "Vouchsafe" daily lenten melodies are changed to regular modes on Friday evening, and back again to their lenten form on Sunday evening. The weekend, focusing on the dominical Eucharist or Divine Liturgy, remains "resurrectional," even during the lenten period.

[29]N.D. Uspensky, *Evening Worship in the Orthodox Church* (New York: St Vladimir's Seminary Press, 1985), p. 19-27; M. Skoballanovich, *The Typikon Interpreted* (Kiev, 1913 — in Russian), Part II, p. 156-158.

[30]Uspensky, p. 58-61, records Moschus' conversation with Nilus of Sinai that specifies the structure of the vigil service familiar to Moschus.

[31]See I. Mansvetov, *Ecclesiastical Ordo (Typikon): Its Formation and Fate in the Greek and Russian Church* (Moscow, 1885 — in Russian), p. 37f.

[32]For a critical edition of his poems, see *Mass-Tyrpanis, Romanos, Cantica Genuina* (Oxford: Clarendon Press, 1963). For English translations, Marjorie Carpenter, *Kontakia of Romanos, Byzantine Melodist*, 2 vols. (Columbia, MO: U. of Missouri Press, 1970, 1973), texts cited from Vol. I (copyright 1970 by the Curators of the University of Missouri), with permission of the University of Missouri Press.

[33]Carpenter, vol. I, p. 4f.

[34]Although the connection with the Water of Life is not explicit, the allusion to quenching the thirst of both Adam and David in B' makes such a connection inescapable.

[35]An allusion to Num 24:17, "a star shall come forth out of Jacob, and a scepter shall rise out of Israel." These royal symbols, referring to David in the OT passage, are taken here as images of the coming Messiah.

[36]The Greek term for "ladder," *klimax*, has been attributed to John of Sinai as a surname.

[37]For the English text, see Climacus, *The Ladder of Divine Ascent*, tr. Luibhead and Russell (New York: Paulist, 1982).

[38]G. Couilleau, art. "Saint Jean Climaque," *Dictionnaire de Spiritualité*, vol. 8, cols. 369-389 (Paris, 1972).

[39]Richard T. Lawrence, "The Three-Fold Structure of the Ladder of Divine Ascent," *SVTQ* 32 (1988), p. 101-118.

[40]P. 106, quoting *Ladder* 186.

[41]The text has been translated and annotated by William MacBain, *The Life of St. Catherine by Clemence of Barking*, Anglo-Norman Text Society #18 (Oxford: Blackwell, 1964). He suggests for its dates c. 1170-80. See as well his *De Sainte Katerine. An Anonymous Picard Version of the Life of St. Catherine of Alexandria* (Fairfax, VA: George Mason University Press, 1987), particularly appendix B, which gives the original Latin *Vulgata* text. I am especially grateful to Prof. MacBain for pointing

out to me the concentric flow of major portions of the former (Barking) work, and for his kindness in offering a literal translation of key passages to reveal their literary structure.

[42]*Barking*, p. 25ff.

[43]D. Obolensky, *The Penguin Book of Russian Verse*, (Harmondsworth, Middlesex, England: Penguin Books, 1962/65), p. xii. English translation, reproduced here, p. 46-49.

[44]"'It is meet in truth to bless thee...', the opening words of a hymn to the Mother of God [the Virgin Mary], which follows the consecration of the Bread and the Wine in the Liturgy of St John Chrysostom" (Obolensky's note, p. 47).

[45]This first strophe was broadcast over clandestine radio by the French Underground, as a code to signal the invasion of Normandy by the Allied Forces on June 6, 1944.

[46]From Ch.-M. Des Granges, *Les Poètes français 1820-1920* (Paris: Librairie A. Hatier, 1935), p. 296.

[47]An editorial note on vv. 13-18 reads: "L'image et le mouvement de la dernière strophe sont en rapport étroit avec les suggestions de la première strophe."

[48]*The English Hymnal with Tunes*, 1933 ed. (London: Oxford University Press).

[49]No. 40, p. 65.

[50]No. 201, p. 290.

[51]No. 643, p. 839.

[52]Sir John Stainer (1840-1901) was organist of St. Paul's Cathedral, London, from 1872 to 1888. Poor eyesight forced him to give up this prestigious position, and in 1889 he was named professor of music at Oxford. Information on the life of Sparrow Simpson is difficult to obtain. He is not even mentioned in the *New Grove Dictionary of Music and Musicians*. His obituary in the *London Times* supplies the following information (for which I am indebted to Kenneth Sivulich): William John Sparrow Simpson, English clergyman (1859-1952), studied at St. Paul's School and Trinity College, Cambridge, where he obtained a first class in theology and the Chancellor's prize for English verse. An author and specialist on St. Augustine, Sparrow Simpson edited the *English Church Review* in the period prior to the First World War. In his article on John Stainer in *New Grove* (ed. Stanley Sadie, London: Macmillan, 1980/87, p. 58), Nicholas Temperley notes that Stainer's anthems and services are "superficially attractive, but their melodic and harmonic resourcefulness is spoilt by an inadequate sense of rhythm and accent: Stainer's fine literary feeling in his choice of texts was not matched by an ability to set them appropriately to music." Aware of his shortcomings in this regard, Stainer even referred to his compositions as "rubbish." The enduring popularity of "The Crucifixion" may well be due rather to the librettist, who skillfully wove together scriptural and doctrinal themes into a moving meditation on the meaning of Christ's passion and death.

[53]Text from G. Schirmer's Edition (New York: G. Schirmer, Inc., n.d.), "The Crucifixion. A Meditation on the Sacred Passion of the Holy Redeemer."

[54]At least one other column by Ms. Goodman displays a chiastic flow as well: "Fear Breeds Technology of Death," published earlier in the same month by the *Washington Post Writers Group*. The present piece is reproduced with her permission.

CONCLUSION: CHIASMUS, A KEY TO INTERPRETATION

The first person to use the term "chiasmus" to designate inverted parallelism seems to be Johannes Bengel, whose *Gnomon novi testamenti* was published in Tübingen in 1742.[1] Nils Lund gives Bengel credit for having first grasped the importance of chiastic forms for New Testament exegesis.[2] With few exceptions, however, scholars still seem to treat chiastic patterns merely as literary curiosities, interesting as examples of an author's artistry but of little significance for interpreting the *meaning* of a text.[3]

Part of the reason for the neglect of chiasmus by exegetes appears to be the Western penchant for narrative form and our lack of familiarity with concentric patterns of thought. Equally important is the fact that the term "chiasmus" has been generally limited to some form of simple inverted parallelism, with the result that the full range of its possibilities and expressions has not been properly appreciated.

It has been my purpose in this book to set forth the characteristics of chiasmus as a specific genre with its own shape and laws, and in the process to suggest a new definition of the term. The usual definition, once again, considers as "chiastic" any combination of two or more lines that includes inverted parallelism: "love is of God... / for God is love" // (1 Jn 4:7f); "the sabbath was made for man / and not man for the sabbath" // (Mk 2:27); "Beauty is truth, / truth beauty" // (Keats). "Parallelism," as we have seen, involves a balance of thought and form between successive members of a literary unit, to provide a feeling of completeness or "closure." In chiastic patterns, parallel elements throw light on the central theme, while the sense of closure is provided by "inclusion" (A:A'). As a development of the "hysteron-proteron" model of reversals, authentic chiasmus thus involves "concentric parallelism": two or more elements (single lines or entire paragraphs) constructed in synonymous, antithetical or inverted parallelism about a one- or two-element central theme, producing patterns such as A:B:A' and A:B:C:C':B':A'. The basic characteristic of such patterns is the central "pivot": the thematic focus that expresses the author's main idea.

Some of this was recognized long ago by specialists in rhetorical criticism, and in recent years, with the advent of the new literary criticism, interest in the characteristics of chiasmus and its potential for biblical interpretation has grown impressively. Hardly a commentary appears today that does not at least note the presence of isolated chiastic micro-units, since they occur in virtually every book of the canon. The number of scholars who attempt a systematic study of the form in any given writing nevertheless remains remarkably small.

Awareness of one further characteristic of chiasmus may lead to a re-evaluation of the genre and a new appreciation of its potential as an important key to biblical interpretation. That other characteristic is the so-called "what's more" factor: the incremental or elevating effect that produces what we have termed the "rhetorical helix." This involves the conjunction of two distinct yet complementary movements within the chiastically structured passage: 1) *heightening* from line to line and strophe to strophe through intensification, specification, contrast or conclusion; and 2) *focusing* upon the thematic center.

Recent studies by James Kugel and Robert Alter, among others, have demonstrated beyond doubt that the basic feature of Hebrew poetry is this principle of "going beyond": the second line of a poetic couplet intensifies, specifies or completes in some essential respect the thought or feeling expressed in the first line. Applying this principle to chiastic patterns, we have discovered that the "what's more" factor is operative there as well. Just as no two lines of Hebrew poetry are ever truly (or simply) synonymous, but the second nearly always serves to heighten or intensify the first, so with the parallel lines balanced before and after the thematic center of a chiastic pattern: the second similarly heightens or intensifies the first. Thus A' is heightened relative to A, B' relative to B, etc. Furthermore, there is a progression in these structures from the extremities toward the center, such that a spiraling effect occurs. Like a coiled watchspring or a spiral galaxy, the movement from A:A' to B:B' to C:C' is also one of heightening or focusing. In a 3:2:1:0:1':2':3' pattern, for example, inclusion will be marked by 3:3'; but the closer one comes to the center (0), the more significant become the parallels for explicating the actual meaning (the "literal sense") of the text. Thus 2:2' is heightened relative to 3:3', as 1:1' is, relative to 2:2'. Just as star clusters are progressively more dense toward the center of a galaxy, so development of the central theme is more direct and intense as one moves from the extremities of a chiastic pattern toward the middle. This, of course, depicts only a general tendency. Such progressive heightening from the outside inward is not always evident. It occurs with such frequency, however (as a quick glance at the chiastic outline of Mark's Gospel, given above, will verify), that we may consider it to be a distinctive and defining mark of the genre.

Given the fact that the laws of Hebrew parallelism govern chiastic structures as well as poetic couplets, we can stipulate a set of principles or laws specific to those structures. Nils Lund proposed seven such laws:[4] 1) "The centre is always the turning point"; 2) "the law of the shift at the centre" (at the center a change occurs in the trend of thought, often introducing antithesis); 3) "identical ideas are often distributed in such a fashion that they occur in the extremes and at the centre of their respective system, and nowhere else in the system"; 4) "the law of shift from centre to the extremes" (ideas occurring in the center of one system recur in the extremities of a corresponding system); 5) a "tendency of certain terms to gravitate toward certain positions within a given system, such as the divine names in the psalms...;" 6) "larger units are frequently introduced and concluded by frame-passages" (the phenomenon of inclusion); and 7) "there is frequently a mixing of chiastic and alternating lines within one and the same unit" (i.e., inverted and direct parallelism).

The following is a modified version of these "laws," reduced to four, that includes examples to illustrate the way they are applied.

1. *Chiastic units are framed by inclusion.* Two parallel lines are set one at the beginning and the other at the end of the unit, so as to provide a sense of completeness or closure. For the reader or hearer, they serve to mark the limits or boundaries of the passage. Like all couplets, they express either direct progression, inversion or antithesis, and they conform as well to the heightening ("what's more") principle. They can involve repetition of *identical terms:*

– the opening and closing doxology of Ps 8

– Mk 13:32-37, "Watch!"

– Phil 2:5-11, Christ Jesus – God // Jesus Christ – God

or the paralleling of *similar ideas:*

– 1 Cor 10:1-11:34, spiritual food and drink of Israel //
spiritual food and drink of the Church

– Jn 16:1-33, "keep you from falling away" //
"be of good cheer"

or they can express *antithesis* through a juxtaposition of opposing or
contrasting themes:

– Lk 14:16-24, many are called to the banquet //
none of those invited shall taste of the banquet

– Mk 9:2-10, Jesus ascends the mountain //
Jesus descends the mountain.

2. *The central element (or pair of elements) serves as the pivot and/or
thematic focus of the entire unit.* As the "pivot," the center serves as a
turning point that shifts the focus from one level of meaning to
another. A good example is Isaiah 60:1-3.

A : Arise,

   B : Shine!

      C : For your light has come,

         D : and the glory

            E : of the Lord

               F : has risen upon you.

                  G : For, behold, darkness shall cover
                     the earth

                  G': and thick darkness the peoples.

               F': But upon you will arise

            E': the Lord,

         D': and his glory will be seen upon you.

      C': And nations shall come to your light,

   B': and kings to the brightness

A': of your rising.[5]

Here the center (G-G') serves as an antithetical pivot or shifting point between strophe I: fallen Zion exhorted to arise and receive "light / the glory of the Lord;" and strophe II: the universal vocation of Israel, called to radiate the light of Yahweh among the nations that dwell in darkness.

Usually, however, the center provides the basic theme of the unit and gives meaning to the entire structure. Consider especially the following central elements of passages we discussed earlier:

- Gen 32:28, Jacob is named *Israel* (victorious in his struggle with God)
- Ezek 36:26b, a *new Spirit* is bestowed upon the people, to transform their heart of stone to a heart of flesh
- Jer 2:28a, the vanity of *idolatry* is stressed by God's ironic question, "Where are your idols...?"
- Ps 8:4, the psalmist's question, "What is man?" receives the answer, *"Little less than God."*

From these few examples in the Pentateuch, Prophets and Psalms, we can turn to the New Testament and note the same importance of the chiastic center.

- Mk 1:13b, Jesus is tempted by Satan
- Mt 3:11c, Jesus baptizes with the Holy Spirit and fire
- Mt 16:17, Peter's confession is granted by divine revelation
- Mk 9:7 // Mt 17:5, the heavenly voice declares, "This is my beloved Son"
- Mt 14:29a, Jesus invites Peter to "Come!"
- Mk 10:49b, the people respond to Bartimaeus with compassion (the universal address to all persons, "Take heart, arise, he is calling you")
- Lk 1:34f, Mary's question / Gabriel's answer (conception will occur by the power of the Holy Spirit)
- Mt 6:7-15, the heart of Jesus' Sermon on the mount is the Lord's Prayer
- Jesus' parables: the focus is on a *crisis* to be resolved
- Mk 14:61b; 15:9,18,31, the chiastic centers are formed respectively by the christological "confessions" of the high priest, Pilate, the soldiers, and the thieves

– 1 Cor 9:1f, Paul as an apostle is *free* in Christ
(the governing theme of the entire epistle)
– Phil 2:8cd, declaring the Death on the Cross
of the pre-existent Son of God.

In each instance (and these examples can easily be multiplied) the author has situated his main theme at the center of a chiastic unit, elucidating it by the careful balancing of parallel lines that move with increasing intensity from the extremities toward the middle.

The same pattern can be found outside the canonical Scriptures, in various forms of literature from a wide variety of cultural, linguistic and historical contexts. Thus the ancient Christian hymn *Phôs hilaron* focuses upon the trinitarian confession, "Father, Son and Holy Spirit: God!" The twelfth century French writer Clemence of Barking employs the chiastic center to convey major themes in her dramatization of the life of St. Catherine. And in John Stainer's late-nineteenth century English oratorio, "The Crucifixion," the librettist W.J. Sparrow Simpson makes similar use of the center to express the depths of Christ's agony, together with his self-offering in the eucharist. Finally, the central paragraph of a contemporary newspaper columnist can likewise serve to drive home the author's point, even when that author is quite unaware that she is drawing on the principles of concentric parallelism.

In each instance, the center both recapitulates the author's principal theme and serves as the leitmotif that provides meaning to the entire composition.

3. *A heightening effect occurs from the first parallel line or strophe to its prime complement.* For example,

– A → B: Whoever sheds the blood of man / (murder) →
by man shall his blood be shed / / (vengeance)
(Gen 9:6)

In his days may righteousness flourish / →
and peace abound, till the moon be no more!
(Ps 72:7)

I have baptized you with water / →
but he will baptize you with the Holy Spirit
(Mk 1:8)

– A → A': The Son of Man must suffer →
The Son of Man will come in the Kingdom and with power.
(Mk 8:31-9:1)

You are in the Spirit who dwells in you →
You will have life through the indwelling Spirit.
(Rom 8:9-11)

– I → II: Mt 17:1-4, Transfiguration / Peter's confusion →
17:6-9, The disciples' fear / Resurrection
(focus = v. 5, the voice from the cloud, "This is my beloved Son.")

Phil 2:5-8b, Incarnation →
2:9-11, Exaltation
(focus = v. 8cd, death on a cross).

4. *The resultant concentric or spiral parallelism, with progressive intensification from the extremities inward, produces a helical movement that draws the reader/hearer toward the thematic center.* A good example is Mark 9:14-29, the healing of the epileptic boy, outlined above (p. 152).

A → A': The illness (spirit possession) →
The solution (prayer)

B → B': The disciples cannot heal →
Why can they not heal?

C → C': The dumb spirit convulses the boy →
It convulses him again and comes out of him

D → D': The possession →
The exorcism

E → E': The father's disbelief →
The father's belief

F: "All things are possible to one who believes."

The helical flow of this passage carries the reader/hearer from the condition and its solution (A:A'), to the disciples' inability to heal (B:B'), to the convulsions (C:C'), to the healing through exorcism (D:D'), to the father's conversion from doubt to belief (E:E'), and culminates in Christ's affirmation: *faith works all things.* Each successive set of parallels focuses with progressively greater intensity on the central theme of faith, illustrated by the father's conversion at the child's healing. The entire sequence centers about, and each set of parallel lines is given meaning by, the central element (F). If this movement goes unrecognized, and the passage is read as plain narrative, then the evangelist's chief point would appear to concern the importance of prayer for accomplishing the miracle. Read chiastically, on the other hand, the ultimate meaning of the passage emerges from the center; and the evangelist's message is seen to concern *faith:* the transition from unbelief to belief, essential for all persons in all situations, but here poignantly and dramatically effected by the healing of the boy with the unclean spirit.

A still more striking example of the value of chiasmus for purposes of interpretation is the Markan crucifixion scene (15:21-39), also outlined above (p. 163). Its helical flow can be analyzed as follows:

A → A':   Simon of Cyrene carries Jesus' cross →
          The centurion confesses Jesus to be Son of God

B → B':   Golgotha, the "Place of the Skull" →
          The death of Jesus

C → C':   Wine mingled with myrrh →
          A sponge full of vinegar

D → D':   They crucify Jesus →
          "My God, why have you forsaken me?"

E → E':   The third hour: crucifixion of the King of the Jews →
          The sixth to ninth hours: darkness over the earth

F → F':   Two robbers are crucified with Jesus →
          The two robbers revile Jesus

G → G':   "Come down from the cross!" →
          "Come down *now* from the cross!"

H: "He saved others; he cannot save himself!"

This passage offers one of the most intricate and interesting examples of chiastic structuring in the entire New Testament. Every phrase in I (A-G) finds its complement in II (G'-A'), and the heightening effect is evident throughout. Read as straight narrative, the passage leads through a jumble of individual incidents and statements, to conclude with the Centurion's unexpected confession. Read concentrically, as the passage was conceived, each gesture and word takes on added significance in relation to its parallel: Simon's bearing of Christ's cross (A) presages the Gentile's confession (A'), confirming that this Jesus who is rejected by his own people is the very Son of God. Golgotha, the "Place of the Skull" (B), becomes preeminently the place of Jesus' death (B'). Having refused drugged wine (C), Jesus also refuses to slake his thirst with vinegar, to abide by his promise of 14:25, but also to drink to the full the "cup" of the

Father's will (C'). The evangelists present the act of crucifixion with extraordinary sobriety, depicting nothing of the anguish and physical torment that accompanied it; yet Mark brings to expression the true force of the act by paralleling the crucifixion (D) with the lament of Psalm 22, "My God, my God...!" (D'). The cosmic aspect of the crucifixion is stressed with the balance between the third hour when Jesus is nailed to the cross (E), and the period from the sixth to the ninth hour when darkness covers the face of the earth (E'). Through this act by which the agent of creation [is Mark aware of this Johannine-Pauline theme?] is willfully put to death at the hands of his sinful creatures, the primeval chaos seems to threaten as it did in the beginning, before the Spirit began to hover over the face of the waters (Gen 1). Although the crucified Jesus is proclaimed by Pilate's inscription to be King of the Jews, the two thieves crucified with him (F) join with their tormentors in reviling him "who saved others" (F'), taunting him to come down from the cross (G-G') and thereby prove the false claims they themselves have put in his mouth.

The focus of the entire passage (H) is this ironic statement that leads the Gospel reader to contemplate the mystery of Jesus' voluntary suffering in the light of the Gethsemane prayer, "Not my will, but thy will be done." Matthew affirms Jesus' control over his destiny by the declaration, "Do you think that I cannot appeal to my Father, and he will at once send me more than twelve legions of angels?" (Mt 26:53). Mark omits that declaration, leaving the reader to understand that Jesus lays down his life as a ransom, a vicarious and voluntary self-offering, whose only purpose is precisely to "save others" (10:45). It is this central affirmation, set in relief through the literary device of chiasmus, that reveals the real significance of Simon's gesture and the Centurion's confession: to take up the cross of the Son of God is to gain one's very life by participating directly and personally in Jesus' suffering and death.

A number of hermeneutic principles or insights can be derived from the study of chiasmus that directly serve the task of exegesis.

(1) Most importantly, recognition of chiastic structures permits the interpreter to locate the *conceptual center* of the unit and thereby determine the primary point the author sought to convey. The significance of this characteristic for grasping the literal sense of a passage can hardly be overstated. Not only does it pinpoint the author's central theme; it also signals a turning point in the flow of

thought. As the pivot or focus of the unit, the center marks a transition — through intensification, specification, antithesis, or the like
— to a new and more significant level of meaning. Strophe II, in other
words, is heightened relative to strophe I. Yet as the illustration of
the conical helix demonstrates (fig. p. 57), that central focus provides
meaning to each of the several parallel elements that surround it.
Whereas the parallels elucidate the center, the center lends content
and form to the entire passage. Detection of that center is impossible
with a purely narrative reading of the text. It can only be discerned
by "reading chiastically."

(2) The *helical flow* through progressive intensification or heightening draws the reader/hearer into the movement of the passage as
into a vortex. Chiastic patterns, as we have found, occur in all forms
of literature, in poetry and prose, in micro-units and macro-units.
They are so flexible — permitting few or many parallels, parallels of
uneven length, overlapping of corresponding passages, etc. — that
they can invest any kind of literary unit with a concentric or helical
flow. In composing their works, authors who employed chiasmus
were caught up in that flow and often expressed it unconsciously
and spontaneously. (Our analytical approach, using letters and
numbers to designate parallel lines, is a regrettably artificial if necessary convention.) In order to interpret a passage accurately, in
terms of its literal sense, the reader (exegete or other) must in similar
fashion become caught up in the flow of meaning inherent in the text.
This means that the reader must learn to *hear* the text, to listen to and
appreciate its rhythms as well as its words, in order to penetrate to
its deepest level of significance.[6] The exegete, then, needs to develop
a "flow of meaning" approach to the text in addition to a more static
search for "themes." The dynamic quality of chiastic structures will
only be appreciated when the interpreter acquires a sense for the
systolic-diastolic pulse of the text, the inward and outward flow by
which the parallels illumine the center and derive their meaning
from it.

(3) Biblical language that assumes a chiastic shape is in essence
poetry. It expresses its meaning most effectively and completely by
what we have termed "holistic impression," by impressing a particular verbal image on the mind of the reader/hearer. Even to those
passages we label "prose," chiasmus lends a poetic quality characterized by "sustained rhythm [through verbal or thematic repetition]
and a continuously operating principle of organization" (B. Smith).
Passages as diverse as the story of Joseph and Potiphar's wife, Jacob's

struggle with God, and Jesus' Bread of Life discourse, all reflect this poetic quality, because each passage has been structured according to the laws of chiasmus. This implies the very opposite of the point made by James Kugel. The heightening or focusing effect suggests not that there is no such thing as "poetry" but only various degrees of heightened prose. It suggests rather that the most basic "shape" of biblical language is poetic. For the interpreter, this means that brute fact is less important than proclamation, that historiography is subordinate to theology. Poetic language expresses meaning in its own way and on its own terms. The true theologian, the Church's spiritual elders affirmed, must be a contemplative. Equally important, the theologian must to some degree be a poet, to hear and assimilate the rhythms and nuances of the Scriptures he or she is called to interpret.

(4) The study of chiastic forms also demonstrates the importance of the *entire semantic context* for a proper interpretation of the text. This is perhaps most clearly illustrated by Psalm 8, where the verbally identical doxologies at the beginning and end conform to the "what's more" principle. The semantic context itself, together with the central question and answer, provide the latter half of the psalm with new meaning: praise of God for placing his created handiwork under the dominion of his human creatures.

This also implies that biblical passages must be read and studied *synchronically* as well as *diachronically*, holistically as well as analytically. The science of structuralism usually opposes these two, whereas in essence they are complementary. A diachronic reading is "disintegrative," in that it examines the historical development of a text "through time," to determine its underlying layers of tradition and the redactional process that led to its present form. A synchronic approach to the text, on the other hand, treats the written work in its actual state as a literary unit, irrespective of questions of historical data or of the author's intended meaning. And it does so with the conviction that the received text itself expresses its own particular theological message via its semantic and syntactic structure.

Interpretation of a chiastic unit requires both approaches, diachronic and synchronic. For each unit has its own history and often incorporates elements from preexisting oral tradition. A given chiastic structure is rarely "self-generating," produced spontaneously by the biblical author in the heat of composition. In most cases it is a composite of elements, received and carefully crafted into a self-contained unit with its own theological point. A properly holistic reading will attempt to ascertain the origin and function of those underlying elements of tradition, as well as the purpose and method of the author who has woven them into a unique proclamation. Yet such a reading will also remain sensitive to the way in which the semantic context as a whole shapes and gives meaning to those elements, independent of historical development and the author's intention. Thereby it will incorporate into its exposition of the text a key insight drawn from structuralism: that the text reflects certain universal "deep structures," an underlying network or system of convictions and meanings that are reflected in the *shape* of a literary passage as well as in its content.

(5) The study of chiastic forms frequently obliges the exegete to reopen questions concerning the *unity of composition* of an individual passage or an entire writing. A basically disintegrative approach to biblical studies has led in recent decades to a plethora of theories concerning multiple authors and the composite structure of individual texts. Few would question today that the Pentateuch is a highly composite work produced by many hands over a period of several centuries. This may be accepted as established fact. Less satisfying are the relentless attempts to demonstrate the disunity of the New Testament Gospels and Epistles. The presence of chiastic patterns often explains, better than theories of multiple authorship or conflation of originally distinct texts, why a given writing seems excessively repetitious or abruptly changes its theme. However the results may be assessed in any particular instance, chiastic analysis has to the minds of many scholars confirmed the unity of composition of such debated works as the Fourth Gospel and Paul's letters to the Philippians and Corinthians.[7] The above analysis of John 6:48-58, to take but one example, would seem to lay to rest once and for all the argument that vv. 51c-58 are a "later eucharistic interpolation." This does not mean that the author composed his work without relying on and incorporating into it diverse, individual units of preexisting tradition. It means, rather, that the true author of the writing in question is the one who provided it with its overall chiastic design. The extent of chiasmus just in the Gospels of John and Mark makes it evident that we can no longer dismiss that figure as a mere compiler or "final redactor."

(6) It happens occasionally that the parallels within chiastic patterns lend weight to one variant reading against another, and thereby aid the exegete in "establishing" the text, or determining its

original wording. We discovered one such example in Psalm 72 above. Another, from the New Testament, is the brief unit, Colossians 3:3-4. Concerned to render the passage in idiomatic English, the *RSV* reproduces these verses in a way that obscures their chiastic shape: "For you have died, and your life is hid with Christ in God. When Christ who is our life appears, then you also will appear with him in glory." The Greek text, however, can be arranged as follows.

   A : απεθανετε γαρ
      B : και η ζωη υμων
         C : κεκρυπται
            D : συν το Χριστω
               E : εν τω θεω˙
            D': οταν ο Χριστος
         C': φανερωθη,
      B': η ζωη υμων,
   A': τοτε και υμεις συν αυτω φανερωθησεσθε εν δοξη.

   A : For you died
      B : and your life
         C : is hidden
            D : with Christ
               E : in God.
            D': When Christ
         C': appears,
      B': your life,
   A': then you also will appear with him in glory.

The correspondence between B and B' strongly supports the reading υμων (your) in v. 4b, rather than ημων (our), accepted as original by the 25th Nestle edition.[8] Paul is addressing his word to those baptized Christians whose "eternal life" is a hidden reality in their present state. He assures them that at the parousia, Christ who is their life will grant them participation in his own glory (cf. 1 John 3:2). Taken in conjunction with the manuscript evidence, the balance between B and B' leaves little doubt about the original reading of v. 4.

Another example would be the difficult passage, 1 John 2:20. Critical editions of the Greek New Testament, followed by the great majority of translations, read οιδατε παντες (with Sinaiticus and Vaticanus) rather than οιδατε παντα (supported by the Majority Text, Alexandrinus and Ephraemi, together with Latin, Syriac and Coptic versions). Accordingly, they translate the verse, "You have an anointing from the Holy One, and you all know," or, "and all of you have knowledge." A close examination of the Siniaticus codex, however, reveals a large number of scribal errors at this point — enough, in fact, to throw into question its reliability as a witness to the παντες reading. This leaves us with a strong witness in "B"; although in 1 Jn 2:27, the scribe has changed the obscure χρισμα into the more familiar χαρισμα, and it is reasonable to suppose that he could have altered the παντα reading in 2:20 to παντες, either through error or to support a polemic against claims by a few to possess esoteric knowledge. Against such hypothetical Christian "gnostics," he would be declaring, "Not only the antichrists, but *all of you* possess knowledge." Aside from the theological and linguistic problems involved with such a reading, however,[9] the alternative παντα is supported by manuscripts representing a broad spectrum of dates, text types and geographical distribution. On the basis of such evidence, the external support for "you know all things" is at least as strong as it is for the reading "you all know."[10]

The literary structure of the unit 1 John 2:18-28 indicates that the proper reading is indeed παντα, inasmuch as it stands in direct parallel with 2:27, ως το αυτου χρισμα διδασκει υμας περι παντων, "as his anointing teaches you about all things." Translated literally, the text reads:

(2:18) Little children, [anacrusis]

   A: It is the last hour,
      B: and just as you have heard
         C: that antichrist is coming,
         C': so now many antichrists have come;
      B': whereby we know
   A': that it is the last hour.

   A: (v.19) They [the antichrists] went out from us,/ but they were not of us;/ for if they were of us/ they would have *abided* with us.// But [they went out from us] that it be *manifest* that none of them is of us.

B: (v.20f) Now *you have* an *anointing* from the *Holy One* and you know *all things* (παντα). I did not *write* to you because you do not know the truth, but because you do know it, and [know] that no *lie* is of the *truth*.

  C: (v.22) Who is the liar if not the one denying that Jesus is the Christ? *This is the antichrist:* the one denying the Father and the Son.

    D: (v.23) No one who denies the *Son* has the *Father;*/ whoever confesses the *Son* also has the *Father.*//

      E: (v.24a) Let what you heard/ from the beginning/ abide in you.//

        E': (v.24b) If in you abides/ what from the beginning/ you heard,//[11]

    D': (v.24c) then you will abide both in the *Son* and in the *Father.*

  C': (v.25) And *this is the promise* which he promised to us: eternal life.

B': (v.26-27d) These things I *wrote* to you about the ones deceiving you. But [as for] you, the *anointing* which *you received from him abides* in you; and you have no need that anyone should teach you, but as *his anointing* teaches you about *all things* (παντων) and is *true* and is not *false,*

A': (v.27e-28) so just as he taught you, *abide* in him. Now little children, *abide* in him, so that when he is *manifested* [in his parousia]...

The evident parallelism between v. 20 and v. 27 offers considerable support to the reading οιδατε παντα. Coupled with textual evidence and other internal considerations, it may be said to tip the balance clearly in favor of the reading, "you know all things" (cf. 1 Jn 3:20b, γινωσκει παντα; Jn 10:41; 16:13, εν τη αληθεια παση).

Detection and appreciation of chiastic patterns, then, can aid significantly in resolving at least some questions of variant readings.

(7) Given the abundance of chiastic structures in the Old and New Testaments, the question remains whether they should be graphically reproduced in popular *translations* of the Bible. Typesetting certain hymnic passages so as to illustrate their poetic form (e.g., Phil 2:6-11; Col 1:15-18) can be helpful to the modern reader, but it can also hinder a full understanding of the text. Chiastic analysis of Philippians 2, for example, shows that the beginning of the unit is

v. 5 rather than v. 6 (as in the Greek-English *RSV*, Nestle 26th ed.); and it is highly debatable whether the Christ-hymn of Colossians 1 comprises only vv. 15-18.

With regard to chiastic structures as such, we should recall that exact or "correct" analyses of given passages are often elusive. If different exegetes produce conflicting yet equally plausible analyses of the same text, it is because the form is fluid and often represents *spontaneous and unconscious* composition by the author.[12] While the four tandem "confessions" of Mark 14:61b; 15:9,18 and 31 can hardly have been placed at the center of their respective chiastic units by anything other than conscious design, the same cannot be said of the macro-unit Mark 5:21-9:29, which contains overlapping and considerable unevenness in the correspondence of parallel lines. It would seem impossible to render such a structure in translation so as to avoid hopeless confusion for the reader. Micro-units, on the other hand, are easier to format chiastically. A translation that makes their structure apparent should prove of great benefit, as long as it is labeled "tentative." In any event, translators would do well to respect chiastic patterns wherever they occur, in order to preserve the balance inherent in the Greek. From most translations, for example, one would never know that Revelation 21:1-4 or Colossians 3:3-4 each constitutes a complete chiasmus, since the correspondence between complementary lines is not preserved in the English version.

The final aim of chiastic analysis should be for us to acquire an intuited sense for the actual shape of biblical language and the flow of meaning that issues from it. This means that we need to grasp and appreciate the helical movement of a chiastically structured passage as the biblical author himself did, and thereby learn to read and to hear the text in the same cadences and with the same accents in which it was composed. Experience has shown that once anyone with a certain "feel" for language learns the key to chiastic structures, they very quickly learn as well to apply that key successfully. In such cases, the Scriptures come to life in a new and vibrant way, and the reader gains fresh insight into the Word of God and a deepened appreciation of it. With this in mind, I have included in Appendix I a simple guide to the process of discerning chiastic forms and "interiorizing" the unique way in which they communicate meaning.

Having reached this point, however, we need to address once again the skepticism expressed by a number of biblical scholars today concerning the very existence of chiasmus. Have we merely cut up the text arbitrarily in order to make it fit a preconceived pattern? Or even if one grants the reality of chiastic structures in isolated micro-units, is it correct for us to conclude that long sections of a work — and even entire writings — were also composed according to the laws of concentric parallelism as we have defined them? If we take individual units such as the Markan temptation scene (1:12-13) or Matthew's version of the Lord's Prayer (6:7-15) and extract them from their respective contexts, then there appears to be good reason for denying that they are chiastic: the helical movement we have described is simply too tenuous in such examples to make a solid case for its presence and consequently for its significance in conveying the author's meaning. Nevertheless, our analysis of the Gospel of Mark, together with passages such as John 6:35-58, make the fact of chiastic structuring undeniable. But that fact can only be appreciated in light of the cumulative evidence that supports it. Although the chiastic "shape" of any given unit might reasonably be questioned, taken as a whole, evidence for the existence of "concentric parallelism" — and its importance for exegesis — is quite simply overwhelming.

One reason chiasmus has been so seldom recognized is because the "prime" line of two parallel verses does not reflect the original statement exactly. Once we learn to feel or sense the heightening or focusing effect from A to A', B to B', etc., the true correspondences emerge with force and clarity. Chiastic "parallelism," in other words, can only be discerned and fully appreciated by taking into account the "what's more" factor, the spiralling concentricity that describes a rhetorical helix.

The persistence of chiasmus throughout history, in a broad variety of cultural and linguistic settings, suggests that the phenomenon is more than just another literary form. Physicists, philosophers and poets today appear to be investigating more than ever the relation between language and the natural order.[13] Their findings are leading them increasingly away from a fragmenting, analytical approach to reality and toward one that is fundamentally holistic. Even superficial reflection on the organization of an integrated universe makes evident the place of balanced elements within it, in the natural world as in art and architecture.[14] There is as well, on the micro- and macro-cosmic scales, a helical movement inscribed in the order of things, from the DNA molecule to the spiral galaxy. The most precise and exquisite example of this form is perhaps the chambered nautilus. It appears as well, though, in a great variety of ocean-side phenomena, from conchs and sea-snail shells to hurricanes, waterspouts and the curl of a breaking wave. Experiments in the new sciences of chaos and fractal geometry have demonstrated a similar movement in the image of the so-called "strange attractor" and the complex, seemingly irregular curve of the "Mandelbrot set."[15] Each of these constructs exhibits a certain concentricity, a spiraling of parallel members toward and about a central axis.[16]

Without extensive research based on an appropriate scientific methodology, it would be too facile to conclude that an analogy can be legitimately drawn between constructs such as these and the shape of a chiastic unit of poetry or prose, or that language replicates a fundamental helical movement inscribed in physical reality. Nevertheless, the movement peculiar to chiasmus suggests that in some sense concentric parallelism is "naturally" imprinted on the fabric of the human mind, on the order of a "deep-structure" such as narrative or myth. This observation, made at the close of the last chapter, offers a plausible explanation for the ubiquity of chiastic structures, irrespective of time and place. Chiasmus is a universal form, both learned and intuited. If it has indeed persisted throughout the centuries, even when its most characteristic features have gone unrecognized, is it not because of its unique ability to communicate a message powerfully and concisely by drawing the reader/hearer into its very center of meaning?

To return to the question posed at the outset of this study, How are we to *read* the Bible? The evidence clearly indicates that we should read it "chiastically," according to the same principles of concentric parallelism by which it was composed. As much as any others, those principles determine the "shape" of biblical language and invest it with both its meaning and its enduring beauty.

ENDNOTES

[1]Reissued as J. Bengel, *New Testament Word Studies*, 2 vols. (Grand Rapids: Kregel, 1971).

[2]*Chiasmus*, p. 35f.

[3]For a welcome corrective, see R.E. Man, "The Value of Chiasm for New Testament Interpretation," and his references to studies by D.R. Miesner.

[4]*Chiasmus*, p. 40f.

[5]*RSV*. See Lund, *Chiasmus*, p. 44, who notes that the first two and the last two lines (A-B // B'-A') create a parallelism of *ideas*, elsewhere of identical terms.

[6]From Jerome (*Preface to Job*) through J. Weiss (*Beiträge zur paulinischen Rhetorik, 1897*), to N. Lund and J. Dewey, scholars have stressed that biblical works were composed for the ear, to be read aloud and heard by a congregation rather than read silently for personal and private edification. See Dewey's article, "Oral Methods of Structuring Narrative in Mark," *Int* 43 (1989), p. 32-44.

[7]See once again P.F. Ellis, *Seven Pauline Letters*, who suggests a chiastic structure for Philippians and the Corinthian correspondence. See as well our above analysis of 1 Corinthians. My student, Vladimir Aleandro, demonstrated in a seminar paper (May, 1990) that 2 Cor 8-9 are not, as is usually thought, two different and divergent accounts of the Jerusalem collection, but a single chiastic unit that serves as the core of the entire letter. His analysis is as follows: A (8:1-2), B (8:3-6), C (8:7-9), D (8:10-11), E (8:12-15), F (8:16-17), G (8:18-19), H (8:20-21 = the focal point: the liberal gift we are administering is honorable to the Lord and to persons), G' (8:22), F' (8:23-24), E' (9:1-4), D' (9:5-7), C' (9:8-10), B' (9:11-12), A' (9:13-15). The inclusion leads from *the grace of God*, the *test of afflictions* and the Macedonians' abundance of joy that produced a wealth of *generosity* (8:1-2), to the Corinthians' *test of service* with obedience and *generosity*, that will lead them to glorify God because of the *grace of God* in them (9:13-14). The entire unit then closes with anacrusis in the form of a cry of praise, "Thanks be to God for his inexpressible gift!" A similar but less complete analysis appears in Ph. Rolland, "La structure littéraire de la Deuxième Epître aux Corinthiens," *Bib* 71 (1990), p. 73-84. (Aleandro's work preceded the appearance of this article.)

[8]Thus favoring the reading of P^{46}, Sinaiticus, A, C and D, against B, D^1, and the Majority text.

[9]The author would hardly have included the antichrists in those who possess (saving) knowledge. In the Johannine Gospel and First Epistle, the term πας is a technical term, synonymous with αληθεια, truth (e.g., Jn 14:26; 16:13; 1 Jn 2:27).

[10]The *NRSV* reading, "and all of you have knowledge," is a paraphrase. For a more detailed discussion of this evidence, see J. Breck, "The Function of πας in 1 John 2:20," *SVTQ* 35/2-3 (1991), 187-206.

[11]The literal translation illustrates the inverted parallelism, a rhetorical form that appears in greater proportion in this writing than anywhere else in the NT.

[12]Cf. R.A. Culpepper's remark, "The Pivot of John's Prologue," p. 17: "the interpreter must...bear in mind that all literary structures are in varying degrees artificial. The prologue of John is a work of art; the artist used structures, but he was

not their slave. To have made the chiastic structure more explicit would necessarily have made it more artificial." This same artistic flexibility explains why chiastic forms can often be analyzed in different ways, revealing different "centers" while the parallelism of surrounding members remains intact.

[13]See, e.g., David Bohm's theory of the "rheomode," in *Wholeness and the Implicate Order* (London: Routledge and Kegan Paul; New York: Methuen, 1980), ch. 2; and Douglas R. Hofstadter's remarkable "metaphorical fugue," *Gödel, Escher, Bach. An Eternal Golden Braid* (New York: Random House, 1979). In his chapter on the "Crab Canon" (p. 199-203), Hofstadter presents a highly contrived and equally amusing dialogue between the Tortoise and Achilles, structured as a perfect chiasmus. The form does indeed persist into modern times!

[14]Most basic is the A:B:A' structure of a flower or a tree (roots → stem → leaves/flower/fruit of the reproductive system). This same pattern appears in animal reproduction: "conception → growth in the womb → birth," or "birth → life → death." A more complicated A:B:C:B':A' pattern appears in the structure of the alimentary canal (mouth → esophagus → stomach → intestine → anus), as it does in tools such as the screwdriver: hand (efficient cause) → handle (point of transferred force) → shaft (the "pivot" through which the force is transmitted from handle to blade) → blade (point of transferred force) → screw (final cause). Frivolous though it may seem, another example is the mechanical toilet: handle (mechanical action to engage the flow) → descent of the water → the "flush" and evacuation (the "focus" of the action) → ascent of the water (the tank fills) → the shut-off (mechanical action to end the flow and prepare for the next usage). Then, of course, there are architectural balances and symmetries, from the ancient ziggurat to the modern skyscraper.

[15]See esp. James Gleick, *Chaos. Making a New Science* (New York: Penguin, 1987) and the photos that demonstrate order and helical structure within chaotic systems; and Paul Davies, *The Cosmic Blueprint* (New York: Simon and Schuster, 1988), esp. chs. 4-5. The helical form is also a common feature of tools, from the woodscrew to the corkscrew (see the preceding note). For an imaginative and intriguing image of the helical structure of space, see Vladimir Volkoff's *Le Tirebouchon du Bon Dieu* (Paris: Presse Pocket, 1982), p. 209-217.

[16]Prof. Peter Cowe of the Graduate School of Arts and Sciences, Columbia University, followed up on a conversation a few years ago with a letter containing other interesting examples (5 February 1990). "...it struck me that there are elements of [chiastic patterns] in the baroque convention of the suite, both solo and orchestral. Basically a combination of dance movements, it would feature smaller units such as the gavotte and musette or minuet and trio. In these latter the gavotte/minuet would normally be composed of two parts, both of which would be played with repeats the first time round. Then the contrasting musette/trio would be played (often in a different but related key and usually with repeats). Finally the gavotte/minuet would be played again (inclusion) but this time its two parts would be played straight through without repeat, constituting a sort of [intensified] a'. Out of the suite developed the classical sonata/symphony in which the first movement was traditionally in "sonata form." This entailed three sections, introduction, development and recapitulation. In the first, two contrasting themes would be announced and in the early days this would be immediately repeated... Usually the final section was much more elaborated than the exposition and might have a long, tumultuous coda as a finale which would undoubtedly qualify as a'... Another thing which struck me is the three distances typically depicted in classical landscape painting,

often with contrasting colours to bring out the play of light and shadow. Often the near distance is darkest, giving way to a flood of light on the middle distance which takes up a large portion of the canvas. That in turn would give way to the far distance which again would be in comparative shade, but not as dark as the foreground, again suggesting a sort of a'." Both psychological and spiritual models have been produced, in many different cultures and periods, that exhibit such a concentric shape, bounded by "inclusion." For examples, see J. Purce, *The Mystic Spiral* (New York: Thames and Hudson, 1974).

APPENDIX I

A Guide to Detecting Chiastic Patterns

To help the reader acquire some facility in detecting chiastic structures throughout the Bible, the following steps are offered as a guide.

1. Acquire a study Bible you can freely mark up with a pencil.

2. Try to detach yourself from the divisions in the printed text, paying as little attention as possible to paragraphs or verse and chapter numbers.

3. Look for units of text — several lines at most — that begin and end with similar terms or themes (A:A' inclusion). When you find such correspondences, mark them off from the rest of the unit with brackets [...].

4. Read the passage through several times to sense its narrative flow (from A to A'), before attempting to discover other parallel elements in it.

5. Move from the extremities toward the center: try to identify the presence and limits of B:B', then C:C', etc.

6. Look for a logical center of meaning (0): one or two lines (whole statements or single words) that seem to summarize the theme of the passage as read "from the outside in." Set it off with brackets.

7. Test the center (0) by moving outward from it in an effort to detect and determine the limits of 1:1'.

8. Re-read the entire passage to verify the parallels (read A then A', then B and B', etc.), and set them off from one another with parentheses (...).

9. On a large sheet of lined paper write out the passage according to its parallel structure (using letters or numbers, and indenting as we have done), in order to *visualize* its form.

10. Read the passage aloud several times as you have written it, in order to *hear* its concentric flow.

11. Work out the helical analysis (A → A'; B → B'; etc.) to test for any *heightening* that may occur from the first parallel line to its complement.

12. Return to the printed text and "read chiastically."

EXAMPLE:

Text (1 John 4:11-12):

"Beloved, if God so loved us, we also ought to love one another. No one has ever seen God; if we love one another, God abides in us and his love is perfected in us."

Marking this as suggested gives the following:

[Beloved, if God so loved us,] (we also ought to love one another.) [No one has ever seen God;] (if we love one another,) [God abides in us and his love is perfected in us.]

Writing it out according to its parallelism gives this:

A : Beloved, if God so loved us,
    B : we also ought to love one another.
        C : No one has ever seen God;
    B': if we love one another,
A': God abides in us and his love is perfected in us.

And we can analyze its concentric flow as follows:

A → A': God loved us →
    God's love is perfected in us.
B → B': We *ought* to love one another (the ethical imperative) →
    If we love one another (the necessary condition)
C : We know God only through his love for us in Christ (4:10).

The central focus (C) links this passage with 4:9-10. We have never seen God, yet we know God sent his Son to give his life as a sacrifice, that through our faith in him we might receive eternal life. The passage 4:11-12 expresses the idea that our faith must issue in love if we are truly to possess that life, that is, if God is to abide in us and perfect his life within us.

Begin this exercise with passages from 1 John that appear at first reading to make up a single unit. Then move on to the Gospel of Mark. Work out your own analyses of several key passages (Jesus' baptism, the transfiguration, healing stories, the crucifixion scene), then compare them with the outline in II.2.C above. For the adventuresome, attempt to work out the parallelism of the Epistle to the Hebrews (clue: the chiastic center appears to be 9:11-14).

APPENDIX II

A Chiastic Outline of the Gospel of John

		Sequences		

: 1:19-52   Jesus: *first coming*   1:19-52   1   (21)
John: first *witness* to Jesus
Jesus and the Apostles in Bethany, across the Jordan
To Peter: "Your name shall be *Cephas*..."

b : 2:1-12   *Woman* at Cana: *Mary*, Jesus' *mother*   2:1-12   2   (20)
Birth of new age: wine

A   c : 2:13-24   *Jewish Passover*   2:13-24   3   (19)
"*Destroy this temple* and..."
"he was talking about the *Temple of his body*."
Destruction and *creation*

b': 3:1-21   *Discourse at night* — to Nicodemus   3:1-21   4   (18)
Birth from above
"Can he return to his *mother's* womb..."

a': 3:22-36   John: last *witness* to Jesus   3:22-36   5   (17)
John says: "*He must increase*..."

a : 4:1-38   Samaritan *Woman*   4:1-38   6   (16)
Believes Jesus
In shadow of *Mount* Gerazim

b : 4:39-42   Samaritans (*non-Jews*)   4:39-42   7   (15)
Believe Jesus
"*Savior of the World*"

B   c : 4:43-52   *Gentile* official and family   4:43-52   8   (14)
Hears and believes without seeing

b': 5:1-47   *Judean Jews* at *Pentecost*   5:1-47   9   (13)
Jesus makes himself "*God's equal*."
Jesus speaks of God as "*his own Father*"

a': 6:1-15   *Passover near*   6:1-15   10   (12)
Jesus on the *mountain*
Galilean Jews *misinterpret bread*
Galilean Jews reject Jesus

a : 6:16-17a   *Disciples* on the *one shore*
   b : 6:17b-18a   Disciples *alone at sea*
C   c : 6:18b   Wind and sea rising (Reed Sea and Exodus)   6:16-21   11
   b': 6:19-21a   *Jesus* like Yahweh ("*It is I*") *comes on water*
a': 6:21b   *Disciples* safe on *other shore*

a : 6:22-72   *Passover near*   6:22-72   12   (10)
Galilean Jews *misinterpret bread*
Galilean Jews reject Jesus
Jesus says: "He who eats ... *I will raise up on the last day.*"

b : 7 - 8   *Judean Jews* at feast of *Tabernacles*   7 - 8   13   (9)
Judean Jews *hear and reject* Jesus
Jesus makes himself *God's equal* ("Before Abraham ... I AM.")
Jesus speaks of God as "*My Father*"

B'   c : 9:1-10:21   *Pharisees* and blind man   9:1-10:21   14   (8)
Pharisees *see* but *do not believe*

b': 10:22-39   *Judean Jews* at feast of *Dedication of the Temple*   10:22-39   15   (7)
Hear and reject Jesus
Jesus is the '*Savior of the flock and other sheep*'

a': 10:40-12:11   *Women*: Martha and Mary   10:40-12:11   16   (6)
Believe Jesus
Lazarus: "*Whoever believes in me ... will come to life.*"
Martha: "I know he *will rise again ... on the last day.*"

a : 12:12-50   Jesus *comes* in triumph to Jerusalem   12:12-50   17   (5)
Crowds cry out "*Blessed is he who comes* in the name of the Lord!"

b : 13 - 17   *Discourse at night* — to the Apostles   13 - 17   18   (4)
Birth from above
About '*absence and presence*'

A'   c : 18 - 19   *Jewish Passover*   18 - 19   19   (3)
Destruction (Jesus' body) and *creation* (the Church)

b': 20:1-18   *Woman* at tomb: *Mary*   20:1-18   20   (2)
About '*absence and presence*'

a': 20:19-21:24   *Jesus and Apostles* at Lake of Galilee   20:19-21:24   21   (1)
Jesus' *last coming*
To Peter: "*Feed* my sheep."

— Judy Ellis

SOME WORDS
AFTER CHIASMUS

by Charles Lock
Professor of English and Religious Studies,
University of Toronto

Throughout Fr. Breck's brilliant and absorbing book the reader must ask the question from the asking of which the author does not himself refrain. When we find such ample evidence of the chiastic structure in Biblical texts, have we found a "key" to an otherwise undisclosed principle of composition? Or have we lit upon a deep structure of language, or at least of writing? The more evidence that Fr. Breck adduces for the universality of chiasmus, in ancient and modern literature, in poetry, prose and journalism — not to mention in one of his own scholarly paragraphs — the less remarkable becomes the case for Scripture. Yet it is of course Fr. Breck's central and dominating insight that the reading of Scripture must itself be modified by the recognition of its chiastic structures. This book is about the language of the Bible, not about language.

Fr. Breck's argument, and the rhetoric of his argument, are themselves not entirely innocent of chiasmus. Northrop Frye explicitly structures his fundamental rethinking of Biblical typology, *The Great Code*, (New York, 1982) on a two-part, mirror-image chiasmus. Fr. Breck's earlier book, *The Power of the Word* (Crestwood, NY, l986), its title a coincidental chiasmus of Frye's second volume *Words with Power* (1990), was concerned with typology. Chiasmus is not, there, mentioned. Given the brilliance of Fr. Breck's treatment of *theoria* and typology in that book, it is remarkable, almost inexplicable that, in this book, typology is hardly mentioned. Such reciprocal silences possess, at least, the significance and the balance of chiasmus.

Typology and Chiasmus are both structured around a centre: as Fr. Breck notes, the shape of chiasmus is properly a helix. The sentence spirals, from A to B and inwards and upwards to the centre of the conical helix (see figure p. 57), and then outwards and upwards to B' and at last to A'. As demonstrated in Part I, Chapter 4, what follows the centre, what is, on the visual model, above the centre, is not a mere repetition of what has gone before, but represents increase, augmentation, intensification. We may compare this with typology, which describes that which comes before as figures or shadows or types, and that which comes after as fulfilment, presence, realization. The mid-point, the neck of the hour-glass, is the Incarnation, the moment when Prophecy becomes Revelation. The Bible in its entirety clearly has the structure of a conical helix, with the New Testament serving not only as a reflection of but also as an increment over the Old Testament. The Incarnation is the mid-point of the conical helix, whose outer- and upper-most point will be the last and pleromatic "what's more" of the Eschaton.

That being so, we might wonder whether chiasmus is not on the local level, the level of syntax and exposition, a model of typology on the level of the collection of books. And we might also wonder what has happened to history, reading and writing, and indeed to the cosmos itself, that the end seems to matter so much more than the middle. We might call this end-fixation a feature of dialectical thought, whose clichés include such numbing denials of the present as "it's not over until it's over," because there can always be another turn of the dialectical screw.

Yet we know, at the moment of the New Testament, that *it is all over*, that the Eschaton is from now on simply deferred, or as Florovsky said, that we live in the inaugurated Eschaton. And when we read chiastically, we know that it is all over when we have reached the mid-point, finding there that which must make of what follows only deferral, dilation, increment ... but nothing made anew, as if from nothing.

In Fr. Breck's most resonant phrase, the literate of the ancient world "were trained throughout their school years to read from the center outwards and from the extremities towards the center." To see the text as linear, progressive, and logical is a sophisticated refinement that characterizes modernity: it is a method of reading appropriate to dialectical thinking, to a thinking by representations in which presence is always deferred. In another, earlier, even "archaic" mode of thinking, presence is here, in the middle of things, in the middle of sentences, in the middle of paragraphs, at the crossing of energies we name the now and here.

Fr. Breck's articulation of the difficulty in arguing the case for chiasmus rests here. Not on Biblical scholarship or hermeneutic nuance, nor on theological slant, but on a vast transformation in the way of reading. We may recognize that reading practices differ, that the reading of alphabets is not the same as the reading of ideograms, that the direction of reading varies, not only to read downwards but also upwards, not only from left to right, but from right to left (when the book's front becomes its back). But what we do not challenge is that reading is directional, that there is in every text a beginning and an ending.

The dialectic of reason, by its very discounting of the mid-point of revelation, effects the change from chiastic to teleological thought. Thought proceeds, and language proceeds, ever onwards to the goal of meaning and presence. In the interim, all sorts of improbable and unpleasant things might occur, whose logic and significance will be made plain "in the long run."

The case for chiasmus evokes two previous ventures into this most contentious territory of the non-linearity of language. The founder of the modern study of linguistics, Fernanand de Saussure (1857-1913), a thinker comparable in profundity and influence to Marx and Freud, took as an axiom that language was "uni-directional," that written words or acoustic signs were strung along a chain, and that speaker and hearer (or writer and reader) attended to each sign sequentially. Yet at the very time that Saussure was teaching his fundamental principles in the *Course in General Linguistics* at the University of Geneva, he was also pursuing a hobby that became a mania. This was a suspicion that in Latin poetry anagrams could be detected dispersed throughout a line of poetry; these he named hypograms. To find a hypogram one takes a line of poetry, and picks out individual letters which, preferably in sequence, spell out a name, typically of the lady to whom the poem is dedicated. The trouble with this "method" is that, in the last sentence, we can find Fiona, Daisy, Diana, Mary, Rachel, Portia, and any number of other girls' names, not to mention thousands of other words. As Jean Starobinski remarks in his revelatory discussion of the great linguist's secret mania for secrets, *Les mots sous les mots* (Paris, 1970), Sausssure must have had a hard time persuading himself of his own sanity.

What is at stake, however, is not the weight of the evidence, but the principle that reading might be performed in a non-linear manner. The statistical absurdities of Saussure's "findings" are irrelevant when it is recognized that Saussure was working exactly against his own axiomatic principle, reading not in sequence but intermittently, registering only those letters that would form a cryptic name. Saussure's research on this topic, which seems to have absorbed a great deal more of his time than did the working out of the theoretical axioms of the *Course*, have long been a source of embarrassment; first published by Starobinski, over fifty years after Saussure's death, the anagrams remain at best a curiosity in the history of scholarship.

Roman Jakobson (1896-1982), another great figure in the modern history of linguistics and semiotics, struggled with Saussure's principle of linearity throughout his life. The key to the undoing of linearity is to be found in Saussure's insistence on the arbitrariness of the sign. "Arbitrariness" at its most simple restates Plato's view in the *Cratylus* that words have no essential connection to those things which they designate. Cratylus's view, similar to that which underlies the notion of the "Edenic language" by which Adam named the creatures in Paradise, is one which has never been entirely forgotten. Ralph Waldo Emerson's belief that all abstract terms came into being as literal and material facts ("right" from "straight," "wrong" from "crooked") must be acknowledged as an echo of Cratylus; so must be the far more sophisticated and extraordinarily learned quest for "etymons" of the great twentieth-century philologist Leo Spitzer. The importance of the arbitrariness of the linguistic sign is that on it depends the principle of the linearity of language. In short, if a sign is not arbitrary, it must be open to self-reflexivity; it may signify in more than one way; it will compromise the linear movement of the text. And this is the axiom on which Saussure's theory depends (as it is also the axiom which is subverted by his Latin anagrams): "The signifier, being auditory, is unfolded in time from which it gets the following characteristics: (a) it represents a span, and (b) the span is measurable in a single dimension; it is a line" (F. de Saussure, *Course in General Linguistics*, trans. W. Baskin, New York, 1966, 70).

Linearity of reading is the fundamental principle by which the text is established in modernity as text. That is to say, when we read a text we do not see an image: the type and size of font, the disposition of the words on the page, the very look of the page, are entirely accidental features. A text might be defined as that which, while being visual, is entirely independent of image, scale and perspective. Yet texts were not always thus. We have learnt to speak of the interaction between text and image in medieval illuminated manuscripts. It might, however, be more accurate to say that before modernity — and especially before the development of printing — there was no fixed distinction between text and image. Both text and image were to be read, as they were likewise each to be *written*: the Greek verb *graphein* exemplifies the unity of what we now take to be the separate activities of writing and drawing, the one pictorial, the other textual.

Linearity is the textual figure by which language is represented as linear, syntactic, progressive and logical. Fr. Breck makes the important point that chiasmus would have been used as a mnemonic device: if one can remember all the phrases from A to F, one will have plenty of cues and clues to complete the chiasmic unit, from F' to A'. And we should therefore assume that chiasmus originated in an oral culture. As oral narratives were written down, and as the written versions safeguarded the narrative details, so the memory of the chiastic structure would fade. We know that sequences of straightforward prose are very hard to memorise. The memorizing of words is best done through poetry, where rhyme, rhythm, alliteration and so forth all contribute to the repetitive patterning by which memory functions. Exceptionally, people are gifted with what is termed "photographic memory," that is, the ability to remember a page which one has not even read — a feat of memory dependent precisely on one's having not read the page, but only — and overwhelmingly — *seen* it, in the twinkling of a snapshot. Reading, however, renders the words on the page invisible. The trick is to see the page as an image, by refusing to read it. If one follows the instructions given by Fr. Breck in Appendix 1, "A Guide to Detecting Chiastic Patterns," one will find in Rule 9 the word *visualize* (visually heightened by italics). That is, indeed, the art: to see the text as an image; to see the page as an image, not to read the page as a text.

Roman Jakobson's last book, published in 1979 (with Linda Waugh as co-author) was entitled *The Sound-Shape of Language*. This most challenging of modern linguistic works consummates the attack on Saussure (the Saussure of the *Course*, not the unknown Knight of the Anagrams) begun by the Danish linguist Otto Jespersen (1860-1943), who in 1922 introduced the notion of "sound-symbolism." Jakobson combined Jespersen's term with the theories of the American pioneer in semiotics, Charles Sanders Peirce (1839-1914). Peirce argued that any sign could be described as either a symbol, or an index, or an icon. For Peirce, the symbol is arbitrary, and most words are symbols. Indices involve pointing: certain words, notably "shifters," those pronouns (me, you) and temporal (then, now) and spatial (here, there) adverbs whose sense depends on knowing the position of the speaker, are to be regarded not as symbols but as indices.

The great question for Jakobson was whether words, which can be indices as well as symbols, could ever function as icons. That is: could a word look like that which it represents? Obviously not, because if it did, it would not be a word but something like a Chinese ideogram. But what if groups of words were possessed of a shape similar to that which those words represent? Answering this in the affirmative, Jakobson spoke of the sound-shape, not of individual words, but of language. As his recent editors remark of the response to Jakobson's breath-takingly audacious claim in his final work: "The issue of nonarbitrariness in language, especially the iconicity relation between sounds and the meanings they carry, has been largely ignored in contemporary linguistics" (Roman Jakobson, *On Language*, Cambridge, MA, 1990, 422). It may be pertinent merely to observe, but to observe here, that in the 1970s Roman Jakobson was received into the Orthodox Church. What is chiasmus but a form of sound-symbolism? We must abstain, as does the author, from encouraging the shadow of chiasmus to fall on the Cross: that would be groundless. But with the help of Peirce and Jakobson, we can say that chiasmus is a manifestation of the iconicity of language. And it is that word, that word for image, Icon, the one word that should never be absent from theology, which even more than *graphein* holds together the text and the image. No icon is complete unless the pictorial surface itself contains the alphabetical symbols identifying the persons depicted. An icon without lettering on its very surface is simply not an icon (and words on a frame, as a label, will not do, and exemplify exactly the text-image divide which modernity has wrought.) And however contentious and problematic readers may find certain aspects and examples in this book, Fr. Breck has demonstrated one vast truth — a truth which modernity has all but forgotten, a truth whose suppression by print and dialectic, has indeed been constitutive of modernity: that no text is complete — no sacred text is properly sacred — unless its words are contained in an iconic structure, unless its language takes the form of an icon. In chiasmus, the word, embodied in print, is not rendered transcendent by reading; the word unread, seen in all the created materiality of its instantiation, remains embodied, visible, a fragment of the chiasmus. Matter alone can never disappear: even the most sacred words can only be crossed out. Chiasmus, a sacred pattern which coincides with and takes the very form of the crossing-out of its erasure, has not disappeared; it has been made visible to those eyes that have learnt, as a profoundly sacramental task, not to read, but to see, and then — now — to make us see.

BIBLIOGRAPHY

Achtemeier, P. *Mark* (Philadelphia: Fortress, 1986).

Allison, D.C. Jr. "The Structure of the Sermon on the Mount," *JBL* 106:3 (1987), 423-445.

Alter, R. *The Art of Biblical Narrative* (New York: Harper Basic Books, 1981).

_____. *The Art of Biblical Poetry* (New York: Harper Basic Books, 1985).

Alter, R. and F. Kermode (eds.). *The Literary Guide to the Bible* (London, 1987).

Auffret, P. "'Allez, fils, entendez-moi!' Etude structurelle du psaume 34 et son rapport au psaume 33," *Eglise et Theologie* 19/1 (Ottawa, 1988), 5-31.

Baker, A. "Parallelism: England's Contribution to Biblical Studies," *CBQ* 35:4 (1973), 429-440.

Barth, M. *Ephesians*, vol. 2 (New York: Doubleday, 1974).

Basser, H. W. "Derrett's 'Binding' Reopened," *JBL* 104 (1985), 297-300.

Beare, F. W. *The Earliest Records of Jesus* (Oxford: Blackwell, 1962).

_____. *The Gospel According to Matthew* (Peabody, MA: Hendrickson, 1981).

Bengel, J. *New Testament Word Studies*, 2 vols. (Grand Rapids, MI: Kregel, 1971).

Berlin, A. *The Dynamics of Biblical Parallelism* (Bloomington, IN: Indiana University Press, 1985).

Bligh, J. *Galatians in Greek: A Structural Analysis of Paul's Epistle to the Galatians* (Detroit: University of Detroit Press, 1966).

Bohm, D. *Wholeness and the Implicate Order* (London: Routledge and Kegan Paul / New York: Methuen, 1980).

Boismard, M. E. *Le prologue de S. Jean* (Paris: Cerf, 1953).

Bonnard, P. *L'Evangile Selon Saint Matthieu*, 2nd ed. (Neuchâtel: Delachaux & Niestle, 1970).

Borgen, P. "Targumic Character of the Prologue of John," *NTS* 16 (1970), 291-293.

Bornkamm, G. "Der Aufbau der Bergpredigt," *NTS* 24 (1978), 419-432.

_____. "Die Eucharistische Rede im Johannes-Evangelium," *ZNW* 47 (1956), 161-169.

Botte, B. *Hippolite de Rome. La Tradition Apostolique* (Paris: Cerf, 1968).

Breck, J. "Biblical Chiasmus: Exploring Structure for Meaning," *BTB*, 17:2 (1987), 70-74.

_____. "Chiasmus in Revelation," in *The Revelation of John* (Proceedings of the Orthodox Biblical Society, Leukosia, Greece, Sept. 26 – Oct. 3, 1991), Ιερα Αρχιεπισκοπη Κυπρου, 1991, p. 247-251 (in Greek).

_____. "John 21: Appendix, Epilogue or Conclusion?," *SVTQ* 36/1-2 (1992), 27-49.

_____. *Spirit of Truth*, vol. I, "The Origins of Johannine Pneumatology" (Crestwood, NY: St. Vladimir's Seminary Press, 1991).

_____. "The Function of ΠΑΣ in 1 John 2:20," *SVTQ* 35/2-3 (1991), 187-206.

_____. *The Power of the Word* (Crestwood, NY: St. Vladimir's Seminary Press, 1986).

Brett, L. F. X. "Suggestions for an Analysis of Mark's Arrangement," in C.S. Mann, *Mark. A New Translation With Introduction and Commentary* (New York, Doubleday, 1986), 174-190.

Brown, R. E. *The Birth of the Messiah: A Commentary on the Infancy Narratives in Matthew and Luke* (New York: Doubleday, 1977).

_____. *The Churches the Apostles Left Behind* (New York: Paulist, 1984).

_____. *The Community of the Beloved Disciple* (New York: Paulist, 1979).

_____. *The Gospel According to John*, 2 vols. (New York: Doubleday, 1966, 1970).

_____. "The Resurrection in Matthew (27:62-28:20)," *Worship* 64/2 (1990), 157-170.

Brown, R. E., Donfried, K. P., Reumann, J., eds. *Peter in the New Testament* (New York: Paulist, 1973).

Bullinger, E. W. *The Companion Bible* (Grand Rapids, MI: Zondervan, 1974).

Bultmann, R. *Das Evangelium des Johannes* (Göttingen: Vandenhoeck & Ruprecht, 1964).

_____. *The History of the Synoptic Tradition* (Oxford: Blackwell, 1963).

Camelot, Th. *Lettres, Martyre de Polycarp, Sources Chrétiennes* 10 (Paris: Cerf, 1969).

Carpenter, M. *Kontakia of Romanos, Byzantine Melodist*, 2 vols. (Columbia, MO: University of Missouri Press, 1970, 1973).

Cassanowicz, I. M. "Parallelism in Biblical Poetry," *TJE* vol. 10, 520-522.

Ceresko, A. R. "The A:B::B:A Word Pattern in Hebrew and Northwest Semitic, with Special Reference to the Book of Job," *UF* 7 (1975), 73-88.

_____. "The Chiastic Word Pattern in Hebrew," *CBQ* 38:3 (1976), 303-311.

_____. "The Function of Chiasmus in Hebrew Poetry," *CBQ* 40:1 (1978), 1-10.

Charles, R. H. *Pseudepigrapha of the Old Testament* (Oxford: Clarendon Press, 1913/1963).

Couilleau, G. "Saint Jean Climaque," *Dictionnaire de Spiritualité*, vol. 8 (Paris, 1972), 369-389.

Culpepper, R. A. "The Pivot of John's Prologue," *NTS* 27 (1980), 1-31.

Dahood, M. "Chaismus," *IDB-S*, (Nashville: Abingdon, 1976), 145.

_____. "A New Metrical Pattern in Biblical Poetry," *CBQ* 29:4 (1967), 574-579.

_____. "Poetry. Hebrew," *IDB-S*, 669-672.

_____. *Psalms*, 3 vols. (Garden City: Doubleday 1966, 1968, 1970).

Davies, P. *The Cosmic Blueprint* (New York: Simon and Schuster, 1988).
de Jong, H. J. "Sonship, Wisdom, Infancy: Luke 2:41-51a," *NTS* 24 (1978), 317-354.
de la Potterie, I. *The Hour of Jesus* (New York: Alba House, 1989).
de Moor, J. C. "Ugarit," *IDB-S*, 928-931.
Derrett, J. D. M. "Binding and Loosing (Matt 16:19; 18:18, John 20:23)," *JBL* 102 (1983), 112-117.
Des Granges, Ch. M. *Les Poètes français 1820-1920* (Paris: Librairie A. Hatier, 1935).
de Waard, J. "The Chiastic Structure of Amos V. 1-17," *VT* 27 (1977), 170-177.
Dewey, J. *Markan Public Debate: Literary Technique, Concentric Structure, and Theology in Mark 2:1-3:6* (Chico, CA, Scholars Press, 1980).
_____. "Oral Methods of Structuring Narrative in Mark," *Int* 43 (1989), 32-44.
Di Marco, A. "Il Chiasmo nella Bibbia," German translation, "Der Chiasmus in der Bibel. 1 Teil," *LingBib* 36 (1975), 21-97; 3 Teil," *LingBib* 39 (1978), 37-85.
Dinkler, E. "Peter's Confession and the 'Satan' Saying: the Problem of Jesus' Messiahship," in *The Future of our Religious Past*, ed. J. M. Robinson (New York: Harper & Row, 1971), 64-68.
Dix, G. *The Shape of the Liturgy* (London: Dacre, 1946/1964).
Dupont-Sommer, A. *The Essene Writings from Qumran* (New York: Meridian/World, 1961).
Eckman, B. "A Quantitative Metrical Analysis of the Philippians Hymn," *NTS* 26 (1980), 258-266.
Ellis, P. F. "The Authenticity of John 21," *SVTQ* 36/1-2 (1992), 17-25.
_____. *The Genius of John: A Composition-Critical Commentary on the Fourth Gospel* (Collegeville: The Liturgical Press, 1984).
_____. *Matthew: His Mind and His Message* (Collegeville: The Liturgical Press, 1986).
_____. "Patterns and Structures of Mark's Gospel," *Biblical Studies in Contemporary Thought*, ed. M. Ward, (Burlington: The Trinity College Biblical Institute, 1975), 88-103.
_____. "Salvation Through the Wisdom of the Cross (I Cor 1:10-4:21)," in *Sin, Salvation, and the Spirit*, ed. D. Durken (Collegeville: The Liturgical Press, 1979), 324-333.
_____. *Seven Pauline Letters*, (Collegeville: The Liturgical Press, 1982).
English Hymnal with Tunes, The (London: Oxford University Press, 1933).
Fay, G. "Introduction to Incomprehension: The Literary Structure of Mark 4:1-34," *CBQ* 51 (1989), 65-81.
Feuillet, A. "L'hymne christologique de l'épître aux Philippiens (2,6-11)," in his *Christologie paulinienne et tradition biblique* (Paris: Desclée de Brouwer, 1973).
_____. *Le prologue du quatrième évangile* (Paris: Desclée de Brouwer, 1968).
Fitzgerald, A. "Hebrew Poetry," *JBC*, (1968), 238-244; and *NJBC* (1990), 201-208.
Fitzmyer, J. A. "The Aramaic Background of Philippians 2:6-11," *CBQ* 50:3 (1988), 470-483.
_____. *The Gospel According to Luke I-IX* (New York: Doubleday, 1981).

Fowler, R. *Loaves and Fishes. The Function of the Feeding Stories in the Gospel of Mark* (Chico, CA: Scholars Press, 1981).

Frankemölle, H. *Jahwebund und Kirche Christi* (Münster, 1974).

Fredericks, D. C. "Chiasm and Parallel Structure in Qoheleth 5:9-6:9," *JBL* 108:1 (1989), 17-35.

Gächter, P. "Die Form der eucharistischen Rede Jesu," *ZKT* 59 (1935), 419-441.

Geller, S. A. "Theory and Method in the Study of Biblical Poetry," *JQR* 73:1 (1982), 65-77.

Gerhard, J. J. *The Literary Unity and the Compositional Method of the Fourth Gospel* (unpub. doctoral dissertation). Catholic University, Washington, DC, May 25, 1981.

Girard, M. *Les Psaumes. Analyse structurelle et interprétation,* vol I, 1-50 (Montreal: Belarmine / Paris: Cerf, 1984).

Gleick, J. *Chaos. Making a New Science* (New York: Penguin, 1987).

Gnilka, J. *Der Philipperbrief* (Freiburg, Basel, Wien: Herder, 1980).

Goodman, E. "Medical Research Ignores Women," Washington Post Writers Group, syndicated column, Friday June 22, 1990.

Gottwald, N. K. "Poetry, Hebrew," *IDB*, v.3, 829-838.

Goulder, M. D. "The Composition of the Lord's Prayer," *JTS* 14 (1963), 32-45.

Gregory Palamas. "Homily on the Transfiguration," PG CLI, col. 448.

Grossberg, D. *Centripetal and Centrifugal Structures in Biblical Poetry* (Atlanta: Scholars Press, 1989).

Guelich, R. A. "Interpreting the Sermon on the Mount," *Int* 41:1 (1987), 117-130.

_____. "The Matthean Beatitudes: Entrance Requirements or Eschatological Blessings?," *JBL* 95 (1976), 415-434.

Harrington, W. *Mark* (Wilmington: Michael Glazier, 1979).

Havener, I. Q. *The Sayings of Jesus* (Wilmington: Michael Glazier, 1987).

Hennecke, E. *New Testament Apocrypha*, vol. I, "Gospels and Related Writings," (London: Lutterworth, 1963).

Hiers, R. H. "'Binding' and 'Loosing': the Matthean Authorizations," *JBL* 104 (1985), 233-250.

Hill, C. E. "Paul's Understanding of Christ's Kingdom in I Corinthians 15:20-28," *NovT* 30 (1988), 297-320.

Hill, D. *The Gospel of Matthew* (Grand Rapids: Eerdmans, 1972).

Hodges, Z. C., and Farstad, A. L. *The Greek New Testament According to the Majority Text*, 2nd ed. (Nashville: Nelson, 1985).

Hofstadter, D. R. *Gödel, Escher, Bach. An Eternal Golden Braid,* (New York: Random House, 1979).

Holladay, W. L. "The Recovery of Poetic Passages of Jeremiah," *JBL*, 58 (1966), 401-435.

Hrushovski, B. "Prosody," *EJ*, v. 13 (New York: Macmillan, 1971), cols. 1195-1203.

Jeremias, J. "Chiasmus in den Paulusbriefen," *ZNW* 49 (1958), 145-156.

_____. "*pais theou,*" *TWNT* V, 698-713.

_____. "Zu Philipper 2,7: *eauton ekenôsen*" *NovT* 6 (1963), 182-188.

_____. "Zur Gedankenführung in den paulinischen Briefen," *Studia Paulina* (ed. J. N. Sevenster) (Haarlem, 1953) 146-154.

Josipovici, G. *The Book of God, a Response to the Bible* (New Haven: Yale University Press, 1988).

Kaiser, O. and Kummel, W. *Exegetical Method* (New York: Seabury, 1981).

Keegan, T. J. *Interpreting the Bible* (New York: Paulist, 1985).

Kelber, W. H. "Gospel Narrative and Critical Theory," *BTB*, 18:4 (1988) 130-136.

Kingsbury, J. D. *Matthew: Structure, Christology, Kingdom* (Philadelphia: Fortress, 1975).

_____. *Matthew as Story* (Philadelphia: Fortress, 1986).

_____. *The Christology of Mark's Gospel* (Philadelphia: Fortress, 1983).

_____. "The Place, Structure, and Meaning of the Sermon on the Mount Within Matthew," *Int* 41/2 (1987) 131-143.

Kodjak, A. *A Structural Analysis of the Sermon on the Mount* (Berlin/New York: Mouton de Gruyter, 1986).

Köhler, L. "Die Offenbarungsformel 'Fürchte dich nicht' im Alten Testament," *STZ* (1919), 33ff.

Kselman, J. S. "Psalm 72: Some Observations on Structure," *BASOR* 220 (1975), 77-81.

_____. "The Recovery of Poetic Fragments from the Pentateuchal Priestly Source," *JBL* 97:2 (1978), 161-173.

Kugel, J. L. *The Idea of Biblical Poetry, Parallelism and Its History* (New Haven: Yale University Press, 1981).

Lake, K. *The Apostolic Fathers*, vols. I-II, (Loeb) (London: Heinemann/New York: Harvard University Press, 1959).

Lambrecht, J. *Die Redaktion der Markus-Apokalypse: Literarische Analyse und Strukturuntersuchung* (Rome: Biblical Institute, 1967).

_____. "Structure and Line of Thought in 1 Cor. 15:23-28," *NovT* 32 (1990), 143-151.

_____. *The Sermon on the Mount: Proclamation and Exhortation* (Wilmington: Michael Glazier, 1985).

Lawrence, R. T. "The Three-Fold Structure of the Ladder of Divine Ascent," *SVTQ* 32 (1988), 101-118.

Leaney, A. R. C. *The Rule of Qumran and Its Meaning* (Philadelphia: Westminster Press, 1966).

Letis, T. P. "The Gnostic Influences on the Text of the Fourth Gospel: John 1:18 in the Egyptian Manuscripts," *The Bulletin of the Institute for Reformation Biblical Studies* (Fort Wayne, IN) 1:1 (1989), 4-7.

Lichtenstein, M. H. "Chiasm and Symmetry in Proverbs 31," *CBQ* 44 (1982), 202-211.

Lindars, B. "The Structure of Psalm CXLV," *VT* 27/1 (1977), 20-30.

Lohmeyer, E. *Der Brief an die Philipper* (Göttingen: Vandenhoeck & Ruprecht, 1929/1964).

_____. *Kyrios Jesus. Eine Untersuchung zu Phil. 2,5-11*, (Heidelberg, 1928; Darmstadt, 1961).

Lossky, V. *The Mystical Theology of the Eastern Church*, (Crestwood, NY: St. Vladimir's Seminary Press, 1976).

Lowth, R. *Lectures on the Sacred Poetry of the Hebrews*, (in Latin, London, 1753; English tr. London, 1787).

_____. *Isaiah: A New Translation with Preliminary Dissertation* (London, 1778).

Luibhead and Russel (trs.). *John Climacus. The Ladder of Divine Ascent* (New York: Paulist, 1982).

Lund, N. *Chiasmus in the New Testament* (Chapel Hill: University of North Carolina Press, 1942).

_____. "Chiasmus in the Psalms," *AJSL* 49 (1933), 281-312.

_____. "The Influence of Chiasmus upon the Structure of the Gospel According to Matthew," *ATR* 13:4 (1931), 405-433.

_____. "The Presence of Chiasmus in the New Testament," *JR* 10 (1930), 74-93.

_____. "The Presence of Chiasmus in the Old Testament," *AJSL* 46 (1930), 104-126.

Luz, U. *Das Evangelium nach Matthäus* (Neukirchen: Neukirchener Verlag, 1985).

MacBain, W. *The Life of St Catherine by Clemence of Barking*, Anglo-Norman Text Society #18 (Oxford: Blackwell, 1964).

_____. *De Sainte Katerine. An Anonymous Picard Version of the Life of St. Catherine of Alexandria* (Fairfax, VA: George Mason University Press, 1987).

Malatesta, E. "The Literary Structure of John 17," *Bib* 52 (1971), 190-214.

Man, R. E. "The Value of Chiasm for New Testament Interpretation," *BS* 141 (1984), 146-157.

Mann, C.S. *Mark. A New Translation with Introduction and Commentary* (New York: Doubleday, 1986).

Mansvetov, I. *Ecclesiastical Ordo (Typikon): Its Formation and Fate in the Greek and Russian Church* (in Russian), (Moscow, 1885).

Mantzaridis, G. I. *The Deification of Man* (Crestwood, NY: St. Vladimir's Seminary Press, 1984).

Marcus, J. "The Gates of Hades and the Keys of the Kingdom," *CBQ* 50/3 (1988), 443-455.

Marrou, H. I. *A History of Education in Antiquity* (New York: Sheed & Ward, 1956).

Martin, R. P. *Carmen Christi: Philippians ii,5-11 in Recent Interpretation and in the Setting of Early Christian Worship* (Cambridge, 1967).

Mass-Tyrpanis. *Romanos, Cantica Genuina* (Oxford: Clarendon Press, 1963).

Matera, F. J. *What Are They Saying About Mark?* (New York: Paulist, 1987).

May, H. G. and Metzger, B. M. *The New Oxford Annotated Bible* (New York: Oxford, 1973).

Metzger, B. M. *The Text of the New Testament*, (New York: Oxford, 1964).

_____. *A Textual Commentary on the Greek New Testament*, (New York: United Bible Societies, 1975).

Meyendorff, J. *St. Gregory Palamas and Orthodox Spirituality*, (Crestwood, NY: St. Vladimir's Seminary Press, 1974).

Muilenberg, J. "Biblical Poetry," *EJ*, v. 13, cols. 671-681.

Murphy-O'Connor, J. *1 Corinthians*, (Wilmington: Michael Glazier, 1979).

Myers, C. D., Jr., "Chiastic Inversion in the Argument of Romans 3-8," *NovT* 35/1 (1993), 30-47.

Navone, J. *Gospel Love, a Narrative Theology* (Wilmington: Michael Glazier, 1984).

Obolensky, D. *The Penguin Book of Russian Verse* (Harmondsworth, Middlesex, England: Penguin Books, 1962, 1965).

O'Connor, M. *Hebrew Verse Structure* (Winona Lake, IN: Eisenbrauns, 1980).

Patte, D. *The Gospel According to Matthew: A Structural Commentary on Matthew's Faith* (Philadelphia: Fortress, 1987).

Perrin, N. *What Is Redaction Criticism?* (New York: Fortress, 1970/79).

Pesch, R. *Das Markusevangelium, Teil I* (Freiburg im B.: Herder, 1976).

_____. "Zur konzentrischen Struktur von Jona 1," *Bib* 47 (1966), 577-581.

Philips, A. *Prayer Book for the New Year* (revised) (New York: Hebrew Publishing Co., 1931).

Phillips, G. A. "This Is a Hard Saying. Who Can Be Listener to It?: Creating a Reader in John 6," *Semeia* 26 (1983), 23-56.

Purce, J. *The Mystic Spiral* (New York: Thames and Hudson, 1974).

Radday, Y. T. "Chiasmus in Hebrew Biblical Narrative," in J. Welch, *Chiasmus in Antiquity*, 50-115.

Roddy, N. "The Form and Function of the Protoevangelium of James," *Coptic Church Review* 14/2 (1993), 35-45.

Rolland, Ph. "La structure littéraire de la Deuxième Epître aux Corinthiens," *Bib* 71 (1990), 73-84.

Rordorf, W. and Tuilier, A. *La Doctrine des Douze Apôtres (Didachê), Sources Chrétiennes* 248 (Paris: Cerf, 1978).

RSV Gospel Parallels (New York: Nelson, 1957).

Sadie, S. (ed.). *New Grove Dictionary of Music and Musicians* (London: Macmillan, 1980/87).

Schirmer, G. *The Crucifixion. A Meditation on the Sacred Passion of the Holy Redeemer* (New York: G. Schirmer, Inc., no date).

Schlier, H. *Der Brief an die Epheser* (Düsseldorf: Patmos Verlag, 1957).

Schnackenburg, R. *Der Brief an die Epheser* (Zürich/Neukirchen-Vluyn: Benziger/Neukirchener Verlag, 1982).

Schweizer, E. *Erniedrigung und Erhöhung bei Jesus und seinen Nachfolgern* (Zürich, 1955).

Scott, M. P. "Chiastic Structure: A Key to the Interpretation of Mark's Gospel," *BTB* 15:1 (1985), 17-26.

Senior, D. *The Passion of Jesus in the Gospel of Matthew*, (Wilmington, DE: Michael Glazier, 1985).

Shirock, R. J. "The Growth of the Kingdom in Light of Israel's Rejection of Jesus: Structure and Theology in Luke 13:1-35," *NovT* 35/1 (1993), 15-29.

Shoemaker, T. P. "Unveiling of Equality: 1 Corinthians 11:2-16," *BTB* 17 (1987), 60-63.

Skoballanovich, M. *The Typikon Interpreted*, (in Russian), (Kiev, 1913).

Smith, B. H. *Poetic Closure* (Chicago, 1968).

Smith, R. F. "Chiasmus in Sumero-Akkadian," in Welch, *Chiasmus in Antiquity*, p. 17-35.

Sparks, J. (ed.) *The Apostolic Fathers* (Nashville, TN: Thomas Nelson, 1978).

Staley, J. "The Structure of John's Prologue: Its Implications for the Gospel's Narrative Structure," *CBQ* 48:2 (1986), 241-264.

Standaert, B. *L'Evangile selon Marc: Composition et genre littéraire* (Brugge: Sint Andriesabdij, 1978).

Stock, A. "Chiastic Awareness and Education in Antiquity," *BTB* 14:1 (1984), 23-27.

_____. *The Message and Method of Mark* (Wilmington: Michael Glazier, 1989).

Sweazey (Cowles), M. *A Chiastic Study of the First Epistle of John* (unpublished M.Div. thesis, St. Vladimir's Seminary, Crestwood, New York, 1986).

Taft, R. *The Liturgy of the Hours in East and West*, (Collegeville: The Liturgical Press, 1986).

Talbert, C. H. "Artistry and Theology: An Analysis of the Architecture of John 1:19-5:47," *CBQ* 32 (1970), 341-366.

_____. *Literary Patterns, Theological Themes and the Genre of Luke-Acts* (Missoula: Scholars Press, 1974).

_____. *Reading Luke. A Literary and Theological Commentary on the Third Gospel* (New York: Crossroad, 1982).

_____. *Reading John, A Literary and Theological Commentary on the Fourth Gospel and the Johannine Epistles* (New York: Crossroad, 1992).

Terrien, S. *Till the Heart Sings: A Biblical Theology of Manhood & Womanhood* (Philadelphia: Fortress, 1985).

Tilley, T. W. *Story Theology* (Wilmington: Michael Glazier, 1985).

Tompkins, J. P. *Reader-Response Criticism* (Baltimore: Johns Hopkins Press, 1980).

Tracy, D. *Plurality and Ambiguity. Hermeneutics, Religion and Hope* (San Francisco: Harper & Row, 1987).

Uspensky, N. D. *Evening Worship in the Orthodox Church* (Crestwood, NY: St. Vladimir's Seminary Press, 1985).

Vanhoye, A. "Der Chiasmus in der Bibel, 1. Teil," *LingBib* 36 (1975), 21-27.

_____. *La structure littéraire de l'Epître aux Hébreux*, 2nd ed. (Paris: Desclée de Brouwer, 1976).

Vermes, G. *The Dead Sea Scrolls in English* (London: Penguin, 1968).

Volkov, V. *Le Tire-bouchon du Bon Dieu* (Paris: Presse Pocket, 1982).

von Allmen, J. J. *La primauté de l'Eglise de Pierre et de Paul* (Fribourg: Editions Universitaires; Paris: Cerf, 1977).

von Wahlde, C. *The Earliest Version of John's Gospel: Recovering the Gospel of Signs* (Wilmington: Michael Glazier, 1989).

Watson, W. G. E. "Chiastic Patterns in Biblical Hebrew Poetry," in J. Welch, *Chiasmus in Antiquity*, 118-168.

_____. "Internal or Half-Line Parallelism in Classical Hebrew Again," *VT* 29:1 (1979), 44-66.

Weiser, A. *The Psalms: A Commentary* (Philadelphia: Westminster, 1962).

Welch, J. W. "Chiasmus in Ancient Greek and Latin Literature," *Chiasmus in Antiquity*, pp. 250-268.

_____. *Chiasmus in Antiquity. Structures Analyses Exegesis.* (Hildesheim, Germany: Gerstenberg Verlag, 1981).

_____. "Chiasmus in the New Testament," *Chiasmus in Antiquity*, 211-249.

_____. "Chiasmus in Ugaritic," *Chiasmus in Antiquity*, 36-49.

Willis, J. T. "The Juxtaposition of Synonymous and Chiastic Parallelism in Tricola in Old Testament Hebrew Psalm Poetry," *VT* 29:4 (1979), 465-480.

Windisch, H. *The Spirit-Paraclete in the Fourth Gospel* (Philadelphia: Fortress, 1968).

INDEX OF SCRIPTURE PASSAGES

INDEX OF NAMES AND SUBJECTS